Gratian's *Tractatus de penitentia*

Studies in Medieval and Early Modern Canon Law

Kenneth Pennington, General Editor

Editorial Advisory Board

Studies in Medieval and Early Modern Canon Law

VOLUME 14

Gratian's
Tractatus de penitentia

A New Latin Edition with English Translation

Edited and translated by

Atria A. Larson

The Catholic University of America Press
Washington, D.C.

Library of Congress Cataloging-in-Publication Data
Names: Gratian, active 12th century, author. I Larson, Atria A., editor. I
Gratian, active 12th century. Tractatus de penitentia. English.
Title: Gratian's Tractatus de penitentia : a new Latin edition with
English translation / edited and translated by Atria A. Larson.
Other titles: Tractatus de penitentia.
Description: Washington, D.C. : Catholic University of America Press,
2016. I Series: Studies in medieval and early modern canon law ;
volume 14 I English and Latin in parallel texts. I Includes bibliographical
references and index.
Identifiers: LCCN 2016010920 I ISBN 9780813237848 (pbk)
Subjects: LCSH: Gratian, active 12th century. Tractatus de penitentia.
I Penance (Canon law)—History—To 1500. I Penance—History of
doctrines—Middle Ages, 600–1500.
Classification: LCC KBR1362.22 .T73 2016 I DDC 262.9/22—dc23 LC
record available at https://lccn.loc.gov/2016010920

F. A. C. Mantello
et
Timothy B. Noone,
viris doctissimis

Contents

Acknowledgments

The work for this edition and translation has been closely connected to my study of Gratian's *Tractatus de penitentia*, which resulted in the monograph *Master of Penance*, also published by the Catholic University of America Press (2014). First thanks should be given to the director of the press, Trevor Lipscombe, for being long interested in this edition and translation, for supporting my choices regarding the program used (Classical Text Editor) and a facing-page format, and for supporting the publication at every step in the process.

Many individuals have given advice along the way to a completed manuscript. I consulted John Wei and Anders Winroth early in the process, seeking their opinion on the manuscripts I was choosing to use. I am grateful for their advice and input. Ken Pennington has been, as always, generous with his time and insights. He encouraged me from the start of my dissertation to work toward this end result, so that the scholarly community could have both a monograph about and a new Latin edition of Gratian's treatise. He was also keen to see an English translation, to benefit students and others. His insights on the manuscript tradition and the scholarly issues surrounding it have enabled him to envision what this edition should be for the current state of *Decretum* scholarship, and I hope it meets his expectations. I am also very grateful to Joseph Goering, who read the entire edition and translation and provided abundant feedback. His generosity in relaying the fruits of his text-editing experience to me will be forever appreciated. If this edition has any long-standing contribution to the scholarship, it is in large part due to the assistance of both Ken and Joe.

My deepest gratitude goes to Joel Kalvesmaki of Dumbarton

Oaks, a fellow doctoral graduate of the Catholic University of America. He took on the enormous task of copyediting this work in its entirety and formatting the Classical Text Editor files for press. His skills in text-editing, Latin, citation style, and English prose have brought improvements in style, ease of use, and consistency on every page of this manuscript.

Finally, I could not have completed this edition and translation if I had not been taught by gifted and passionate professors who shared with me their knowledge of medieval Latin and the process of editing Latin texts. My skill is far inferior to theirs, but even this modest effort is inconceivable without their patient teaching. I am especially indebted to F. A. C. Mantello and to Timothy B. Noone, of the Catholic University of America's Department of Greek and Latin and School of Philosophy, respectively. They are men of different scholarly interests, different teaching styles, and different personalities, but they share great facility in Latin, great skill in editing texts, and great passion for the preservation and printing of medieval works. This book is dedicated to them with sincere gratitude for all that they taught me.

Abbreviations

Authors

Ambros.	Ambrosiaster
Ambr. Med.	Ambrosius Mediolanensis (Ambrose of Milan)
Ans. Laud.	Anselmus Laudunensis (Anselm of Laon)
Aug. Hipp.	Augustinus Hipponensis (Augustine of Hippo)
Bas. Caes.	Basilius Caesarius (Basil of Caesarea)
Bed. Uen.	Beda Uenerabilis (the Venerable Bede)
Caes. Arel.	Caesarius Arelatensis (Caesarius of Arles)
Cass.	Cassiodorus
Chrom. Aquil.	Chromatius Aquileiensis
Cypr. Carth.	Cyprianus Carthaginensis (Cyprian of Carthage)
Genn. Mass.	Gennadius Massiliensis
Greg. Magn.	Gregorius Magnus (Pope Gregory I, the Great)
Halit. Cam.	Halitgarius Cameracensis (Halitgar of Cambrai)
Haymo Antis.	Haymo Antisiodorensis (Haymo of Auxerre)
Haymo Halb.	Haymo Halberstatensis (Haymo of Halberstadt)
Hier.	Hieronimus (Jerome)
Ioh. Chrys.	Iohannes Chrysostomus (John Chrysostom)
Isid. Hisp.	Isidorus Hispalensis (Isidore of Seville)
Jul. Pom.	Julianus Pomerius
Orig.	Origenes (Origen)
Paul. Aquil.	Paulinus Aquileiensis (Paulinus of Aquileia)
Prosp. Aquit.	Prosper Aquitanus (Prosper of Aquitaine)
Ps.-Aug.	Pseudo-Augustine
Rab. Maur.	Rabanus Maurus

Journals, Series, and Reference Works

AKKR	*Archiv für katholisches Kirchenrecht*
BMCL	*Bulletin of Medieval Canon Law*, New Series
JK	Jaffé-Kaltenbrunner, *Regesta pontificu romanorum* (an. 64?–599)
RDC	*Revue de droit canonique*
SG	*Studia Gratiana*
ZRG Kan. Abt.	*Zeitschrift der Savigny-Stiftung für Rechtsgeschichte, Kanonistische Abteilung*

Series of Ancient and Medieval Texts

CCSL	Corpus Christianorum, Series latina
COGD	Corpus Christianorum: Conciliorum Oecumenicorum Generaliumque Decreta
CSEL	Corpus scriptorum ecclesiasticorum latinorum
GCS	Griechischen christlichen Schriftsteller der ersten drei Jahrhunderte
MIC	Monumenta Iuris Canonici
Ser. B	Series B: Corpus Collectionum
Ser. C	Series C: Subsidia
MGH	Monumenta Germaniae Historica
Conc.	Concilia
Epp. sel.	Epistolae selectae
PG	Jacques-Paul Migne, ed., Patrologia Graeca (Paris 1857–66)
PL	Jacques-Paul Migne, ed., Patrologia Latina (Paris 1844–80)
SChr	Sources chrétiennes
TU	Texte und Untersuchungen zur Geschichte der altchristlichen Literatur

Gratian's Sources and Related Texts

3L	*Collectio canonum trium librorum*
83 quaest.	*De diuersis quaestionibus octaginta tribus*
9L	*Collectio nouem librorum*
Aduers. Jou.	*Aduersus Jouinianum*
Bh	*Baptizato homine*

Cod.	*Codex Justiniani*
Coll. sermonum ps.-Ambr.	*Collectio sermonum pseudo-Ambrosiana*
Comm. in epist. ad Rom.	*Commentarius in epistulam ad Romanos*
Comm. in euang. Matt.	*Commentarii in euangelium Matthaei*
De cons. euang.	*De consensu euangelistarum*
De corr. et grat.	*De correptione et gratia*
De eccles. dog.	*De ecclesiasticis dogmatibus*
De Gen. ad litt.	*De Genesi ad litteram libri duodecim*
De grat. et lib. arb.	*De gratia et libero arbitrio*
De Is. uel an.	*De Isaac uel anima*
De lib. arb.	*De libero arbitrio*
De pecc. mer. et rem.	*De peccatorum meritis et remissione et de baptismo paruulorum*
De salut. doc.	*De salutaribus documentis ad Henricum comitem*
De serm. Dom.	*De sermone Domini in monte*
De uera	*De uera et falsa penitentia*
Decr. ps.-isid.	*Decretales pseudo-isidorianae*
Dial.	*Dialogorum libri iv*
Dig.	*Digesta* (Justinian's *Digest*)
Enarr.	*Enarrationes in Psalmos*
Ench.	*Enchiridion de fid , spe, et caritate*
Exp.	*Expositio* (on various books of the Bible)
F	*Sententie de caritate et penitentia* in Firenze, Biblioteca Medicea Laurenziana, Plut. V sin 7, fols. 70ra–84rb
Gl. ord.	*Glossa ordinaria* (on the Bible)
Hom. evang.	*Homeliarum evangelii libri ii*
Hom. in euang.	*Homiliae in euangelia*
Hom. in Heb.	*In epistolam ad Hebraeos homiliae*
Hom. in Hiezech. proph.	*Homiliae in Hiezechielem prophetam*
In epist. B. Pauli ad 2 Cor.	*In epistolam Beati Pauli ad Corinthios secundam*
In Ioh. epist. ad Parthos tract.	*In Iohannis epistulam ad Parthos tractatus*
In Ioh. evang. tract.	*In Iohannis evangelium tractatus CXXIV*
In Luc. euang. expos.	*In Lucae euangelium expositio*
Pro Aug. respons.	*Pro Augustino responsiones*
Quaest. in hept.	*Quaestionum in heptateuchum libri septem*

Abbreviations

Reg. epist.	*Registrum epistularum*
Reg. past.	*Regula pastoralis*
Synon.	*Synonyma de lamentatione animae peccatricis*
Trip.	*Collectio tripartita*
Vt autem	*Vt autem hoc euidenter*

Introduction

In the 1120s and the 1130s, the Italian city of Bologna contained within its walls a few individuals who would begin to change the legal system of Europe. Intellectuals had recently rediscovered key texts of ancient, Roman law (collectively the *Corpus iuris civilis* of the emperor Justinian issued in 533) and in particular the collection of Roman juristic opinions on the law, compiled in the part of the *Corpus* known as the *Digestum*, or Digest. Individuals such as Bulgarus and Martinus studied the texts of the law intently and taught them to students, creating *de facto* schools of Roman law several decades before the official founding of the University of Bologna. Meanwhile, a man named Gratian was teaching the church's canons in a new way. He stood in a line of individuals of the previous several decades who were returning to the ancient sources of the Christian church's doctrine and regulations and composing works based on their reevaluation of the tradition. His work founded a *de facto* school of canon law in the same city that was now training civilian, or Roman law, jurists. The two schools fed off one another, they influenced academic enterprises elsewhere in the Italian peninsula and north of the Alps in French, Anglo-Norman, imperial, and other realms, and soon those who studied both laws filled ecclesiastical and secular administrations. The expertise in law filled a need that the various demographic, social, economic, commercial, political, and religious changes had thrust upon governing bodies in the late eleventh and early twelfth century, and helped propel these governing bodies toward new heights of organization and centralized power.

At the same time, in the 1120s and 1130s, significant developments in Paris made it the key intellectual center in northern Christendom.

A great teacher had recently, in 1117, died in the town of Laon. His name was Anselm, and his work in scriptural exegesis and his methods of applying dialectic and grammar to the interpretation of the Bible and the Church Fathers influenced contemporary developments in the burgeoning field of systematic theology, far more than the work of his more famous namesake and contemporary, Anselm of Canterbury (d. 1109).[1] For various reasons, in the next decade, great minds began to congregate in nearby Paris, where they attracted numerous students, again several decades before the formal appearance of the University of Paris. Guillaume de Champeaux, Peter Abelard, Gilbert de la Porrée, Hugh of St Victor, and Peter Lombard are only the most famous intellectuals who made or began to make their career in Paris in those years. Their work established theology as a scientific discipline, setting it on a firm foundation to become the "queen of the sciences" for the remainder of the Middle Ages.[2]

The *Tractatus de penitentia*, the treatise edited and translated in this volume, played a role in both developments, the legal and the theological. It established firm principles on which to base ecclesiastical judicial decisions about how and when to administer penance. It also quickly became the work that contemporaries had to read before they themselves wrote anything on penance, and it comprised one of the most, if not the most, important sources for Peter Lombard's (d. 1160) treatment of penance in his *Sentences*, the standard introductory textbook for theology students over the next several centuries. The treatise was influential in both realms, the legal or canonical and the theological, because it was created and circulated in an age when these two spheres were not yet clearly divided in academic culture. Further, the man who wrote it was equally comfortable

1. On Anselm of Laon and his school, see most recently Cédric Giraud, *Per verba magistri: Anselme de Laon et son école au XIIe siècle*, Bibliothèque d'histoire culturelle du Moyen Âge 8 (Turnhout: Brepols, 2010).

2. The developments noted in the first two paragraphs constitute part of what has been termed the "Twelfth-Century Renaissance." See an overview in R. N. Swanson, *The Twelfth-Century Renaissance* (New York: Manchester University Press, 1999). Individual, nuanced accounts on various aspects of the period may be found in Thomas F. X. Noble and John Van Engen, eds., *European Transformations: The Long Twelfth Century* (Notre Dame, Ind.: University of Notre Dame Press, 2011). The essays in Robert L. Benson and Giles Constable, eds., *Renaissance and Renewal in the Twelfth Century* (Cambridge, Mass.: Harvard University Press, 1982) are still valuable.

in contemplating the complex legal situations that arose in the life of the church and in reflecting on the scriptural and patristic basis of the church's teachings. A few more words about this man, Gratian, and his work are in order before discussing the nature of the present edition and translation.

Gratian's Life and the *Concordia discordantium canonum* (*Decretum*)

Unfortunately not much of certainty can be said about Gratian's life. Scholarly consensus states that he was most likely born in the final decade or two of the eleventh century and was probably dead by the mid-1140s. He taught in Bologna—absolutely in the 1130s, most likely also in the 1120s, and possibly even earlier. He very well could have been a monk, but the old identification of him as a monk of the Camaldolese order has been shown to be based on very late and shaky information. Certainly he was a cleric, and, if he was a monk, he was also ordained, for scholars now have very good evidence to support the old idea that he became a bishop.[3] Perhaps he became bishop of the city of Chiusi; perhaps he was from Chiusi but became bishop elsewhere after his tenure as master, or *magister*, in Bologna. Where Gratian was educated prior to his teaching career remains unproven, but good evidence exists to suppose that Gratian studied in Laon or at least studied under a master who had studied under Anselm of Laon, evidenced by the way Gratian's work is deeply connected to literature and a methodology originating in Laon at the time.[4]

3. Anders Winroth, "Where Gratian Slept: The Life and Death of the Father of Canon Law," ZRG Kan. Abt. 100 (2014): 106–28; idem, *The Making of Gratian's* Decretum, Cambridge Studies in Medieval Thought and Life (Cambridge: Cambridge University Press, 2000), 5–8. The most significant article in English to raise doubts about what scholars once thought they knew about Gratian was John T. Noonan, Jr., "Gratian Slept Here: The Changing Identity of the Father of the Systematic Study of Canon Law," *Traditio* 35 (1979): 145–72. See also the helpful biographical review in Stephan Kuttner, "Research on Gratian: Act and Agenda," in *Proceedings of the Seventh International Congress of Medieval Canon Law, Cambridge, 23–27 July 1984*, ed. Peter Linehan, MIC Ser. C–8 (Vatican City: Biblioteca Apostolica Vaticana, 1988), 5–9. While Winroth believes Gratian became bishop of Chiusi, Kenneth Pennington has questioned the point but also presented good manuscript evidence that Gratian did become a bishop: "The Biography of Gratian, the Father of Canon Law," *Villanova Law Review* 59, no. 4 (2014): 679–706.

4. Atria A. Larson, "The Influence of the School of Laon on Gratian: The Us-

Scholars can attribute but one work to Gratian, a massive text-book that he entitled the *Concordia discordantium canonum,* or *The Har-mony of Discordant Canons.* In this title, Gratian announced his project: to bring the apparently differing rules in the church's tradition into a coherent whole.[5] The title also alludes to the legacy of the conten-tious debates from the second half of the eleventh century, called to-day the Investiture Controversy, which caused many to realize that a clear answer to certain questions could not always be reached sim-ply by checking the local canonical collection to see what the church had always maintained. The harder one looked at the source ma-terial, the more contradictions and uncertainties one found.[6] While authors sometimes revealed a sensitivity to these conundrums, par-ticularly in prologues to their works, they did not implement a meth-odology to resolve those differences in the works themselves. They compiled their own collections of canons, highlighting those canons they deemed best represented what the church had maintained or should now practice. In the 1120s, in his *Sic et Non,* dealing most-ly with theological questions, the great thinker Peter Abelard listed various texts from the Christian tradition that could be used to argue pro and contra a certain statement, but he did not demonstrate how to reconcile the differences. Gratian's *Concordia discordantium cano-num,* which eventually came to be known simply as the *Decretum,* did not resolve every contradiction that it addressed, but scholars agree that Gratian took the *concordia* methodology to new heights, apply-

---

age of the *Glossa ordinaria* and Anselmian *Sententie* in *De penitentia* (*Decretum* C.33 q.3)," *Mediaeval Studies* 72 (2010): 197–244; see also chapters 1–4, 7 in eadem, *Master of Penance: Gratian and the Development of Penitential Thought and Law in the Twelfth Century,* Studies in Medieval and Early Modern Canon Law 11 (Washing-ton, D.C.: Catholic University of America Press, 2014).

5. On this concept, see Stephan Kuttner, *Harmony from Dissonance: An Interpre-tation of Medieval Canon Law,* Wimmer Lecture 10 (Latrobe, Pa.: Archabbey Press, 1960); reprinted in idem, *The History of Ideas and Doctrines in the Middle Ages,* 2nd ed. (Aldershot: Ashgate, 1992), no. 1.

6. Among the vast literature, I direct students and non-specialists to: *Prefac-es to Canon Law Books in Latin Christianity: Selected Translations, 500–1245,* ed. and trans. Robert Somerville and Bruce C. Brasington (New Haven: Yale University Press, 1998). As Somerville and Brasington note in their introduction to "The Era of Reform: 1050–1140" (i.e., leading up to Gratian), "The focus of jurisprudence ... shifted decisively over the century treated here, from concerns about sources and their arrangement to the problem of harmonization of contradictions found in those sources" (105).

ing it more thoroughly and extensively to a wider spectrum of issues than anyone else had. Regardless of other works where Gratian may have encountered the methodology, he certainly found it in a somewhat obscure text from northern France (modern-day Belgium), Alger of Liège's *Liber de misericordia et iustitia* (c. 1095–1121), which he drew upon directly in one section (*Causa* 1) of the *Decretum*.[7] The methodology also constituted the core of how Anselm of Laon, also in northern France, presented the Christian tradition, and it constituted a chief part of Anselm's pedagogy.[8] His innovation consisted of applying such methods to the study of Scripture and the Fathers, which paved the way for the development of systematic theology. It is this methodology that Gratian adopted and applied to the entire Christian tradition.

Like Anselm's, Gratian's intellectual output was directed to his students. He was a teacher, and his great work was a textbook. Gratian did not just want to teach his students what the Christian tradition said on various matters; he wanted them to wrestle with how to understand the truth and unity of the Christian tradition even when certain parts of it seemed not to fit. The analysis of *auctoritates* (authoritative texts) in terms of their grammar, historical context, specific or limited application, and relationship to one another proved just as important as understanding what they said. In fact, such analysis represented what it truly meant to understand them. As a result, Gratian interspersed the various chapters or *capitula* of *auctoritates* with many *dicta*, sections where he explained what the texts meant, created logical arguments following from one *auctoritas* to another, and demonstrated how one should (or at least could) harmonize discordant canons. These *dicta* made Gratian's textbook stand out from what the literature refers to as "pre-Gratian canonical collections," which were collections of ecclesiastical canons and papal decretals (papal letters of legal consequence) plus some Roman

7. Critical edition: Robert Kretzschmar, *Alger von Lüttichs Traktat "De misericordia et iustitia": Ein kanonistischer Konkordanzversuch aus der Zeit des Investiturstreits; Untersuchungen und Edition*, Quellen und Forschungen zum Recht im Mittelalter 2 (Sigmaringen: Jan Thorbecke, 1985). Alger's preface is translated in Somerville and Brasington, *Prefaces*, 165–69. See also the editors' comments on 117–18. On Gratian's usage of Alger, see Gabriel Le Bras, "Alger of Liège et Gratien," *Revue de sciences philosophiques et théologiques* 20 (1931): 5–26.

8. See Giraud, *Per verba magistri*, 187, and my *Master of Penance*, 287–91.

law in use in the barbarian kingdoms. The compilers of these collections, even though often skilled and knowledgeable, included no extensive analysis.[9] They were creating texts largely for administrative purposes or, at certain times, within the context of specific political or polemical fights within the ecclesiastical hierarchy.[10] Even though they would have been educational to those wanting to learn the church's regulations, they were not composed for teaching, and they did not include the thoughts and arguments of a *magister*. By including many *dicta*, Gratian broke new ground and established an altogether different genre.

The *Decretum* contains three parts; Gratian's thoughts and arguments intermingle with *auctoritates* in parts one and two, whereas the third part consists almost exclusively of *auctoritates*.[11] The first part, or *prima pars*, is also referred to as the *distinctiones* because it is divided into 101 distinctions. The first twenty (DD.1–20) treat the nature and types of law.[12] The remaining eighty-one (DD.21–101) deal with holy orders: the different types and ranks of clerics, what their qual-

---

9. A few of the collectors provided limited analysis by summarizing the point of each canon with an original rubric. Such work is, for instance, evident in Anselm of Lucca's *Collectio canonum*; see Kathleen G. Cushing, *Papacy and Law in the Gregorian Revolution: The Canonistic Work of Anselm of Lucca* (New York: Oxford University Press, 1998), esp. examples at 75–76 and in appendix IA.

10. On pre-Gratian collections, see introductory material in James A. Brundage, *Medieval Canon Law*, The Medieval World (New York: Longman, 1995), 18–43, the introductions to chapters 2–4 in Somerville and Brasington, *Prefaces*, and, on the reform collections, Gérard Giordanengo, "*Auctoritates et auctores* dans les collections canoniques (1050–1140)," in *Auctor et Auctoritas: Invention et conformisme dans l'écriture medieval; Actes du colloque de Saint-Quentin-en-Yvelines (14–16 juin 1999)*, ed. Michel Zimmermann, Mémoires et documents de l'école des Chartres 59 (Paris: École des Chartres, 2001), 99–129. Several recent works in English on the major pre-Gratian figures have been published, including Greta Austin, *Shaping Church Law around the Year 1000: The Decretum of Burchard of Worms*, Church, Faith and Culture in the Medieval West (Burlington, Vt.: Ashgate, 2009), Christof Rolker, *Canon Law and the Letters of Ivo of Chartres*, Cambridge Studies in Medieval Life and Thought (Cambridge: Cambridge University Press, 2010), and Cushing, *Papacy and Law in the Gregorian Revolution*.

11. For a more detailed discussion of the structure of Gratian's work, see Peter Landau, "Gratian and the *Decretum Gratiani*," in *The History of Medieval Canon Law in the Classical Period, 1140–1234: From Gratian to the Decretals of Pope Gregory IX*, ed. Wilfried Hartmann and Kenneth Pennington, History of Medieval Canon Law 6 (Washington D.C.: The Catholic University of America Press, 2008), 35–38.

12. This is the one section that has been translated into English (along with the corresponding *Glossa ordinaria*): Gratian, *The Treatise on Laws (Decretum DD.1–20) with Ordinary Gloss*, trans. Augustine Thompson, O.P. and James Gordley, in-

ifications are, how they achieve their offices, what their roles in the church are, and so forth. The second part, or *secunda pars*, is also referred to as the *causae* because it is divided up into thirty-six cases. Besides later references by other writers to Gratian as a *magister*, this section provides the greatest evidence for Gratian's teaching activity, for it organizes and presents the church's canons in an ideal way to catch the student's attention and deal with several canonical questions in imitation of real-life cases. Each case in the *secunda pars* sets up a scenario; some of the scenarios might have been possible, but many were clearly hypothetical and perhaps even created in order to provide a context within which Gratian could teach about a given topic addressed by a certain *auctoritas*.[13] After the presentation of the scenario in the "case statement," the *causa* lists a series of questions (*quaestiones*) pertaining to the case, and then treats (sometimes at great length) each *quaestio*. The majority of the *causae* pertain to issues of relevance to clerics (secular and religious, with a special focus on monks in CC.16–20), including various types of offences that merit punishment by an ecclesiastical superior, and here issues of judicial procedure come to the fore: who can accuse a cleric, how charges and investigations should occur, and so forth. Beginning with C.27, Gratian turns his attention to the laity and in particular to the institution of marriage. All ten fi al *causae* (CC.27–36) deal with marriage cases. As will be explained in more detail below, the *Tractatus de penitentia* appears within this general section. The third part of the *Decretum*, or *tertia pars*, is called *De consecratione*, and, roughly speaking, treats issues related to the sacraments and to the liturgy.

As the preceding should make apparent, the *Decretum* is no slight or simple volume. The sheer size (1424 columns in the edition from 1879) would suggest that Gratian did not compose it all in a short time; its complexity would suggest that Gratian's conception of what the work should be and how it should be organized developed over time. Many internal textual clues have led scholars to presume that the work developed in different stages or recensions; certain structural features, such as the fact that the entire third part, *De consecratione*,

---

tro. Katherine Christensen, Studies in Medieval and Early Modern Canon Law 2 (Washington D.C.: The Catholic University of America Press, 1993).

13. For the latter hypothesis, see John Nöel Dillon, "Case Statements (*themata*) and the Composition of Gratian's Cases," ZRG Kan. Abt. 92 (2006): 306–39.

contains no *dicta* (except one minor one) while the other sections are replete with *dicta*, have also led scholars to suspect that not every section of the *Decretum* was part of Gratian's original plan.[14] The unique structure of the second part, organized around cases and questions, meanwhile, suggests that these *causae* were the original heart of Gratian's work, that much of the content there constituted his earliest teaching material.[15]

We now have definitive proof that Gratian wrote a recension of the *prima pars* and *secunda pars* earlier than the one preserved in most medieval manuscripts of the *Decretum* and all early modern and modern printed editions. Anders Winroth built on much previous scholarship on twelfth-century *Decretum* manuscripts and made the key discovery that a few of these manuscripts contained an earlier recension of the text.[16] This earlier recension, completed as early as 1133, received substantial augmentation within a few years' time, by 1140, possibly by Gratian or possibly by a circle of his students, and then later scholars continued to add texts to the *Decretum* through the third quarter of the twelfth century.[17] Even before the end of the twelfth century, those who studied the *Decretum* labeled these later, additional texts, understood not to be the work of Gratian, as *paleae*. The version of Gratian's *Decretum* incorporating the *paleae* and reproduced countless times in late medieval manuscripts, early printings, and modern editions is known as the vulgate version.[18] For the law of the church, the most important edition was the *Editio Romana*, officially sanctioned in 1582, but this edition often replaced Gratian's rendition of his material sources (e.g., Augustine's *De Trinitate* or canons from the Council of Nicaea) with what those in charge of

14. See a challenge to the then-prevailing understanding of *De consecratione* in John H. Van Engen, "Observations on 'De consecratione'," in *Proceedings of the Sixth International Congress of Medieval Canon Law, Berkeley, California, 28 July–2 August 1980*, ed. Stephan Kuttner and Kenneth Pennington, MIC Ser. C-7 (Vatican City: Biblioteca Apostolica Vaticana, 1985), 309–20, esp. 311–12.

15. There may be proof of this supposition in a manuscript currently housed in Sankt Gallen (Stiftsbibliothek 673; Sg in the literature), which contains only *causae* and no *prima pars* or *tertia pars*. See Appendix A for more information and a transcription of its C.30 q.3 (the section equivalent to *De penitentia*).

16. Winroth, *Making of Gratian's* Decretum; idem, "The Two Recensions of Gratian's *Decretum*," ZRG Kan. Abt. 83 (1997): 22–31.

17. On dating, see below, n. 34.

18. On the *paleae*, see Landau, "Gratian and the *Decretum Gratiani*," 47.

the *Editio Romana* thought to be the best version of Gratian's sources. The best modern edition appeared in volume one of Emil Friedberg's two-volume *Corpus iuris canonici* in 1879.[19] Unlike those who produced the *Editio Romana*, Friedberg attempted to recreate Gratian's original composition and also attempted to identify all the *paleae*. Thus, in his edition, Friedberg included later additions to the text certainly not made by Gratian and he also sought to be faithful to Gratian's original work. Friedberg was, in short, sensitive to issues of authorial intent and textual development, but he did not have the benefit of knowing that certain manuscripts produced an earlier recension of Gratian's text. His edition therefore does not adequately represent the earlier recension identified by   inroth.[20]

C.33 q.3: *De penitentia*

The basic textual history of the *Decretum* just outlined bears upon the *Tractatus de penitentia* in the following ways. First, the earlier recension identified in extant manuscripts by Winroth contained the treatise. The twentieth century witnessed many doubts about the authenticity of the treatise and Gratian's authorship of it, but Winroth's discovery proved that Gratian wrote *De penitentia* and purposefully included it in his *Concordia discordantium canonum* at a relatively early stage of his work. Second, like other parts of the *Decretum*, the original *De penitentia* was subject to later changes and additions, so the final version of *De penitentia* looks somewhat different from the earlier recension. Third, neither Friedberg nor later scholars have identified any *paleae* within *De penitentia*. This means that Gratian or his immediate students made some changes to the treatise within a decade or so after its original composition, but the version in place by c. 1150 became the final and vulgate version, without any further supplementation. In general it is that version that appears in Friedberg's edition.

If *De penitentia* was included in Gratian's earlier recension and was part of an early stage of Gratian's plan for his entire textbook, then

---

19. *Decretum magistri Gratiani*, vol. 1 of *Corpus iuris canonici* (Leipzig: B. Tauchnitz, 1879; repr. Graz: Akademische Druck und Verlagsanstalt, 1959).

20. Winroth is leading a team to produce an online edition of this recension for the entire *Decretum*.

it is imperative to grasp the textual context of the treatise. Where did Gratian put it? Why did he put it there? Gratian incorporated *De penitentia* into one of the marriage cases in the final section of the *secunda pars* of the *Decretum*. C.33 put forward the scenario of an impotent husband whose wife then began a relationship with another man. The treatment of the case makes clear that the man's impotence did not result from a congenital condition or any conceivable natural cause. The impotence was a "magically induced impotence" (or *maleficiu*), meaning that some malicious individual had targeted the man (or his marriage) and put a spell on him.[21] Since the man had been susceptible to such an act of divination, he must have committed some sin for which he had not repented, for any person who was right with God would have been impervious to such machinations. Consequently, if the man wanted to regain potency, he would have to reconcile himself to God. The third *quaestio* of the case thus asked whether someone could be reconciled to God through contrition of the heart and confession to God alone or whether a sin could be remitted only through oral confession to a priest and an act of satisfaction.

Gratian wrote *De penitentia* in answer to that question and addressed many subsidiary questions about penance along the way.[22] Gratian composed it as a lengthy theological treatise, originally untitled. This section of the *Decretum* can be labeled a "theological treatise" for several reasons. Gratian would not have labeled it as such, for "theology" was still in its nascent form and even a "treatise" or *tractatus* was not yet a clearly defined genre, but this phrase is the best modern term to describe what Gratian created, and, it is argued,

21. Cf. Catherine Rider, *Magic and Impotence in the Middle Ages* (Oxford: Oxford University Press, 2006), and my discussion of C.33 in my introduction to *Master of Penance*, 13–16.

22. John Wei believes Gratian wrote his treatise on penance before many of the *causae*, including C.33, of the *Decretum*. Once he had his penitential treatise, Gratian concocted the scenario of C.33 about the impotent husband in order to accommodate the treatise within his textbook. I am not convinced of Wei's arguments, partly because I lean toward viewing the manuscript Sankt Gallen, Stiftsbibliothek 673 (see Appendix A) as representing an earlier stage in the development of the *Decretum*. The manuscript contains a reduced C.33 (there C.30) q.3, which I believe was in place, and then Gratian later expanded that *quaestio* into a full-fledged treatise. See John Wei, *Gratian the Theologian*, Studies in Medieval and Early Modern Canon Law 13 (Washington, D.C.: Catholic University of America Press, 2016).

self-consciously so.[23] First, *De penitentia* is a self-standing work revolving around questions pertaining to a single topic, namely penance, and so it is a treatise or *tractatus* in that sense. Although Gratian clearly wanted it to be read or taught within the *Decretum*, one does not have to read it within the *Decretum* to understand it. It could have been copied and studied separately. Second, *De penitentia* deals with more limited source material than does the rest of the *Decretum*. Over the previous several centuries, medieval authors had developed different genres, and those genres were determined largely by the source material informing and treated in each. One could treat "the canons," or one could treat "the sacred page."[24] The *Decretum* bridged that divide. But in the original version of *De penitentia*, Gratian quotes no canons (no conciliar decrees, no papal decretals, and no other legal texts); he restricts his *auctoritates* to those sources that were used in the study of *sacra pagina*, namely Scripture itself, writings of the church Fathers, and some papal letters with theological content. The third reason pertains to rubrics. Elsewhere in the *Decretum*, Gratian composed a summarizing rubric for almost every *capitulum*. These rubrics were fairly common (though not applied everywhere) in earlier canonical collections; they gave the user a summary of the canon and revealed the main point the compiler wished the user to gather from the text. But Gratian provided no *auctoritas* in the original *De penitentia* with a rubric. Rather, the *auctoritates* functioned much more as commentary by others and were closely interwoven with Gratian's own commentary (the *dicta*) in order to create one coherent composition, much like they were in Alger of Liège's treatise. Gratian did not view the different *auctoritates* as ecclesiastical rules requiring a summary statement of their main canonistic point, and he did not conceive of his treatise in C.33 q.3 as the type of work in which such rules and regulations were required or fitting. The manuscripts confirm Gratian's purpose. The earliest manuscripts do not divide the texts Gratian cited individually as they do in the

---

23. On the lack of clarity by the term *tractatus*: Wolfgang P. Müller, "Toward the First Iconographical Treatise of the West: Huguccio and Sicard of Cremona," in *Mélanges en l'honneur d'Anne Lefebvre-Teillard*, ed. Bernard d'Alteroche et al. (Paris: Éditions Panthéon-Assas, 2009), 778–79.

24. Atria A. Larson, "The Reception of Gratian's *Tractatus de penitentia* and the Relationship between Canon Law and Theology in the Second Half of the Twelfth Century," *Journal of Religious History* 37.4 (2013): 458–59.

other parts of the Decretum. In sum, considering the academic fields and the genres that were then developing, *De penitentia* can best be described as a theological treatise.

Like the *prima pars* and the *tertia pars* (*De consecratione*), *De penitentia* is divided into distinctions, in this case seven.[25] The first discusses the issue mentioned in the statement of the *causa*, namely at what moment the remission of sins occurs within the process of penance. It does not ask whether confession to a priest is necessary (Gratian always and everywhere assumed oral confession would happen), but the issue is whether the oral confession plus an act of satisfaction (the external aspect of penance) is that which actually causes a sin to be forgiven or whether internal contrition, silently and privately expressed before God alone, is responsible for reconciling a sinner with God. This distinction famously ends with Gratian claiming he could not decide which position was correct or better. The second and third distinctions are closely related, as the arguments of the second support those of the third. The issue is the nature of true penance and whether sin is compatible with it. Can someone be truly penitent and then fall back into sin (thereby requiring one to repeat penance)? In Gratian's argumentation, the situation is analogous to love, or *caritas*. Can someone ever truly possess *caritas* and then later lose it, as evidenced by a fall into sin? D.2 discusses this possibility (with side discussions of the angels and the fall of Lucifer), and then D.3 considers the specific terms of penance. Gratian argues that someone cannot be truly penitent and simultaneously sin but that one can be truly penitent and then later fall back into sin. He thus affir s that Christians may (and almost always do) need to perform penance more than once. But what happens if a person performs penance once or multiple times but then falls deeply into sin without ever coming to repentance before dying? Will God punish that person (an apostate) only for the final sins for which he or she did not repent? Or will the older sins, previously repented of, return, as it were, to the apostate's account so that he or she will also be punished for them? Gratian turns to that question in D.4 and simultaneously incorporates a treatment of predestination.

The final three distinctions are shorter, have fewer *dicta*, and are

25. For detailed treatment of these seven distinctions, see the first five chapters of my *Master of Penance*.

more practical in nature. D.5 deals with the proper attitude and actions of a penitent—what things he should meditate on and what things he should or should not do while repenting of a sin. The next distinction turns to the confessor: who the confessor should be (one's own priest, but, in cases of emergency, whoever is present), what qualities a confessor-priest should have, how he should conduct himself in relationship to a penitent, and what happens to him if he reveals the content of a confession (i.e., breaks the seal of confession). The fi al distinction, D.7, handles deathbed repentance, affirming that it is possible to be reconciled to God at death's door but making stern warnings against those inclined to live with an "eat, drink, and be merry" philosophy and who trust that they can always set things right at the end.

The distinction divisions in *De penitentia* and even the identific - tion of the various sections as "distinctions" did not originate with Gratian, even though these developed quite early. Gratian himself seems to have conceived of the various sections in terms of questions, for, in the only cross-reference to *De penitentia*, he or a later redactor refers to "the first question."[26] No matter the label, the start and stop of each *distinctio* fall in logical places in the progression of Gratian's argument and treatment, and the material in each section is coherent. For this reason, and not wishing to cause confusion by overturning nearly nine centuries of scholarly tradition in referring to different sections of the treatise, this edition maintains the long-standing division into seven distinctions.

The Purpose of the *Decretum* and *De penitentia*

The thorough analysis of any work involves the question of purpose. Why did the author write the work? What did he aim to achieve? Gratian left no prologue signaling his intentions. Previous scholarship highlighted a possible relationship to the body of Roman law texts being studied in Bologna at the same time. Perhaps Gratian intended to compose a comprehensive body of law for the church in imitation of or even in opposition to Justinian's *Corpus iuris ciuilis*.[27]

26. C.11 q.3 d.p.c.24.
27. While some had thought Gratian disapproved of any application of Roman

Or perhaps he intended to replace all earlier canonical collections by creating the ultimate collection of the church's law.[28] Several aspects of the *Decretum* make such hypotheses difficult to defend. First, the structure of the *causae* organized around questions pertaining to real-life scenarios do not allow for a systematic treatment of canon law. Second, the entire *De penitentia* and many *dicta* include paragraph after paragraph of theological argumentation, none of which parallels (or directly opposes) anything in Justinian's corpus and little of which has parallels in earlier canonical collections. Third, the earlier recension of the *Decretum* omits several issues of canon law common in earlier collections, most notably liturgical and sacramental regulations.[29] It also did not include a strict penitential. In short, if Gratian was intending to produce the best, most organized, most comprehensive collection of canon law, he failed miserably. More recent scholarship has subsequently focused on Gratian's identity as a *magister* and on the *Decretum* as a teaching text.[30]

The discussion of Gratian's purposes must take into account the early inclusion of *De penitentia* in the *Decretum*, an inclusion that must have contributed to his goals. Gratian was teaching clerics, and he wanted to teach them not only the content of the church's traditional canons but also how to analyze and interpret such legal texts in relation to the Christian tradition as a whole. Such analysis, as *De penitentia* and many other sections of theological argumentation showed,

---

law to the church, Kuttner found the view difficult to accept: Kuttner, "Research on Gratian," 20.

28. This viewpoint was summed up by Kuttner's question pertaining to the issue of Gratian's purpose ("Research on Gratian," 10): "Did Gratian merely want to produce a canonical collection that would be more comprehensive than any single compilation before him, combining the materials of the Italian reformers with those assembled by Ivo of Chartres; and one that would apply the new dialectical methods of the age to those traditional but often discordant *canones*?"

29. See the excellent discussion, based on the omission of *De consecratione* from the earlier recension, in Wei, *Gratian the Theologian*.

30. The comments in this and the following paragraph reflect those in my *Master of Penance*, 300–312. The emphasis on Gratian as a teacher now pervades the field, both among scholars working on very detailed textual matters (e.g., José Miguel Viejo-Ximénez; see, for instance, his "La composición del Decreto de Graciano," *Ius Canonicum* 45.90 [2005]: 441) and those who have emphasized Gratian's position in the larger legal developments of the Middle Ages (see, for instance, James A. Brundage, *The Medieval Origins of the Legal Profession: Canonists, Civilians, and Courts* [Chicago: University of Chicago Press, 2008], 102).

required training and exercises in the burgeoning field of theology and therefore the application of methods of the *trivium* (grammar, dialectic, rhetoric) to the study of the *sacra pagina* (the Scriptures), of the Fathers, and, for Gratian (as to a certain extent for Anselm of Laon), also of the canons.

Thus, Gratian sought to create an educated priesthood. This was no novel endeavor, but he went about it in a novel way. His concern for priestly ignorance lies just under the surface throughout his work, but his complaints come to the fore in DD.36–39. *De penitentia* too expresses concern for uneducated clerics since, in his view, ignorant priests could not bind and loose sinners, that is, they could not properly administer penance to the benefit of their parishioners' souls. Ignorant priests put Christians' souls at risk and thus also placed the chief enterprise of the church on earth at risk. Ignorance about penance particularly places the church in danger because it not only affects whether laypeople can properly reconcile themselves to God but it also affects who inhabits the clerical hierarchy. The ecclesiastical hierarchy is filled necessarily with sinners, but it cannot be filled with those who commit grievous, scandalous offences and neglect to exhibit and practice true penance afterward. The judges of the church had to know from the canons what qualities were needed for a man to be ordained in the first place, what offences threatened an ordained cleric's position in the church, and how charges and investigations against a cleric should be undertaken (all issues dealt with in the *prima pars* and the first 26 *causae*). Nonetheless, they also had to be trained in what true penance looked like (this is what *De penitentia* does) so that, for instance, they could determine whether a lapsed priest could be reinstated (D.50).

In short, as a *magister*, Gratian aimed to train clerics who would serve as legal advisors, representatives, or judges in ecclesiastical courts or who would judge the sin and contrition of individual souls, lay or cleric. For all of these tasks, knowledge of the canons was essential, and for many of them, an understanding of penance was as well. An education in these matters would contribute to a reform in the governance of the church, and Gratian sought to provide that education for his students in Bologna. *De penitentia* was important for the developing fields of canon law and theology and it contributed to the efforts of church reform that from the mid-eleventh century onward worked to create a distinctive, morally pure, and knowledgeable clergy, separate from and spiritually responsible for the laity.[31]

Textual Issues and Manuscripts for the Edition

The Recensions of the Text

In this edition, the major stages of textual development in *De penitentia* are presented simultaneously, using manuscript evidence of *De penitentia* combined with a critical evaluation of the recent literature on other sections of the *Decretum*. The edition adopts new nomenclature incorporating the general terminology of one group of scholars (represented most visibly by Anders Winroth) and the conceptual framework of another (represented most visibly by Carlos Larrainzar). Some background is in order before explaining and defining the conventions used in this edition

Different conceptualizations about the development of the text of the *Decretum* have generated different terminology, most clearly seen in the terms used for the earlier recension discovered in extant manuscripts and for the pre-vulgate version of text (i.e., vulgate minus the *paleae*). Winroth and others refer to the earlier recension as the "first recension" and the pre-vulgate version as the "second recension."[32] In their opinion, only these two versions have clear testimony in the manuscripts, and they conceive of the second recension in its totality as a conscientiously formed composition in which all

31. As introductions to this era of reform, one can consult Colin Morris, *The Papal Monarchy: The Western Church from 1050 to 1250* (Oxford: Clarendon Press, 1989), 11–180, and Kathleen G. Cushing, *Reform and the Papacy in the Eleventh Century: Spirituality and Social Change* (Manchester: Manchester University Press, 2015).

32. This terminology may be found, for instance, in Winroth, *Making of Gratian's* Decretum; idem, "Recent Work on the Making of Gratian's *Decretum*," BMCL 26 (2004–6): 1–30; idem, "Neither Slave nor Free: Theology and Law in Gratian's Thoughts on the Definition of Marriage and Unfree Persons," in *Medieval Church Law and the Origins of the Western Legal Tradition: A Tribute to Kenneth Pennington*, ed. Wolfgang P. Müller and Mary E. Sommar (Washington, D.C.: The Catholic University of America Press, 2006), 97–109, and idem, "Marital Consent in Gratian's *Decretum*," in *Readers, Texts and Compilers in the Earlier Middle Ages: Studies in Medieval Canon Law in Honour of Linda Fowler-Magerl*, ed. Martin Brett and Kathleen G. Cushing (Burlington, Vt.: Ashgate, 2009), 111–21. Among literature in German, see, e.g., Titus Lenherr, "Zur Redaktionsbeschichte von C.23 q.5 in der '1. Rezension' von Gratians Dekret: 'The Making of a Quaestio'," BMCL 26 (2004–6): 31–58. Landau also adopts this terminology in his "Gratian and the *Decretum Gratiani*," 38–41.

the additional texts were added to the first recension in one continuous effort, either by Gratian himself or by others in Bologna (most likely Gratian's disciples). Some Spanish scholars, especially Carlos Larrainzar and José Miguel Viejo-Ximénez, adhere to a more organic model of textual development, whereby the earlier recension defined by Winroth is not the "first," and several stages of redaction stand between the so-called first and second recensions.[33] Since they fundamentally object to the idea of a clearly defined "second recension" and believe manuscript evidence exists for a recension earlier than the "first," they refer to the stage equivalent to Winroth's "firs recension" as the *Concordia* stage (adopting Gratian's original title for his work), whereas they refer to the pre-vulgate text as the *Decretum* stage (adopting the title that the work eventually obtained). These scholars insist that the development between the *Concordia* and *Decretum* stages occurred by several irregularly sized steps, some of which have manuscript testimony. The first identifiable step is clearly defined in the manuscripts (and perhaps is the only step that is so clearly defined), especially in the appendix to the Florence manuscript of the earlier recension (Fd). The additional texts added in this first step on the way from the *Concordia* to the *Decretum* receive the name the *additiones bononienses*, or "Bolognese additions," because of their purported origin in Bologna.

The present edition attempts to utilize the best aspects of both models. Larrainzar's has the benefit of being rooted in the manuscript evidence and highlights the progressive development of the

33. Larrainzar and Viejo-Ximénez's articles are numerous; see especially Carlos Larrainzar, "La formación del Decreto de Graciano pore tapas," ZRG Kan. Abt. 87 (2001): 5–83; idem, "La edición critica del Decreto de Graciano," BMCL 27 (2007): 71–105; and idem, "Métodos para el anàlisis de la formación literaria del Decretum Gratiani: 'Etapas' y 'esquemas' de redacción," in *Proceedings of the Thirteenth International Congress of Medieval Canon Law: Esztergom, 3–8 August 2008*, ed. Péter Erdö and Anzelm Szabolcs Szuromi, MIC Ser. C–14 (Vatican City: Biblioteca Apostolica Vaticana, 2010), 85–116; Viejo-Ximénez, "La composición del Decreto," 438–42 (with a very helpful summary of Larrainzar's stages, or *etapas*, on 440); idem, "La recepción del derecho romano en la derecho canónico," *Annaeus* 2 (2005): 139–69; idem, "Variantes textuales y variants doctrinales en C.2 q.8," in *Proceedings of the Twelfth International Congress of Medieval Canon Law, Washington DC, 1 August – 7 August 2004*, ed. Uta-Renate Blumenthal, Kenneth Pennington, and Atria A. Larson, MIC C–13. (Vatican City: Biblioteca Apostolica Vaticana, 2008), 161–190; idem, "'Costuras' y 'Descosidos' en la version divulgada del Decreto de Graciano," *Ius Ecclesiae* 21 (2009): 133–54.

text in Bologna; Winroth's has the virtue of simplicity and captures the fact that the two main recensions achieved wider dissemination. This edition employs the nomenclature of "R1" for Winroth's "firs recension" and Larrainzar's "*Concordia* stage." It employs the nomenclature of "R2" to refer broadly to the finalized pre-vulgate text, the version referred to as the "second recension" by Winroth and the "*Decretum* stage" by Larrainzar. The short-hand "R1" and "R2" allows for further, intermediate stages to be defined. In this context, recension R2a stands equivalent to the "Bolognese additions," or the firs major set of additions to R1 that a finalized R2 incorporated. Post-R2a stages can be referred to by "R2b," "R2c," and so forth. In one place, *De penitentia* D.7 cc.2–4, the edition and translation necessarily separates out textual versions R1, R2a, and R2b. In other places, text certainly does not belong to R1 and seems unlikely to belong to R2a, but it remains unclear whether it can be squarely identified with R2b or some later stage.[34]

The R2 alterations to R1 consisted not only of whole additional texts (*auctoritates* or *dicta*) but also of changes to individual words or phrases. These latter types of changes did not occur all at once, but it is impossible to assign each alteration of this kind to R2a, R2b, R2c, and so forth, and so no attempt has been made to do so here. These changes can be understood simply and generically as R2 changes to R1 text that scribes soon incorporated into new copies of the *Decretum*.

34. The issue of dating these recensions remains contested. Winroth and others maintain that the earlier recension (in my terminology, R1) was not completed until after the Second Lateran Council of 1139, while I have argued that the link to Lateran II is far more tenuous than some have assumed, that there are good reasons to suppose that a reference in R1 to a "synod held under Innocent II in Rome" might not refer to Lateran II. Werckmeister accepted my note of caution on this issue. A gathering of ecclesiastics and lay nobles at the imperial coronation of Lothar III in June 1133 may in fact constitute the Roman synod and provide the *terminus post quem* of R1. R2 includes several canons that have been assumed to come from the legislation of Lateran II, which would place the completion of the first major set of additions to R1 at c. 1140. After a careful textual comparison, Pennington has expressed doubts that Gratian's text of decrees from Innocent II was a copy of the canons of Lateran II. Pennington would date R1 to the mid-1130s, like myself, and R2 possibly even pre-1139, with those canons derived from pre-Lateran II councils and writings by Innocent II. See my "Early Stages of Gratian's *Decretum* and the Second Lateran Council: A Reconsideration," BMCL 27 (2007): 21–56; Werckmeister, Introduction to *Décret de Gratien, Causes 27 à 36: Le Mariage*, ed. and trans. Jean Werckmeister, Sources canoniques 3 (Paris: Éditions du Cerf, 2011), 39–40; Pennington, "The Biography of Gratian," 682–88.

The Manuscripts

More than 600 manuscripts of the *Decretum* still survive. This edition uses a mere seven and improves upon the edition of Friedberg, who used eight. The justification for such a selection rests on the work of scholars who have identified many twelfth-century (and thus the earliest) manuscripts and have produced some working editions of other, comparatively short, sections of the *Decretum* that have shed light on the nature and quality of these manuscripts.[35] The present edition utilizes the following:[36]

Aa = Admont, Stiftsbibliothek 23 and 43. Date: 1160s. Provenance: Austria, at Admont itself.[37]   The two codices making up this *Decretum* manuscript contain a complex arrangement of the text, including a division after C.14 and main sections of R1 text interpolated with some R2 texts. Codex 23 contains an interpolated R1 text of the *prima pars* and CC.1–14 followed by an appendix or supplement of most,

35. On C.24 q.1: Titus Lenherr, *Die Exkommunikations- und Depositionsgewalt der Häretiker bei Gratian und den Dekretisten bis zur Glossa ordinaria des Johannes Teutonicus*, Münchener Theologische Studien III, Kan. Abt. 42 (St Ottilien: EOS Verlag, 1987), edition at 18–56; other studies stemming from the work for this monograph: Lenherr, "Die Summarien zu den Texten des 2. Laterankonzils von 1139 in Gratians Dekret," AKKR 150 (1981): 528–51; idem, "Arbeiten mit Gratians Dekret," AKKR 151 (1982): 140–66; idem, "Fehlende 'Paleae' als Zeichen eines überlieferungsgeschichtlich jüngeren Datums von Dekrethandschriften," AKKR 151 (1982): 495–507. On C.30 qq. 1, 3, and 4: Enrique de León, *La 'cognatio spiritualis' según Graciano* (Milan, 1996), edition at 138–68. On D.16: Regula Gujer, *Concordia Discordantium Codicum Manuscriptorum? Die Textentwicklung von 18 Handschriften anhand der D.16 des Decretum Gratiani*, Forschungen zur kirchlichen Rechtsgeschichte und zum Kirchenrecht 23 (Cologne: Böhlau, 2004). For R1 D.20: Tatsushi Genka, "Hierarchie der Texte, Hierarchie der Autoritäten: Zur Hierarchie der Rechtsquellen bei Gratian," ZRG Kan. Abt. 95 (2009): 100–127, edition at 126–27. None of these editions utilized Fd. This edition does so based on Winroth's unveiling of its true nature as a manuscript containing an earlier recension. Its value has been highlighted in the numerous studies by Larrainzar and Viejo-Ximénez; see above, n. 33. Fs was also not used in these editions; it has only recently been identified as an early manuscript of good qualit .

36. I provide a much more detailed analysis of the textual quality and nature of all seven manuscripts in my "Gratian's *De penitentia* in Twelfth-Century Manuscripts," BMCL 31 (2014): 57–110. I also put the manuscripts into three categories: R1 manuscripts plus *additiones* (Aa, Fd), mixed or intermediate manuscripts (Fs, Pf, Sb), and finalized or completed R2 manuscripts (Bi, Mk)

37. Gujer, *Concordia Discordantium Codicum Manuscriptorum?* 223–27. See table 1 (pp. xxxviii) for all manuscript *sigla* and the folios on which *De penitentia* appears.

but not all, of the remaining R2 *auctoritates* and *dicta* of these sections, while codex 43 has, again, an interpolated R1 text of the rest of the *causae* (CC.15–36) followed by additional material pertaining to clerical orders, *De consecratione*, and an appendix or supplement of most, but not all, of the remaining R2 *auctoritates* and *dicta* for CC.15–36.[38] The manuscript has relatively few marginal or interlinear additions or corrections. Its R1 text sometimes includes the R2 changes to individual words and phrases.

In this edition, the *siglum* AaB refers to the appendix of Aa. The AaB text for *De penitentia* appears within the same codex as the main text of *De penitentia* in Aa (specifically codex 43), but for textual analysis, it is convenient to indicate when a text appears in the appendix, not the main section of Aa, through the usage of this different *siglum*.

Bi = Biberach an der Riss, Spitalarchiv B 3515. Date: third quarter of 12th century. Provenance: northern Italy.[39]   The manuscript appears less professional than Mk and Pf and contains many uncorrected errors. The quality of its text is, nevertheless, generally quite good; it often contains correct readings in both R1 and R2 passages. The manuscript contains several early glosses, few *paleae*, and several added texts called *extrauagantes*, and it has received scholarly attention for these reasons.[40] Its *De penitentia* contains all additional R2 texts and all R2 changes to individual words and phrases in R1 text; there are no remnant R1 readings at the points of these changes. In brief, it is a manuscript of the finalized second recension

Fd = Firenze, Biblioteca Nazionale Centrale, Conv. Soppr. A.I.402. Date: mid-12th century.[41] **Provenance: Bologna.**   This manuscript

38. For a more precise description of the contents, see Winroth, *Making of Gratian's* Decretum, 25–26. Melodie H. Eichbauer, "From the First to the Second Recension: The Progressive Evolution of the *Decretum*," BMCL 29 (2011–12): 119–67, has highlighted the incomplete nature of the supplemental, R2 texts.

39. Gujer, *Concordia Discordantium Codicum Manuscriptorum?* 228–36.

40. Weigand, "Die Dekrethandschrift B 3515 Spitalarchivs Biberach an der Riss," BMCL 2 (1972): 76–81; Lenherr, "Arbeiten," 164, and idem, "Summarien," 551; Stephan Kuttner, "The 'Extravagantes' of the Decretum in Biberach," BMCL 3 (1973): 61–71.

41. The relevant script(s) of Fd is (are) dated variously to the second half of the twelfth century (Winroth based on the work of Adriana Di Domenico) or pre-1150 (Larrainzar). Giuseppa Zanichelli has personally related to me her opinion that Di Domenico erred and that the main script (though not necessarily the illu-

stands incomplete, beginning at D.28 d.p.c.13. For the rest of the *Decretum*, the first 104 folios contain a complete, pure (non-interpolated) R1 with some R1 corrections and some R2 additions in the margins. The next sixty folios contain an appendix or supplement of the majority of other R2 texts, mostly in the main columns of the folios but sometimes in a different hand and ink in the margins.[42] The main body of the manuscript was left incomplete in its decorated initials but was relatively professional in production, evidenced by its even lines and justified columns. The appendix has a rougher appearance with unjustified columns. Two chronologically consecutive systems of identifiers cue the texts in the appendix to their proper location in the sequence of text in the first part of the manuscript.[43] The R1 text was heavily corrected.

As in the case of Aa, this edition makes use of a modified *siglum*, namely FdB, for text that appears in the Fd appendix. Given the importance of marginal texts written in a different hand in this manuscript, a third *siglum* related to this codex is also adopted. "FdG" refers to marginal texts in either Fd or FdB that are not obviously corrections to originally omitted texts in those sections but seem to represent later textual additions.[44]

Fs = Firenze, Biblioteca Medicea Laurenziana, Plut. 1 sin. 1. Date: second half of 12th century with mid-13th-century gloss apparatus. Provenance: Bologna/central Italy. This manuscript has recently been identified by Kenneth Pennington as an early vulgate manuscript

minations) is without a doubt mid-twelfth century, specificall , in her opinion, of the decade 1150–1160.

42. For a more precise description of the contents, see Winroth, *Making of Gratian's* Decretum, 28–30. As in the case of Aa, all the texts do not add up to a complete R2; see Eichbauer, "From the First to the Second Recension."

43. The first system used incipits; the second system, put in place after the addition of some other (R2b, R2c, etc.) texts, utilized tie-marks. See my *Master of Penance*, 218–35.

44. In my opinion and that of Carlos Larrainzar, many of these marginal additions represent later stages in the development of R2, namely some stage post-R2a. Some of the marginal additions may in fact represent the work of a later scribe filling in what had been omitted earlier by the original scribe. In his review essay of my book, John Wei argues that most of the marginal additions in all of Fd fall into this latter category. He does not, however, provide a systematic study of all such additions; nor does he address my specific arguments about D.7 cc.2–4. See his "The Importance and Influence of Gratian's Tract *De penitentia*," ZRG Kan. Abt. 101 (2015): 373–88.

of superior textual quality. The twelfth-century *Decretum* text was originally accompanied by early glosses. These were later erased, when
Bartholomeus Brixiensis's expanded version of Johannes Teutonicus's
Glossa ordinaria was copied into the margins. The text of the *Decretum*
was professionally produced in a clear script with a frequent, even
excessive, use of the e-cedilla. It contains all R2 additions plus some
additional lines in two of the Roman law chapters in *De pen.* D.1 that
either do not appear or appear only in the margins of the other R2
manuscripts used here. Nevertheless, it also retains several R1 readings altered by R2. For this reason, it is an intermediate or mixed manuscript, not a pure manuscript of the finalized second recension

Its copy of *De penitentia* is incomplete, missing D.4 c.8 *dicitur. Cur
ergo* through D.6 c.1 *plorantem que unicum*. The break comes after
fol. 315v. Those numbering the folios identified the next folio as fol.
320r to account for the missing text. These folios apparently were
already missing by the late thirteenth century, when the new gloss
was added in the margins.

**Mk = München, Bayerische Staatsbibliothek lat. 28161. Date: sec-
ond half of 12th century. Provenance: central/northern Italy.**[45]   This
manuscript has received privilege of place since the work of Lenherr.
He recommended its use and employed it for determining his base
text. Gujer found it problematic. For *De penitentia*, it is most closely
related to the pre-corrected Bi but often has inferior readings. It is
heavily corrected. It is a manuscript of the finalized second recension
and contains only negligible traces of R1 readings.

**Pf = Paris, Bibliothèque Nationale lat. 3884 II. Date: third quarter
of 12th century. Provenance: northern France, probably Paris (possibly Sens).**[46]   This manuscript is probably the earliest extant French

45. Gujer, *Concordia Discordantium Codicum Manuscriptorum?* 196–202, 281–90.

46. Ibid., 302–8. Gujer did not offer a specific theory on provenance. My suggestion, based on art history combined with current scholarship on the early Parisian school of canon law, is the cumulative result of consultation of the following (many thanks to Susan L'Engle for directing my attention to Nordenfalk and
Cahn): Carl Nordenfalk, Review of *The Corpus of the Miniatures in the Manuscripts
of Decretum Gratiani* by Anthony Melnikas, *Zeitschrift für Kunstgeschichte* 43, no. 3
(1980): 318–37; Rosy Schilling, "The *Decretum Gratiani* formerly in the C. W. Dys-
on Perrins Collection," *Journal of the Archaeological Association* 26 (1963): 27–39
(in terms of art history, Pf is in a family of manuscripts including the *Decretum*
manuscript now at the Getty Museum); Walter Cahn, *Romanesque Manuscripts:*

copy of the *Decretum*. It contains several editorial changes and unique variants. The scribe attempted to improve the grammar and flow of the text. In places where R2 made changes to R1 text, it sometimes preserves the R1 readings. It is therefore a mixed or intermediate manuscript, containing all additional R2 texts but not containing all R2 changes to R1 text.

Sb = Salzburg, Stiftsbibliothek St. Peter a.XI.9. Date: third quarter of 12th century. Provenance: Bologna/central Italy.[47]   This manuscript is the least corrected of the seven manuscripts here. It contains many unique and faulty variants. Like Fs and Pf, it is a mixed or intermediate manuscript, but it is exceptional for the number of R1 readings it retains. In more places than any other manuscript collated, it preserves R1 readings later changed in R2. Despite its failings from the perspective of general textual quality, it is invaluable for its preservation of these R1 readings.

In addition, the following two editions have been consulted:

EdF = Emil Friedberg, *Decretum Gratiani* (Leipzig, 1879).   Friedberg's edition has been included given its continued importance in *Decretum* scholarship and since it provides a witness to other manuscripts. Most of these are manuscripts of the finalized second recension. At least one, Friedberg's manuscript A (Köln, Dombibliothek 127, currently designated Ka), is very early (c. 1160s) and constitutes a mixed or intermediate manuscript, that is to say, one that at times preserves R1 readings.

EdRom = *Editio Romana*, as cited in the notes of Friedberg.   By papal decree, the 1582 *Editio Romana* was the version of the *Decretum* used in canon law studies in Catholic regions and in Catholic ecclesiastical courts from its printing until the *Codex iuris canonici* of 1917 went into effect in 1918. The present edition has not collated the EdRom in full, but it does at times note certain EdRom variants as

---

The Twelfth Century, 2 vols., A Survey of Manuscripts Illuminated in France (London: H. Miller, 1996); Peter Landau, "Master Peter of Louveciennes and the Origins of the Parisian school of Canon Law around 1170," in *Proceedings of the Fourteenth International Congress of Medieval Canon Law, Toronto, August 2012,* ed. Joseph Goering, Andreas Thier, and Stephan Dusil, MIC Ser. C–15 (Vatican City: Biblioteca Apostolica Vaticana, forthcoming).

47. Gujer, *Concordia Discordantium Codicum Manuscriptorum?* 327–32.

Table 1. *Sigla* and the folios on which *De penitentia* appears

Siglum	Manuscript, Manuscript Section, or Edition	Folios of *De penitentia*
Aa	Admont, Stiftsbibliothek 43	145ʳ–183ᵛ
AaB	Aa appendix	329ᵛ–337ʳ
Fd	Firenze, Biblioteca Nazionale Centrale Conv. Soppr. A I.402	88ʳᵇ–99ᵛᵃ
FdB	Fd appendix	159ᵛᵃ–162ʳᵇ
FdG	Fd marginal additions in Fd and FdB	*passim*
Bi	Biberach, Spitalarchiv B 3515	292ᵛᵇ–315ʳᵇ
Fs	Firenze, Biblioteca Medicea Laurenziana Plut. 1 sin. 1	294ʳᵇ–321ʳᵃ
Mk	München, Bayerische Staatsbibliothek lat. 28161	235ʳᵃ–255ᵛᵇ
Pf	Paris, Bibliothèque Nationale de France lat. 3884 II	99ᵛᵇ–127ᵛᵃ
Sb	Salzburg, Stiftsbibliothek St. Peter a.XI.9	258ʳᵃ–282ʳᵇ
EdF	Friedberg, ed., *Decretum Magistri Gratiani*	cols. 1159–1247

indicated in Friedberg's apparatus, which reveal that the *correctores Romani* had at their disposal some early, good manuscripts and sometimes chose readings superior to Friedberg's.

Principles and Practices of This Edition and Translation

This book is an edition and translation both of R1 as defined predominantly by Fd and, separately, of R2 as determined by the multitude of manuscript witnesses, with no manuscript given consistent preference. In early drafts, this edition utilized EdF as the base text; Fd came to provide the base text for R1 text. R2 text was ascertained through various methods: quantitative analysis of variants, comparison with material and possible formal sources, consideration of meaning and grammar, and evaluation of the apparent family lineages among manuscripts. The R1 text attempts to present what Gratian originally wrote in his original treatise (at least the earliest version that can be detected); the R2 text attempts to reconstruct what *De penitentia* looked like by c. 1140–1150.[48] The formatting of the

48. I have not included manuscripts of the Σ family and P family. The former emerged early but with heavy editorial changes; the latter appeared later in the twelfth century and could have been the dominant version in Bologna in Huguccio's day. My edition therefore does not indicate the various versions of *De penitentia* preserved in these groups of manuscripts as they came into being in the second half of the twelfth century. Gujer, *Concordia Discordantium Codicum Manuscriptorum?* 357–62; John C. Wei, "A Discussion and List of Manuscripts Belong-

edition shows successive developments in the R2 text, although the *emendationes*, or small changes to R1 text, can be presented as belonging to R2 only generally speaking, regardless of when, in fact, they came to dominate the manuscript transmission.

The edition and translation present *De penitentia* in light of its original design, that of a theological treatise, as revealed in twelfth-century manuscripts. As in Fd and the other manuscripts, no R1 *auctoritas* is separated out as a "canon" or "chapter." Rather, each one is placed within paragraphs so as to reflect the flow of argumentation. Paragraph divisions do not follow any single manuscript; they follow modern conceptions of paragraph organization in order to assist readers with understanding Gratian's text. Sometimes several *auctoritates* appear in one paragraph, at times combined with some of Gratian's own words. Sometimes a longer *auctoritas* is a paragraph unto its own or is divided into multiple paragraphs.

This is the first edition of any part of the *Decretum* to present a critical edition of R1 and to show the progressive development of R2 text. It is the first edition of *De penitentia* to improve upon EdF for R2 text.[49] It also constitutes the first translation of *De penitentia* into any vernacular language. The late Jean Werckmeister produced an edition and French translation of the marriage causae (CC.27–36), but exclusive of C.33 q.3, or *De penitentia*. He reproduced Friedberg's edition for all R2 texts in the marriage *causae* and provided the variant readings of Fd and Aa on R1 texts. Since he did not collate additional early manuscripts of the mixed or intermediate type (e.g., Fs, Ka, Pf, Sb), his work cannot claim to produce a critical edition of "first recension" text.[50] Werckmeister adhered to a strict first-versus-second-recensio understanding of the textual development of the *Decretum* and did not give any indication of the progressive development of the text. The only other English translation of any section of the *Decretum* is Augustine Thompson and James Gordley's translation of *prima pars* DD.1–20 (the *Tractatus de legibus*) with ordinary gloss.[51] The English-speaking

---

ing to the Σ-group (S-group)," available at https://sites.google.com/site/repertori umiuriscanonici/home/gratian/s-group; accessed 12 October 2013. Wei identifies 23 manuscripts of the group and lists several other potential candidates in n. 8.

49. Note that I am in no way claiming to produce a critical edition of R2.

50. Werckmeister made this claim in his introduction to *Décret de Gratien, Causes 27 à 36*, 69.

51. See n. 12 above.

community looks forward to the publication of Giulio Silano's translation of the entire *Decretum*, which, like Thompson's publication, will translate the *Editio Romana* of 1582, the version of the *Decretum* that was the official church edition from that year until 1918

Abbreviations in the Edition

The following abbreviations are used in the *apparatus critici* and margins:

ac	ante correctionem
add.	addidit
c.	canon/capitulum
corr.	correxit
d.a.c.	dictum ante canonem/capitulum
d.p.c.	dictum post canonem/capitulum
inc.	incipit
interlin.	inter lineas
hom.	homoeoteleuton
mg.	in margine
om.	omisit
pc	post correctionem
pr.	prologus
praem.	praemisit
rep.	repetivit
rub.	rubrica
tr.	transposuit

Formatting

1. Regular, larger font = R1 text, as determined by main text of Fd and Aa (sometimes combined with readings in Fs, Pf, and Sb), with preference given to Fd; significant variant readings from all manuscripts and EdF in bottom apparatus; R2 changes to specifi   words/phrases noted in special, middle apparatus (see below).

2. Smaller Scala typeface = R2 text, as determined by FdB, FdG, AaB and all other manuscripts plus EdF; variant readings from all manuscripts, EdF, and occasionally EdRom in bottom *apparatus*.

   a. Smaller font without any brackets = R2a text, as determined by FdB.

   b. Smaller font in square brackets ([...]) = R2b, possibly R2c, text, as determined by FdG (the texts are present in Fd but only in the margins in a different hand and ink).

   c. Smaller font in curly brackets ({...}) = indeterminate, post-R2a stages of R2; not present anywhere in Fd (main body, appendix, or margins).

3. Italics = scriptural quotations, whether within another *auctoritas* or cited on its own.

4. Bold-faced, left-aligned type = rubrics to select R2 *auctoritates*, as determined by FdB, FdG, AaB and all other manuscripts plus EdF.

5. Other Editorial Interventions

   a. Italicized, left-aligned text within angle brackets (<...>) = editor's inserted subheadings to aid the reader in following the topics under discussion and Gratian's argument (pro, contra, etc.).

   b. Regular text within parentheses, e.g., (Et infra), = text present in manuscripts that is technically incorrect in relationship to the material source; if a phrase *Et infra* or *Post pauca* appears in parentheses, it means that the passage quoted after this phrase in fact follows without break from the preceding passage in the material source.

   c. Ellipsis (...) = a break in the material source, or a switch from one material source to another, that is not indicated in the manuscripts.

   d. Marginal (inner) text-identifiers (e.g., c.2, d.p.c.12) = numbering of the various texts (*dicta* and *capitula*) as determined in the late medieval tradition, early modern printings, and EdF. With the exception of opening *dicta* in each distinction (which might include a "pr.," i.e., *prologus*, and a "d.a.c.1," i.e., *dictum ante* c.1), for simplicity's sake the edition labels every other *dictum* a *dictum post* (d.p.c.), even though in some cases it would be appropriate to associate Gratian's words with the following *auctoritas* rather than the preceding one. A number in parentheses indicates that the so-called "chapter" is in fact Gratian's own words.[52]

   e. Marginal (outer) folio-markers (e.g., Fd 97ra) = notation of where each manuscript collated changes folio or column.

---

52. These are D.1 (c.20), the second half of D.1 c.30, or (c.30b), and D.4 (c.12). EdF's D.3 d.p.c.4 is a continuation of Pseudo-Augustine's *De uera et falsa penitentia* quoted in c.4; I have provided no separate number for it in the margin.

Some R2 texts are so short that they are contained within a single column or margin of FdB, FdG, or AaB. The edition still identifies the locations of these texts in FdB or FdG and AaB but puts the folio number in parentheses.

f. Text in small caps (e.g., AUGUSTINUS IN EODEM LIBRO) = represents the rough equivalent of an inscription, indicating the author and sometimes the work being quoted. The usage here is meant above all to help the reader take note of when Gratian begins to quote a new source, whether in a series of quoted *auctoritates* or embedded within what has traditionally been identified as a *dictum Gratiani*. The usage of small caps does not, therefore, line up strictly with separate chapter numbers in EdF.

Orthography and Punctuation

Spelling has been made uniform in accord with modern expectations but attempts to remain close to mid-twelfth-century Italian practice. Where great variation existed (e.g., usage of e-cedilla, -ci v. -ti), the edition uses: 'e' for all classical 'ae' and 'oe' spellings or e-cedilla; '-ti' in words such as *penitentia* where later and some contemporary usage often chose '-ci'; 'u' for lowercase 'u' and 'v' but 'V' for uppercase 'u' and 'v'; 'i' for 'i' and 'j'; *inquid* for the classical *inquit*; *set* for *sed*; *cum* for EdF's *quum*; *caritas* for EdF's *karitas*.

Punctuation follows modern American usage and is intended, as many other conventions of the edition, to assist the reader in understanding Gratian's text.

Apparatus critici

The Latin edition contains two *apparatus critici*.

1. Bottom apparatus (on every page): This apparatus corresponds to the most familiar type of *apparatus criticus*, in negative, noting manuscript readings departing from the established text. Unique variant readings are reproduced only in rare instances and most often from Aa (or AaB) and Fd (or FdB or FdG).

Example:

D.3 c.4 uindicat] uindicans Fd Bi Mk$_{ac}$ Pf EdF

= Fd, Bi, Mk prior to correction, Pf, and EdF all read *uindicans*, while the remaining manuscripts (Aa, Fs, Sb) read *uindicat*.

2. Middle apparatus (on select pages): This apparatus presents R2 changes to R1 text, or, in other words, changes to the original treatise that became standard. This middle apparatus is never used with reference to R2 text. Following the lemma from R1 text, this apparatus firs presents the R2 reading. Then all R2 variants (including unique ones) are noted in parentheses. The material within the parentheses acts as a negative apparatus, but it is positive with reference to Fd and Aa.

Examples:

D.1 c.68 regni] regis R2

= all manuscripts except Fd and Aa (viz. Bi, Fs, Mk, Pf, Sb) have *regis* where R1 reads *regni*.

D.1 c.88 in figura] figuraliter R2 (in figura S

= all manuscripts except for Aa, Fd, and Sb read *figuralite* ; R1 reading is *in figur* , which Sb retains. The bottom apparatus notes a unique R1 variant reading in Aa (*figurat*).

D.2 d.p.c.12 caritatem] *add.* semel R2 (*interlin.* Aa, *om.* Sb)

= R1 does not have a *semel* after *caritatem*, but manuscripts Bi, Fs, Mk, and Pf do. Aa adds the *semel* interlineally. The *semel* is not present in Sb; therefore Sb preserves the R1 reading.

The English translation has footnotes, some of which contain comments corresponding to the middle apparatus on the facing page. These comments explain in sentence form the R2 changes to R1 text when such changes in the Latin make a difference for the English translation. Other footnotes provide brief information on things such as obscure names or offer explanatory comments on text that is difficult to interpret. The notes do not offer extensive commentary, which may be found in chapters 1–5 of my *Master of Penance*.

In sum, the reader of either Latin or English can read R1 by following the text in the larger font and can read R2 by reading all text, in larger font and smaller, Scala font, in combination with the Latin middle apparatus of R2 changes to R1 text or the English footnotes explaining later R2 changes to R1 text.

Biblical Citations, Cross-references, and Apparatus fontium

All biblical citations are listed exclusively in the outer margin of the English translation, as are any and all cross-references to other sections of *De penitentia* or other parts of the *Decretum Gratiani*.

The Latin edition's top apparatus consists of an *apparatus fontium*,

specifically references to material sources and the best modern edition available. These material sources are the patristic, papal, conciliar, or Roman law texts from which Gratian's excerpts ultimately
derive. Many of them were known to Gratian only through formal sources, i.e., medieval compilations and florilegia. A few works
can be considered simultaneously Gratian's material and his formal
source. These are medieval texts from which Gratian directly copied,
including (1) Pseudo-Augustine's *De uera et falsa penitentia*,[53] (2) the
Glossa ordinaria on the Bible, which served as Gratian's formal source
for several patristic texts (see Appendix C) but which also at times
served as a material source in its original commentary and its cre-
ative paraphrasing of patristic material, and (3) a ninth-century collection of sermons that survives in various forms in numerous manuscripts. The collection bears no name, even in its modern edition. I
have chosen to call it the *Collectio sermonum pseudo-Ambrosiana*, since
most of the sermons circulated with an attribution to Ambrose of
Milan and were included among the dubious works of the bishop
in earlier editions, including Migne's Patrologia Latina. Gratian used
one of these sermons for D.1 c.39 and for D.3 c.1, which is a shorter
excerpt of the same text in D.1 c.39. The manuscript evidence sup-
ports the idea that Gratian had access to a copy of this sermon collection in some form in Bologna in the second quarter of the twelfth
century. Many of the extant manuscripts have a provenance of cen-
tral or northern Italy, and many survive from the second and third
quarters of the twelfth century, including manuscripts with the key
variant in D.1 c.39: the addition of *acceptabile* in the first sentence.[54]
Finally, it is clear that Gratian had access to complete manuscripts of
select patristic works and that Gratian copied his excerpts from them
directly, not via a *florilegiu* . Titus Lenherr has done excellent work
uncovering a family of manuscripts of Gregory the Great's *Moralia
in Iob* to which Gratian's manuscript must have belonged.[55] Besides

53. Karen Wagner, "*De vera et falsa penitentia*: An Edition and Study" (Ph.D.
dissertation, University of Toronto, 1995).

54. Cf. the introduction to Paul Mercier, ed., *XIV Homélies du IXe siècle*, SChr
161 (Paris: Éditions du Cerf, 1970), and the *apparatus fontium* to *Sermo* 7.

55. Titus Lenherr, "Langsame Annäherung an Gratians Exemplar der 'Mora-
lia in Iob'," in *Proceedings of the Thirteenth International Congress of Medieval Canon
Law, Esztergom, 3–8 August 2008*, ed. Peter Erdö and Sz. Anzelm Szuromi, MIC Ser.
C–14 (Vatican City: Biblioteca Apostolica Vaticana, 2010), 311–26.

the *Moralia*, Augustine's *De correptione et gratia* and Jerome's *Aduersus Iouinianum* are patristic texts that Gratian might have used in full manuscripts since his quotations from these two works in *De penitentia* are very lengthy.[56] Only if one locates *florilegia* with numerous excerpts of similar length from these works could one suppose that Gratian worked from a *florilegiu* in these cases and not from complete manuscripts of the patristic texts.[57]

Much recent literature on Gratian's *Decretum* has focused on Gratian's formal sources, or the collections of texts from which Gratian or later redactors directly copied the material source texts. Kuttner advocated for a critical edition of the *Decretum* that would identify all of Gratian's formal sources. As he well understood, that task presents major obstacles to completing such an edition.[58] Those Spanish scholars, led by Larrainzar, who have dreamed of and labor toward an eventual critical edition, have also found the issue of formal sources to inhibit the work.[59] Identifying which major pre-Gratian canonical collections contain a particular text is time consuming but not overly difficult. Friedberg did as much, and Werckmeister, acknowledging the difficulty of doing anything more, followed the same practice in his recent edition.[60] In short, Friedberg and Werckmeister present parallel passages in collections such as Burchard of Worms's *Decretum*, the *Decretum*, *Panormia*, and *Tripartita* associated with Ivo of Chartres, the *Collectio canonum* of Anselm of Lucca, and the *Collectio canonum trium librorum* for each *capitulum* in Gratian. Identifying which collection Gratian or later redactors used in each case, however, is a daunting task hindered by the lack of critical editions of these texts, not to mention untold numbers of lost manuscripts and even lost collections unknown to any modern scholar.

Because research on Gratian's formal sources has advanced much

56. Another possibility is Julianus Pomerius's *De uita contemplatiua*, wrongly attributed to Prosper of Aquitaine. Note that Gratian's copy of Augustine's text would have entitled it *De correctione et gratia*.

57. Peter Landau, "Patristische Texte in den beiden Rezensionen des *Decretum Gratiani*," BMCL 23 (1999): 77–82, assumed *florilegi* as the formal source for patristic passages not found in earlier canonical collections, but I believe in the cases named above, complete manuscripts of the material source are more likely.

58. Kuttner, "Research on Gratian," 10–11.

59. Cf. the comments in José Miguel Viejo-Ximénez, "La composición del Decreto," 438.

60. Werckmeister, Introduction to *Décret de Gratien, Causes 27 à 36*, 42.

in recent decades, I have chosen to be selective and not simply list all parallel texts in earlier works, but because in so many instances one cannot be sure whether Gratian did in fact use one or another collection or text, I have placed the current state of research into the formal sources of *De penitentia* into an appendix (Appendix C) rather than into the edition itself. As scholars such as Kenneth Pennington have noted, pinpointing a formal source frequently proves to be impossible.[61] Even after Peter Landau identified five main collections from which Gratian worked, he himself found instances in which Gratian (or a later redactor) took a few canons from other collections, such as Burchard's *Decretum*, or directly from the papal register of Gregory I, and he has admitted numerous instances where Gratian drew many of his texts from local collections or *florilegi* that remain unidentified, if ever they will be.[62] John Wei attempted to identify the formal source for every *capitulum* in *De penitentia*.[63] While he had much success and my own edition could not have been completed without his work, many of his conclusions had to remain tentative, and, in some cases, he could find no known text from which Gratian could have drawn his. In other cases where he did identify a formal source, his identification has not convinced me fully. At this point of research, a simple list of presumed formal sources could do more to hinder further research than to advance it; the appendix thus lists possible formal sources along with other, similar, near-contemporary texts to which additional research could fruitfully be applied.

61. Kenneth Pennington, "Gratian, Causa 19, and the Birth of Canonical Jurisprudence," *La cultura giuridico-canonica medioevale: Premesse per un dialogo ecumenico* (Rome: 2003), 215–36 and an expanded version in *"Panta rei": Studi dedicati a Manlio Bellomo*, ed. Orazio Condorelli (4 volumes; Roma: Il Cigno, 2004), 4.339–55; available online with manuscript image details at http://faculty.cua.edu/pennington/Canon%20Law/Causa19Rome.htm; accessed 30 September 2013.

62. The literature on Gratian's formal sources is now quite large. See the overview in José Miguel Viejo-Ximénez, "La investigación sobre las fuentes formales del Decreto de Graciano," *Initium* 7 (2002): 217–39. Landau's major contribution appeared in his "Neue Forschungen zur vorgratianischen Kanonessammlungen und den Quellen des gratianischen Dekrets," *Ius Commune* 11 (1984): 1–29. Later contributions include P. Landau, "Burchard de Worms et Gratien: À propos des sources immédiates de Gratien," RDC 48 (1998): 233–45, and idem, "Das Register Papst Gregors I. im Decretum Gratiani," in *Mittelalterliche Texte: Überlieferung, Befunde, Deutung; Kolloquium der Zentraldirektion der Monumenta Germaniae Historica am 28.–29. Juni 1996* (Hannover, 1996), 125–40.

63. John C. Wei, "Law and Religion in Gratian's *Decretum*," (Ph.D. diss., Yale University, 2008).

Finally, a note of methodology with regard to the usage of formal sources. Knowing a formal source can be immensely valuable in determining a correct reading in the text. If a reading in some manuscripts matches the reading in the formal source while others do not, more likely than not, the reading shared with the formal source is correct. The theory is neat but not without serious objection. For example, Gratian changed and created rubrics; why could he not also have altered a text in front of him?[64] Peter Lombard edited texts when he took them from Gratian; how can we be sure that Gratian did not as well?[65] In practice, the methodology is fraught with difficult . First, as noted above, few of Gratian's formal sources have been critically edited, so scholars often lack access to a reliable text and a critical apparatus to show manuscript variants. For *De penitentia*, the three major editions that I could consult were Joseph Motta's edition of 3L, Martin Brett's online working edition of the *Tripartita*, and Karen Wagner's edition of *De uera et falsa penitentia* (also a material source).[66] Second, one can never be sure what particular version Gratian had in front of him. This makes identifying a formal source in certain instances difficult, if not impossible, and choosing a reading in Gratian based on a reading in a supposed formal source highly objectionable. As Martin Brett has pointed out, there is a circular type of reasoning in this approach: one decides which formal source or version of a formal source Gratian (or some other figure) used based on how closely Gratian's text matches the text in said source or version of said source, but one also decides the best reading in Gratian's text based on whether it is the reading in the formal source.[67] All the same, as

64. This issue has long been recognized. Kuttner voiced his concern in "Research on Gratian," 10–11.

65. See an analysis of the Lombard's editing of certain texts from *De penitentia* in chapter 8 of my *Master of Penance*.

66. *Collectio canonum trium librorum*, vol. 2, *Pars altera: Liber III et Appendix*, ed. Joseph Motta, MIC Ser. B–8.2 (Vatican City: Biblioteca Apostolica Vaticana, 2008); *Collectio tripartita*. Working edition by Martin Brett and Przemysław Nowak. Available at http://project.knowledgeforge.net/ivo/tripartita.html; Wagner, "*De vera et falsa penitentia*."

67. Brett, "Creeping up on the *Panormia*," *Grundlagen des Rechts: Festschrift für Peter Landau zum 65. Geburtstag*, ed. Richard Helmholz (Paderborn: F. Schöning, 2000), 205–70, was referring specifically to the issue of the relationship between Ivo of Chartres's *Decretum* and the *Panormia*, a case in which it is clear that the *Panormia* was based on a text of the *Decretum* that is far superior to any of the extant *Decretum* manuscripts.

in so many other points of methodology, one works on a case-by-case basis, gathers all the evidence, and makes as informed a judgment as one can. At times, then, the edition reflects a particular reading on the basis of comparison with a formal source when the formal source is certain or nearly so. For instance, Gratian quoted *De uera et falsa penitentia* extensively. Fortunately, the work survives in several manuscripts and has been critically edited. Although making a decision on any one reading in Gratian based on the reading in the critical edition of *De uera* or a variant reading in its apparatus would be problematic, examining large portions of Gratian's quotations in tandem with the critical edition reveals that Gratian's manuscript of *De uera* must have been in the same family as Wagner's manuscripts B (Bologna, Biblioteca Comunale dell'Archiginnasio A148) and Vb (Città del Vaticano, Biblioteca Apostolica Vaticana, Reg. lat. 135). When my manuscripts of *De penitentia* differed on readings in texts taken from *De uera*, then, I could confidently give preference to a reading that matched its critical edition or, when the *De penitentia* readings did not match the *De uera* edition but one or more of my manuscripts did contain the variant reading from the B-Vb family of *De uera* manuscripts, I could confidently give preference to that reading. In such situations, comparison with the formal source helped determine the readings in the edition; in many other situations, however, the edition's text could be decided based only on considerations of grammar, meaning, and the general reliability of each manuscript collated.

Gratian's *Tractatus de penitentia*

Distinctio prima

<Quaestio>

His breuiter decursis, in quibus extra negotii finem aliquantulum pr.
euagati sumus, ad proposite cause tertiam questionem pertractan-
5 dam, qua queritur utrum sola cordis contritione, et secreta satisfactione, absque oris confessione quisque possit Deo satisfacere, redea-
mus.

<Sententia prima>

Sunt enim qui dicunt, quemlibet criminis ueniam sine confes- d.a.c.1
10 sione ecclesie et sacerdotali iudicio posse mereri, IUXTA ILLUD LEO-
NIS PAPE,

{"Petrus doluit et fleuit, quia errauit, ut homo. Non inuenio quid dixerit, scio c.1
quod fleuerit.}

"Lacrimas Petri lego, satisfactionem non lego." ITEM IOHANNES
15 CHRISOSTOMUS: "Lacrime lauant quod pudor est confiteri." ITEM c.2
PROPHETA: *Sacrificium Deo spiritus contribulatus, cor contritum et humi-* c.3
liatum, Deus, non despicies. ITEM: *Dixi, confitebor aduersum me iniusti-* c.4
tiam meam Domino, et tu remisisti inpietatem peccati mei. QUOD AUGU-
STINUS EXPONENS, AIT, "Magna pietas Dei, ut ad solam promissio- c.5
nem peccata dimiserit. | Nondum pronuntiat | ore, et tamen Deus
iam audit in corde, quia ipsum dicere quasi quoddam pronuntiare
est. Votum enim pro opere reputatur."

Sb 258rb | Aa
145^v

1,12 Petrus... **14** lego²] Ambr. Med., *Exp. euangelii secundum Lucam* 10.87 (CCSL
14:371.845–847)   **15** Lacrime... confiteri] Ibid. 371.848   **19** Magna... **20** dimi-
serit] cf. Cass., *Exp. psalmorum* 31.5 (CCSL 97:278)   **20** Nondum... **22** est] cf.
Aug. Hipp., *Enarr.* 31.2 (CCSL 38:236.15.22–32)   **22** Votum... reputatur] *Gl.
ord. in Ps.* 31:6 (ed. Rusch, 2.490–91)

1,10 Leonis... **11** pape] Ambrosii super Lucam R2 (Aa_pc)   **14** Petri] eius R2
(p<etri> Bi)

1,3 His] *praem.* Tractatus pulcher et utilis de confessione Aa   **9** quemlibet]
quamlibet Mk Pf   **10** mereri] promereri EdF Sb   **15** lauant] *add.* delictum Aa
EdF Fs Mk (*interlin.* Aa)   **17** despicies] *om.* Bi despicit Fs Sb   **19** Dei] Domini Aa
Bi | ut] *interlin.* Fd *om.* Bi   **20** dimiserit] *add.* uel <dimi>sit *interlin.* Fd remisserit
Sb

Distinction 1

<Question>

pr.   Now that we have made it through these matters, in which we have digressed somewhat from the business at hand, let us return to the third question of the case before us, which should be treated thoroughly, by which it is asked if each person is able to make satisfaction to God by contrition of the heart alone and secret satisfaction without oral confession.

<First Position>

d.a.c.1   There are those who say that anyone can merit mercy for an evil deed without confession to the church and to the judgment of a priest. They say this based on THAT TEXT OF POPE LEO:[1]

c.1   {"Peter grieved and wept because he sinned as a man. I do not find what he said; I know that he wept.}

"I read about Peter's tears; I do not read about satisfaction."
c.2   LIKEWISE, JOHN CHRYSOSTOM: "Tears wash away what is shame-
c.3   ful to confess." LIKEWISE, THE PROPHET: *A sacrifice to God, a crushed*
c.4   *spirit, a contrite and humble heart, God, you will not despise.* LIKEWISE: *I* Ps 50:19
have said, "I will confess against myself my injustice to the Lord," and you | Ps 31:5
have remitted the wickedness of my sin. AUGUSTINE EXPLAINS THIS
c.5   WHEN HE SAYS, "Great is the kindness of God that he has forgiven sins according to his promise alone. I do not yet announce with my mouth, and yet God already hears in my heart, for to say this very statement, ['I will pronounce,'] is just like pronouncing the thing. For the will is taken to be the work."

---

1. The second recension corrected this attribution, so that later versions of the Decretum read "that text of Ambrose in his commentary on Luke."

CODICE LIBRO I TITULO "DE EPISCOPIS ET CLERICIS," IMPERATOR IOUINIA-
NUS: "Si quis non dicam rapere, set attemptare tantum matrimonii iungendi causa   c.6
Fs 294va   sacratissimas | uirgines ausus fuerit, capitali ferietur pena."

LIBRO EODEM TITULO "DE POSTULANDO," IMPERATORES LEO ET AN-
TONINUS NICOSTRATO P. P.: "Nemo uel in foro magnitudinis tue, uel in prouin-   c.7
ciali iudicio, uel apud quemquam iudicem accedat ad togatorum consortium, nisi
sacrosanctis catholice religionis fuerit inbutus misteriis. Sin autem aliquid quoquo
AaB 330^r   modo uel quadam machinatione factum | uel attemptatum fuerit, offitium quidem
sublimitatis tue centum librarum auri iacturam pro condempnatione sustineat.
Pf 100ra   Idem uero quicumque ausus fuerit contra prouidum | nostre serenitatis decretum   c.8
offitium aduocationis per subreptionem arripere, et prohibitum patrocinium presti-
terit, aduocationis offitio remotus stilum proscriptionis atque perpetui exilii speciali-
35   ter sustinebit; scituris etiam prouinciarum rectoribus, quod is, sub cuius administratione aliquid huiusmodi fuerit attemptatum, partis bonorum dimidie proscrip-
tionem, et penam exilii per quinquennium sustinebit."

ITEM LIBRO IX TITULO AD LEGEM IULIAM MAIESTATIS: "Quisquis cum militi-   c.9
bus cogitauerit..., eadem enim seueritate, uoluntatem sceleris, qua effectum puniri
40   iura uoluerunt."

ITEM AD LEGEM CORNELIAM "DE SICARIIS": "Is qui cum telo ambulauerit hominis necandi causa, sicut is, qui hominem occiderit, uel cuius, dolo malo, factum
erit conmissum, legis Cornelie de sicariis pena coherceatur."

Mk 235rb   IMPERATORES VALENTINIANUS, VALENS, ET GRATIANUS: "Si quis | necandi   c.10
Bi 293ra   infantis piaculum aggressus | aggressaue fuerit, sciat, se capitali supplicio esse pu-
niendum."

IMPERATORES GRATIANUS ET VALENTINIANUS: "Si forte mulier marito mortis   c.11
parasse insidias, uel quolibet alio genere uoluntatem occidendi habuisse inueniatur,

---

24 Si...25 pena] Cod. 1.3(6).5   27 Nemo...37 sustinebit] Cod. 2.6.8   38 Quisquis...40 uoluerunt] Cod. 9.8.5   41 Is...43 coherceatur] Cod. 9.16.6(7)
44 Si...46 puniendum] Cod. 9.16.7(8)   47 Si...51 defensione] Cod. 9.16.8(9)

24 causa] causas Bi_ac Pf   26 Libro] praem. Item in Fs | eodem] Codicis Bi EdF
Mk Pf | Antoninus] recte Anthemius   31 tue] sue AaB Bi   33 prestiterit] om.
FdB   34 offitio] om. FdB | specialiter] spiritualiter Fs   38 Iuliam] Iulie Pf, Aqui-
lam Sb | Quisquis] Si quis FdB Quis Bi   40 iura] om. Fs   41 Is qui] Si quis
EdRom Fs   42 malo] malum AaB FdB Sb   43 erit] fuerit Fs Mk   44 Valentinia-
nus] om. Bi | Valens] Valerius AaB EdF Fs Pf om. Sb   45 supplicio] iudicio Bi Fs
47 Valentinianus] Valerius Fs Sb

c.6 CODEX BOOK 1, IN THE TITLE ON BISHOPS AND CLERICS, EMPEROR JOVIN-
IAN: "If anyone dares, not I say to rape, but only to attempt to rape most holy virgins for the purpose of creating a binding marriage, he will be subject to capital
punishment."

c.7 IN THE SAME BOOK, IN THE TITLE ON LITIGATION, EMPERORS LEO AND AN-
TONINUS[2] TO NICOSTRATUS, PRAETORIAN PREFECT: "No one may be admitted
to practice, either in the court of your greatness, or in a provincial one, or in the
house of any judge unless he has been instructed in the sacrosanct mysteries of the
Catholic religion. If he should, however, do or attempt something in any way whatsoever or by a certain machination, your lofty office is indeed to suffer the expense

c.8 of one hundred pounds of gold as your condemnation. But whoever dares to pro-
cure the office of an advocate through deception against the prudent decree of Our
Serenity, and performs the prohibited pleading in court, this same man will be removed from the office of advocate and undergo the sentence of confiscation [of
property] and of perpetual exile. Even the governors of the provinces will be ready to
make inquires, because he under whose administration something of this sort is attempted will undergo the confiscation of half of his property and the punishment of
a five-year exile."

c.9 LIKEWISE BOOK IX ON JULIAN'S LAW CONCERNING TREASON: "Whoever considers with soldiers..., for the laws wanted the intention to commit a crime to be
punished with the same severity as its execution."

LIKEWISE ON CORNELIUS'S LAW CONCERNING ASSASSINS: "He who walks
with a weapon with the intention of killing a man, just as he who kills a man or by
whose evil plan the deed is committed, is to be restrained by the penalty of Cornelius's law concerning assassins."

c.10 THE EMPERORS VALENTINIAN, VALENS, AND GRATIAN: "If anyone, male or
female, should undertake the crime of killing an infant, let him know that he must
be penalized with capital punishment."

c.11 EMPERORS GRATIAN AND VALENTINIAN: "If a woman should happen to be
discovered to have prepared a deadly ambush for her husband or in whatever other
way to have had an intention to kill him, or by chance a husband will in this way

2. This name should read "Anthemius," emperor of the western half of the Roman Empire, 467–472.

uel forte maritus eo modo insequitur uxorem, in eadem questione ab omni familia
50 non solum mariti, set etiam uxoris que tamen tunc temporis domi fuerit querendum est, sine cuiusquam defensione."

ITEM DIGESTA TITULO "DE INIURIIS," LEGE "SET EST QUESTIONIS": "Si quis   c.12
tam masculum quam feminam, siue ingenuos siue libertinos, inpudicos facere at-
temptauerit, iniuriarum tenebitur. Set et si serui pudicitia attemptata sit, iniuria lo-
55 cum habet.... Attemptari pudicitia dicitur, cum id agitur, ut ex pudico inpudicus
fiat....| Non solum is iniuriarum tenetur, qui fecit | iniuriam, hoc est qui percussit,
uerum ille quoque continetur, | qui dolo fecit uel qui curauit ut cui mala pugno per-
cuteretur."

ITEM APUD LABEONEM: "Si quis pulsatus quidem non est, uerum manus   c.13
60 aduersus eum leuate, et sepe territus, quasi uapulaturus, non tamen percussus,
iniuriarum | actione tenetur."

CONTRA LIBRO EODEM TITULO "DE PENIS": "Cogitationis penam nemo patia-   c.14
tur."

TITULO "DE EXTRAORDINARIIS CRIMINIBUS": "Sollicitatores alienarum nuptia-   c.15
65 rum, itemque matrimoniorum interpellatores, etsi effectu sceleris potiri non possunt, propter uoluntatem perniciose libidinis extra ordinem puniuntur.... Qui puero
stuprum (abducto uel corrupto comite) persuaserit, aut mulierem aut puellam in-
terpellauerit, quidue inpudicitie gratia fecerit, domum prebuerit pretiumue, quo is
persuadeat, dederit, perfecto flagitio punitur capite, imperfecto in insulam deporta-
70 tur. Corrupti comites summo supplicio afficiuntur."

ITEM TITULO "DE FURTIS": | "Vulgaris est questio, an is, qui ex aceruo frumenti   c.16
modium sustulit, totius rei furtum faciat, an uero eius tantum, quod abstulit. Offi-
lius totius acerui furem esse putat. Nam et qui aurem alicuius tetigit, inquit Trebatius, totum eum uidetur tetigisse. Proinde et qui dolium aperuit, et exinde parum

Marginal references:
Fs 294vb | FdB 159vb Sb 258va
Pf 100rb
AaB 330^{v}

---

52 Si...**58** percuteretur] Dig. 47.10.9.4, 47.10.10, 47.10.11   **59** Si...**61** tenetur]
Dig. 47.10.15.1   **62** Cogitationis...patiatur] Dig. 48.19.18   **64** Sollicitatores...
70 afficiuntur] Dig. 47.11.1, 47.11.1.2   **71** Vulgaris...**81** manifestus] Dig.
47.2.21

49 insequitur] insequetur Bi EdF insequatur Pf insectetur Mk   **52** Set est] secunde Fs Mk   **54** serui pudicitia] secundum pudicitiam FdB Sb   **57** quoque
continetur] quoque tenetur Fs qui tenetur Pf   **59** uerum] uesum (!) Bi, ausus
AaB Pf_{pc} Sb, *add.* ausus *interlin.* Mk   **60** leuate] leuae Bi_{ac} leuare AaB Mk Pf
Sb_{pc}, *add.* sunt *interlin.* Bi | percussus] percussit Mk, *add.* sit Pf   **70** afficiuntur]
affliciuntur Bi Sb   **74** uidetur] uideri Pf Sb EdF

hostilely pursue his wife, there is to be an inquiry with the same examination by torture of the entire household, not only of the husband but also of the wife, who were in the house at the time, without anyone maintaining their legal right."

c.12 LIKEWISE, THE DIGEST IN THE TITLE ON INSULTS, IN THE LAW "BUT IT IS A QUESTION": "If anyone attempts to rob either free-born or freed persons, whether male or female, of their chastity, he will be held guilty of wrongs. But even if the chastity of a slave is assailed, a wrong still applies.... Chastity is said to be assailed when there is an action done in order for an unchaste person to be made out of a chaste one.... Not only is he who commits the wrong, that is he who struck the blow, held guilty of wrongs, but also he is included who acted out of evil intent or who made preparations to strike someone a blow."

c.13 LIKEWISE IN THE WORKS OF LABEO: "If anyone has not indeed been beaten, but hands have been raised against him, and he has often been terrified as if about to be flogged, but nevertheless has not been struck, a charge of wrong-doing is upheld."

c.14 AGAINST THIS POSITION, HOWEVER, IS THIS STATEMENT IN THE SAME BOOK IN THE TITLE ON PUNISHMENTS: "No one may suffer punishment for a thought."

c.15 IN THE TITLE ON EXTRAORDINARY CRIMES: "The seducers of married persons and likewise the spoilers of marriage, even if they are not able to avail in the carrying out of their crime, are punished by an extraordinary process on account of their will for pernicious desire.... He who persuades a boy (either an abducted or corrupted companion) to commit debauchery, who seduces either a woman or a girl (or whatever he does for the sake of unchastity), who offers a home or gives a reward as the means of his persuasion receives capital punishment for his disgraceful act if it has been completed and is deported to an island if it has not been fully carried out. Corrupt companions undergo the utmost punishment."

c.16 LIKEWISE IN THE TITLE ON THEFTS: "It is a common question whether he who carries away a measure of corn from the heap commits a theft of the whole entity or truly only of that which he takes away. Ofilius[3] believes that it is a theft of the entire heap. For also he who has touched someone's ear, says Trebatius,[4] seems to have touched all of him. Then, also, he who has opened a large jar and then has removed

---

3. Aulus Ofilius (fl. 1st century BC): Roman law jurist and friend to Cicero and Julius Caesar.
4. Gaius Trebatius Testa (fl. 1st century BC): Roman law jurist and legal adviser to Julius Caesar and Caesar Augustus.

75 uini abstulit, totius furtum uidetur fecisse. Set uerum est, in tantum eum furti actione teneri, quantum abstulerit. Nam et si quis armarium, quod tollere non poterat, aperuit, et omnes res, que in eo erant, contractauerit, atque ita discesserit, deinde reuersus unam ex his abstulerit, et antequam se reciperet quo destinauerat,

Bi 293rb deprehensus fuerit, eiusdem rei et | manifestus, et nec manifestus fur erit. Set et si quis segetem ante lucem secat et contractat, eius, quod secat, manifestus fur est nec manifestus."

ITEM LIBRO II TITULO "QUOD QUISQUE IURIS," LEGE PRIMA: "Hec autem c.17 uerba: 'Que statuerit qui iurisdictioni preest,' cum effectu accipimus, non uerbote-

Mk 235va nus; et ideo, si, cum uellet statuere, prohibitus sit, nec effectum decretum habuit, |

Fs 295ra cessat edictum. Nam 'statuit' | uerbum rem perfectam significat, et consummatam iniuriam, non ceptam."

"Pene," sicut IN DIGESTIS TITULO "DE PENIS" legitur, "legum interpretatione c.18 molliende sunt potius, quam nimis exasperande." Atque ideo proprium casum non d.p.c.18 excedunt.

Pf 100va | Set que de raptu uirginum, uel aduocatis, seu de crimine maiestatis, uel de sicariis dicta sunt, fauore religionis et fidei atque principali exordio sicariorum introducta sunt.

Sb 258vb Iniuriarum uero pro earum uarietate multipliciter quis reus fieri potest. | Varietas itaque criminum uarietatem inducit penarum. VNDE IN DIGESTIS TITULO "DE PE-

95 NIS": "Aut facta puniuntur, ut furta cedesque; aut dicta, ut conuitia et infide aduoca- c.19 tiones; aut scripta, ut falsa et famosi libelli; aut consilia, ut coniurationes, aut conscientia latronum, quosque alios suadendo monuisse sceleris est instar.

"Set hec quatuor genera consideranda sunt septem modis: causa, persona, loco, tempore, qualitate, quantitate, euentu. Causa, ut in uerberibus, que inpunita

100 sunt a magistro illata uel parente, quoniam emendationis animo, non iniurie gratia

---

82 Hec...86 ceptam] Dig. 2.2.1.2 87 Pene...88 exasperande] Dig. 48.19.42
95 Aut...112 puniat] Dig. 48.19.16

76 abstulerit] abstulit EdF Mk 77 aperuit] aperuerit EdF Pf 78 abstulerit] abstulit Fs 79 fur erit] fuerit Fs *add.* qua de re maximus apud grecos orator Demostene sic ait Fs (*cf. l.* 108) 80 eius quod] his que FdB | quod] quam Pf qui Sb
81 nec] *praem.* et Bipc EdF (*interlin.* Bi) 83 iurisdictioni] iurisdictioni Bi Mk
91 principali] principum Pf | exordio] et odio AaB Bi Pf Sb odio EdF Fs Mk
93 uero] *add.* non FdB Sb (*interlin.* Sb) 96 ut1] aut FdB Pf | ut2] aut FdB Pf *om.*
Fs | aut3] ut Fs | conscientia] *add.* ut AaB FdB Sb 100 gratia] gratie FdB Mk

a little of the wine seems to have committed theft of it all. But the truth is that they are held responsible for theft for as much as they have taken. For even if someone opened a chest which he had not been able to lift and touches all the things which were in it, and in this way departs but then turns back and removes one of these things, and, before he withdraws to where he had intended, should be apprehended, he will be both a manifest thief and a non-manifest thief of the same thing. But even if someone should cut and steal away a crop before dawn, he is a manifest and non-manifest thief for that which he cuts."

LIKEWISE IN BOOK 2, IN THE FIRST LAW IN THE TITLE "THE SAME RULE

c.17   WHICH ANYONE MAINTAINS," "But we receive these words: 'What things he who has charge of the jurisdiction will have established,' in terms of their effect, not in terms of their words alone; and thus, if, even though he desired to establish something, he was hindered and did not have a decree that was carried out, the edict is invalid. For the word 'established' signifies a completed thing and a 'wrong' something consummated, not merely begun."

c.18   "Punishments," just as is read IN THE DIGEST IN THE TITLE ON PUNISH-

MENTS, "should be lightened by the interpretation of laws rather than made

d.p.c.18   harsher." And thus punishments do not exceed their own case.

But the things which have been said about the rape of virgins, or advocates, or high treason, or murderers have been introduced into this discussion in support of religion and faith and because of the chief starting-point of murderers.

Now someone can become guilty in a multitude of ways for a variety of these wrongs. The varied aspects of crimes therefore bring about a variety of punish-

c.19   ments. AND THUS IN THE DIGEST IN THE TITLE ON PUNISHMENTS: "Either deeds are punished, like thefts and murders, or spoken words, like insults and false pleadings, or written words, like forgeries and libel, or plans, like conspiracies or the guilty knowledge of robbers; to have urgently advised each one of the others is a form of crime.

"But these four types should be considered in seven aspects: motive, person, place, time, quality, quantity, outcome. Motive, as in the case of lashings, which are left unpunished when they have been inflicted by a master or a parent, since they seem to be employed for sake of the correction of the mind rather than for injury.

uidentur adhiberi. Puniuntur cum quis per iram ab extraneo pulsatur. Persona dupliciter spectatur, eius qui fecit, et eius qui passus est. Aliter enim puniuntur ex eisdem facinoribus serui, quam liberi; et aliter qui in dominum parentemue ausus est,
quam qui in extraneum et in magistratum quam qui in priuatum. In huius rei consi-
105   deratione etatis quoque ratio habetur. Locus facit ut idem uel furtum uel sacrilegium sit, et capite luendum uel minore supplicio. Tempus discernit uel furem diur-
num ac nocturnum. Qualitate, factum uel atrocius, uel leuius est, ut furta manifesta
FdB 160ʳᵃ   a non manifestis discerni solent, | rixa a crassaturis, expilationes a furtis, petulantia.
Quantitas discernit furem ab abigeo. Nam qui unum suem subripuerit, ut fur coher-
AaB 331ʳ   cebitur: qui gregem, | ut abigeus. Euentus spectatur, ut a clementissimo queque
facta; quamquam lex non minus eum, qui occidendi hominis causa cum telo fuerit
inuentus, quam eum, qui occiderit, puniat."

Bi 293ᵛᵃ Fs | Cogitatio non meretur penam lege ciuili cum suis terminis contempta est. Di-   (c.20)
295ʳᵇ   scernuntur | tamen a maleficiis ea, que de iure effectum desiderant. In his enim non
Pf 100ᵛᵇ   nisi animi iudicium consideratur. Vɴᴅᴇ ɪɴ Dɪɢᴇsᴛɪs ᴛɪᴛᴜʟᴏ "Dᴇ ʀᴇᴘᴜᴅɪɪs": "Di-   c.21
uortium non est nisi uerum, quod animo perpetua constitutione dissensione fit. Itaque quicquid calore iracundie fit uel dicitur, non aliter ratum est quam si perseuerantia apparuerit iudicium animi fuisse. Ideoque per eum calorem misso repudio, si
breui reuersa uxor est, nec diuertisse uidetur."

---

115 Diuortium…119 uidetur] Dig. 24.2.3

101 Puniuntur] *add.* autem Mk Pf   104 magistratum] magistrum Mk Pf
105 habetur] habeatur Pf EdF   106 et…luendum] ex capite ligandum Fs | di-
scernit] *add.* et manore a furtiuo uel effractorem Fs, *add.* emansorem a fugitiuo,
et effractorem Biₚc EdF Pf (*interlin.* et et *om.* Bi, *mg.* Pf)   108 petulantia] *praem.* a
uiolentia Bi EdF (*mg.* Bi) *add.* ac uiolentia Fs *add.* a uiolentia *mg.* Mk Pf; *add.* de
qua (*tr.* Fs) re maximus apud Grecos orator Demosthenes sic ait EdF Fs Mk Pf
(*mg.* Mk Pf)   109 suem] *om.* Sb   110 a clementissimo] ad ementissimo Bi Fs
ademtissimo AaB Mk clementissime Pf | queque] que Fs Sb   111 non] *om.* AaB
Biₐc FdB Fs Sb   112 puniat] *add.* et ideo apud grecos ex illo uoluntarie fortuitu
casu lugebatur apud partium poetarum scriptum est EdF Fs   113 Cogitatio]
praem. Gratianus Fs | meretur] ueretur AaB Bi | contempta est] contemptare Fs
contenta est AaB EdF Pf Sb   116 nisi uerum] *tr.* AaB EdF Fs Mk | perpetua con-
stitutione] perpetuam constituendi EdF | dissensione] dissensionem AaB Sb EdF
discensione (!) FdB Bi in dissensione Pf | fit] sunt Pf facit AaB FdB Sb

They are punished when someone is struck by an outsider out of wrath. Person is viewed in two ways: he who acted, and he who was acted upon. For slaves are punished differently from freemen for the same evil deeds, and those who dared commit a crime against his lord or parent are punished differently from those who dared commit a crime against an outsider, and against a magistrate as compared with against a private citizen. The person's age is also taken into account in the consideration of this issue. Place makes it so that the same thing may be either theft or sacrilege, and should be paid with capital or a minor punishment. Time distinguishes[5] a daytime and nighttime burglar or thief. By quality, a deed is either atrocious or less severe, as obvious thefts are customarily distinguished from nonobvious ones, disputes from highway robbery, pillaging from thefts, and petulance.[6] Quantity distinguishes a thief from a rustler. For he who snatches one pig will be restrained as a thief, but he who snatches a herd as a rustler. Outcome is looked at, just as each and every deed done by a very merciful man, although the law punishes the one who was found with a weapon with the intent to kill a man no less than the one who killed."

(c.20)   A thought does not deserve punishment by civil law when it is deemed insignificant on its own terms. Nevertheless, such thoughts that lack an effect as far as the law is concerned are distinguished from crimes. For nothing but the mind's judgment is considered in thoughts without legal consequence. THUS IN THE DIGEST

c.21   IN THE TITLE ON DIVORCES: "There is no divorce except a valid one, which occurs with a mind fixed on a perpetual separation. Thus, whatever occurs or is said in the heat of anger is not deemed to be something else until it should persistently appear that such was the judgment of the mind. Therefore, if a wife is returned after a short time after she was sent away, it seems to have been a repudiation through the heat of anger and not to have been a true divorce."

5. Quite early in the manuscript transmission, a scribe added here, "the soldier who exceeds his furlough from a deserter," which is included in the text of the Digest and which Friedberg also included.

6. The person who added this text from the Digest seems to have mistakenly omitted the conclusion of this thought. The original text read, "petulance from violence." Some manuscripts of the *Decretum* added both "from violence" and the next clause from the *Digest*, which read, "on which topic the greatest of the Greek orators, Demosthenes, thus speaks." The *Digest* had followed this clause with Demosthenes' text in Greek, but the medieval scribes were content to cite Demosthenes by name only; they did not copy his Greek text.

120   HINC ETIAM IN CANONIBUS: "Si quis iratus crimen alicui obiecerit," etc.   c.22

Ex consilio autem uelut ex facto aliquem teneri AUGUSTINUS PROBAT, ita dicens:

Non solum qui manibus occidunt, set etiam quorum consilio et fraude alii occiduntur, homicide probantur.

Sb 259ra | Mk   "Periculose decipiunt, | qui existimant, eos | tantum homicidas esse, qui mani-   c.23
235vb   bus hominem occidunt, et non potius eos, per quorum consilium, et fraudem, et exhortationem homines exstinguntur. Nam Iudei Dominum nequaquam propriis manibus interfecerunt, sicut scriptum est: *Nobis non licet interficere quemquam.* Set tamen illis Domini mors imputatur, quia ipsi eum lingua interfecerunt, dicentes, *Cru-*
130   *cifige, crucifige eum.* Vnde unus Euangelista dicit, Dominum crucifixum esse hora tertia, alius sexta, quia Iudei crucifixerunt eum hora tertia lingua, milites hora sexta manibus. Qui ergo hominem tradidit, ille interfecit eum, Domino dicente, *Maius peccatum habet qui me tradidit tibi.* Vnde Psalmista: *Filii hominum, dentes eorum arma et sagitte, et lingua eorum gladius acutus.* Subiciant ergo se penitentie quorum
135   consilio sanguis funditur, si ueniam promereri uoluerint."

ITEM EX EPISTOLA CLEMENTIS:

Interfectores fratrum, detractores eorum, eosque odientes homicide habentur.

"Homicidiorum uero tria genera esse dicebat Beatus Petrus, et penam eorum   c.24
140   parilem fore docebat. Sicut enim homicidas interfectores fratrum, ita detractores eorum, eosque odientes, homicidas esse manifestabat, quia et qui occidit, et qui odit
Fs 295va   fratrem suum, et qui ei detrahit | pariter homicide esse demonstrantur."

---

120 Si… etc] C.2 q.3 c.5; Ps.-Fabian, *Decr. ps.-isid.* c.25 (ed. Hinschius, 168)
125 Periculose…**135** uoluerint] cf. Aug. Hipp., *De cons. euang.* 3.13 (CSEL
43:327, 335–36); *Enarr. in Psalmos* 56.12 (CCSL 39:702.26–32) et 63.5 (CCSL
39:810.26–811.14); *In Ioh. evang. tract.* 114.4 (CCSL 36:642.22–28)   **139** Homicidiorum…**142** demonstrantur] Ps.-Clement, *Decr. ps.-isid.* c.40 (ed. Hinschius,
43–44)

120 obiecerit"] obicit Fs obicitur Sb   **124** occiduntur] occidunt Bi occiderint Sb
125 Periculose] *add.* se Mk EdF | decipiunt] decipiuntur Fs Pf   **131** alius…tertia[2]] *om. hom.* FdB   **132** interfecit] interficit Bi Fs Sb   **137** Interfectores…**138**
habentur] *om.* Pf | homicide…**138** habentur] homicidas Fs   **138** habentur] probantur AaB   **140** docebat] dicebat EdF FdB Fs Pfac Sb   **142** homicide esse] *om.*
FdB Biac, *tr.* Fs Mk (homicide *interlin.* Mk), esse *interlin.* Bi, homicida esse AaB

c.22   HERE ALSO IN THE CANONS: "If anyone should reproach someone for a crime while in a state of anger," etc.[7]

AUGUSTINE PROVES that someone is bound by his plan just as by his deeds, saying in this way:

Not only those who kill with their hands but also those by whose counsel and deceit others are killed, are proven to be murderers.

c.23   "They are dangerously deceived who believe that only those who kill a man with their hands are murderers and not rather those through whose counsel and deceit and urging men's lives are extinguished. For the Jews in no way killed the Lord with their own hands, as it is written, *We are not allowed to kill anyone*. But, nevertheless,   Jn 18:31
the death of the Lord is imputed to them because these same people killed him with their tongue, saying, *Crucify him, crucify him*. One Evangelist thus says that the Lord   Lk 23:21
was crucified at the third hour and again at the sixth hour, for the Jews crucified him at the third hour with their tongue, and the soldiers crucified him at the sixth hour with their hands. He who betrays a man, therefore, has killed him, since the Lord says, *He who has handed me over to you has committed the greater sin*. And thus the   Jn 19:11
Psalmist: *Sons of men, their teeth are weapons and arrows, and their tongue is a sharp sword*. Therefore, let those by whose counsel blood is poured submit them-   Ps 56:5
selves to repentance if they should desire to be promised mercy."

LIKEWISE FROM A LETTER OF CLEMENT:

Those who kill, disparage, and hate their brothers are considered murderers.

c.24   "Now the blessed Peter was teaching that there are three types of homicides. For just as those who kill their brothers are murderers, so also did he make clear that those who disparage them and those who hate them are murderers, because both he who kills his brother, and he who hates, and he who disparages him are shown equally to be murderers."

---

7. D.1 cc.6–30 comprise the largest set of R2 additions to any distinction of *De penitentia*. The first dozen or so authorities, namely cc.6–21, comprise the only Roman law R2 additions to *De penitentia*. Here at c.22, R2 switches to early Christian source material. This particular text cites in brief an R2 text inserted into another section of the *Decretum* at C.2 q.3 c.5. The medieval (and modern) reader could look up the text in full at that place.

ITEM IERONIMUS IN YSAIA:

In maleficiis uoluntas pro opere reputatur.

Pf 101ʳᵃ   "Omnis iniquitas et oppressio et iniustitia iudicium | sanguinis est: et, licet gla-   c.25
dio non occidas, uoluntate tamen interficis."

ITEM CIPRIANUS:

De eodem.

"Numquid Cayn, cum Domino munus offerret, peremerat fratrem? Et tamen   c.26
150   parricidium mente conceptum Deus prouide ante dampnauit. Vt illic cogitatio mala
Bi 293ᵛᵇ   et perniciosa conceptio Deo prouidente prospecta est, ita et in | Dei seruis, apud
quos cogitatur, et martirium mente concipitur, animus ad bonum deditus Deo iu-
AaB 331ᵛ   dice coronatur. | Aliud est martirio animum deesse, aliud animo defuisse marti-
rium. Qualem te inuenit Dominus, cum uocat, talem pariter et iudicat, quando ipse
155   testatur et dicit: *Et scient omnes ecclesie, quia ego sum scrutator renum et cordis.*"

ITEM AUGUSTINUS:

Homicida est qui fratri suo mala suadet.

"Noli putare, te non esse homicidam, quando fratri tuo mala persuades. Si fratri   c.27
tuo mala persuades occidis. Et ut scias, quia occidis, audi Psalmum: *Filii hominum,*
160   *dentes eorum arma et sagitte, et lingua eorum machera acuta.*"

IDEM:

Occidit qui ad nocendum mouetur.

Sb 259ʳᵇ   "Homicidium lege uetitum | putabatur non aliud esse, nisi corporis peremptio.   c.28
Aperuit ergo Dominus, omnem iniquum motum ad nocendum fratri in homicidii
165   genere deputari."

145 Omnis... 146 interficis] Hier., *Comm. in Isaiam* 10.33 (CCSL 73:416.52–54)
149 Numquid... 155 cordis] Cypr. Carth., *De mortalitate* 17 (CCSL
3A:26.286–295)   158 Noli... 160 acuta] Aug. Hipp., *In Ioh. evang. tract.* 42 (CCSL
36:370.11.16–20)   163 Homicidium... 165 deputari] Aug. Hipp., *Contra Faustum*
19 (CSEL 25:521.21–24)

144 In... reputatur] *om.* Pf   148 De eodem] *om.* AaB   150 prouide ante] prouidit ante Fs prouidit et Pf prouidus ante EdF   155 dicit] dicat AaB Mk Sb
157 Homicida... suadet] *om.* Pf   161 Idem] Item Mk *om.* Pf   162 Occidit... mo-
uetur] *om.* Pf

In wicked deeds, the will is taken to be the work.

c.25   "All iniquity and oppression and injustice is the judgment of blood: and, although you do not kill with the sword, you nevertheless kill with your will."

LIKEWISE CYPRIAN:

On the same matter.

c.26   "Cain had not already slain his brother when he offered his gift to the Lord, had
he? And yet the provident God had already condemned the fratricide conceived in
his mind. Just as there an evil thought and pernicious idea was foreseen by the
provident God, so also in the servants of God, in whose minds martyrdom is
thought and mentally conceived, the mind devoted to good is crowned by God in
his justice. It is one thing for the mind to be absent from martyrdom; it is another
for martyrdom to have been absent from the mind. In equal measure to how the
Lord finds you when he calls does he judge, inasmuch as he himself testifies and
says, *And let all the churches know that I scrutinize the reins and the heart*."   Rv 2:23

LIKEWISE AUGUSTINE:

He who urges his brother to do evil is a murderer.

c.27   "Do not think that you are not a murderer when you persuade your brother to
evil deeds. If you persuade your brother to evil deeds, you kill him. And, so that you
may know that you kill him, hear the Psalm: *Sons of men, their teeth are weapons
and arrows, and their tongue is a sharp sword*."   Ps 56:5

THE SAME AUTHOR:

He who is moved to do harm kills.

c.28   "The murder forbidden by the law used to be thought to be nothing other than
the killing of the body. The Lord thus explained that every wicked inclination to do
harm to a brother is considered to be in the genus of homicide."

Furti tenetur qui solo timore non furatur.

"Si propterea non facis furtum, quia times ne uidearis, intus, in corde fecisti;   c.29
furti teneris, et nil tulisti."

FdB160^rb | Idem de libero arbitrio:

Non ideo minus delinquit, cui sola deest facultas.

"Si cui etiam non contingat facultas concumbendi cum coniuge aliena, planum   c.30
tamen aliquo modo sit eum cupere, et, si potestas detur, esse facturum, non minus
Mk 236ra | reus est, quam si in ipso facto deprehenderetur."

175   Item, si, ut auctoritas testatur, uoluntas remuneratur, non opus,   (c.30b)
uoluntas autem in cordis contritione est, opus uero in oris confessione, luce clarius constat cordis contritione, non oris confessione
peccata dimitti.

Item Prosper: "Porro illi, quorum peccata humanam notitiam   c.31
180   latent, non ab ipsis confessa, nec ab aliis publicata, si ea confiteri
uel emendare noluerint, Deum, quem habent testem, ipsum habi-
Pf 101rb | Fs   turi sunt et ultorem. | Et quid eis prodest | humanum uitare iudi-
295vb   cium, cum, si in malo suo permanserint, ituri sunt in eternum, Deo
Fd 88va | retribuente, supplicium? Quod si sui ipsi iudices fiant, et ueluti sue
185   iniquitatis ultores, hic in se uoluntariam penam seuerissime anima-
duersionis exerceant, temporalibus penis mutabunt eterna supplicia, et lacrimis ex uera cordis conpunctione fluentibus restinguent
eterni ignis incendia." Et infra: "Facilius sibi Deum placabunt illi,   c.32
qui non humano conuicti iudicio, set ultro crimen agnoscunt, qui
190   aut propriis illud confessionibus produnt, aut nescientibus aliis quales occulti sint, ipsi in se uoluntarie excommunicationis sententiam
ferunt, et ab altari, cui ministrabant, non animo, set officio separati
Bi 294ra   uitam suam tamquam mortuam plangunt, | certi, quod reconciliati

---

168 Si... **169** tulisti] Aug. Hipp., *Sermo* 17 (CCSL 41:239.84–86)   **172** Si... **174**
deprehenderetur] Aug. Hipp., *De lib. arb.* 1.3.20 (CCSL 29:215.50–53)
179 Porro... **196** perueniant] Jul. Pom., *De vita contemplativa* 2.7.2–3 (PL
59:451C–452B)

175 si ut] sicut R2 (Fd_pc)

167 Furti] *praem.* Reus FdB   **169** furti] *praem.* reus FdB   **175** ut] *om.* Fd_ac
176 autem] enim Fs | uero] enim Bi_ac Pf   **191** sint] sunt Fd_ac Pf Sb EdF

ALSO AUGUSTINE:

He who does not steal because of fear alone is held responsible for theft.

c.29   "If, moreover, you do not steal because you fear that you will be seen, you have stolen within, in your heart; you are held guilty of theft even though you have borne nothing away."

THE SAME AUTHOR IN *De libero arbitrio*:

He is thus not less delinquent who lacks opportunity alone.

c.30   "If, though the opportunity to lie with the spouse of another should not befall someone, but nevertheless it should be clear in some way that he desires [to do so] and, if the power were granted him, he would do it, he is not less guilty than if he were caught red-handed."

(c.30b)   Likewise, if, as the authoritative text testifies, the will is re-   cf. c.5
warded, not the work, but the will consists of contrition of the heart, but the work of confession of the mouth, then it is most clearly established that sins are forgiven by contrition of the heart, not by oral confession.

c.31   LIKEWISE PROSPER: "Indeed if those whose sins lie hidden from human notice, not having been confessed by them and not having been publicized by others, were not to want to confess or correct them, they are about to have God himself, whom they have as a witness, also as an avenger. And what does avoiding human judgment profit them when, if they were to persist in their evil, they are going to eternal torture as God gives the retribution? But if these same people should become their own judges and, as the avengers of their own iniquity, should exercise upon themselves here a voluntary penalty of the most severe chastisement, they will exchange eternal tortures for temporary penalties, and, with tears flowing out of true compunction of the heart, they will extinguish

c.32   the flames of the eternal fire." And later he writes, "They will more easily reconcile themselves to God who have not been convicted by human judgment but recognize their misdeed of their own will and either disclose it by their own confessions or bring a sentence of voluntary excommunication upon themselves with others unaware of what kind of things have been hidden, and, having been separated not in mind but in duty from the altar which they used to

sibi efficacis penitentie fructibus a Deo non solum amissa recipiant,
195 set etiam ciues superne ciuitatis effecti ad gaudia sempiterna perueniant."

HOC IDEM PROBATUR AUCTORITATE ILLA PROPHETICA: *In qua-*   d.p.c.32
cumque hora peccator conuersus fuerit, et ingemuerit. Non enim dicitur
"ore confessus fuerit," set tantum *conuersus et ingemuerit, uita uiuet, et*
200 *non morietur.* HINC ETIAM IDEM PROPHETA AIT, *Scindite corda uestra,*   c.33
et non uestimenta uestra, ostendens contritione cordis, que in eius-   d.p.c.33
dem scissione intelligitur, non in confessione oris, que pars est ex-
terioris satisfactionis, quam scissuram uestium nominauit, a parte
Sb 259ᵛᵃ totum intelligens, peccata dimitti. HINC ETIAM PER EUNDEM | PRO-
205 PHETAM DOMINUS AIT: *Conuertimini ad me et ego conuertar ad uos.*   c.34
Conuersio autem dicitur quasi cordis undique uersio. Si autem cor   d.p.c.34
nostrum undique a malo ad Deum uertitur, mox sue conuersionis
fructum meretur, ut Deus ab ira ad misericordiam conuersus peccati prestet indulgentiam, cuius primo preparabat uindictam.

210 Vnde datur intelligi quod etiam ore tacente ueniam consequi
possumus. Hinc etiam leprosi illi, quibus Dominus precepit ut
ostenderent se sacerdotibus, in itinere, antequam ad sacerdotes uenirent, mundati sunt. Ex quo facto nimirum datur intelligi quod
antequam sacerdotibus ora nostra ostendamus, id est peccata confi-
215 teamur, a lepra peccati mundamur. Hinc etiam Lazarus de monu-
Fs 296ʳᵃ | Pf mento uiuus | prodiit; non prius de monumento est eductus, et po-
101ᵛᵃ stea a Domino suscitatus, | set lapide remoto, quo monumentum
Aa 146ʳ claudebatur, in sepulchro reuixit, et foras uiuus prodiit. Hinc etiam,
ut Dominus ostenderet, quod non sacerdotali iudicio, set largitate
220 diuine gratie peccator emundatur, leprosum tangendo mundauit, et
Mk 236ʳᵇ postea ut sacerdoti | sacrificium ex lege offerret precepit. Leprosus
enim tangitur, cum respectu diuine pietatis mens peccatoris illu-
strata conpungitur. Vnde post trinam negationem Petrus, Domino
eum respiciente, profudit amaras lacrimas, quibus culpam sue ne-
225 gationis diluit. Leprosus semetipsum sacerdoti representat, dum
peccatum suum sacerdoti penitens confitetur. Sacrificium ex lege
offert, dum satisfactionem ecclesie iudicio sibi inpositam factis ex-

---

194 amissa] *add.* bona Fs   **199** conuersus] *add.* fuerit Bi Fd_{pc} Fs Mk EdF
201 contritione] contritionem Aa Bi Fd Mk Pf Sb   **215** mundamur] emunda-
mur Aa Bi Mk Sb   **224** negationis] negotiationis Fd_{ac} Pf_{ac}

serve, bewail their as it were dead life, certain that, since God has been reconciled to them by the efficacious fruits of penance, they will not only receive pardons but also, having been made citizens of the supernal city, will attain everlasting joys."

d.p.c.32   THIS SAME POINT IS PROVEN BY THAT PROPHETIC AUTHORITY, *In whatever hour the sinner turns and laments*, etc. For it is not said   Ezek 33:12 "confesses with his mouth," but only *turns and laments, he will live*

c.33   *with life and not die.* HENCE THE SAME PROPHET ALSO SAYS, *Tear*   Jl 2:13

d.p.c.33   *your hearts, and not your clothes*, showing that sins are forgiven by contrition of the heart, which is understood in the tearing of it, not in oral confession, which is part of external satisfaction, which he called the tearing of clothes, understanding the whole from the

c.34   part. HENCE THROUGH THE SAME PROPHET THE LORD SAYS, *Turn*   Zech 1:3

d.p.c.34   *round to me and I will turn round to you.* But turning round or "conversion" bespeaks, as it were, a turning of the heart in all respects. If our heart entirely turns to God from evil, soon the fruit of its conversion merits that God be turned from wrath to mercy and offer remission for the sin, even though he had been preparing its punishment.

For this reason, it is given to be understood that we are also able to attain mercy without saying a word. Hence also those lepers whom the Lord ordered to show themselves to the priests were cleansed before they came to the priests. From this fact, it is indeed given to be understood that we are cleansed from the leprosy of sin before we show ourselves to priests with our mouth, that is, before we confess our sins. And thus also Lazarus came out of the tomb alive; he was not led forth from the tomb first and afterward resuscitated by the Lord, but, after the stone had been removed by which the tomb was closed off, he became alive again in the sepulcher and came forth alive. And thus also, so that the Lord might   cf. Jn show that the sinner is cleansed not by sacerdotal judgment but by   11:43–44 the greatness of God's grace, he cleansed the leper by his touch and afterward ordered him to offer a sacrifice to the priest according to the law. For the leper is touched when the mind of the sinner is il-   cf. Mt 8:4 luminated with respect to divine kindness and feels remorse. For this reason, after his threefold denial, when the Lord gazed back at him, Peter poured forth bitter tears with which he diluted the guilt of his denial. The leper presents himself to the priest when the pen-   cf. Mt itent confesses his sin to a priest. The leper offers a sacrifice accord-   26:69–75 ing to the law when the penitent carries out with deeds the satis-

equitur. Set antequam ad sacerdotes perueniat, emundatur, dum
per contritionem cordis ante confessionem oris peccati uenia indul-
230 getur.

Hinc etiam medici negantur resuscitare aliquem, ut resuscitatus
confiteatur, DUM PER PROPHETAM DICITUR, *Numquid medici resusci-*
Bi 294ʳᵇ *tabunt, et confitebuntur tibi?* ITEM: *A mortuo,* ut auctoritas |dicit, uelut
ab eo, qui non est, *perit confessio.* VNDE PENITENS ILLE, qui timore
235 octaue territus EXCLAMAUERAT, *Domine, ne in furore tuo arguas me,*
postea supplicans aiebat, Saluum me fac propter misericordiam tuam,
quoniam non est in morte qui memor sit tui; in inferno autem nullus confi-
tebitur tibi. Si ergo nullus confitetur, nisi suscitatus, nemo autem uiuit eterne gehenne filius, et perpetua dampnatione dignus, patet,
240 quod antequam quisque confiteatur peccatum, a reatu sue preuaricationis, quo eterna sibi debebantur supplicia, per gratiam interne
conpunctionis absoluitur.

Item: Si antequam quisque confiteatur, a Domino resuscitatur,
Sb 259ᵛᵇ uel resuscitatus uiuit, dum confitetur, uel post resuscitationem | ite-
245 rum mortuus est, et confitetur. Set, sicut antequam resuscitaretur
Fs 296ʳᵇ | Pf mortuus confiteri non poterat, sic post resuscitationem | mortuus
101ᵛᵇ confiteri non ualet. Restat ergo, ut resuscitatus uiuat, dum peccatum confitetur. Habet itaque resuscitatorem suum sibi presentem,
seque inhabitantem. VT ENIM AUGUSTINUS AIT IN PSALMO LXII:
250 "Resuscitatus corpore uiuit absente suscitatore.... Non autem sic re-   c.35
suscitatus in anima." Cum enim Deus sit uita anime, anima uero   d.p.c.35
uita corporis, sicut corpus uiuere non potest anima absente, ita non
Fd 88ᵛᵇ nisi Deo presente anima uiuere | ualet. Habet itaque anima sibi
Deum presentem per gratiam, que uiuens peccatum suum confite-
255 tur, eamque uita, que Deus est, inhabitat, quam inhabitando uiuere
facit.

---

250 Resuscitatus…**251** anima¹] cf. Aug. Hipp., *Enarr.* 70.2 (CCSL
39:962.49–50, 56), *Gl. ord. in Ps.* 70:17 (ed. Rusch, 2.542) **251** Cum…**253** ua-
let] cf. ibid. (CCSL 39:962.58–60)

232 resuscitabunt] suscitabunt Aa Fs Pf **233** dicit] ait Aa EdF Fs **236** aiebat] a-
gebat Bi Mk **237** nullus] aliquis? Aaₚc quis Pf **241** debebantur] debentur Aa
debeantur Fs **242** absoluitur] absoluerit Fs **246** resuscitationem] resurrectio-
nem EdF Pf **248** itaque] utique Bi Pf **250** suscitatore] resuscitatore Aa
251 uero] *interlin.* Fd

faction imposed on him by the judgment of the church. But the leper is cleansed before he reaches the priests when remission of a sin is granted through contrition of the heart before oral confession.

Hence also physicians are denied the ability to resuscitate someone so that, having been resuscitated, he may confess, WHEN THROUGH THE PROPHET IT IS SAID, *Will physicians resuscitate them,* Ps 87:11 *and will they confess to you?* LIKEWISE, *Confession from a dead man,* as Ecclus 17:26 the authority says, just as from the man who does not exist, *perishes.* FOR THIS REASON THAT PENITENT who, terrified with the fear of the eighth hour, had EXCLAIMED, *Lord, do not accuse me in your* Ps 6:1 *furor,* afterward said in supplication, *Save me for your mercy's sake, for* Ps 6:4–5 *there is no one in death who is mindful of you; but in hell no one will confess to you.* If, therefore, no one confesses except he who has been made alive, but no son of eternal hell and no one worthy of perpetual damnation lives, it is clear that, before each person confesses his sin, through the grace of internal compunction he is absolved from the guilt of his transgression by which eternal punishments were owed to him.

Likewise: If someone is resuscitated by the Lord before he confesses, either, having been resuscitated, he is alive when he confesses, or, after the resuscitation, he died again and confesses. But, just as the dead man had not been able to confess before he was resuscitated, so also after the resuscitation a dead man is not able to confess. Therefore it remains that a man who has been resuscitated is alive when he confesses his sin. He thus has his resuscitator present to him and living within him. AS AUGUSTINE SAYS COMc.35 MENTING ON PSALM 62: "The man resuscitated in body lives without his reviver being present.... But this is not so for a man resuscid.p.c.35 tated in his soul." For since God is the life of the soul, but the soul is the life of the body, just as the body cannot live with the soul being absent, so also the soul cannot live except by God being present. Therefore the soul has God present to itself through the grace by which a living person confesses his sin, and the Life which God is indwells that soul, which it causes to live by its indwelling.

Si autem illam inhabitat, ergo templum Spiritus sancti facta est, ergo illuminata est, ergo a tenebris peccatorum expiata est, ergo templum diaboli esse desiit, que ad lucem uenit, cuius respectus te-
260 nebras fugat. Nulla enim (UT AIT APOSTOLUS) conuentio Christi ad Belial, nulla participatio lucis ad tenebras, nulla conmunicatio iustitie et iniquitatis, nullus consensus templo Dei cum ydolis. ITEM, UT CHRISTUS AIT, *Omnis, qui odit malum, in luce agit.* Qui autem in luce
Aa 146ᵛ agit | cum Deo operatur, sicut Augustinus ait. Qui autem in Christo
265 operatur, eius filius probatur. Cuius enim opera quisque facit, eius filius esse perhibetur. VNDE QUIBUSDAM DOMINUS AIT, *Si filii Abrae estis, opera Abrae facite.* Item: *Vos ex patre diabolo estis quia opera patris uestri facere uultis.* Nemo autem filius Dei et diaboli simul esse
Mk 236ᵛᵃ potest. | *Nemo enim, UT IPSE AIT, duobus Dominis potest seruire.* ITEM,
270 UT IOHANNES AIT IN EPISTOLA SUA, *Qui natus est ex Deo non peccat.*   c.36
Ergo nec est filius diaboli; solo enim peccato diaboli filii sumus.   d.p.c.36
Ergo de eius regno translati sumus in regnum claritatis filii Dei, sumus erepti de potestate tenebrarum, et facti sumus filii lucis.

Bi 294ᵛᵃ   Cum ergo ante confessionem, | ut probatum est, sumus resusci-
275 tati per gratiam, et filii lucis facti, euidentissime apparet, quod sola contritione cordis sine confessione oris, peccatum remittitur. ITEM: c.37
Pf 102ʳᵃ *Omnis qui non diligit | manet in morte.* Si ergo uiuit, et diligit; si diligit,   d.p.c.37
dilectio in eo est; dilectio autem in malo non est. Est enim proprius fons bonorum, in quo non conmunicat alienus. Ergo bonus est iste
280 factus per gratiam ante confessionem peccati; non itaque malus est,
Fs 296ᵛᵃ bonus | enim et malus aliquis simul esse non potest. Quod si malus non est, membrum diaboli non esse probatur: nec ergo est dignus gehenna, que diabolo et membris eius solummodo debetur, sicut
Sb 260ʳᵃ eterna beatitudo solummodo membris | Christi paratur.

---

278 Est…**279** alienus] cf. Aug. Hipp., *Contra Cresconium* 2.15 (CSEL 52:377.25–26)

272 claritatis] caritatis EdF **273** sumus] *om.* Bi Mk Pf EdF, *interlin.* Fd **276** peccatum remittitur] peccata remittuntur Fs | Item] *add.* epistola Iohannis Fs *add.* Iohannes *interlin.* Pf **277** Omnis] *om.* Aa Fs **282** est²] *interlin.* Aa Fd **284** paratur] operatur Fd_{ac}

If, however, Life indwells that soul, it has therefore been made the temple of the Holy Spirit, which means it has been illuminated, which means it has been purged of the shadows of sins, which means that, having come to the light, whose consideration causes shadows to flee, it has ceased being the temple of the devil. For, AS THE APOSTLE SAYS, there is no agreement between Christ and Belial, no participation of light with darkness, no communication of justice and iniquity, no consensus between the temple of God and idols. LIKEWISE, AS CHRIST SAYS, *All who hate evil walk in the light.* He who walks in the light, however, strives in Christ, just as Augustine says. He who strives in Christ is proven to be his son. For each person is said to be the son of him whose works he performs. AND THUS THE LORD SAYS TO CERTAIN MEN, *If you are the sons of Abraham, do Abraham's works.* Likewise: *You are of your father, the devil, because you desire to do the works of your father.* But no one can be the son of God and of the devil at the same time. *For no one,* AS HE SAYS, *can serve two masters.* LIKEWISE, AS JOHN SAYS IN HIS EPISTLE, *He who is born of God does not sin.* Therefore he is not the son of the devil. For by sin alone are we sons of the devil. Therefore we have been transferred from his kingdom to the kingdom of the radiance of the Son of God, and we have been seized out of the power of darkness and have been made sons of light.

Since therefore, as has been proven, we have been resuscitated through grace and have been made sons of light before confession, it is most evidently apparent that sin is remitted by contrition of the heart alone without oral confession. LIKEWISE: *All who do not love remain in death.* Therefore, if he lives, he also loves; if he loves, love is in him; but love is not in an evil person. It is the proper fount of good things in which no one foreign to God takes part. Therefore, he has been made good through grace before the confession of sin; he is thus not evil, for someone is not able to be good and evil at the same time. But if he is not evil, he is proven not to be a member of the devil and consequently is undeserving of hell, which is owed only to the devil and his members, just as eternal beatitude is prepared only for the members of Christ.

Margin notes:
cf. 2 Cor 6:14–16
Jn 3:20
Jn 8:39
Jn 8:44
Mt 6:24
1 Jn 3:9
c.36 | d.p.c.36
1 Jn 3:14
c.37
d.p.c.37

285   Non ergo in confessione peccatum remittitur, quod iam remissum esse probatur. Fit itaque confessio ad ostensionem penitentie,
non ad inpetrationem uenie. Sicut circumcisio data est Abrae in signum iustitie, non in causam iustificationis, sic confessio offertur
sacerdoti in signum uenie accepte, non in causam remissionis acci-
290   piende.

\<Sententia secunda\>

Alii e contra testantur, dicentes sine confessione oris et satisfactione operis neminem a peccato posse mundari, si tempus satisfaciendi habuerit. VNDE DOMINUS PER PROPHETAM AIT, *Dic tu iniqui-*
295   *tates tuas, ut iustificeris.*

ITEM AMBROSIUS IN LIBRO DE PARADYSO: "Non potest qui-   c.38
squam iustificari a peccato, nisi fuerit peccatum ante confessus."
IDEM IN SERMONE QUADRAGESIME: "Ecce nunc tempus accepta-   c.39
bile adest, in quo confessio a morte animam liberat, confessio aperit
300   paradysum, confessio spem saluandi tribuit. Vnde scriptura dicit,
Dic tu iniquitates tuas, ut iustificeris. His uerbis ostenditur quia non
meretur iustificari qui in uita sua peccata non uult confiteri. Illa
confessio uos liberat que fit cum penitentia. Penitentia uera est dolor cordis et amaritudo anime pro malis que quisque conmisit. Pe-
305   nitentia est et mala preterita plangere et plangenda iterum non
conmittere." ITEM IOHANNES OS AUREUM: "Perfecta penitentia co-   c.40
git peccatorem omnia libenter sufferre.... In corde eius contritio, in
Pf 102rb   ore confessio, in | opere tota humilitas—hec est fructifera peniten-
tia."

310   {IDEM: "Non potest quis gratiam Dei celestis accipere nisi purgatus fuerit ab   c.41
omni sorde peccati per penitentie confessionem, per donum baptismi salutaris."}

---

296 Non...**297** confessus] Ambr. Med., *De paradiso* 14.71 (CSEL
32.1:329.15–16)   **298** Ecce...**306** conmittere] *Coll. sermonum ps.-Ambr.* 7 (ed.
Mercier, SChr 161, 186.2–16); olim Ambr. Med. (dub.), *Sermo* 25 (PL 17:655A)
306 Perfecta...**309** penitentia] Haymo Halb., *De amore coelestis patriae* 2.64 (PL
118:929A)   **310** Non...**311** salutaris] Chrom. Aquil., *Tract. in Mattaeum* 15
(CCSL 9A, 261.70–73); cf. *De cons.* D.4 c.4

285 remittitur] dimittitur Aa Sb uel re-[mittitur] *mg.* Sb   **288** offertur...**289** sa-
cerdoti] *tr.* Aa EdF Fs Sb   **293** mundari] emundari Bi Pf   **297** iustificari] absolui
Aa   **304** conmisit] consensit uel conmisit Fs Sb (uel conmisit *mg.* Sb)

Therefore, sin is not remitted in confession, because it is proven to have already been remitted. Confession is thus made as a demonstration of penance, not as a searching after forgiveness. Just as circumcision was given to Abraham as a sign of righteousness, not as the cause for justification, so also confession is offered to the priest as a sign of forgiveness already received, not as the cause for remission yet to be received.

cf. Rom 4:1–12

<Second Position>

Others testify to the contrary, saying that no one is able to be cleansed without oral confession and a work of satisfaction, if he has the time to make satisfaction. WHENCE THE LORD SAYS THROUGH THE PROPHET, *Say your iniquities so that you may be justified.*

Is 43:26

c.38   LIKEWISE AMBROSE IN HIS BOOK *DE PARADISO*: "No one is able to be justified from a sin unless he has previously confessed the c.39   sin." THE SAME IN HIS LENTEN SERMON: "Behold, now the acceptable time is here in which confession liberates the soul from death, confession opens up paradise, and confession grants the hope of salvation. And so Scripture says, *Say your iniquities so that you may be justified.* With these words it is shown that he who refuses to confess his sins does not deserve to be justified. Therefore that confession which is done with penance frees us. True penance is the heart's grief and the soul's bitterness for the evil deeds which one has committed. Penance is also the lamentation of past evils and not committing the evils to be lamented again." LIKEWISE JOHN c.40   CHRYSOSTOM: "Perfect penance drives the sinner to gladly suffer all things.... Contrition in his heart, confession in his mouth, total humility in his work—this is fruitful penance."

Is 43:26

Final sentence, cf. D.3 c.1

c.41   {THE SAME: "No one can receive the grace of the heavenly God unless he first has been purged from all the filth of sin through penitential confession, through the gift of salutary baptism."}

ITEM AUGUSTINUS: "Nullus debite grauioris pene accipit ue- c.42
niam nisi qualemcumque, etsi longe minorem quam debeat, soluerit penam. Ita enim inpertitur a Deo largitas misericordie, ut non
Aa 147ʳ relinquatur iustitia discipline." IDEM VINCENTIO: "Neminem | putes c.43
Fs 296ᵛᵇ | Bi ab errore ad ueritatem, | et a quocumque | seu magno seu paruo
294ᵛᵇ peccato ad correctionem, | sine penitentia posse transire."
Mk 236ᵛᵇ

IDEM DE PENITENTIA: "Agite penitentiam qualis agitur in eccle- c.44
sia, ut oret pro uobis ecclesia. Nemo dicat sibi, 'Occulte ago, apud
320 Deum ago; nouit Deus, qui mihi ignoscit, quia in corde ago.' Ergo
sine causa dictum est, *Que solueritis in terra soluta erunt et in celo.* Ergo
sine causa claues date sunt ecclesie Dei. Frustramus euangelium
Dei. Frustramus uerba Christi. Promittimus uobis quod ille negat.
Nonne uos decipimus? Iob dicit, *Si erubui in conspectu populi peccata*
325 *mea confiteri.* Atque ideo, si non potuistis habere uel noluistis pudi-
Sb 260ʳᵇ citiam | coniugalem, seu continentiam, et deuiastis a proposito, uel
uinculo coniugali, uel deuotione continentie, sit in uobis dolor et
Fd 89ʳᵃ humilitas penitentie. Apertius dico: nemo | dicat, 'Non intellexi.'
Qui post uxores uestras illicito concubitu uos maculastis, si preter
330 uxores uestras cum aliqua concubuistis, agite penitentiam," etc.

(FdB 160ʳᵇ) | ITEM IERONIMUS SUPER EXODUM: "*Et uenit,* inquid, *Aaron, et omnes presbi-* c.45
teri de Israel, manducare panem cum socero Moysi in conspectu Dei. Omnia ergo,
que faciunt sancti, in conspectu Dei faciunt, peccator autem a conspectu Dei fugit.
Denique scriptum est quia Adam, postquam peccauit, fugit a conspectu Dei, et in-
Pf 102ᵛᵃ terrogatus respondit, *Audiui,* inquit, *uocem tuam, et* | *abscondi me quia eram nudus.*
Set et Cayn, de fratricidio condempnatus a Deo: *Exiit,* inquit, *a facie Dei, et habitauit*
in terra Naim. Exiit ergo a facie Dei qui indignus est eius conspectu. Sancti autem

---

312 Nullus...315 discipline] Aug. Hipp., *De continentia* 6 (CSEL 41, 158.8)
315 Neminem...317 transire] Aug. Hipp., *Epistula* 93 (CSEL 34.2, 496.9)
318 Agite...330 etc] Aug. Hipp. (dub.), *Sermo* 392 (PL 39:1711) 331 Et...345
peccantem] Orig. (trans. Rufinus), *In Exodum homiliae* 11 (GCS 29, 258.4–19)

312 debite] debitor Fs debito Sb 318 Idem] Item Aa Bi Mk 321 solueritis] sol-
ueris Mk Pf | et] *om.* Bi Pf 323 uobis] uerbis Fs, uerbis uerbum Pf, *add.* uerbis
Bi uerbum Mk 326 deuiastis] deruiastis uel Aa diruiastis Pf | uel] *add.* a Bi Mk
Pf 329 Qui] Quia Aa EdF Mk Pf 336 inquit] *om.* Fs *interlin.* Sb

c.42   LIKEWISE AUGUSTINE: "No one receives the pardon of a very serious punishment that is due him unless he suffers some kind of punishment, even if it is far less serious than he owes. For the abundance of loving-kindness is bestowed by God in such a way that the justice of his discipline is not given up." THE SAME IN HIS

c.43   LETTER TO VINCENT: "You are to believe that no one can pass from error to truth and from whatever sin, whether great or small, to correction without penance."

c.44   THE SAME, SPEAKING ABOUT PENANCE: "Do the kind of penance that is done in a church so that the church may pray for you. Let no one say to himself, 'I act secretly, I act in the presence of God; God, who forgives me, knows because I act in my heart.' Then without reason is it said, *What things you loose on earth will also have been loosed in heaven.* Then without reason have the keys been given   Mt 16:19
to the church of God. We frustrate the gospel of God. We frustrate the words of Christ. We promise to you what he denies. We deceive you, do we not? Job says, *If I have felt ashamed to confess my sins*   Jb 31:33–34
in the sight of the people.... And thus, if you have not been able to possess or have refused conjugal virtue, or continence, and you have deviated from your intention or from the conjugal bond or from devotion to continence, let the grief and humility of penance be in you. I speak more frankly: Let know one say, 'I have not understood.' You who, after your wives, defile yourselves with illicit copulation—if you lie with any woman besides your wives, do penance," etc.

c.45   LIKEWISE JEROME IN HIS COMMENTARY ON EXODUS: "*And Aaron and all the elders of Israel came,* he says, *to eat bread with Moses' father-in-law in the sight of God.* Therefore all the things that holy men do, they do in the sight of God, while the   Ex 18:12
sinner flees from the sight of God. Indeed, it is written that Adam, after he sinned, fled from the sight of God and, when he was questioned, he answered, *I heard your voice, and I hid myself, for I was naked.* But also concerning Cain, after he had been   Gn 3:10
condemned by God for his fratricide, it says, *He thus departed from the face of God and lived in the land of Nod.* Thus he who was unworthy of God's sight departed   Gn 4:16

manducant et bibunt in conspectu Dei, et omnia, que agunt, in conspectu Dei
agunt. Ego amplius adhuc locum presentem discutiens uideo quia, qui pleniorem
340 scientiam Dei accipiunt et plenius diuinis inbuti sunt disciplinis, isti, etiamsi malum
faciunt, coram Deo faciunt, et in conspectu eius faciunt, sicut ille qui dixit, *Tibi soli
peccaui, et malum coram te feci.* Quid ergo plus habet qui malum coram Deo facit?
Continuo penitet et dicit, 'Peccaui.' Qui autem discedit a conspectu Dei, nescit conuerti et peccatum penitendo purgare. Hoc ergo interest, malum coram Deo facere,
Fs 297ra   et a Dei conspectu discessisse | peccantem."

ITEM AUGUSTINUS: "Set et continuo qui dixerat, *Sicut Adama faciam te, et sicut*   c.46
Seboym, que due urbes ex uicinia Sodomorum parilis excidii traxere consortium,
Conuersum est, Inquld, *cor meum. In me ipso conturbata est anima mea; non faciam*
Bi 295ra   *secundum iracundiam furoris mei.* Nonne ergo apparet quod ideo nobis | peccanti-
350 bus indignatur Dominus Iesus, ut indignationis sue nos terrore conuertat? Indigna-
tio ergo eius non ultionis executio, set magis absolutionis operatio est."

AaB 332r | ITEM AMBROSIUS IN LIBRO DE PARADYSO: "*Serpens decepit me, et mandu-*   c.47
caui. Veniabilis culpa quam sequitur professio delictorum. Ideo non desperata mulier, que non reticuit Deo, set magis confessa peccatum est quam medicabilis sen-
Mk 237ra   tentia secuta est. Bonum est condempnari in peccato et flagellari | in delicto, ut cum
Sb 260va | hominibus flagellemur. Denique Cayn, qui uoluit crimen negare, indignus iudica-
Pf 102vb   tus est. Qui puniretur in peccato, set remissus est sine prescripto | pene, fortasse
non tam maiore crimine parricidii (illud enim conmisit in fratrem) quam sacrilegii,
quod Deo credidit mentiendum, dicens, *Nescio; numquid ego custos fratris mei sum?*
360 Et ideo accusatori diabolo eius accusatio reseruata est, ut cum eius angelis flagelle-
tur qui cum hominibus noluit flagellari." "Nam pastor ille euangelicus lapsam ouem
uexisse legitur, non abiecisse, et Salomon ait: *Noli esse nimis iustus.* Debet enim iustitiam temperare moderatio. Nam quemadmodum tibi curandus prebeatur, quem
fastidio habeas, qui contemptui se, non conpassioni medico suo putet futurum?"

---

346 Set...351 est] Ambr. Med., *De paenitentia* 1.5 (SChr 179:70.14–23)
352 Serpens...361 flagellari] Ambr. Med., *De paradiso* 14.71 (CSEL 32.1,
328.20–329.9)   361 Nam...364 futurum] Ambr. Med., *De paenitentia* 1.1 (SChr
179:52.11–54.17)

339 Ego] Ergo Fs Sb   353 Veniabilis] venialis Bipc EdF Fs Pf   354 peccatum est]
tr. Mk EdF Pf   358 maiore] maiori Mk Pf maioris FdB Fs Sb | conmisit] conmis-
sum AaB Bi Fs Mk | conmisit...sacrilegii] sacrilegium conmissum est Pf
359 ego] *om.* Bi FdB, *pos.* sum EdF Pf

from his face. But holy men eat and drink in the sight of God, and all the things that they do, they do in the sight of God. Discussing still more fully the present text, I see that those who receive a fuller knowledge of God and have been imbued more fully with divine learning, even if they do evil, act in the presence of God and they act in his sight, just like he who said, *I have sinned to you alone, and I have done evil in your presence.* What more does he who does evil in the presence of God have? He Ps 50:6 continually repents and says, 'I have sinned.' But he who departs from the sight of God does not know how to turn back and purge sin by repenting. Thus, this is important: that the sinner does evil in the presence of God and has departed from the sight of God."

c.46 LIKEWISE AUGUSTINE: "But immediately, he who had said, *I will do to you just as Admah and just as Zeboiim,* which two cities, from their affinity with Sodom, con- Hos 11:8 tracted a fellowship of equal destruction, said, *My heart has been turned round: my soul has been disturbed within me; I will not do according to the wrath of my fury.* It is Hos 11:8–9 apparent, is it not, that the Lord Jesus is so angry with us when we sin that he turns us round by the terror of his anger? Thus his anger is not the carrying out of revenge, but more the working out of his absolution."

c.47 LIKEWISE AMBROSE IN HIS BOOK *De paradiso:* "*The serpent deceived me, and I ate.* It is venial guilt that a profession of wrongs follows. Thus the woman was not Gn 3:13 brought to despair, for she did not stay silent toward God but rather confessed her sin, and a medicinal sentence followed this confession. To be condemned in our sin and to be beaten in our wrongdoing in such a way that we are beaten with men is good. Indeed Cain, who wanted to deny his crime, was judged unworthy. He who would be punished in his sin was sent back without a prescription for punishment, perhaps being guilty not so much of the crime of parricide (for he committed that act against his brother) as that of sacrilege, because he believed he should lie to God, saying, *I do not know. Am I my brother's keeper?* And thus the accusation has Gn 4:9 been reserved for his accuser, the devil, in such a way that he who does not want to be beaten with men is beaten with the devil's angels." "For that gospel shepherd is read to have carried the fallen sheep, not to have cast him out, and Solomon says, *Do not be excessively just.* For moderation ought to temper justice. How is he to of- Eccl 7:17 fer himself to take care of you if you consider him with loathing or if he thinks that he will serve as an object of contempt and not as a source of curative compassion?"

365   IDEM: "Libenter ignosco, prompte indulgeo, misericordiam malo quam sacrifi-   c.48
cium, quia per sacrificium iustus conmendatur, per misericordiam peccator redimi-
tur. *Non ueni uocare iustos, set peccatores ad penitentiam.* In lege sacrificium, in
euangelio misericordia est. *Lex per Moysen data est*, per me gratia."

ITEM LEO EPISCOPUS THEODORO, FOROIULIENSI EPISCOPO:
370   "Multiplex misericordia Dei ita lapsibus humanis subuenit, ut, non   c.49
solum per baptismi gratiam, set etiam per penitentie medicinam
spes uite reparetur eterne, ut qui regenerationis dona uiolassent,
Fs 297rb   proprio se iudicio | condempnantes, ad remissionem criminum per-
uenirent, sic diuine uoluntatis presidiis ordinatis, ut indulgentia
375   Dei, nisi supplicationibus sacerdotum, nequeat obtineri. Mediator
Dei et hominum homo dominus Iesus Christus hanc prepositis ecclesie tradidit potestatem, ut confitentibus penitentie satisfactionem
darent, et eadem salubri satisfactione purgatos ad conmunionem
sacramentorum per ianuam reconciliationis admitterent."

380   Et post pauca: "Si autem aliquis eorum, pro quibus Domino
supplicamus, quocumque interceptus obstaculo a munere indulgentie presentis excesserit, et priusquam ad constituta remedia perueniat, temporalem uitam humana conditione finierit, quod ma-
Bi 295rb   nens in corpore | non recepit, consequi exutus carne non poterit."

385   Et post aliqua: "His autem, qui tempore necessitatis et periculi
urgentis instantia presidium penitentie et mox reconciliationis in-
plorant, nec satisfactio interdicenda est, nec reconciliatio deneganda, quia misericordie Dei nec mensuras possumus ponere, nec

---

365 Libenter...**368** gratia] Ibid. 1.12 (SChr 179:100.20–26)   **370** Multiplex...
399 peccauerunt] Leo I, *Epistola* 108 (PL 54:1011B–1014A) = JK 485

375 Mediator] *add.* enim R2

365 malo] uolo FdB Sb   **369** Episcopus] *om.* Aa | Foroiuliensi] forolunensi Bi
Fd_pc Mk Sb foroliminensi Fs   **373** se iudicio] *tr.* Aa Sb EdF   **375** nisi] non nisi
Fs, *interlin.* Fd | nequeat] nequeant Bi Fs Mk | Mediator] *add.* enim *interlin.* Fd
384 recepit] receperit Fd_pc Fs   **386** urgentis] urguentis Bi Fs Sb   **388** mensuras]
mensuram Pf Sb

c.48   THE SAME: "Freely I forgive; readily do I bestow pardon; I prefer mercy to sacrifice, for through sacrifice the righteous man is commended, but through mercy the
sinner is redeemed. *I did not come to call the righteous but sinners to repentance.* In   Lk 5:32
the law is sacrifice; in the gospel, mercy. *The law was given through Moses*; grace   cf. Jn 1:17
was given through me."

LIKEWISE BISHOP LEO TO THEODORE, BISHOP OF CIVIDALE
c.49   DEL FRUILI: "The many-sided mercy of God comes to the aid of
fallen humans in such a way that the hope of eternal life is restored
not only through the grace of baptism but also through the medicine of penance, so that those who had violated the gift of regeneration might condemn themselves by their own judgment and thus
achieve the remission of sins. The watchful assistance of the divine
will, however, has been ordained in such a way that the mercy of
God cannot be obtained except by the supplications of priests. The
Mediator between God and men, the man, the Lord Jesus Christ,
handed this power down to the leaders of the church so that they
might give the satisfaction of penance to those who confess and
might admit those purged by that same salubrious satisfaction to
the communion of sacraments through the door of reconciliation."

And a little further on: "If anyone of them, however, for whom
we make supplication to the Lord, should be hindered by some sort
of stumbling block and depart from the gift of the present mercy,
and, before he reaches the established remedies, should end his
temporal life in a human condition, that which he did not receive
while remaining in his body, he would not be able to obtain once
he had been divested of the flesh."

And a little later: "But to those who desperately seek the assistance of penance and then of reconciliation at the time of necessity
and the instant of urgent danger, neither is satisfaction to be forbidden, nor is reconciliation to be denied, for we can neither place

tempora diffinire, apud quem nullas patitur moras uenire conuer-
390 sio."

Sb 260vb   Et item: "Ita ergo | necessitati auxiliandum est, ut nec actio illis
Pf 103ra penitentie nec conmunionis | gratia denegetur, si eam, etiam amis-
so uocis officio, per indicia integri sensus querere conprobentur.
Quod si ita aliqua egritudine fuerint aggrauati, ut quod paulo ante
395 poscebant sub presenti significare non ualeant, testimonia eis fidelium circumstantium prodesse debebunt. Simul tamen et penitentie
Aa 147^v Mk et reconciliationis beneficium consequantur. Seruata | tamen cano-
237rb num regula paternorum circa eorum personas qui in dominica fide
discedendo peccauerunt."

400   ITEM AMBROSIUS: "Nemo potest bene agere penitentiam nisi c.50
qui sperauerit indulgentiam. Set negant his oportere reddi conmunionem qui preuaricatione lapsi sunt.... Deus autem nullius crimen
excepit, qui peccata omnia donauit."

(FdG 89ra)   [| AMBROSIUS: "Verbum Dei dimittit peccata, sacerdos et iudex; sacerdos qui- c.51
(AaB 332^r) dem offitium suum exhibet, et nullius potestatis iura exercet."]

Et paulo post: "Dominus par ius et soluendi esse uoluit et ligandi, qui utrumque pari conditione permisit. Ergo qui soluendi ius
non habet nec ligandi habet."

Fs 297va   Et infra: "Certum est, quod ecclesie utrumque | licet, heresis
410 utrumque non habet. Ius enim hoc solis permissum est sacerdoti-
bus. Recte igitur ecclesia hoc uendicat, que ueros habet sacerdotes;
heresis uendicare non potest, que sacerdotes Dei non habet."

---

400 Nemo...403 donauit] Ambr. Med., *De paenitentia* 1.1–2 (SChr
179:54.36–40, 56.5–6)   404 Verbum...405 exercet] cf. Ambr. Med., *De Cain et
Abel* 2.4.15 (CSEL 32.1, 391.7–10)   406 Dominus...412 habet] Ambr. Med., *De
paenitentia* 1.2 (SChr 179:58.26–29, 35–39)

389 moras uenire] moram ueni *mg.* Fd | uenire] uenie EdF Fs Mk Pf
392 etiam] *interlin.* Fd   393 indicia] indicium Fd_{pc} indutias Fd_{ac} Pf   397 benefi-
cium] remedium Pf   398 eorum] earum Aa Sb   401 sperauerit] sperauit Sb
402 nullius] *add.* mouenti Pf   403 omnia] omnium Aa   404 Ambrosius] *praem.*
Idem Fs Item EdF Pf, Et paulo post FdG Sb | et] est Bi_{pc} EdF Fs Pf   408 habet²]
om. Aa Fs   410 est] *interlin.* Bi Mk

measures on nor delimit times for the mercy of God, from whose viewpoint conversion does not allow any delays to occur."

And below: "Therefore, there should be help for such necessity in such a way that neither the act of penance nor the grace of communion would be denied to them, if they should be proven to seek it through signs of genuine sentiment, even if they have lost the ability to speak. But if they should be afflicted by some illness in such a way that what they were demanding only a little earlier they should not be able to signify in the presence of a priest, the testimonies of the faithful who were in their presence ought to serve them. The benefit of both penance and reconciliation, however, should follow simultaneously. Nevertheless, the rule of the canons of the Fathers about the persons of those who have sinned by departing from the Lord's faith has been preserved."

c.50 LIKEWISE, AMBROSE: "No one is able to do penance well except he who has hoped for mercy. But they deny that communion should be rendered to those who fell by violating their duty.... But God, who has forgiven all sins, makes an exception for no one's wicked deed."

c.51 [AMBROSE: "The Word of God forgives sins, as do the priest and judge; indeed the priest displays his office but does not exercise any rights of power."]

And a little later: "The Lord, who granted the right both to loose and to bind on equal condition, desired both to be equal. Therefore, he who does not possess the right to loose also does not have the right to bind."

And below: "It is certain that both are permitted to the church but that both are not permitted to a heretical sect. For this right has been granted to priests alone. Thus the church which has true priests correctly claims this, but a heretical sect, which does not have priests of God, cannot claim it."

Item in eodem: "Potest fieri ut aliquis uictus suppliciis sermone   c.52
neget et corde adoret. Numquid eadem causa eius, qui sponte ne-
415   gat, et eius, quem tormenta inclinauerunt ad sacrilegium? Non.
Quam indignum autem est, cum apud homines ualeat certaminis
gratia, ut apud Deum non ualere asseratur? Nam sepe in hoc athle-
tarum seculari certamine etiam uictos, quorum fuerunt certamina
probata, hominum uulgus cum uictoribus coronare consueuit, ma-
420   xime quos uiderit aut forte, dolo, aut fraude excussos uictoria. Et
Christus athletas suos, quos uiderit grauibus paulisper cessisse suppliciis, sine uenia patietur manere? Numquid non habebit remunerationem laboris, qui etiam aliquos proiecit?"

Et infra: "Dicis Petro, excusanti ne eius pedes lauares, *Nisi lauero*
425   *tibi pedes, non habebis partem mecum.* Quod ergo isti possunt consortium tecum habere, qui claues regni non suscipiunt, negantes quod
Bi 295ᵛᵃ   peccata dimittere | debeant? Quod recte quidem de se fatentur. Non
habent enim Petri hereditatem qui Petri sedem non habent, quam
inpia diuisione discerpunt."

Sb 261ʳᵃ   Et paulo post: "Egritudo | carnis peccatum repellit, luxuria au-
tem carnis culpam adolet. Illuditur ergo diabolus ut se ipsum morsu
suo uulneret, et contra se armet, quem debilitandum putauit."

Et infra: "Quod nocet corpori, iuuat spiritum."
Et paulo post: "Sicut semel pro omnibus inmolatus est Christus,
435   ita, quotiescumque peccata donantur, corporis eius sacramentum
Pf 103ʳᵇ   sumimus, ut per sanguinem eius remissio peccatorum | detur. Ergo
euidentissime Domini predicatione mandatum est etiam grauissimi
criminis reis, si ex toto corde et manifesta confessione peccati penitentiam gerant, sacramenti celestis perfundendam gratiam."

(AaB 332ʳ) | Idem: "Quantuslibet ergo mortui fetor sit, aboletur omnis, ubi sacrum redole-   c.53

---

413 Potest…**423** proiecit] Ibid. 1.4 (SChr 179:68.31–44)   **424** Dicis…**429** di-
scerpunt] Ibid. 1.7 (SChr 179:80.27–34)   **430** Egritudo…**433** spiritum] Ibid.
1.13 (SChr 179:106.54–57, 108.82)   **434** Sicut…**439** gratiam] Ibid. 2.3 (SChr
179:144.50–146.57)   **440** Quantuslibet…**452** uenit] Ibid. 2.7 (SChr
179:170.54–172.74)

425 Quod] quid EdF Fd Fs Mk Pf Sb

c.52   And again, Ambrose, in the same work: "It is possible that someone who has been overcome with tortures denies with his mouth
and yet worships in his heart. The case of he who denies of his own
volition is not the same as the case of he whom torments bend to
sacrilege, is it? No. How unseemly would it be, when the esteem of
a contest counts for something among men, that it is declared to
count for nothing with God. For the mob of the people were often
accustomed to crown the defeated, whose struggles had been ap-
proved, along with the victors in this worldly contest of athletes,
especially those whom it saw excluded from victory by accident,
deceit, or trickery. Does Christ then allow his athletes, whom he
has seen gradually yield to grave tortures, remain without mercy?
He has indeed also cast out some, but he will not not have a reward
for labor such as this, will he?"

And below: "When Peter objects to you washing his feet, you
say to him, *If I do not wash your feet, you will have no part of me.* What   Jn 13:8
fellowship, then, can those have with him when they do not re-
ceive the keys of the kingdom and so deny that they are responsible for forgiving sins? They rightly confess this about themselves,
for those who do not have the seat of Peter, which they tear into
pieces by a wicked division, do not have his inheritance."

And a little later: "Sickness of the flesh drives back sin, but
fleshly ease and comfort magnify guilt. The devil thus makes a
laughing-stock of himself such that he wounds himself by his own
bite and arms against himself the person whom he thought should
have been debilitated."

And below: "Because he harms the body, he assists the spirit."

And a little later: "Just as Christ was sacrificed once for all, so
also, however many times sins are offered, we take the sacrament
of his body so that the remission of sins may be given. The grace of
the heavenly sacrament is to be poured out even for those guilty of
a very serious crime, if they do penance with their whole heart and
with a clear confession of sin."

c.53   The same: "Therefore, however great the stench of a dead man is, it is eliminated in its entirety when the deceased smells like holy perfume, and he rises up,

uerit unguentum, et surgit defunctus, et solui iubentur eius uincula, qui adhuc in
peccato est. Tollitur uelamen de facie eius, quod ueritatem gratie, quam acceperat,

Mk 237va obumbrabat. Set | quia uenie donatus est, reuelare faciem, aperire uultum, iubetur.
Fs 297vb Non enim habet | quod erubescat, cui peccatum dimissum est. In tanta enim Do-
FdB 160va mini gratia tantoque diuini muneris miraculo cum oporteret uniuersos | letari, con-
mouebantur inpii et aduersus Christum concilium congregabant, Lazarum quoque
interficere uolebant. Nonne merito eorum successores uos fore cognoscitis, quorum duritie heredes estis? Nam et uos indignamini, et contra ecclesiam congregatis
concilium, quia uidetis mortuos in ecclesia reuiuiscere, et peccatorum indulgentia
450 resuscitari. Itaque (quod in uobis est) per inuidiam rursus uultis interficere suscita-
tos. Set Iesus non reuocat beneficia; immo cumulo libertatis amplificat: reuiuiscit
sollicite suscitatus, et celebrata resurrectionis gratia letus ad cenam uenit."

Fd 89rb Item: "His potestatis | sue gratiam negat, que in remissione pec-   c.54
catorum est, qui celestem eius potestatem diabolico spiritu separant
455 ab ecclesia Domini, ut omnium temporum hereticos et scismaticos
conprehenderet, quibus indulgentiam negat, quod omne peccatum
Aa 148r circa singulos est ac | uniuersos."

Et infra: "Quid mirum, si salutem negatis aliis, qui uestram re-
cusatis, licet illi nichil a uobis differant, qui a uobis penitentiam pe-
460 tunt? Arbitror enim, quod et Iudas potuisset tanta miseratione Domini non excludi a uenia, si penitentiam non apud Iudeos, set apud
Christum gessisset."

Et paulo post: "Qui agit penitentiam, non solum diluere lacrimis
debet peccatum set etiam emendationibus operire, et tegere delicta
465 superiora, ut non inputetur ei peccatum."

---

453 His...**462** gessisset] Ibid. 2.4 (SChr 179:148.45–52, 150.74–79)   **463** Qui...
465 peccatum] Ibid. 2.5 (SChr 179:156.60–63)

447 fore] forte AaB Bi$_{ac}$ Fs Mk esse forte FdB esse fortes Sb   **448** duritie] diuitie
AaB$_{ac}$ durie Pf$_{ac}$ **449** concilium] consilium Fs conscilium (!) Bi   **450** rursus] ite-
rum *pos.* uultis Fs, *pos.* uultis Pf, *om.* Sb | suscitatos] resuscitatos EdF Pf Sb
451 cumulo] cumulos AaB Mk Pf cumulose FdB   **459** nichil] *ant.* differant Aa
Pf   **460** et] *om.* Aa Bi   **461** non²] *add.* solum Fs Mk (*interlin.* Mk)   **465** ei] *ant.*
non Fd Fs Mk

and the chains of him who is still in sin are ordered to be released. A veil is lifted from his face. This veil used to cover the truth of the grace which he had accepted, but, because he has been given over to mercy, he is ordered to reveal his face, to show his countenance. For he for whom sin has been remitted does not have that which causes shame. In the midst of such immense grace of the Lord and such a great miracle of the divine gift,[8] at a time when it would be justified for all men of the world to be slain, the wicked were roused and assembled together a gathering against Christ, and also desired to killed Lazarus. You know, do you not, that you will deservedly be successors of them, since you are the heirs to their hard-heartedness? For you also are unworthy, and you gather together an assembly against the church, because you see that the dead come to life again in the church and are brought back to life by the pardon of sins. Thus, because envy is in you, on account of it you want to kill again those raised to life. But Jesus does not call back his blessings; instead, he makes them larger with a heap of liberality: the person brought to life is vigorously renewed in strength and comes joyfully to dinner when the grace of the resurrection has been celebrated."

c.54   Likewise: "He denies the grace of his power, which consists of the remission of sins, to those who, by a diabolical spirit, separate his heavenly power from the church of the Lord, so that he might apprehend the heretics and schismatics of all times, to whom he denies pardon because every sin encompasses them individually and as a whole."

And below: "What wondrous thing is it if you who refuse your own salvation deny salvation to others, despite the fact that those who seek penance from you differ from you in nothing? For I think that even Judas would have been able not to be excluded from mercy, from such great compassion of the Lord, if he had yielded up penance, not among the Jews but before Christ."

And a little later: "He who does penance ought not only to wash away his sin with tears but also to conceal it with more proper behavior and to cover over higher offences so that the sin may not be imputed to him."

---

8. The miracle refers to the raising of Lazarus from the dead in John 11.

Sb 261rb   Item in eodem: "Nonnulli ideo poscunt penitentiam, ut statim | c.55
sibi reddi conmunionem uelint. Et non tam soluere se cupiunt,
Bi 295vb   quam sacerdotem ligare. Sua enim conscientia se non tam | exuunt,
quam sacerdotem indui cupiunt, cui preceptum est: *Nolite sanctum*
Pf 103va   *dare canibus, neque miseritis | margaritas uestras ante porcos,* hoc est, in-
mundis spiritibus sacre conmunionis non sunt facile tribuenda con-
sortia."

       In eodem: "Sunt qui arbitrentur hanc esse penitentiam: si absti-   c.56
neant a sacramentis celestibus. Hii seueriores in se iudices sunt, qui
475   penam prescribunt si remedium declinant, quos ob penam conue-
niebat dolere, quia celesti fraudarentur gratia."

Fs 298ra   Et paulo post: "Facilius autem inuenis | qui innocentiam serua-
uerit quam qui congrue egerit penitentiam peccati. Vbi acquirende
ambitio dignitatis, ubi uini effusio, ubi ipsius copule coniugalis
480   usus? Renunciandum seculo est, et ipsi somno minus indulgendum
quam natura postulet, interpellandum est gemitibus, interrumpen-
dum est suspiriis, sequestrandum orationibus, uiuendum ita, ut ui-
tali huic moriatur usui; se ipsum homo abneget, et totus inmute-
tur."

485   Et infra: "Nemo in peccatis positus arrogare sibi debet auctoritatem aut usurpationem sacramentorum, quia scriptum est: *Peccasti?*
quiesce."
Mk 237vb   Et paulo post: "Dicimus ergo, agendam | penitentiam et eo tem-
pore agendam, quo culpa deferuescat luxurie, et in peccati captiui-
490   tate positos reuerentiores, non usurpatores esse debere."

466 Nonnulli...**476** gratia] Ibid. 2.9 (SChr 179:186.43–188.49, 188.56–60)
477 Facilius...**484** inmutetur] Ibid. 2.10 (SChr 179:192.43–51)   **485** Nemo...
490 debere] Ibid. 2.11 (SChr 179:196.44–47, 198.76–200.79)

467 Et] Hii *seu add.* hii R2

467 uelint] et Mk Sb | Et] Hii Bi Pf *add.* hii Mk Sb   **468** sacerdotem] sacerdotes
Aa   **474** seueriores] seuiores Fs Mk seceriores? Pf | sunt] fuerint Bi Mk Sb fiunt
Fs   **476** dolere] delere Bi Sb_{ac}   **478** congrue] congruenter Pf incongrue Sb
482 sequestrandum] *add.* est Aa Pf

c.55   The same author in the same book: "Some demand penance in such a way that they want communion immediately returned to them, and they[9] do not desire to free themselves so much as to bind the priest. For they do not divest themselves of their conscience so much as they want the priest to be entangled. Nevertheless, priests were commanded, *Do not give holy things to dogs, and do not cast your pearls before swine*, that is to say, the fellowship of holy communion is not to be given indiscriminately to unclean spirits."   Mt 7:6

c.56   In the same work: "There are those who think that this is penance: if they abstain from the heavenly sacraments. These are more severe judges of themselves if they prescribe this punishment and so shun their remedy. It was fitting to grieve for them on account of this punishment because they were defrauded of heavenly grace."

And a little later: "But you find more easily those who preserve their innocence than those who have done penance for their sin in a fitting manner. When is there place for striving after worldly stature or obtaining libations of wine or the enjoyment of the conjugal bond itself? The penitent is to renounce the world, to indulge in sleep less than nature demands, to cause disruptions with lamentations, to break apart with sighs, to give himself over to prayers, to live in such a way that he dies to this vital enjoyment; as a man he is to deny himself, and his entire being is to be changed."

And below: "No one in sin ought to adopt to themselves authority or make use of the sacraments, for it is written, *You have sinned? Be still.*"   Ecclus 21:1

And a little later: "We therefore say that penance should be done, and it should be done at the time in which the abundance of guilt ceases its raging, and those held in the captivity of sin should be very reverent and not be usurpers."

---

9. The second recension adds a pronoun, making the subject of "desire" more pronounced: "These people do not desire...."

(Et infra:) "Nam si Moysi proprius accedere gestienti ut cognitionem misterii celestis hauriret dicitur, *Solue calciamentum pedum tuorum*, quanto magis nos anime
nostre pedes exuere uinculis corporalibus et nexu mundi istius gressus eius debe-
AaB 332ᵛ   mus | absoluere?"

495   Et infra: "Nichil est, quod tam summi doloris sit, quam si unusquisque positus sub captiuitate peccati recordetur unde lapsus sit
atque unde deciderit et quod ad corporea atque terrena ab illa spe-
ciosa atque pulchra diuine conditionis intentione defluxerit."

ITEM CIPRIANUS: "Miror autem quosdam sic obstinatos esse, ut dandam non   c.57
500 putent lapsis penitentiam, aut penitentibus existiment ueniam denegandam, cum
scriptum sit: *Memento unde cecideris, et age penitentiam, et fac priora opera.* Quod
utique ei dicitur quem constat cecidisse, et quem Dominus hortatur per opera rursus exurgere, quia scriptum est, *Elemosina a morte liberat*, non utique ab illa morte
quam semel Christi sanguis exstinxit, et a qua nos salutaris baptismi et redemptoris
505 nostri gratia liberauit, set ab ea que per delicta postmodum serpit."

Sb 261ᵛᵃ   ITEM IERONIMUS: |"Inportuna in euangelio mulier tandem meruit audiri, et   c.58
Pf 103ᵛᵇ   clauso cum seruis ostio, media | licet nocte, ab amico panes amicus accepit. Deus
Bi 296ʳᵃ | Fs   ipse, qui nullis | intra se superari | uiribus potest, publicani precibus uincitur. Niniue
298ʳᵇ   ciuitas, que peccato periit, fletibus stetit. Quorsum ista tam longo repetita princi-
510 pio? Videlicet ut paruum magnus aspicias, ut diues pastor morbidam non contemp-
nas ouem. Christus in paradysum de cruce latronem etiam tulit, et, ne quis aliquando seram conuersionem putaret, fecit homicidii penam martyrium. Christus,
inquam, prodigum filium reuertentem letus amplectitur, et, nonaginta nouem pecu-
dibus derelictis, una ouicula que remanserat humeris boni pastoris aduehitur." "Vbi
515 uero peccator intelligens uulnus suum tradit medico se curandum, ibi non est uirga
necessaria, set spiritus lenitatis."

---

491 Nam...**494** absoluere] Ibid. (SChr 179:200.79–83)   **495** Nichil...**498** deflu-
xerit] Ibid. (SChr 179:196.32–37)   **499** Miror...**505** serpit] Cypr. Carth., *Epistula* 55.22.1 (CCSL 3B:281.356–364)   **506** Inportuna...**514** aduehitur] Hier.,
Epistula 16 (ed. Hilberg, CSEL 54, 68.3–14)   **514** Vbi...**516** lenitatis] Hier.,
Comm. in iv epistulas paulinas, Ad Galatos 3 (PL 26:426A)

491 Et infra] *om.* EdF Sb, Set infra Fs Mk   **492** hauriret] audiret FdB Sb
493 corporalibus] corporis Bi corporeis Mk   **495** Et infra] *om.* Bi | infra] *recte* su-
pra   **497** deciderit] ceciderit Pf Sb   **507** seruis] seris Biₚᶜ EdF Fs Mkₚᶜ Pf EdF
508 nullis] nullius Fs Mk | uincitur] uel uincitur uel superatur Fs   **510** aspicias]
accipiat FdB accipias Pf   **511** etiam tulit] intulit Pf EdF   **513** letus] leuis Bi
515 tradit] tradet AaB Sb

(And below:) "For if it is said to Moses, who longed to come nearer so that he might drink up the knowledge of a heavenly mystery, *Take off the shoes from your feet*, how much more should we divest the feet of our souls of bodily chains and free their steps from the bond of this wretched world?" Ex 3:5

And below: "There is nothing which is so great a source of grief as when someone held under the captivity of sin recollects from where he slipped and from where he fell and that he descended to the corporeal and earthly from that illustrious and beautiful directing of the mind to the divine condition."

c.57   LIKEWISE CYPRIAN: "But I am amazed that certain people are so inflexible that they believe that penance ought not be given to the lapsed, or they think that mercy ought to be denied to penitents, even though it is written, *Remember from where you have fallen and repent, and do the deeds you did at first.* Assuredly this is said to Rv 2:5 him who it is agreed has fallen and whom the Lord urges to rise up again through works, for it is written, *Alms liberate from death*, and surely not from that death Tob 4:11 which the blood of Christ extinguished once and for all and from which the grace of our salutary baptism and our redeemer freed us, but from that death which creeps up afterward through sins."

c.58   LIKEWISE JEROME: "The troublesome woman in the gospel at last earned a hearing, and, after his friend's door had been shut by his servants,[10] although it was the middle of the night, the man received loaves of bread from him. God himself, who cannot be overcome by any strength brought against him, is conquered by the prayers of the publican. The city of Nineveh, which perished by its sin, stayed standing as a result of its weeping. To what end have these tales been repeated here at the start at such length? Namely so that you, a great man, may look to the small man, so you, a rich shepherd, may not loathe the sickly sheep. Christ even brought the thief from the cross into paradise, and, lest anyone at any time consider a late conversion, he made martyrdom the penalty for murder.[11] Christ, I say, gladly embraces the prodigal son as he returns, and, having left behind the ninety-nine [other] sheep, the good shepherd bears the one remaining lamb on his shoulders." "For where a sinner who understands his wound has handed himself over to a physician to be healed, a rod is not necessary, but a spirit of leniency."

---

10. The text originally seems to have used a word meaning "servants" (*seruis*), but the text was later corrected with the removal of the "u" to read "late in the evening" (*seris*)

11. That is, the thief on the cross became a martyr through his murder at the hands of those who crucified him, but this is a rare occurrence and not the norm in any sense, and therefore people should not delay conversion and penance in the hopes of attaining what the thief on the cross did.

Quod autem omni peccanti auctoritate Ambrosii uenia promittitur falsum uide-   d.p.c.58
tur. Quibusdam enim uenia denegatur, aut ex magnitudine peccati aut ex gradu offi-
tii. VNDE IOHANNES IN EPISTOLA: *Est peccatum ad mortem—quis orabit pro eo?*
520 ALIBI QUOQUE LEGITUR, *Quis medebitur incantatori uulnerato a serpente?* ITEM: *Si*   c.59
sacerdos peccauerit, quis orabit pro eo?

Set huiuscemodi interrogationes non semper negationem inferunt, set potius   d.p.c.59
difficultatem uel raritatem notant, ut est ILLUD EUANGELII: *Quis, putas, est fidelis*
seruus et prudens, etc. HINC ETIAM AMBROSIUS: *"Deus, quis similis erit tibi?* non
525 utique nullus; quia imago patris filius est." Similiter accipiendum *Quis orabit pro*
eo? hoc est, singularis uite aliquis debet orare pro eo, qui peccauit in Domino.
Mk 238ʳᵃ   "Nam quomodo Iohannes | diceret, non orandum pro delicto grauiori, qui legisset,
Moysen rogasse, et inpetrasse, ubi erat preuaricatio uoluntaria, qui sciret etiam Iere-
miam rogasse?"

530   Potest etiam SECUNDUM AUGUSTINUM aliter intelligi ILLUD IO-
HANNIS, *Est peccatum ad mortem,* etc. ut nulla sit eius et superiorum
contrarietas. AIT ENIM: *"Est peccatum ad mortem, non pro illo dico ut*
roget quis. De quo peccato, quoniam expressum non est, possunt
multa et diuersa sentiri. Ego autem dico hoc peccatum esse: fidem,
535 que per dilectionem operatur, deserere usque ad mortem." Hec
Fs 298ᵛᵃ   etiam est blasphemia in Spiritum sanctum, quam | neque in hoc se-
AaB 333ʳ   culo, neque in futuro remittendam | in euangelio Dominus asseruit.
Siue autem delectatione peccati siue desperatione uenie usque ad
mortem quis in peccato perseueret, iustum est ut sine fine puniatur
Pf 104ʳᵃ | Sb | qui sine fine peccauerit. VNDE GREGORIUS: "Voluissent iniqui, si | c.60
261ᵛᵇ   potuissent, sine fine uiuere, ut potuissent sine fine peccare. Ostendunt, quia in peccato semper uiuere cupiunt, qui numquam desi-
Bi 296ʳᵇ   nunt peccare, dum uiuunt. Ad magnam ergo iustitiam iudicantis |
FdB 160ᵛᵇ   pertinet ut numquam careant supplicio qui in hac | uita numquam
545 uoluerunt carere peccato."

---

524 Deus…**525** est] Ambr. Med., *De paenitentia* 1.9 (SChr 179:88.29–30)
527 Nam…**529** rogasse] Ibid. 1.10 (SChr 179:92.13–16)   **532** Est…**535** mor-
tem] Aug. Hipp., *De corr. et gratia* (PL 44:938)   **540** Voluissent…**545** peccato]
Greg. Magn., *Dial. libri IV* 4.46.3 (SChr 265, 162.22–28)

517 omni] *om.* FdB Sb   **518** enim] autem Bi Fs Mk Sb   **528** qui] quis Fs Sb
533 quo] eo FdB Sb   **540** peccauerit] peccauit AaB Fs Pf Sb   **544** pertinet] permanent Fs pertinent Sb

d.p.c.58   But the idea, according to the authority of Ambrose, that mercy is promised to every sinner seems false. For mercy may be denied to certain persons, either because of the magnitude of their sin or because of the degree of their office. FOR THIS REASON JOHN [WRITES] IN HIS EPISTLE, *There is a sin unto death—who will pray for*   1 Jn 5:16 *him?* ELSEWHERE IT IS ALSO READ, *Who will heal the charmer wounded*   Ecclus 12:13

c.59   *by the serpent?* LIKEWISE: *If a priest sins, who will pray for him?*   Lv 4:3, 1 Sm 2:25; cf. D.50

d.p.c.59   But, one could answer that questions of this kind do not always bear a negative   c.67 answer; rather they point out a difficulty and rarity, as is the case with THAT TEXT OF THE GOSPEL: *Who do you think is the loyal and prudent slave,* etc.? FOR THIS   Mt 24:45 TYPE OF QUESTION THERE IS ALSO AMBROSE: "God, who is like you? Surely not   Ps 82:2 nothing, because the Son is the Image of the Father." Similarly should *Who will pray for him?* be understood, that is, someone of a singular life ought to pray for him who sinned against the Lord. "For how could John say that there is to be no prayer for a very serious offence when he would have read that Moses had petitioned and received, after he had willfully violated his duty, and when John also would know that Jeremiah had petitioned?"

That PASSAGE OF JOHN, *There is a sin unto death,* can also be un-   1 Jn 5:16 derstood differently in accord with Augustine's interpretation so that there is no contradiction between him and his forebears. FOR AUGUSTINE SAYS, *"There is a sin unto death, but I do not say that some- one should petition for this.* Concerning this sin, since it is not ex- pressly stated, many and diverse opinions can be held. But I say that this is the sin: deserting the faith which works through love all the way until death." This is also the blasphemy against the Holy Spirit, which the Lord in the gospel has declared is to be remitted neither in this world nor in the next. But if someone were to perse- vere in sin, whether by delighting in the sin or by despairing of mercy, all the way to death, it is just that he who would have sinned without end be punished without end. AND THUS GRE-

c.60   GORY: "If they had been able to, the wicked would have wanted to live without end so that they could have sinned without end. For those who never stop sinning while they are alive show that they desire always to live in sin. It is thus appropriate for the great jus- tice of the Judge that those who never wanted to be without sin in this life never lack punishment."

Ex his itaque apparet quod sine confessione oris et satisfactione   d.p.c.60
operis peccatum non remittitur. Nam si necesse est, ut iniquitates
nostras dicamus, ut postea iustificemur; si nemo potest iustificari a
peccato nisi peccatum antea fuerit confessus; si confessio parady-
550 sum aperit, ueniam acquirit; si illa solum confessio utilis est, que fit
Aa 148ᵛ cum penitentia (in quo notatur | aliud esse confessio, aliud peniten-
tia, siue interior siue exterior accipiatur); si ille, qui promittit ueniam occulte apud Deum non apud ecclesiam penitentiam agenti,
frustrat euangelium et claues datas ecclesie, promittit etiam quod
555 Deus negat delinquenti; si nemo potest ueniam consequi, nisi
quantulamcumque, etsi minorem quam debeat, peccati soluerit penam; si solis sacerdotibus ligandi soluendique potestas a Deo tradita
est; si nullus ueniam accipit, nisi ecclesie supplicationibus ipsam inpetrare contendat—concluditur ergo, quod nullus ante confessio-
560 nem oris et satisfactionem operis peccati abolet culpam.

Denique, ut perspicue appareat neminem sine confessione a
peccato mundari, ab ipsius humani generis principio sumamus exordium. Peccato transgressionis primi parentes corrupti a Domino
sunt requisiti de culpa, ut peccatum, quod transgrediendo conmise-
565 rant, confitendo delerent. Serpens autem de culpa requisitus non
est, quia per confessionem non reuocabatur ad uitam. Cayn quoque, cum prime preuaricationi fratricidium addidisset, similiter a
Domino de culpa requisitus est, dum dicitur ei, *Vbi est Abel frater
tuus?* Set quia superbus peccatum suum confiteri noluit, potius
570 mendaciter negando Dominum fallere conatus est, dicens, *Numquid
custos fratris mei sum ego?* indignus uenia iudicatus est. Vnde in de-
Fs 298ᵛᵇ | Mk sperationis | profundum | mersus, dum ait, *Maior est iniquitas mea,*
238ʳᵇ *quam ut ueniam merear.* Vagus et profugus exiit a facie Domini, si-
Fd 89ᵛᵃ gnificans, eos, | qui peccatum suum confiteri dissimulant, respectu
575 diuine miserationis indignos haberi.

---

549 peccatum] *pos.* confessus EdF Fs Sb, *ant.* confessus Pf   555 ueniam conse-
qui] *tr.* Aa EdF Sb sequi ueniam Fs Pf   556 soluerit] persoluerit Aa   558 accipit]
accipit Fd_{pc} Sb   566 reuocabatur] reuocabitur Fd Sb   572 iniquitas mea] *tr.* Fd
Fs Sb

d.p.c.60 From these things it is thus clear that sin is not remitted without oral confession and a work of satisfaction. For if it is necessary that we say our iniquities so that we may afterward be justified; if no   cf. d.p.c.37 one can be justified from a sin unless he has previously confessed the sin; if confession opens up paradise and obtains mercy; if that   cf. c.38 confession is alone useful that occurs with penance (in which it is | cf. c.39 noted that confession is one thing, penance another, whether an interior or exterior entity is understood); if he who promises mercy   cf. within c.39 to the person doing penance secretly before God and not before the church frustrates the gospel and the keys given to the church, and if he also promises what God denies to the transgressor; if no one   cf. c.44 can obtain mercy unless he pays his sin's penalty, however small, even if it is less than he owes; if the power of binding and loosing   cf. c.42 has been bestowed by God on priests alone; if no one receives   cf. c.49, c.51 mercy unless he strives to procure it by the supplications of the church—it is therefore concluded that no one may do away with   cf. c.49 the guilt of sin before oral confession and a work of satisfaction.

And then, so that it may be perfectly clear that no one is cleansed of sin without confession, let us take our start from the beginning of the human race itself. Our parents, having been corrupted by the sin of the first transgression, were questioned by the Lord about their guilt so that, by their confession, they might destroy the sin which they had committed by their transgression. The serpent, however, was not questioned about his guilt because he was not called back to life through confession. Cain as well, when   cf. Gn 3:9–14 he had added fratricide to the first failure of duty, was similarly asked about his guilt by the Lord, when it was said to him, *Where is*   Gn 4:9 *your brother, Abel?* But, because he was proud and refused to confess his sin and instead tried to deceive God with lies and a denial, saying, *Am I my brother's keeper?*, he was judged unworthy of mercy. He   Gn 4:9 was thus plunged into the depth of despair when he said, *My iniq-*   Gn 4:13 *uity is greater than that I may deserve mercy.* A vagabond and fugitive, he departed from the face of the Lord, signifying that those who neglect to confess their sins are considered unworthy with respect to divine compassion.

Pf 104rb   Reges quoque, qui ignorantia ducti in Abraam | deliquerant,
non nisi eodem orante sanari meruerunt. In quo figuratur, quod
Sb 262ra   passiones morum non sanantur | nisi orationibus ecclesie. Moysi
quoque precepit Dominus, ut lepra, siue in cute, siue in domo, siue
580   in ueste, appareret, sacerdoti ostenderetur, et, iuxta eius arbitrium
separata, eius iudicio contaminaretur, uel mundaretur. Saul quoque, cum a spiritu maligno uexaretur, non poterat ad sane mentis
Bi 296va   officium | redire nisi prius Dauid psalterium arriperet et coram eo
psalleret, et ita ab eius uexatione diabolus cessaret. In quo mistice
585   ostenditur, quod quicumque diabolo per peccatum mancipatur ab
eius dominio eripi non ualet, nisi Dauid, id est ecclesia, psalterium
arripiat et coram eo psallat, id est spiritualis gratie ipsum participem
faciat, et, salubriter ammonendo et pie pro eo orando et exempla
boni operis sibi prebendo, diabolum ab eius inuisibili uexatione
590   conpescat.

Dauid quoque, cum adulterium conmisisset et homicidium, non
ante audiuit a Propheta, *Transtulit Dominus peccatum tuum a te*, quam
Aa 149r   ipsum peccatum confiteretur. Prius enim Prophete redarguenti |
peccatum confessus est, et postea audiuit, *Transtulit Dominus pecca-*
595   *tum tuum a te*. Achab quoque, cum de innocentis sanguinis effu-
sione sententiam conminantis Dei audiret, induit se ipsum cilicio,
satisfaciens Deo per penitentiam. Vnde Dominus ad Helyam ait,
Quoniam Achab reueritus est faciem meam, non inducam malum in diebus
eius. Niniuite, cum audirent, *Adhuc quadraginta dies, et Niniue subuer-*
600   *tetur,* ex edicto regis et principum penitentiam egerunt, dicentes,
Quis scit, si conuertatur, et ignoscat Deus, et relinquat post se benedictio-
nem? Hac humilitate satisfactionis inminentem subuersionem euadere meruerunt.

Quorum exemplis euidenter ostenditur, ut nullus a Deo conse-
605   quatur ueniam nisi primum satisfecerit sibi per penitentiam. Nabuchodonosor propter superbiam suam a rationabili mente in bestia-

---

576 deliquerant] deliquerunt Fd   **585** per] propter Aa EdF Fs Pf Sb   **587** arri-
piat] accipiat Aa Bi EdF Fs Mk   **591** et] *om.* Aa Sb   **592** a te] ante Aa Fs *om.* Sb
te] *add. ante interlin.* Fd   **595** a te] *om.* Aa Fs Sb   **604** ut] quod Bi Mk Pf EdF
consequatur] consequitur Fd Fs Mk Sb   **605** primum] prius Fs primus Pf
606 propter] quoque per Fs Pf | rationabili] rationali Mk Sb

Also the kings who, led by ignorance, had sinned against Abraham did not deserve to be healed except by this same man's prayers. In this it is portrayed that the illnesses of one's character cf. Gn 20 are not healed except by the prayers of the church. Also, the Lord commanded Moses that leprosy, whether it appeared on the skin or on a home or on a garment, be shown to the priest, and, having been considered separately in accord with the priest's assessment, be contaminated by his judgment or cleansed. Also Saul, when he cf. Lv 14 was vexed by a malignant spirit, could not return to the functioning of a healthy mind until David first took up the Psalter and sang psalms in his presence, and in this way the devil ceased his vexation. In this story it is mystically shown that, whoever is delivered cf. 1 Sm up to the devil through his sins cannot be snatched away from his 16:14–23 dominion unless David, that is, the church, snatches up the Psalter and sings psalms in his presence, that is, makes him a participant of spiritual grace, and, through salubrious admonition and pious prayer on his behalf and the offering to him of examples of good works, restrain the devil from his invisible vexation.

Also, David, when he had committed adultery and murder, did not hear from the Prophet, *The Lord has removed your sin from you,* 2 Sm 12:13 before he confessed that very sin. For first he confessed his sin to the Prophet who was convicting him, and afterward he heard, *The Lord has removed your sin from you.* Also Ahab, when he heard the sentence for his shedding of innocent blood from a threatening God, clothed himself with a hair shirt, making satisfaction to God through penance. Hence the Lord said to Elijah, *Since Ahab has revered my face, I will not inflict evil in his days.* When they heard, *Forty* 1 Kgs 21:29 *days more and Nineveh will be destroyed,* the Ninevites did penance at Jon 3:4 the order of their king and princes, saying, *Who knows? If we should turn back, God may both forgive and leave his blessing after him.* By the Jon 3:9 humility of their satisfaction, they merited an evasion of imminent destruction.

By these examples, it is clearly shown that no one obtains mercy from God if he has not first made satisfaction for himself through penance. Because of his pride, Nebuchadnezzar was changed from

lem animum conmutatus, atque a regno suo profugus recedens,
non ante regnum recepit, quam conuersus Deum predicauit. Denique plebs Israelitica, ob culpam sue transgressionis captiuitati tra-
Fs 299ra   dita, non ante liberari | meruit, quam peccata sua confitens Danielis
et aliorum sanctorum precibus ueniam accepit. In euangelio quo-
que, uenientes ad Iohannem ut baptizarentur ab eo baptismo penitentie, primum confitebantur peccata sua, ostendentes quod quisque debet peccata sua dampnando confiteri et innouationem melio-
Pf 104va   ris uite promittere, si regenerationis gratiam desiderat | accipere.

Christus quoque alios legitur suscitasse a mortuis, alios a lepra
mundasse, alios illuminasse, aliorum membra paralisi dissoluta
Mk 238va | Sb   consolidasse; | omnium tamen sanitatem | petitio proprie uocis uel
262rb   amicorum legitur precessisse. Luca enim referente didicimus, quod
Bi 296vb   pro socru Petri prius rogatus est, quam eam sanitati redderet. | Le-
prosus uero ille, quem descendens de monte mundauit, prius cla-
mauit ad eum: *Domine, si uis, potes me mundare*, quem postea tangendo mundauit. Cecus quoque dum clamaret ad eum, *Miserere mei,*
fili Dauid, interrogauit Iesus, *Quid uis, ut faciam tibi?* Ait, *Rabboni, ut*
625   *uideam lumen*. Tres quoque mortuos audiuit, quos aliis orantibus
reddidit uite. Quartum quoque discipulo nuntiante audiuit, set,
quia defuerunt uiui, qui pro eo precarentur, resuscitari non meruit.

Quibus nimirum exemplis euidentissime datur intelligi, quod
ille, quem macula grauioris culpe inficit, nisi confessione proprii
630   oris uel ecclesie intercessione suffragante sanari non poterit. Hinc
penitens ille, qui prius tacendo peccata flagellari meruerat, postea
correctus dicebat, *Quoniam tacui, inueterauerunt ossa mea, dum clama-*
Aa 149^v   *rem tota die*. Hinc Christus ex persona | membrorum ait, *Non absor-*
beat me profundum, neque urgeat super me puteus os suum. QUOD AU-

---

608 recepit] suscepit Aa accepit Fs   621 descendens] *praem.* Dominus Fs Mk (*in-*
terlin. Mk), *add.* Dominus EdF   623 dum] cum Aa Pf   624 interrogauit] *add.*
eum Pf EdF   628 euidentissime] euidenter Bi Mk   631 peccata…meruerat] fla-
gella meruit Pf | meruerat] meruit Fs   632 correctus] correptus Bi Mk EdF
mea] *om.* Bi Mk

a rational mind to bestial passions, and, after he had withdrawn from his kingdom as a fugitive, he did not receive back his kingdom before he converted and proclaimed God. Finally, the Israelite people, having been handed over to captivity on account of the guilt of their transgression, did not deserve to be freed before they confessed their sins and received mercy by the prayers of Daniel and other saints. In the gospel as well, those coming to John to be baptized by him by the baptism of repentance first confessed their sins, showing that each person ought to make confession by condemning his sins to promise the renewal of a better life, if he should desire to receive the grace of regeneration. cf. Dn 4:28–37 cf. Dn 9 cf. Mt 3:6

Also we read that Christ raised some from the dead, cleansed others of leprosy, caused others to see, and made firm the loose limbs of the paralyzed. Nevertheless, we read that the pleading of these people's own voice or that of their friends had preceded the healing in every case. For by the report of Luke we learn that Christ was asked for on behalf of Peter's mother-in-law before he returned her to health. The leprous man whom Christ healed while descending the mountain first cried out to him, *Lord, if you want, you can cleanse me*; afterward the Lord cleansed him by his touch. Also when the blind man cried out to him, *Have pity on me, Son of David*, Jesus asked, *What do you want me to do to you?* He replied, *Rabbi, that I may see light*. He also heard about three dead people whom he returned to life by the pleas of others. Moreover he heard of a fourth by the announcement of a disciple, but, because there failed to be any living who would plead for him, this dead person did not deserve to be raised to life. cf. Lk 4:38–39 Mt 8:2 Mk 10:46–52 cf. Lk 7:9–10, 14–15; 8:40–56 cf. Mt 8:21–22?

By these examples, it is certainly most clearly given to be understood that he whom the stain of serious guilt taints will not be able to be healed except through the confession of his own mouth or through the supporting intercession of the church. For this reason, that penitent who by initially staying silent about his sins had deserved to be whipped, afterward, after he was corrected, said, *Because I stayed silent, my bones were made old until I shouted the whole day long*. For this reason Christ said in the persona of his members, *Let* Ps 31:3

635 GUSTINUS EXPOSUIT, dicens, "Puteus est profunditas humane iniquitatis, in quam, si cecideris, non claudet super te os suum, si tu
non claudis os tuum. Confitere ergo, et dic, *De profundis clamaui ad*
te, Domine, et euades. Claudet super illum, qui in profundo con-
Fd 89vb tempnit, a quo mortuo, uelut ab eo, qui non est, perit confessio." |
640 HINC IDEM PROPHETA AIT, *Introite portas eius in confessione,* ostendens ad portas misericordie non nisi per confessionem peccati aliquem posse pertingere. HINC ETIAM BEATUS IOHANNES BAPTISTA,
ET SALUATOR NOSTER exordium sue predicationis a penitentia
sumpserunt, dicentes, *Penitentiam agite, appropinquabit enim regnum*
Fs 299rb *celorum,* ostendentes neminem ad regna celorum posse pertingere, |
nisi primum per penitentiam Deo curauerit satisfacere. HINC ETIAM
IN ACTIBUS APOSTOLORUM LEGITUR, quod *credentes ueniebant* ad
Apostolos, *annunciantes actus suos.*

Ex his omnibus facile monstratur, sine confessione nullum ue-
650 niam posse mereri. HINC ETIAM LEO PAPA AIT: "Sufficit penitenti   c.61
confessio, que primum Domino offertur, deinde sacerdoti, qui pro
Pf 104vb delictis penitentium precator accedit." | IDEM: "Penitentia, que di-   c.62
lata est, cum studiosius petita fuerit, non negetur, ut eo modo ad
indulgentie medicinam anima uulnerata perueniat."

655   ITEM AUGUSTINUS IN SERMONE DE PENITENTIA: "Non sufficit   c.63
mores in melius conmutare et a preteritis malis recedere, nisi etiam
Sb 262va de his, que facta sunt, | satisfaciat Domino per penitentie dolorem,
per humilitatis gemitum, per contriti cordis sacrificium, cooperanti-
bus elemosinis et ieiuniis." ITEM AMBROSIUS: "Nouit Deus mutare   c.64
Bi 297ra sententiam, si tu noueris emendare delictum." ITEM LEO PAPA: |

---

635 Puteus...**639** confessio] cf. Aug. Hipp., *Enarr.* 68.1.19 (CCSL
39:916.14–23); *Gl. ord. in Ps.* 68:16 (*interlin. et marg.,* ed. Rusch, 2.538b)
650 Sufficit...**652** accedit] Leo I, *Epistola* 168 (PL 54:1211A-B) = JK 545
652 Penitentia...**654** perueniat] Leo I, *Epistola* 167, *Ad Rusticum* (PL 54:1206A)
= JK 544   **655** Non...**659** ieiuniis] Aug. Hipp., *Sermo* 351 (PL 39:1549)
659 Nouit...**660** delictum] Ambr. Med., *Expositio euangelii secundum Lucam* 2.33
(CCSL 14:45.470–471)

635 exposuit] exponit Aa Bi EdF   **636** quam] quem Bi Mk Pf EdF   **644** enim]
om. Fs Mk Sb   **650** etiam] *om.* Aa Fs Mk Pf *interlin.* Sb | Sufficit] sufficiat Fd_ac
Mk   **657** satisfaciat] satisfiat Bi Mk Sb

not the deep swallow me, nor let the pit close its mouth upon me. AUGUS- Ps 68:16
TINE EXPLAINED THIS, SAYING, "The pit is the depth of human iniquity, which, if you fall into it, does not shut its mouth upon you,
if you do not shut your mouth; therefore confess and say, *From the
depths have I cried unto thee, o Lord,* and you will escape. The Lord Ps 129:1
will shut out the man who stands defiant in the depth. Confession
perishes from this dead man, just as from a person who does not
exist." FOR THIS REASON THE SAME PROPHET SAID, *Enter his gates
in confession,* showing that someone cannot reach the gates of mercy Ps 99:4
except through the confession of sin. FOR THIS REASON ALSO THE
BLESSED JOHN THE BAPTIST AND OUR SAVIOR took the basis for
their preaching from repentance, saying, *Repent, for the Kingdom of
Heaven is approaching,* showing that no one can reach the realms of Mt 3:2, 4:17
heaven unless he first takes care to satisfy God through penance.
For this reason also we read in the ACTS OF THE APOSTLES that *believers used to come* to the apostles, *declaring their acts.* Acts 19:18

 From all these examples, it is easily shown that no one can merit
c.61   mercy without confession. AND THUS ALSO POPE LEO SAID, "That
confession is sufficient for the penitent which first is offered to God,
then to the priest, who comes near as the intercessor for the of-
c.62   fences of penitents." THE SAME: "The penance which has been de- cf. D.1 c.89
layed, when it has been sought zealously, will not be denied, so
that the wounded soul may obtain the medicine of a pardon in this
way."

c.63   LIKEWISE AUGUSTINE IN A SERMON ON PENANCE: "It is not sufficient to change one's character for the better and to withdraw
from former evils if, regarding the things which have been done,
one does not also make satisfaction to God through the grief of repentance, the groaning of humility, the sacrifice of a contrite heart,
along with the works of almsgiving and fasting." LIKEWISE AM-
c.64   BROSE: "The Lord knows how to change his judgment if you know
c.65   how to correct your offence." LIKEWISE POPE LEO: "Indeed it is

"Aliud quidem est debita iusta reposcere, aliud propria perfectionis c.65
Mk 238vb amore contempnere. | Illicitorum ueniam postulantem oportet
etiam a multis licitis abstinere, dicente Apostolo, *Omnia mihi licent,
set non omnia expediunt.* Vnde si penitens habeat causam, quam ne-
665 gligere forte non debeat, melius expetet ecclesiasticum quam fo-
rense iudicium."

ITEM IERONIMUS IN MALACHIA: "Qui sanctus sacerdos est et c.66
comedit Pasca Domini, accingatur baltheo castitatis, et audiat cum
Apostolis, *Sint lumbi uestri precincti, et lucerne ardentes in manibus ue-*
670 *stris.* Qui autem peccator est, et quem remordet propria conscientia,
cilicio accingatur, et plangat uel propria delicta uel populi; et ingre-
diatur ecclesiam, de qua propter peccata fuerat egressus; et cubet
uel dormiat in sacco, ut preteritas delicias, per quas Deum offende-
rat, uite austeritate conpenset."

675 IDEM IN AMOS PROPHETA: "Si agamus penitentiam, ipsum quo- c.67
Aa 150^r que | sue penitebit sentie. Rursus iuxta eundem Ieremiam pro-
mittit prospera si penitentiam egerimus. Quod si negligentia dissol-
uamur, et illum penitebit sponsionis, promissaque mutabit. Cuius
rei exemplum Samariam et Iherusalem habere possumus, quorum
680 alii de inminentibus suppliciis liberati sunt, alii que patribus pro-
missa fuerant perdiderunt."

IDEM SUPER DANIELEM: "*Quamobrem, consilium meum placeat tibi:* c.68
Fs 299va *et peccata tua elemosinis | redime et iniquitates tuas in misericordiis paupe-*
rum; si forte ignoscat Deus delictis tuis. Si predixit sententiam, que mu-
685 tari non potest, quomodo hortatur ad elemosinas pauperum et misericordiam, ut Dei sententia permutetur? Quod facile soluitur exemplo regis Ezechie, quem Ysaias dixit esse moriturum, et Niniuitarum, quibus dictum fuerat: *Adhuc tres dies, et Niniue subuertetur.* Et

---

661 Aliud...**666** iudicium] Leo I, *Epistola* 167, *Ad Rusticum* (PL 54:1206A–B) =
JK 544   **667** Qui...**674** conpenset] Hier., *Comm. in prophetas minores, In Ioelem*
1.13–14 (CCSL 76:172.410–418)   **675** Si...**681** perdiderunt] Hier., *Comm. in*
prophetas minores, In Amos 3.9 (CCSL 76:344.324–330)   **682** Quamobrem...**706**
repromittitur] Hier., *Comm. in Danielem* 1.4 (CCSL 75A:816.928–817.957)

688 tres] quadraginta R2 | dies] *add.* sunt R2 (Fd_pc, *om.* Fs)

665 expetet] expectet Aa Bi Mk Pf Sb expectent Fs   **667** sanctus] *add.* et Fd Pf
(*interlin.* Fd)   **668** comedit] *add.* in Aa Fd_pc Fs Bi Mk Sb   **673** uel] et Bi Pf
688 dies] *add.* sunt *interlin.* Fd_pc

one thing to lay claim to one's just debts and another to disdain them with a proper love of perfection. The one demanding mercy for illicit deeds should also abstain from many licit ones. As the Apostle states, *Many things are permitted for me, but not all things are profitable.* Hence, if a penitent has a situation which he perhaps ought not neglect, it is better for him to seek out an ecclesiastical judgment rather than one in public courts."

1 Cor 6:12

c.66   LIKEWISE JEROME IN HIS COMMENTARY ON MALACHI: "He who is a holy priest and who eats the Lamb of the Lord is to gird himself with the belt of chastity, and let him hear with the apostles, *Let your loins be girded, and let your lamps be burning in your hands.* He who is a sinner, however, and whom his own conscience vexes, is to gird himself with a hair shirt, and let him bewail either his own sins or those of the people; enter the church, from which he had exited on account of his sins; and lie down or sleep in sackcloth so that he may make compensation for his past allurements, through which he had offended God, with an austere life."

Lk 12:35

c.67   THE SAME IN HIS COMMENTARY ON THE PROPHET AMOS: "If we should repent, he also will repent of his sentence. Again, according to the same Jeremiah, he promises prosperity if we should repent. But if we should loosen ourselves from our negligence, he will both repent of his solemn pledges and change his promises. We have Samaria and Jerusalem as an example of this phenomenon, of which the one people were freed from imminent destruction while the other lost what had been promised to their fathers."

c.68   THE SAME IN HIS COMMENTARY ON DANIEL: "*For this reason, king, may my counsel be pleasing to you: redeem both your sins with alms and your iniquities through compassion on the poor; perhaps God will forgive your offences.* If he proclaimed a sentence that cannot be changed, why does he urge alms and compassion for the poor so that the sentence of God may be altered? This issue is easily resolved by the example of King Hezekiah, whom Isaiah had said was about to die, and of the Ninevites, to whom it was said, *Three[12] days*

Dn 4:24

---

12. Gratian seems to have had a slip of the mind. He seems to have copied this Jerome text as saying "three," even though he and every other even semiliterate medieval Christian would have known that the correct number here was forty. Copyists quickly made the correction, and it became standard in the second recension. The second recension also added the verb "to be," making the first clause of the verse read something like, "There are yet forty days...."

tamen ad preces Ezechie et Niniue Dei sententia commutata est.
690 Rursum bona agenti se asserit polliceri et indulgentiam, alioquin et
Pf 105ʳᵃ in reuerentiam | loquitur Deus se mala minari super gentem, et, si
bona fecerit, minas clementia commutare. Rursum asserit polliceri,
et, si male fecerit, dicit suam mutare sententiam, non in homines,
set in opera, que mutata sunt. Neque enim Deus hominibus irasci-
Sb 262ᵛᵇ tur, set uitiis, que, cum in homine non fuerint, | nequaquam punit
quod mutatum est. Dicamus quidem et aliter. Fecit igitur Nabuchodonosor iuxta Danielis consilium misericordias in pauperes, et idcirco usque ad mensem duodecimum in eo dilata est sententia. Set
Bi 297ʳᵇ quia postea, ambulans in aula Babylonis, gloriatur et dicit, | *Nonne*
700 *hec est Babilon magna, quam ego edificaui in domum regni et in robore for-*
titudinis mee et gloria nominis mei? bonum misericordie perdidit malo
superbie. *Forsitan ignoscat Deus delictis tuis.* Cum Beatus Daniel pre-
Mk 239ʳᵃ scius futurorum de sententia Dei dubitet, rem temerariam faciunt |
qui audacter peccantibus ueniam pollicentur. Et tamen sciendum
705 est, quod Nabuchodonosor bona opera facienti uenia repromitti-
tur."

IDEM: "Vide benignum Dominum, misericordiam cum seueritate miscentem et   c.69
ipsius pene modum iusta et clementi liberatione pensantem. Et ideo non in perpe-
tuum tradidit delinquentes, set quanto, inquid, tempore seruierunt Chusarsathon,
710 hoc est octo annis. Disce et hoc, o tu auditor, quisquis ille es, qui tibi conscius es
alicuius erroris, et quanto tempore errasse te nosti: quanto tempore deliquisti, tanto
nichilominus tempore humilia te ipsum Deo, et satisfacito ei in confessione penitentie. Non expectes, ut humiliet te Chusarsathon, et inuito necessitas extorqueat
Fs 299ᵛᵇ penitentiam. Set ipse preueni tortoris istius | duritiam, quia, si te ipse emendaueris,
715 si te ipse correxeris, pius est Dominus et misericors, qui uindictam temperet ab eo,
qui illam penitendo preueni. Set et illud consideremus, quia, donec seruierunt Chusarsathon hi, qui traditi fuerant pro delictis suis et non clamauerunt ad Dominum,

---

707 Vide...719 eos] Orig. (trans. Rufinus), *Homiliae in librum Iudicum* 3.2 (GCS
30:482.12–20)

700 regni] regis R2 (*add.* uel regis Fd_{pc})

689 commutata] mutata Bi Fs Mk   691 reuerentiam] reuerentia Aa Sb
700 domum] domo Bi Fs Mk Pf   701 mei] *om.* Bi Fs Mk   704 audacter] aucdac-
ter (!) Bi audaciter Mk Pf   707 Idem] Item Ieronimus AaB   708 iusta] iuxta
Bi_{ac} Pf | Et ideo] *interlin.* Mk, *om.* Bi Pf EdF   709 tradidit] tradit AaB Mk Pf

more and Nineveh will be destroyed. And nevertheless God's sentence Jon 3:4 was changed in accord with the prayers of Hezekiah and Nineveh. God in reverence says that he threatens evil upon a people, but, again, God asserts that he promises both pardon to the person doing good and, if the person does good, that he changes out his threats for mercy. Again he asserts that he makes promises, and, if a person acts wickedly, he changes his sentence, not against the men, but against the works, which have changed. For God does not grow angry with men but with vices. When they no longer exist in a man, God in no way punishes him, for they have been changed. Let us also speak in another manner. Nebuchadnezzar did indeed show compassion on the poor in accord with Daniel's counsel, and for that reason, his sentence was delayed against him until the twelfth month. But, because afterward, while walking in the palace of Babylon, he boasts and says, *Is not this Babylon great, which I have built as the house of the kingdom*[13] *in the might of my strength and in the glory of my name?*, he damaged the good of compassion with the evil Dn 4:27 of pride. *Perhaps God will forgive your offences.* Since the blessed Dn 4:24 Daniel, prescient of future things, expresses doubt about the sentence of God, those who boldly promise pardon for sins do an imprudent thing. And nevertheless, it should be known that mercy is promised again to Nebuchadnezzar should he do good works."

c.69　　THE SAME: "See the kindness of the Lord, who mixes mercy with severity and ponders the mode of the punishment itself with just and clement acquittal. And so he did not hand the delinquent over to punishment forever, but for how long, he says, they served Cushan-rishathaim, that is, for eight years. Learn also this, o you hearer, whoever you are, you who are aware of some fault in you and know how long you have erred: in spite of it all, humble yourself before God and make satisfaction to him in penitential confession for how long you have been delinquent. You are not to wait for Cushan-rishathaim to humble you and for necessity to extort penance from an unwilling heart. But I myself have prevented having to endure that tormenter, because, if you amend yourself, if you correct yourself, God is kind and compassionate; he restrains vengeance from the one who prevents it by repenting. But let us also consider this, that, as long as these people who had been handed over for their offences served Cushan-rishathaim and did not cry out to the Lord, no

---

13. The second recension reads "king," not "kingdom."

nemo suscitatus est, qui saluare eos posset. Cum uero clamauerunt ad Dominum, tunc suscitauit Dominus saluatorem Israel, et saluauit eos."

720   IDEM: "Ecclesia Christi est, non habens maculam neque rugam, aut aliquid   c.70 istiusmodi. Qui ergo peccator est, aliqua sorde maculatus, de ecclesia Christi non potest appellari nec Christo subiectus dici. Possibile autem est, ut, quomodo eccle-

Pf 105rb   sia, | que prius rugam habuit et maculam et inmunditiam postea restituta est, ita et peccator currat ad medicum (quia non habent opus sani medico set male haben-

725   tes) ut curentur uulnera ipsius et fiat de ecclesia, que est corpus Christi."

IDEM: "*Super tribus sceleribus Damasci et super quatuor, non conuertam eum.*   c.71 Iuxta tropologiam hoc possumus dicere: primum peccatum est cogitasse que mala sunt; secundum, cogitationibus acquieuisse peruersis; tertium, quod mente decre-

Sb 263ra   ueris | opere conplesse; quartum, post peccatum non agere penitentiam, et suo sibi

730   conplacere delicto."

IDEM: "Secunda post naufragium tabula est culpam simpliciter confiteri. Imitati   c.72 estis errantem, imitamini et correctum. Errauimus iuuenes, emendemur senes. Iun-gamus gemitus et lacrimas copulemus."

IDEM: "Quia diuinitatis natura clemens est et pia, magisque ad indulgentiam   c.73

735   quam ad uindictam prona, quia *non uult mortem peccatoris, set ut conuertatur et ui-*

AaB 333v   *uat*—si quis post lapsum peccatorum ad ueram penitentiam se conuertit, | cito a

Bi 297va   misericorde iudice ueniam | inpetrabit."

IDEM IN MALACHIA: "Ne forsitan peccati memores tardius reuertantur, *adhuc,*   c.74 inquid, *sedere uos faciam in tabernaculis, sicut in diebus festiuitatis,* ut, quod facit

740   baptisma, hoc faciat penitentia, et habitent in tabernaculis Saluatoris, hoc est in ec-clesia."

Mk 239rb   IDEM: "Predixerat Ieremias septuaginta | annos desolationis templi, post quos   c.75

Fs 300ra   rursum | ueniret populus in Iudeam, et edificaretur ibi templum et Iherusalem. Que

720 Ecclesia…**725** Christi] Hier., *Comm. in iv epistulas Paulinas, Ad Ephesios* 3 (PL 26:531B–C)   **726** Super…**730** delicto] Hier., *Comm. in prophetas minores, In Amos* 1.1 (CCSL 76:219.224, 231–35)   **731** Secunda…**733** copulemus] Hier., *Epistula* 84.6 (CSEL 55:128.5–8)   **734** Quia…**737** inpetrabit] Rab. Maur., *Expositionis super Jeremiam prophetam libri viginti* 19.3 (PL 111:1224D)   **738** Ne…**741** ecclesia] Hier., *Comm. in prophetas minores, In Osee* 3.12 (CCSL 76:137.243–247)   **742** Predixerat…**753** offensam] Hier., *Comm. in Danielem* 3.9 (CCSL 75A, 860.16–861.32)

718 posset] possit AaB Pf Sb   **721** est] *add.* et Bi EdF   **723** habuit] habuerit Bi Fs Mk EdF   **725** curentur] curent Fs Sb EdF curet Bi Mk | Christi] *om.* AaB Bi Mk eius FdB Fs Sb   **732** correctum] corrigentem FdB correptum Bi   **737** misericorde] misericordie Pf EdF

one was raised up in order to be able to save them. But when they cried out to the Lord, then the Lord raised up a savior for Israel, and he saved them."

c.70   THE SAME: "The church is of Christ, not having blemish or wrinkle or anything of the sort. Therefore, he who is a sinner and has been stained by some filth cannot be called a member of the church of Christ, nor can he be said to be subject to Christ. It is possible, however, that, in the way in which the Church, which previously had wrinkle and blemish in its youth, as well as uncleanness, afterward was restored, so also the sinner may run to the physician (for the healthy have no need for a physician but those in a bad condition) so that his wounds may be healed and so that he may become one of the church, which is the body of Christ."

c.71   THE SAME: "*For three crimes of Damascus and for four, I will not turn back its [punishment]*. According to tropology, we can say this: the first sin is to have   Am 1:3
thought what is evil; the second, to have acquiesced to perverse thoughts; the third, to have completed in deed what you have decided in mind; the fourth, not to do penance after a sin, and to take great pleasure in one's offence."

c.72   THE SAME: "Simply confessing one's guilt is the second plank after a shipwreck. You have imitated an erring man; imitate also a reformed one. We erred in our youth, we improve in our old age. Let us yoke together our lamentations and join together our tears."

c.73   THE SAME: "Because the divine nature is clement and kind and prone more to pardon than to vengeance, because *he does not desire the death of the sinner but that he be turned back and live*—if, after a fall into sins, anyone turns himself   Ezek 18:23
around to true penance, he will quickly obtain mercy from the compassionate judge."

c.74   THE SAME IN HIS COMMENTARY ON MALACHI: "Lest by chance those mindful of sin be turned back too late, he says, *I will yet make you abide in tents just as in the days of the festival*, so that, what baptism does, penance may do, and they may live   Hos 12:9
in the tents of the Savior, that is, in the church."

c.75   THE SAME: "Jeremiah had prophesied seventy years of the temple's desolation, after which the people would return once more to Judaea, and the temple would be built in Jerusalem. That prophecy does not make Daniel negligent, but rather pro-

res non facit Danielem negligentem, set magis prouocat ad rogandum, ut, quod
745 Deus per suam promisit clementiam, per eorum inpleat preces, ne negligentia et
superbia pariat offensam. Denique in Genesi legimus, centum et uiginti annos penitentie constitutos ante diluuium. Quia tanto tempore, hoc est centum annis, nolue-
runt agere penitentiam, nequaquam expectat, ut et uiginti alii conpleantur, set infert
ante quod postea fuerat conminatus. Vnde et Ieremie dicitur ob duritiam cordis po-
750 puli Iudeorum, *Ne ores pro populo hoc, quia non exaudiam te.* Et ad Samuel: *Vsque-*
quo luges super Saul? Et ego abieci eum. In cinere igitur et sacco postulat inpleri
Pf 105ᵛᵃ quod promiserat Deus, | non quod esset incredulus futurorum, set ne securitas ne-
gligentiam, et negligentia pareret offensam."

ITEM AMBROSIUS IN SERMONE IN DOMINICA DE ABRAHAM:

755 Operibus misericordie non Deum emimus, set nosmetipsos redimimus.

"*Medicina misericordie tollit peccata magna.* Habemus plura subsidia, quibus   c.76
peccata nostra redimimus. Pecuniam habes; redime peccatum tuum. Non uenalis
est Dominus, set tu ipse uenalis es. Peccatis tuis uenundatus es; redime te operi-
FdB161ʳᵃ bus tuis, redime te pecunia tua. Vilis pecunia, | set preciosa est misericordia. *Elemo-*
760 *sina,* inquid, *a peccato liberat.*"

Crimina ergo elemosinis redimuntur. ITEM IOHANNES OS AUREUM: "Medica-   d.p.c.76 | c.77
Sb 263ʳᵇ mentum fortius, quod maxime operatur in | penitentia, hoc est. Sicut in preceptis
medicine medicamentum multas quidem herbas accipit, unam autem dominantis-
simam, sic et in penitentia ista herba dominantior et potentior est, et uniuersum
765 ipsa efficit. Audi enim quid dixit diuina scriptura: *Date elemosinam, et omnia munda*
sunt uobis."

ITEM AMBROSIUS IN LIBRO DE PENITENTIA: "Deus diffinitionem   c.78
non facit, qui misericordiam suam omnibus promisit, et relaxandi
licentiam sacerdotibus suis sine ulla exceptione concessit. Set qui
Fd 90ʳᵃ culpam exaggerauerit | exaggeret penitentiam. Maiora enim cri-
mina maioribus abluuntur fletibus." Idem: "Fleat pro te mater ec-   c.79
clesia, et culpam tuam lacrimis lauet. Videat te Christus merentem,

---

756 Medicina...**760** liberat] Ambr. Med., *De Helia et ieiunio* 20.76 (CSEL
32.2:458.4–10)   **761** Medicamentum...**766** uobis] Ioh. Chrys., *Hom. in Heb.* 9
(PG 63:81)   **767** Deus...**771** fletibus] Ambr. Med., *De paenitentia* 1.3 (SChr
179:60.9–14)   **771** Fleat...**775** resuscitauit] Ibid. 2.10 (SChr 179:190.14–18)

749 quod] quam FdB Sb | et] *om.* Bi Fs Mk Pf EdF   **750** Vsquequo] Quousque
Bi Fs Mk   **753** pareret] prepararet AaB preparet Bi Fs Mk EdF appareret FdB
771 Idem] Item Bi Fs Mk

vokes him to ask that they bring to fulfillment through their prayers what God promised through his clemency, lest negligence and pride produce an offence. Finally, we read in Genesis that one hundred and twenty years of penance were established before the flood, which, because they refused to do penance for so great a time, that is, one hundred years, it certainly is not anticipated that another twenty must also be completed, but he inflicts earlier what had been threatened to occur later. Hence to Jeremiah it is said on account of the hardness of heart of the Jewish people, *Do not pray for this people, for I will not hear you.* And to Samuel: *For how long will you mourn for Saul when I have cast him out?* Therefore in ashes and sackcloth he begs that what God had promised be fulfilled, not that he was unbelieving with regard to future events, but so that a sense of security might not produce negligence, and negligence produce an offence."

Jer 7:16

1 Sm 16:1

LIKEWISE, AMBROSE IN HIS LORD'S DAY SERMON ABOUT ABRAHAM:

We do not buy God off with works of compassion, but we do redeem ourselves.

c.76   *"The medicine of compassion removes great sins.* We have more aids by which we redeem our sins. You have money; redeem your sin. The Lord is not for sale, but you are. You were sold with your sins; redeem yourself with your works, redeem yourself with your money. Money is of little value, but compassion has great value. *Alms,* he says, *liberate from sin."*

Eccl 10:4

Tob 4:11

d.p.c.76 | c.77   Crimes are thus redeemed with alms. AND SO JOHN CHRYSOSTOM: "[Alms] are a very strong drug which work especially in penance. Just as in the rules of medicine a drug certainly includes many herbs but one which is most dominant, so also in penance that herb is more dominant and powerful and is universally efficacious. For hear what the divine scriptures say: *Give alms, and everything has been cleansed for you."*

Lk 11:41

c.78   LIKEWISE AMBROSE IN HIS BOOK ON PENANCE: "God does not make a definite prescription—he promised his mercy to all, and he granted the license to relax punishments to his priests without exception. But he who has heaped up guilt should also heap up penance. For greater crimes are washed away with greater weep-
c.79   ing." The same: "Let your mother, the church, weep for you, and

Bi 297vb | et dicat, *Beati tristes, quia gaudebitis.* Amat, ut pro uno multi rogent.

Fs 300rb   Denique | in euangelio motus uidue lacrimis, quia plurimi pro ea
775   flebant, filium eius resuscitauit."

Aa 150^v   Idem: "Adam post culpam statim de paradyso Deus | eiecit. Non   c.80
distulit, set statim separauit a deliciis ut ageret penitentiam; statim
tunica uestiuit eum pellicia, non serica."

ITEM AUGUSTINUS AD FELICIANUM: "Tres sunt autem actiones   c.81
780   penitentie, quas mecum uestra eruditio recognoscit.... Vna est, que
nouum hominem parturit, donec per baptismum salutare omnium
preteritorum fiat abolitio peccatorum.... Omnis enim, qui iam uo-

Mk 239va | Pf   luntatis sue arbiter | constitutus est, cum accedit ad sacramenta fi-
105vb   delium, nisi eum peniteat uite ueteris, nouam non potest inchoare.
785   Ab hac penitentia cum baptizantur soli paruuli inmunes sunt. Nondum enim uti possunt libero arbitrio. Quibus tamen ad consecratio-
nem remissionemque originalis peccati prodest eorum fides, a quibus offeruntur.... Altera uero penitentia est cuius actio per totam
uitam istam, qua in carne degimus mortali, perpetua supplicationis
790   humilitate subeunda est. Primo, quia nemo uitam eternam, incor-
ruptibilem inmortalemque desiderat, nisi eum uite huius tempora-
lis, corruptibilis, mortalis peniteat. Non enim sic quisque in uitam
nouam per sanctificationem baptismi nascitur, ut, quemadmodum
ibi deponit omnia peccata preterita, ita etiam statim mortalitatem
795   ipsam carnis corruptionemque deponat.... Tertia est actio penitentie, que pro illis peccatis subeunda est, que legis Decalogus continet

Sb 263va   et de quibus Apostolus ait, *Si enim nos iudicaremus, a Domino non* | *iu-*
dicaremur."

---

776 Adam...**778** serica] Ibid. 2.11 (SChr 179:194.10–13)   **779** Tres...**798** iudi-
caremur] Aug. Hipp., *Sermo* 351 (PL 39:1537–42)

784 nouam] *add.* uitam R2 (*pos.* inchoare Sb, *om.* Pf)   **797** non] *add.* utique R2

778 pellicia] pellicea Aa_{ac} Bi Mk Sb EdF   **780** recognoscit] cognoscit Aa Bi
781 baptismum] baptisma Bi Fs Mk   **784** inchoare] *ant.* non Bi Fs Mk   **790** incor-
ruptibilem...**791** inmortalemque] inmortale<m> incorruptibilemque Fs
791 inmortalemque] *mg.* Bi inmortalem *interlin. ant.* incorruptibilem Mk | eum]
cum Fd Mk   **792** uitam...**793** nouam] *tr.* Aa Bi Fs Mk Pf EdF

let her wash your guilt with her tears. Let Christ see that you are deserving, so that he may say, *Blessed are the sad, for you shall rejoice.*   Mt 5:5 He loves that many pray for one. Indeed, in the gospel, moved by the tears of the widow, he raised her son to life, for several people were weeping for her."

c.80   The same: "God cast Adam out of paradise immediately after his guilt. He did not delay but immediately separated [him] from delights so that he might do penance; he immediately clothed him with a tunic made of animal skins, not silk."

c.81   LIKEWISE AUGUSTINE TO FELICIANUS: "There are three actions of penance which you in your erudition recognize with me.... The first, which generates a new man, is when the abolition of all past sins occurs through salutary baptism.... Every person, who already has been established as the arbiter of his own will, when he approaches the sacraments of the faithful, cannot begin a new life unless he repents of his old one. Only children are immune from this penance when they are baptized. For they are not yet able to exercise free will. Nevertheless, the faith of those who offer them for baptism profits them for consecration and the remission of original sin.... The second penance is the activity of which we are to undergo with the perpetual humility of supplication throughout that whole life in which we carry on in mortal flesh. This is so in the first place because no one desires eternal, incorruptible, and immortal life unless he repents of this temporal, corruptible, and mortal life. For not every person is born into a new life through the sanctification of baptism in such a way that he immediately puts aside the very mortality and corruption of the flesh in the same way as he then sets aside all past sins.... The third is the act of penance which we are to undergo for those sins which the Ten Commandments contain and concerning which the Apostle says, *For if we were judging ourselves, we*[14] *would not be being judged by the Lord.*"   1 Cor 11:31

---

14. The second recension adds an "indeed" or "certainly": "We certainly would not be...."

ET INFRA: "Est etiam penitentia humilium et bonorum fidelium pena cottidiana,
800 in qua pectora tundimus, dicentes, *Dimitte nobis debita nostra,* etc. Neque ea dimitti nobis uolumus, que dimissa in baptismo non dubitamus, set illa utique, que
humane fragilitati, quamuis parua, tamen crebra, subrepunt, que, si collecta contra
nos fuerint, ita nos grauabunt et oppriment, sicut unum aliquod grande peccatum.
Quid enim interest ad naufragium utrum uno grandi fluctu nauis operiatur et ob-
805 ruatur, an paulatim subrepens aqua in sentinam, et, per negligentium culpam dere-
licta atque contempta, inpleat | nauem | atque submergat? Propter hec ieiunia, ele-
mosine, et orationes inuigilant. In quibus cum dicimus, *Dimitte nobis, sicut et nos
dimittimus,* etc., manifestamus | nos habere quod nobis dimittatur, atque in his uer-
bis humiliantes animas nostras cotidianam quodammodo agere penitentiam non
810 cessamus."

ITEM GREGORIUS: "Si peccatum Dauid Dominus transtulit tam detestabile, c.82
quid est, quod post omnia que de eodem peccato per Prophetam ei a Domino dicta
sunt, postmodum tanta tollerauit? Set proculdubio Dominus delictum sine ultione |
non deserit. Aut enim ipse homo in se hoc penitus punit, aut hoc Deus cum ho-
815 mine uindicans percutit. Nequaquam igitur peccatum parcitur, quia nullatenus sine
uindicta laxatur. Sic enim Dauid audire post confessionem meruit, *Dominus transtulit peccatum tuum,* et tamen multis post cruciatibus afflictus ac fugiens reatum
culpe, quam perpetrauerat, exsoluit; sicut nos salutis unda a culpa primi hominis
absoluimur, set tamen, reatum eiusdem culpe diluentes, absoluti quoque adhuc
820 carnaliter obimus, quia delicta nostra, siue per nos siue per semetipsum resecat,
etiam cum laxat. Ab electis enim suis iniquitatum maculas studet temporali afflic-
tione tergere, quas in eis in perpetuum non uult uidere." |

ITEM AUGUSTINUS: "Sicut primi homines postea iuste uiuendo merito credun- c.83
tur per Domini sanguinem ab extremo iudicio liberari, non tamen illa uita merue-

AaB 334^r | Fs 300va

Bi 298ra

Pf 106ra

Mk 239vb

---

799 Est...**810** cessamus] Aug. Hipp., *Epistula* 265.8 (CSEL 57:646.3–18)
811 Si...**822** uidere] Greg. Magn., *Moralia in Iob* 9.34 (CCSL
143:495.82–496.96); *sententia prima deest* **823** Sicut...**838** ademit] Aug. Hipp.,
De pecc. mer. et rem. 2.34.55–56 (CSEL 60:125.1–20)

---

800 in qua] cum AaB Fs | qua] *add.* cum FdB Mk Sb   **801** dubitamus] dubitaba-
mus Bi Fs   **802** collecta] coniecta FdB   **805** per...culpam] pro negligentiam
culpa AaB | negligentium culpam] negligentiam Pf EdF   **808** nos habere] *tr.*
AaB Fs Mk Sb   **814** penitus] penitens Pf EdF   **815** uindicans] iudicans AaB FdB
peccatum] peccato AaB Pf EdF   **817** fugiens] refugiens FdB   **820** obimus] obici-
mus Bi_ac luimus AaB Pf | siue²] seu AaB Mk Sb   **821** laxat] relaxat Bi Mk EdF
824 iudicio] supplicio AaB Pf Sb | liberari] liberati AaB FdB Sb EdF

AND BELOW: "Penance is also the daily punishment of the good and humble faithful in which we strike our breasts and say, *Forgive us our debts,* etc. For we do   Mt 6:12 not want those debts to be forgiven us which we do not doubt were forgiven in our baptism, but those debts which, even if small, nevertheless frequently creep up on human weakness, which, if they are gathered against us, will burden and oppress us in the same way as some one, large sin. For what does it matter to a shipwreck whether the ship is covered over and overwhelmed by a large wave or whether water gradually creeps into the hold, is left behind deemed unimportant by men guilty of negligence, and fills up and submerges the ship? Fasts, alms, and prayers hold vigil on account of these small sins. In these actions, when we say, *Forgive us our debts as we also forgive,* we show that we have that which is forgiven us, and, humbling   Mt 6:12 our souls daily, in these words we do not cease doing penance daily in a certain way."

c.82   LIKEWISE GREGORY: "If the Lord removed David's sin, which was so detestable, how is it that, after all the things which were said about that same sin by the Lord through the Prophet to him, he afterward tolerated such things? But, without a doubt, the Lord does not leave an offence unrevenged. For either the person fully punishes this offence in himself, or God avenges it with the man and strikes. Thus by no means is sin spared, because in no way is there a relaxation of punishment without vengeance. Just as, after his confession, David deserved to hear, *The Lord has removed your sin,* and, nevertheless, he was later afflicted afterward by many tor-   2 Sm 12:13 ments, fled the guilt of the crime which he had perpetrated, and so paid his debt, so also we are absolved of the guilt of the first man by the wave of salvation, but, nevertheless, we still also wash away the guilt of the same crime, are absolved, and so die carnally, for [the Lord] cuts off our offences either through us or through his own doing, even when he relaxes punishment. He is eager to cleanse the stains of iniquities from his elect with temporal affliction, which stains he does not want to see on them forever."

c.83   LIKEWISE AUGUSTINE: "Just as the first humans are justifiably believed to have been freed from extreme judgment through the blood of the Lord by living right-

825 runt ad paradysum reuocari; sic et caro peccati, etiamsi remissis peccatis homo in
ea iuste uixerit, non continuo meretur eam mortem non perpeti, quam traxit de pro-
pagine peccati. Tale aliquid nobis insinuatum est de patriarcha Dauid in libro Re-
gnorum, ad quem cum Propheta missus esset, eique propter peccatum quod admi-
Sb 263vb serat euentura mala | conminaretur, confessione peccati ueniam meruit, respon-
830 dente Propheta quod illud ei flagitium facinusque remissum sit. Et tamen consecuta
sunt que Deus fuerat conminatus, ut sic humiliaretur a filio. Quare et nunc dicitur:
si Deus propter peccatum illud fuerat conminatus, cur, dimisso peccato, quod erat
ei minatus inpleuit, nisi quia rectissime, si dictum fuerit, respondetur, remissionem
illam peccati factam, ne homo a percipienda uita inpediretur eterna; subsecutum
835 uero illud conminationis exemplum, ut pietas hominis etiam in illa humilitate exer-
Fs 300vb ceretur atque | probaretur. Sic et mortem corporis propter peccatum Deus homini
inflixit, et post peccatorum remissionem propter exercendam iustitiam non ade-
mit."

IDEM IN OMELIA DE PENITENTIA:

840 **Doloris mensura potius quam temporis in actione penitentie**
consideranda est.

"In actione penitentie, ubi tale conmissum est, ut is qui conmisit a Christi etiam   c.84
Bi 298rb | Pf   corpore separetur, non tam | consideranda | est mensura temporis, quam doloris:
106rb   *Cor enim contritum et humiliatum Deus non spernit.* Verum quia plerumque dolor
845 alterius cordis occultus est alteri, nec in aliorum notitiam nisi per uerba uel quecumque alia signa procedit, cum sit coram illo cui dicitur, *Gemitus meus a te non est*
FdB 161rb | *absconditus.* | Recte constituuntur ab his, qui | ecclesiis presunt, tempora penitentie,
AaB 334^v   ut satisfiat etiam ecclesie, in qua remittuntur ipsa peccata. Extra eam quippe non remittuntur.... Ergo cum tanta est plaga peccati atque inpetus morbi, ut medicamenta
850 corporis et sanguinis Domini differenda sint, auctoritate antistitis debet se quisque
ab altario remouere ad agendam penitentiam et eadem auctoritate reconciliari."

---

842 In...**863** tumorem Aug. Hipp., *Ench.* 17 (CCSL 46:84.29–39); *Epistula* 54
(CSEL 34.2:162.8)

828 cum] *pos.* propheta Fs, dum *pos.* propheta AaB Pf | propter] hoc FdB hoc
propter Pf ob AaB Sb   **832** propter] *add.* hoc Fs Mk (*interlin.* Mk)   **834** a...uita]
ad percipiendum uitam AaB | eterna] eternam AaB   **835** etiam] et FdB Fs Sb,
om. Mk Pf EdF   **840** mensura] *add.* pecuniis FdB | in actione] satisfactione AaB
Bi Fs Sb satisfactio Pf   **844** spernit] despiciet Bi Fs Mk EdF   **848** satisfiat] satisfaciat AaB Sb   **849** morbi] mortis FdB

eously afterward, [but] they nevertheless did not deserve in that life to be called back to paradise, so also the flesh tainted with sin does not immediately deserve not to endure that death which a man attracted from the progeny of sin, even if he has lived righteously in that flesh after his sins were remitted. Some such situation was suggested to us concerning the Patriarch David in the Book of Kings. When the Prophet had been sent to him, and warned him that evil things would occur by the wrath of God because of the sin which he had committed, by the confession of his sin, he merited mercy, since the Prophet responded that that shameful act and crime was remitted him. Nevertheless, what God had threatened came to pass so that he was humbled accordingly by his son. And so it is also now said: if God had threatened on account of that sin, why, after the sin had been remitted, did he bring to pass what he had threatened, unless because it will be most correctly answered, if it is said thus, that that remission of sin occurred lest the person be hindered from attaining eternal life, but the subsequent example, that of the threatening, happened so that the piety of the person might also be practiced and proven in that humility. So also God inflicted the death of the body on account of the sin of man, and, on account of the exercising of his justice, he did not take it away after the remission of sins."

THE SAME IN HIS HOMILY ON PENANCE:

The amount of grief rather than of time ought to be considered in an act of penance.

c.84   "In an act of penance, when such an evil deed has been committed that he who committed it is separated as well from the body of Christ, the amount of time of the penance should not be considered as much as the amount of grief: *For a contrite and lowly heart God will not despise.* This is certainly so, because for the most part   Ps 50:19
the grief of one person's heart is hidden from another, and it does not come to the attention of others except through words or whatever other signs, although that grief is in the presence of him to whom it is said, *My lamentation has not been hidden from you.* The lengths of penance are rightly established by those in charge of   Ps 37:10
the church so that [the penitent] may also satisfy the church, in which the sins are themselves remitted. Indeed, outside of the church, no sins are remitted.... Therefore, when the pestilence of sin and the attack of illness are so great that the medicines of the body and blood of the Lord have to be put off, by the authority of the bishop the sinner ought to be removed from the altar in order to do penance and be reconciled by the same authority."

ITEM IN EADEM: "Iudicet se ipsum homo uoluntate dum potest, et mores con-   c.85
uertat in melius, ne, cum iam non poterit, preter uoluntatem a Domino iudicetur. Et
cum in se protulerit seuerissime medicine set tamen utilissime sententiam, ueniat
855   ad antistites, per quos illi claues in ecclesia ministrantur tamquam bonus iam incipiens esse filius, maternorum membrorum ordine custodito, a prepositis sacramentorum accipiat satisfactionis sue modum. In offerendo sacrificio contribulati cordis
deuotus et supplex, id tamen agat, quod non solum ipsi prosit ad recipiendam salutem, set etiam ceteris ad exemplum, ut, si peccatum eius non solum in graui eius
860   malo, set etiam in tanto scandalo aliorum est, atque hoc expedire utilitati ecclesie
Mk 240ra   uidetur antistiti, in notitia | multorum uel coram totius plebis multitudine agere pe-
Sb 264ra   nitentiam non recuset nec resistat, ne letali et | mortifere plage per pudorem addat
tumorem...." "Multi enim corriguntur, ut Petrus; multi tollerantur, ut Iudas," etc.

ITEM IERONIMUS:

865   Mortificatio uitiorum magis quam abstinentia ciborum penitentie est
necessaria.

"Mensuram autem temporis in agenda penitentia idcirco non satis aperte prefi-   c.86
Fs 301ra   gunt canones | pro unoquoque crimine, ut de singulis dicant qualiter unumquodque
emendandum sit, set magis in arbitrio sacerdotis intelligentis relinquendum sta-
870   tuunt, quia apud Deum non tam ualet mensura temporis, quam doloris, nec absti-
Pf 106va   nentia tantum ciborum, quam mortificatio uitiorum. Propter quod tempora | peni-
tentie pro fide et conuersatione penitentium abbreuianda precipiunt, et pro negligentia protelanda existimant. Tamen pro quibusdam culpis modi penitentie sunt in-
positi."

---

863 Multi...etc Aug. Hipp., *Sermo* 351 (PL 39:1546)   **867** Mensuram...**874** in-
positi] *Praefatio ad dictum 'Poenitentiale Romanum'*: Halit. Cam., *De vitiis et virtuti-*
bus et de ordine poenitentium libri quinque, Praefatio de poenitentiae utilitate (PL
105:657A–B); *etiam: Poenitentiale*, praef. (ed. Schmitz, 2.266)

852 Item] Idem Mk Pf EdF   **854** protulerit] tulerit FdB Sb | utilissime] utillime
AaB FdB Fs Mk Sb   **861** notitia] notitiam Pf Sb | coram] Bi_ac Mk Sb EdF com-
munione Bi_pc | multitudine] *om.* Bi Fs Mk Pf   **865** penitentie] penitenti AaB Fs
Mk Pf Sb EdF   **868** dicant] agatur FdB dicatur Pf   **871** quod] *add.* ipsa AaB FdB
Sb

c.85   LIKEWISE IN THE SAME WORK: "Let a man voluntarily judge himself in these things while he is able, and let him change his character for the better, lest, when he is no longer able, he also be judged against his will by the Lord. And when he brings forth a sentence of a very severe, although very beneficial, medicine against himself, let him come to the bishops, through whom those keys are managed in the church. And, like a good man already beginning to be a son, since the order of his maternal members has been preserved, let him receive the manner of his satisfaction from the overseers of holy matters. Devout and suppliant in offering the sacrifice of an afflicted heart, let him nonetheless aim at this, that he not only benefit himself for receiving salvation, but also that he serve as an example to the others, so that, if his sin not only entails his serious evil but also entails a great scandal to others, and if it seems to the bishop that this is advantageous for the benefit of the church, he may not refuse and resist doing penance under the eyes of many or in the presence also of a crowd of all the people. Let him not add a tumor to a lethal and mortal pestilence through shame...." "For many are corrected, like Peter, but many are merely put up with, like Judas," etc.

LIKEWISE JEROME:

The mortification of vices is more necessary for the penitent than abstaining from food.

c.86   "Now the canons indeed do not fix in a sufficiently clear manner the amount of time for doing penance for each evil deed so as to say concerning each individual deed how each one is to be emended, but rather they state that it is to be left to the judgment of an intelligent priest, because, for God, the amount of time does not have as much value as the amount of grief, and abstinence from food does not on its own have as much value as the mortification of vices. For this reason, the canons order that the lengths of penance ought to be shortened on account of the penitents' faith and way of life, and they judge that lengths of penance ought to be prolonged on account of negligence. Nevertheless modes of penance have been imposed for certain guilty actions."

875   ITEM IOHANNES CRISOSTOMUS: "Quis aliquando uidit clericum   c.87
cito penitentiam agentem? et si deprehensus humiliauerit se, non
Bi 298ᵛᵃ ideo dolet | quia peccauit, set confunditur quia perdidit gloriam
suam."

His auctoritatibus asseritur, neminem sine penitentia et confes-   d.p.c.87
880 sione proprie uocis a peccatis posse mundari.

\<Argumenta ex sententia secunda contra sententiam primam\>

Vnde premisse auctoritates, quibus uidebatur probari sola contritione cordis ueniam prestari, aliter interpretande sunt quam ab
885 eis exponantur. Negationem namque Petri secuta est satisfactio lacrimarum, et trina confessio dominice dilectionis, qua penitus dele-
uit peccatum trine negationis. Non ergo necessaria sibi erat certa
satisfactio peccati, cuius totum uite tempus obedientie inpendeba-
tur sui conditoris. Imitabatur enim ILLUD PROPHETICUM: *Declina a*
890 *malo et fac bonum,* et ILLUD YSAIE: *Derelinquat inpius uiam suam et uir*
iniquus cogitationes suas, et reuertatur ad Dominum et miserebitur eius.
Amplius horum a peccatore nichil exigitur. Non ergo illa auctoritate
Leonis Pape satisfactio penitentie negatur esse necessaria cuilibet
delinquenti, set ei tantum qui Beatum Petrum imitatus huic seculo
895 penitus abrenuntiat et cunctorum uitiorum fomitem in se funditus
mortificat.

Item illud IOHANNIS CRISOSTOMI: "Lacrime lauant quod pudor
Aa 151ʳ est confiteri;" et illud | aliud, quod scribit IN EPISTOLA AD EBREOS:
"Non tibi dico, ut te prodas in publicum, neque apud alios te accu-
900 ses, set obedire te uolo Prophete dicenti, *Reuela uiam tuam ante*
Sb 264ʳᵇ *Deum.* Ergo tua confitere peccata, apud uerum iudicem cum | ora-
tione delicta tua pronuntia, non lingua, set conscientie tue memo-

---

875 Quis…**878** suam] *fons materialis non inuenitur*   **899** Non…**905** tenebis] Ioh.
Chrys., *Hom. in Heb.* 31 (PG 63:216–217)

880 mundari] emundari Aa Mk Pf Sb   **884** ueniam] *add.* posse Pf   **886** penitus]
add. Petrus Pf   **891** et¹…eius] etc. Aa Bi EdF Mk Pf, *om.* Fs   **893** Leonis Pape]
recte Ambrosii   **895** funditus] penitus Pf   **897** Lacrime lauant] *tr.* Bi EdF Fs Mk
lauant] *add.* delictum Biₚc EdF Pf   **899** te²] *om.* Bi EdF Fd Fs Mk Pf Sb
901 Deum] Dominum Bi Sb EdF

c.87   LIKEWISE JOHN CHRYSOSTOM: "Who has ever seen a cleric who quickly did penance? But even if he humbles himself after he is caught, he does not grieve because he sinned, but he is disturbed because he has lost his reputation."

d.p.c.87   By these authorities it is asserted that no one can be cleansed from sins without penance and the confession of his own mouth.

\<Arguments from the Second Position against the First Position\>

Hence the formerly mentioned authorities, by which it appeared to be proved that mercy is offered by contrition of the heart alone, are to be interpreted in another manner than they are explained by [the adherents of the first position]. For the satisfaction of tears fol-   cf. c.1
lowed Peter's denial, as did the threefold confession of love for the   cf. Jn
Lord, by which he completely did away with the sin of the three-   21:15–17
fold denial. Therefore a fixed satisfaction for sin was not necessary
for him whose entire lifetime was being devoted to the obedience
of his Maker. For he was expressing that STATEMENT OF THE
PROPHET: *Turn away from evil and do good,* and THE ONE OF ISAIAH: Ps 36:27
*Let the wicked man abandon his way of life and the man of iniquity his
thoughts, and let him return to the Lord, and he will have mercy on him.*   Is 55:7
Nothing more of these things is required of the sinner. Thus the
satisfaction of penance is not denied to be necessary for any delinquent person whomsoever by that authority of Pope Leo,[15] but
only to him who has imitated the Blessed Peter in completely re-
nouncing this world and utterly mortifying the kindling-wood of all
vices in himself.

Likewise, that statement of JOHN CHRYSOSTOM: "Tears wash
away what is shameful to confess," and that other text which he   c.2
writes IN HIS COMMENTARY ON THE EPISTLE TO THE HEBREWS: "I
do not say to you that you should make a public report, nor that
you should accuse yourself among others, but I want you to obey
the Prophet, who says, *Lay bare your way before the Lord.* Therefore   Ps 36:5
confess your sins; declare your offences before the true Judge with

---

15. Although the second recension corrected the inscription at c.1 (to Ambrose), the attribution to Pope Leo remained uncorrected here.

ria. Et tunc demum spera te misericordiam posse consequi. Si ha-
bueris in mente peccata tua continue, numquam malum aduersus
Fs 301ʳᵇ   proximum in corde tenebis," | non ita intelligendum est, ut sine
confessione oris peccata dicantur dimitti, set sine publica satisfactione. Secreta namque peccata secreta confessione et occulta sati-
Mk 240ʳᵇ   sfactione purgantur, nec est necesse, ut que semel | sacerdoti con-
Pf 106ᵛᵇ   fessi fuerimus denuo | confiteamur, set lingua cordis, non carnis
910   apud uerum iudicem ea iugiter confiteri debemus.

(FdG 161ʳᵇ)   [| Hinc etiam idem Iohannes Crisostomus: "Nunc autem si recorderis peccato-
(AaB 334ᵛ)   rum tuorum et frequenter ea in conspectu Dei pronunties et pro eis clementiam
eius depreceris, citius illa delebis. Si autem nunc obliuiscaris peccatorum tuorum,
tunc eorum recordaberis nolens, quando in toto mundo publicabuntur et in con-
915   spectu proferuntur omnium tam amicorum tuorum quam inimicorum, et sanctorum angelorum celestiumque uirtutum. Non enim ad Dauid solum dicebat, *Tu se-
creto fecisti ego cunctis manifestabo*, set etiam ad omnes nos hoc dicitur."]

Bi 298ᵛᵇ   Similiter et illud Prosperi intelligitur: "Qui crimen suum ultro |
agnoscunt et aut propriis illud confessionibus produnt aut nescien-
920   tibus aliis quales occulti sint," etc. "Aliis nescientibus," id est occulta
confessione istis peccatum suum confitentibus, non publice illud
manifestantibus. Item illud Prophete: *Dixi, Confitebor, et tu remisisti*,
Fd 90ʳᵇ   id est remissibilem iudicasti, *inpietatem peccati | mei*. Ita et illud Augu-
stini intelligitur: "Magna pietas Dei, ut ad solam promissionem pec-
925   cata dimiserit," id est remissibilia iudicauerit. Item: "Votum pro
opere reputatur" cum deest facultas operis. Vnde uotum confessionis reputatur pro opere uocis cum deest facultas confessionis. Item:
"Voluntas remuneratur, non opus," ita intelligitur: uoluntas facit
opus remunerabile, non opus uoluntatem. Item illud: *In quacumque*
930   *hora peccator conuersus fuerit*, conuerti dicitur qui omnino uertitur;
omnino uertitur cuius opus, uox, et cogitatio ita mortificationi de-
sudat peccati, sicut prius seruierat iniquitati. Ita et illud intelligitur:
Conuertimini ad me, etc. Item: *Scindite corda uestra, et non uestimenta*

---

911 Nunc…**917** dicitur] Ibid. (PG 63:217)

915 proferuntur] proferentur Pf EdF   **920** sint] sunt Bi Mk Pf EdF   **930** pecca-
tor] ingemuerit peccator et Pf

prayer, not with your tongue but with the memory belonging to your conscience, and then at last hope that you can attain compassion. If you perpetually have your sins in mind, you will never retain evil in your heart against your neighbor." These things should not be understood in such a way that sins are said to be forgiven without oral confession but rather without public satisfaction. For secret sins are purged by secret confession and occult satisfaction, and it is not necessary for us to confess a second time what we have confessed once to a priest. But we ought to confess these things continually before the true Judge with the tongue of our heart, not of our flesh.

[Also on this topic, the same John Chrysostom: "But now, if you call to mind your sins and frequently declare them in the presence of God and plead for his mercy for them, you will very soon destroy them. But if you now forget your sins, then you will call them to mind even when you don't want to, when they will be made public in the whole world and are made known in the sight of all your acquaintances, both friends and enemies, and of holy angels and the heavenly powers. For he was not saying to David alone, *What you have done in secret, I will show them to all*; but this is said also to all of us."]   2 Sm 12:12

That text of Prosper is understood similarly: "Those who recognize their misdeed of their own will and disclose it either by their own confessions or with others unaware of what kind of things have been hidden," etc. "With others unaware," that is with those   D.1 c.32
confessing their sin by a secret confession, not publicly making it known. Likewise that text of the Prophet: *I said, "I will confess," and you have remitted,*—that is, you have judged remissible—*the wicked-*   c.4
ness of my sin. In this way also that text of Augustine is understood: "Great is the kindness of God, that he has forgiven sins according to his promise alone,"—that is, he judges them remissible. Likewise: c.5
"The will is taken to be the work" when the opportunity for a work   c.5
is lacking. Thus, the will to confess is considered to be a work of the voice when the opportunity for confession is lacking. Likewise: "The will is rewarded, not the work" is understood in this way: the   c.30b
will makes a work remunerable, not vice versa. Likewise that statement, *In whatever hour the sinner turns,* etc., he who turns entirely is   d.p.c.32
said to have been turned around, and he turns entirely whose thoughts, words, and deeds perform with exertion the mortification of sin in the same way that they had previously served iniquity. So also is that text understood, *Turn round to me,* etc. Likewise, *Tear*   c.34

uestra, eis dicitur qui nulla interiori satisfactione precedente sola ex-
935 teriori se Deum posse placare confidunt.

Sb 264ᵛᵃ   Item cuncta que de leprosis mundatis uel de Lazaro resuscitato |
inducuntur ad contritionem cordis, non ad ueniam remissionis re-
Fs 301ᵛᵃ ferenda sunt. Obstinatio | enim animi et confessionis contemptus
quedam mors est inpietatis et lepra superbie, a qua quisque reuiui-
940 scit dum sibi per gratiam dolor delicti et uotum confessionis inspira-
tur. Ad hunc etiam articulum pertinent ea, que de uiuentibus, uel
Pf 107ʳᵃ in luce ambulantibus, uel dilectionem | Dei habentibus, uel de habi-
taculum Spiritus sancti factis dicta sunt, ut hec omnia quisque dicatur assecutus ex cordis contritione, quam habet, non ex plenaria
Aa 151ᵛ peccati remissione, quam nondum inuenit. | Sicut enim in bapti-
smate peccatum remittitur, et tamen eius pena reseruatur, sic per
contritionem cordis quisque a Deo resuscitari dicitur, licet adhuc
peccati reatu teneatur. Non ergo premissis auctoritatibus uel argu-
mentis sine confessione oris et satisfactione operis aliquis probatur
950 a peccato mundari.

\<Argumenta ex sententia prima contra sententiam secundam\>

Mk 240ᵛᵃ   Econtra auctoritas illa Iohannis Crisostomi et Prosperi contra |
mentem auctoris extorta uidetur. Non enim dicitur, "non tibi dico,
955 ut te publice accuses," set, "non tibi dico, ut apud alios te accuses."
Sic et Prosper non ait, "omnibus," set simpliciter, "aliis nescientibus." Vnde euidentissime datur intelligi quod sine confessione oris
peccata possunt deleri. Ea uero que ad exhortationem penitentie et
Bi 299ʳᵃ confessionis dicta sunt non huic sententie | contraire uidentur. Vel
960 enim sunt uerba exhortationis, non iussionis, sicut illud: *Confitemini
alterutrum peccata uestra*, uel si qua iubendo dicta sunt, non ad oris

---

936 resuscitato] suscitato Aa Pf EdF resuscitati Fd_ac   **938** enim] autem Aa
939 superbie] superbia Pf EdF   **942** habitaculum] habitacuculum (!) Aa habita-
culis EdF habitaculi Fs habitaculo Pf   **944** ex plenaria] explanaria Aa_ac Fs
948 teneatur] *add.* astrictus Aa   **954** auctoris] auctori Fd_ac auctoritatis Fd_pc ac-
toris Bi Fs   **958** peccata] *add.* non Aa | deleri] dimitti Pf   **959** contraire] contra-
ria Aa Pf EdF

your hearts, and not your clothes is said to those who trust that they   c.33
can placate God with an external satisfaction alone without a preceding internal one.

Likewise, all those texts which are introduced about the
cleansed lepers and the revived Lazarus should be related to contrition of the heart, not to the mercy of remission. For obstinacy of
the mind and contempt for confession are a certain death, that of
impiety, and a certain leprosy, that of pride, from which everyone
becomes alive again when grief for an offence and longing for confession is breathed into him through grace. Those things which
have been said concerning those who live or walk in the light, or
who have love for God, or who have become a dwelling-place of
the Holy Spirit also pertain to this point, in that each individual
may be said to have procured all these things as a result of contrition of the heart, which he has, not as a result of the plenary remission of sin, which he has not yet found. For just as sin is remitted
in baptism and yet its punishment is reserved, so also each person
is said to be revived by God, although he is still held onto by the
guilt of sin. Thus, by the aforementioned authorities or arguments,
someone is not proven to be cleansed from sin without oral confession and a work of satisfaction.

\<Arguments from the First Position against the Sec-
ond Position\>

On the other hand, that authority of John Chrysostom and of
Prosper seems twisted against the intention of the author. For it is
not said, "I do not tell you to accuse yourself publicly," but, "I do
not tell you to accuse yourself among others." So also Prosper does   cf. previous
not say "with all" but simply "with others unaware." Hence it is   argument
  c.32
most clearly given to be understood that sins can be done away
with without oral confession. Those things which have been said as
an exhortation to penance and confession do not seem contrary to
this opinion. For these are words of exhortation, not of command,
just like that statement, *"Confess your sins to one another,"* etc. Or, if   Jas 5:16

confessionem, set cordis, non ad exteriorem satisfactionem, set ad interiorem referenda sunt.

Est enim penitentia alia interior, alia exterior. Interior peniten
965 tia est illa de qua AUGUSTINUS AIT, "Omnis, qui sue uoluntatis arbiter est constitutus, non potest inchoare nouam uitam nisi peniteat eum ueteris uite." Item de eadem PETRUS IN ACTIBUS APO
STOLORUM legitur dixisse, *Penitentiam agite, et baptizetur unusquisque*
uestrum. Quod de interiori penitentia, non de exteriori dictum acci
970 pitur. De exteriori uero penitentia AMBROSIUS AIT SUPER EPISTO
LAM AD ROMANOS: "Gratia Dei in baptismate non requirit gemitum uel planctum, non opus aliquod, set solam confessionem cordis, et omnia gratis condonat." Quecumque ergo de penitentia iubendo dicta sunt, non ad exteriorem, ut diximus, set ad interiorem
Fs 301ᵛᵇ referenda sunt, sine qua nullus umquam Deo reconciliari | potuit.

ILLUD AUTEM AUGUSTINI, quo quisque negatur ueniam consequi, nisi prius quantulamcumque peccati soluerit penam, non huic
Sb 264ᵛᵇ sententie inuenitur | aduersum. Nullus enim asseritur a peccato
mundari, nisi penam peccati passus fuerit. Set aliud est peccatum
Pf 107ʳᵇ sacerdoti confiteri et eius arbitrio | de peccato satisfacere, atque
aliud Deo corde confiteri, et secreta satisfactione peccatum in se
ipso punire. Est enim penitentia, ut Augustinus ait, dolor cordis,
quo quisque in se punit quod deliquit. De hac iterum satisfactione
IDEM AIT IN PSALMO L, EXPONENS, "*Quoniam iniquitatem meam ego*
985 *cognosco,* tu ne punias, quia ego punio: ignosce, quia ego cognosco
non dissimulo." Et infra: "Sic Deus misericordiam dat, ut seruet ueritatem, ut nec peccata eius sint inpunita, cui ignoscit. Ignoscit
enim se ipsum punienti. Misericordia est quod homo liberatur; ue
Aa 152ʳ ritas, quod peccatum punitur." Idem in Psalmo LXXXIV: "*Veritas de* |
990 *terra oritur,* id est confessio de homine, ut se accuset, et sic *iustitia de*

---

964 Est...**973** condonat] cf. *Summa sententiarum* 5.5 | Interior penitentia] cf. *interlin. gl. in Rom.* 11:29 (ed. Rusch, 4.298b)   **965** Omnis...**967** uite] Aug. Hipp., *Sermo* 351 (PL 39:1537)   **971** Gratia...**973** condonat] Ambros., *Comm. in epist. ad Rom.* 11.29 (CSEL 81.1:385)   **984** Quoniam...**986** dissimulo] Aug. Hipp., *Enarr.* 50.7 (CCSL 38:603.16–18)   **986** Sic...**989** punitur] Ibid. 50.11 (CCSL 38:607.4–8)   **989** Veritas...**994** penitenti] cf. ibid. 84.14 (CCSL 39:1174.16–29)

962 ad²] *om.* Bi Fs Pf Sb   **967** Item] Idem Fs Pf   **975** umquam] *om.* Aa | potuit] potest Aa   **977** penam] penitentiam Aa   **985** cognosco¹] agnosco Aa Sb *add.* non dissimulo Aa   **989** LXXXIV] LXXIV Bi Fs septuagesimo iiii Mk

they have been said by way of command, they should not be related to confession of the mouth but of the heart, not to external
but to internal satisfaction.

For internal penance is one thing and external penance another.
Internal penance is that of which AUGUSTINE SAYS, "Everyone
who is made the arbiter of his own will is not able to begin a new
life unless he repents of his old life." Likewise we read IN THE ACTS
OF THE APOSTLES that PETER spoke of the same thing: *Each one of
you repent and be baptized*. This is understood to have been said re- Acts 2:38
garding internal penance, not external. But AMBROSE SPEAKS
about external penance IN HIS COMMENTARY ON THE EPISTLE TO
THE ROMANS: "The grace of God does not seek groaning or lamentation in baptism, nor some work, but only contrition of the heart,
and he pardons all things freely." Therefore, whatever has been
said about penance by way of command, should not be related to
external penance, as we have said, but to internal penance, without which no one will has ever been able to be reconciled to God.

BUT THAT TEXT OF AUGUSTINE in which each person is said to
be unable to attain mercy unless he first pays however small a
penalty, is not found to be against this opinion. For we are not as- cf. c.42
serting that anyone is cleansed from a sin if he has not suffered the
penalty of that sin. But confessing a sin to a priest and satisfying his
judgment about the sin is one thing, and confessing with the heart
to God and punishing the sin in oneself by a secret satisfaction is
another. For penance, as Augustine says, is heartfelt grief, by which cf. D.3 cc.4–5
each person punishes in himself that in which he has been delinquent. Again, concerning this satisfaction, THE SAME AUTHOR EX-
PLAINS IN HIS COMMENTARY ON PSALM 50, "*Since I recognize my iniquity*, do not punish, for I am punishing; forgive, for I acknowledge Ps 50:5
my iniquity and am not disingenuous." And below: "God grants
compassion in such a way that he preserves truth, and the sins of
him whom he forgives do not go unpunished. For he forgives the
one punishing himself. There is compassion because the man is
freed; there is truth because the sin is punished." The same author
says about Psalm 84: "*Truth arises from the earth*, that is, confession
from man, in that he accuses himself, *and righteousness has looked out*

Fd 90ᵛᵃ *celo prospexit,* ut publicanus confitens rediit iustificatus. | *Iustitia pro-*
spicit, quasi Deus dicat, 'Parcamus huic, quia non parcit sibi; igno-
scamus, quia agnoscit.' *De celo ergo iustitia prospexit,* id est, a Deo data
est iustificatio penitenti." Hec ergo secreta satisfactio leuium siue
995 occultorum criminum Deo offerenda est, nec sine pena relaxari
Mk 240ᵛᵇ probantur que | sic expiari creduntur.

Ea uero, que de publica satisfactione uel oris confessione dicun-
Bi 299ʳᵇ tur, in publicis et manifestis criminibus intelligenda sunt. | Peccata
namque Nabuchodonosor, que Propheta misericordiis et elemosinis
1000 redimi suasit, peccata quoque Niniuitarum, que publica satisfactione expiata sunt, cunctis nota erant. Et publica noxa (ut Augustinus testatur) publico eget remedio. Premissis itaque auctoritatibus
pro manifestis criminibus manifesta probatur offerenda satisfactio
et oris confessio. Latentia uero peccata non probantur sacerdoti ne-
1005 cessario confitenda et eius arbitrio expianda.

<Argumenta ultima ex sententia secunda contra sententiam primam>

Econtra ea que in assertione huius sententie dicta sunt partim
Fs 302ʳᵃ ueritate nituntur, | partim pondere carent. Sine contritione etenim
1010 cordis nullum peccatum posse dimitti, occulta uero peccata secreta
satisfactione, publica quoque manifesta penitentia expiari debere,
firmissima constat ratione subnixum. Porro sine confessione oris, si
facultas confitendi non defuerit, aliquod graue delictum expiari
auctoritati penitus probatur aduersum. Quomodo enim secundum
Sb 265ʳᵃ | Pf auctoritatem Leonis Pape sine supplicationibus | sacerdotum | in-
107ᵛᵃ dulgentia nequit obtineri si sine confessione oris a peccato possumus emundari? Quis enim supplicabit pro peccato, quod nescit?
Item, quomodo secundum Augustinum frustrat claues ecclesie qui
sine arbitrio sacerdotis penitentiam agit si sine oris confessione cri-

---

994 Hec…**995** est] cf. *Gl. ord. in Marcum* 5 (ed. Rusch, 4.153a)   **1001** publica…
1002 remedio] cf. ibid.

991 prospexit] *om.* Aa prospicit Fd Sb *add.* uel [prosp]exit *interlin.* Fd_{pc}
993 agnoscit] ignoscit Fd_{ac} Sb   **1016** peccato] *add.* non Aa Pf

from heaven in such a way that the confessing publican returns justi-   Ps 84:12
fied. *Righteousness has looked out from heaven*—as if God is declaring,
'Let us spare him because he does not spare himself; let us forgive,
because he acknowledges his sin'. Therefore *righteousness has looked
out from heaven*, that is, justification has been granted by God to the
one confessing." Thus, this secret satisfaction for light or secret offences should be offered to God, and those which are believed to be
expiated in this manner are not proven to be loosened without
punishment.

But those things that are said about public satisfaction or oral
confession should be understood in public and manifest offences.
For the sins of Nebuchadnezzar, which the Prophet urged to be   cf. Dn 4, Jon
3
paid back with compassion and alms, and also the sins of the
Ninevites, which were expiated with public satisfaction, had been
known to all. And public injury (as Augustine testifies) requires a
public remedy. And so, by the aforementioned authorities it is
proven that manifest satisfaction and oral confession must be offered up for manifest sins. But it is not proven that hidden sins
must necessarily be confessed to a priest and expiated by his judgment.

<Final Arguments from the Second Position against
the First Position>

On the other hand, the things that have been said in support of
this opinion partly rely on truth and partly lack weight. For it is
agreed that it is a notion relying upon the firmest reason that no sin
can be forgiven without contrition of the heart, and that secret sin
ought to be expiated with secret satisfaction and also public ones
with manifest penance. But indeed, the idea that some serious offence is expiated without oral confession, if a person does not lack
the opportunity to confess, is proven to be entirely contrary to authority. For how, according to the authority of Pope Leo, is pardon   cf. c.49
able to be attained only with the supplications of priests if we can
be cleansed from our sin without oral confession? For who will
make supplication on behalf of a sin of which he is unaware? Likewise, how, according to Augustine, does he who does penance   cf. c.44
without the judgment of the priest frustrate the keys of the church

1020 minis indulgentia inpetratur? Item, quomodo secundum Ambro-
sium ius ligandi et soluendi solis sacerdotibus a Domino creditur
permissum, si quisque suo arbitrio se ipsum peccando ligat; uel secreta penitentia, secundum Prosperum, in se ipso sententiam pro-
fert excommunicationis atque post satisfactionem absque sacerdo-
1025 tali iudicio se ipsum Deo uel altario eius reconciliat?

Non sunt hec premissis auctoritatibus consentanea set multorum exemplis probantur aduersa. Filiam namque archisynagogi
turbis eiectis Dominus resuscitauit, non tamen nisi presentibus patre et matre puelle, Petro quoque, Iacobo, et Iohanne, uite reddita
1030 est. In quo moraliter instruimur ut secreta peccata, que per mortem
puelle intelliguntur, non nisi supplicationibus ecclesie, que per patrem et matrem puelle designatur, et sacerdotum ministerio, qui
Aa 152ᵛ   per Petrum et ceteros | intelliguntur, a Domino existimentur di-
mitti.

1035   ITEM IN LEUITICO: *Qui domum suam uel agrum Domino uouendo
consecrauerit non potest eam redimere nisi syclo sanctuarii sacerdote quoque
(non ipso) supputante annorum numerum usque ad iubileum.* In quo similiter docemur quod quicumque domum consciencie uel agrum
conuersationis per penitentiam Domino offerre atque pretio bono-
1040 rum operum de uana uite sue conuersatione se ipsum redimere
Bi 299ᵛᵃ   uoluerit non potest hoc facere nisi syclo sanctuarii, | id est operibus
Fs 302ʳᵇ   penitentie sacra | scriptura prefixis. Vnde uenientibus ad se turbis
Mk 241ʳᵃ   BEATUS IOHANNES non ait simpliciter, "Facite penitentiam" | uel
"fructus penitentie," set addidit, *dignos*, ut pro qualitate uidelicet
1045 peccatorum qualitas offeratur bonorum operum. Non par debet
esse fructus boni operis eius, qui nichil uel parum deliquit, atque
eius, qui grandia conmisit. Ille, tamquam nullius criminis sibi conscius, usum sibi in rebus licitis prebet; hunc tamquam multis grauatum etiam a licitis temperare oportet. In iubileo plena remissio pre-
1050 stabatur; unde per eum perfecta peccati remissio figuratur. Sacerdos

---

1021 creditur] *add.* esse R2 (*add. interlin.* Aa)   1045 Non] *add.* enim R2 (*add.*
mg. Aa)

1020 indulgentia inpetratur] indulgentiam inpetrat Mk Pf EdF   1032 designa-
tur] designantur Aa Bi_{pc?} EdF Mk Pf designatum Fs

if pardon may be procured for his offence without oral confession? Likewise, how, according to Ambrose, is the right to bind and loose cf. c.51b believed to be granted by the Lord to priests alone if everyone who sins binds himself by his own judgment? Or how, according to Prosper, does he bring a sentence of excommunication against him- cf. c.32 self by means of a secret penance, and, after satisfaction, reconcile himself to God or the altar without priestly judgment?

For these opinions do not stand in agreement with the afore-mentioned authorities but are proven to be contrary by many ex-amples. For the Lord raised the daughter of the synagogue priest af-ter he cast out the crowds, but, nevertheless,. she was not returned cf. Mk 5:35–42 to life except with the father and mother of the girl being present as well as Peter, James, and John. In this we are instructed according to the moral sense of the text that secret sins, which are understood through the death of the girl, are not judged by the Lord to be for-given except with the prayers of the church, which is designated through the mother and father of the girl, and the ministry of priests, who are understood through Peter and the other apostles.

LIKEWISE, IN LEVITICUS: *He who has dedicated or consecrated his* Lv 27:18 *house or field to the Lord cannot redeem it unless a priest also (not he him-self) counts up, by the shekel of the sanctuary, [the value based upon] the number of years until the Jubilee.* In this text we are similarly taught that whoever wants to offer the house of his conscience or the field of his way of life through penance to the Lord and wants to redeem himself from his empty way of life with the price of good works cannot do this unless by the shekel of the sanctuary, that is, by works of penance fixed beforehand by Holy Scripture. Thus, to the crowds coming to him, THE BLESSED JOHN does not simply say, "Do penance," or "the fruits of penance," but he adds, *worthy*, so Lk 3:8 that the quality of the good works may be offered as a match for the quality of the sins. The fruit[16] of the good work of him who has done nothing or only a little wrong should not be equal to that of him who has committed great sins. The former man, who, as it were, is aware of no evil deed in himself, grants the enjoyment of licit things to himself; the latter man, who, as it were, has been weighed down by many wicked deeds, should abstain even from licit things. In the Year of Jubilee full remission was offered, and

---

16. The second recension adds a connecting "for" at the start of this sentence: "For the fruit...."

Pf 107ᵛᵇ ergo numerum annorum usque ad iubileum | supputat cum eius
Sb 265ʳᵇ arbitrio penitentie tempora diffiniuntur quibus quisque plenam |
peccati remissionem inueniat. Non enim (sicut Esitius ait super
eundem locum) statim post diffinitam penitentiam quisque a pec-
1055 cato plene mundatur.

Cum ergo, ut ex premissis colligitur, tempora penitentie sacerdotis arbitrio diffiniantur, euidentissime apparet sine confessione
proprie uocis peccata non dimitti. Quis enim tempora penitentie
Fd 90ᵛᵇ alicui prefiget nisi primum peccata sua | sibi manifestare curauerit?

1060 Item, taciturnitas peccati ex superbia nascitur cordis. Ideo enim
peccatum suum quisque celare desiderat, ne iniquitas sua aliis manifesta fiat, ne talis reputetur apud homines foris, qualem se iam-
dudum exhibuit diuino conspectui. Quod ex fonte superbie nasci
nulli dubium est. Species etenim superbie est se uelle iustum uideri,
1065 qui peccator est, atque ypocrita conuincitur qui ad imitationem pri-
morum parentum uel tergiuersatione uerborum peccata sua leui-
gare contendit uel, sicut Cayn, peccatum suum reticendo penitus
supprimere querit. Vbi autem superbia regnat uel ypocrisis, humilitas locum habere non ualet. Sine humilitate uero alicui ueniam
1070 sperare non licet. Nec ergo, ubi est taciturnitas confessionis, uenia
speranda est criminis.

Probatur hoc idem AUCTORITATE AUGUSTINI, QUI IN LIBRO DE
PENITENTIA AIT, "Quem penitet omnino peniteat, et dolorem lacri-   c.88
mis ostendat, representet uitam suam Deo per sacerdotem, preue-
1075 niat iudicium Dei per confessionem. Precepit enim Dominus mun-
Aa 153ʳ dandis | ut ostenderent ora sacerdotibus, docens corporali presentia
confitenda peccata, non per nuntium, non per scriptum manife-
Fs 302ᵛᵃ standa. | Dixit enim, *Ora monstrate*, et, *Omnes*, non 'unus pro omni-
bus.' Non alium statuatis nuntium, qui pro uobis offerat munus a
Bi 299ᵛᵇ Moyse statutum, set qui per uos peccastis per uos erubescatis. | Eru-

1064 Species…1068 querit] cf. Greg. Magn., *Moralia in Iob* 23.6 (CCSL
143B:1153) 1073 Quem…1136 meritum] Ps.-Aug., *De uera* 10–11 (PL
40:1122–23; ed. Wagner, linn. 538–611)

1064 etenim] enim Aa Bi Mk 1074 representet] representat Fs Sb

thus completed remission of sin is figuratively represented in it. Therefore the priest counts the number of years until the Jubilee when he, by his judgment, defines the duration of penance after which each person may find full remission of his sin. For (as Esitius[17] says in his commentary on the same text) each person is not fully cleansed from his sin immediately after the penance has been designated.

Therefore, since, as is gathered from the preceding, the duration of penance is defined by the judgment of the priest, it is most evidently apparent that sins are not forgiven without the confession of one's own mouth. Now who will fix the duration of penance for someone unless he has first been concerned to make known his sins to him?

Moreover, silence about a sin is born of pride of the heart. For everyone desires to hide his sin so that his iniquity may not become manifest to others, so that he may not be considered publicly by people to be the kind of person he long ago since showed himself to be in the sight of God. No one doubts that this is born of the fount of pride; for indeed, that he who is a sinner wants to seem righteous is a species of pride; and he who strives to make his sins small by a shifting of words in imitation of our first parents or, like Cain, seeks to fully suppress his sin by keeping silent is convicted as a hypocrite. But where pride or hypocrisy reigns, humility cannot have a place. Without humility, no one can hope for mercy. Therefore, where there is silence in confession, mercy for the offence should not be hoped for.

c.88   This same point is proven BY THE AUTHORITY OF AUGUSTINE, WHO SAYS IN THE BOOK ON PENANCE, "Let he who repents fully repent, and let him show grief with tears, let him show his life to God through a priest, let him come before the judgment of God through confession. For the Lord commanded those to be cleansed to show their mouths to the priests, teaching that sins must be confessed in person; they are not to be made known through a messenger or in writing. For he said, *Show your mouths*, and, *All of you*, cf. Lk 17:14 not one on behalf of all. You are not to establish another person as a messenger who may offer up the offering established by Moses, but you who have sinned on your own should feel ashamed on

17. Hesychius of Jerusalem (fl. mid-fifth century), who purportedly wrote commentaries on all the books of the Bible, but only his works on Leviticus and the Psalms are extant *in toto*.

bescentia enim ipsa partem habet remissionis. Ex misericordia enim hoc precepit Dominus, ut neminem peniteret in occulto. In hoc enim, quod per se ipsum dicit sacerdoti et erubescentiam uincit timore offensi, fit uenia criminis. Fit enim ueniale per confessionem quod criminale erat in operatione, et, si non statim purgatur, fit tamen uitale quod conmiserat mortale. Multum enim satisfactionis obtulit qui erubescentie dominans | nichil eorum, que conmisit, nuntio Dei denegauit. Deus enim qui misericors et iustus est; | sicut conseruat misericordiam in iustitia, | ita et iustitiam in misericordia. Opus enim est misericordie peccanti peccata dimittere, set oportet ut iustus misereatur iuste. Oportet enim ut non solum quid, set in quo, doleat consideret, si dignus est, non dico iustitia, set misericordia. Iustitia enim sola dampnat, set dignus est misericordia qui spirituali labore petit gratiam. Laborat enim mens patiendo erubescentiam, et, quoniam uerecundia magna est pena, qui erubescit pro Christo fit dignus misericordia. Vnde patet, quia quanto pluribus confitebitur in spe uenie turpitudinem criminis, tanto facilius consequitur gratiam remissionis.

"Ipsi enim sacerdotes plus iam possunt proficere, plus confitentibus parcere; quibus enim remittunt remittit Dominus. Lazarum enim de monumento iam suscitatum obtulit discipulis soluendum, per hoc ostendens potestatem soluendi concessam sacerdoti. Dixit enim, *Quodcumque solueritis super terram soluetur et in celis*, hoc est, 'Ego Deus, et omnes celestis militie ordines, et omnes sancti in gloria mea laudant uobiscum et confirmant quos ligatis et soluitis.' Non dixit, 'quos putatis ligare et soluere,' set in quos exercetis opus iustitie aut misericordie. Alia autem opera uestra in peccatores non cognosco.'

"Quare qui confiteri uult peccata ut inueniat gratiam querat sacerdotem scientem ligare et soluere, ne, cum negligens circa se extiterit, negligatur ab illo, qui eum misericorditer monet et petit, ne ambo in foueam cadant, quam stultus euitare noluit. Tanta itaque

---

1082 neminem] nemo Fs Mk **1086** uitale] ueniale Fs Pf **1090** est misericordie] *tr.* Aa Bi Fs Mk Sb **1094** petit] querit Bi Fs Mk **1100** Dominus] Deus Bi EdF Fs Mk Sb **1101** suscitatum] resuscitatum Aa suscitauit Bi$_{ac}$ **1103** solueritis] solueris Fs Pf **1105** soluitis] *add.* super terram Fs Pf

your own. Shame itself has a part in remission. The Lord commanded this, that no one repent in secret, out of compassion. For mercy for an evil deed occurs in this, that the offender speaks to the priest on his own and conquers his shame with fear of the offence. Now what was a mortal sin in act becomes a venial sin through confession, and, if it is not immediately purged, what mortal sin the person had committed nevertheless becomes venial. For he who, mastering his shame, has denied none of the things which he has done to the messenger of God has offered a good portion of satisfaction. For God is merciful and just; just as he preserves mercy in his justice, so also does he preserve justice in his mercy. Forgiving the sins of a sinner is a work of mercy, but the righteous should exercise mercy justly. It is proper for him to consider not only what, but in what manner, a sinner grieves, to consider if he is worthy of, I do not say justice, but mercy. For justice alone condemns, but he is worthy of mercy who seeks grace with spiritual labor. The mind labors by suffering shame, and, since great disgrace is a punishment, he who is ashamed for the sake of Christ becomes worthy of mercy. For this reason it is clear that the more he will confess to many the foulness of his wicked deed in the hope of mercy, the easier he will attain the grace of remission.

"For priests are now increasingly able to be of use and to spare those confessing, for those whom they forgive, the Lord forgives. He presented Lazarus to the disciples to be loosed after he had already been raised from the grave, showing through this occurrence that the power to loose has been granted to priests. For he said, *Whatever you have loosed on earth will be loosed also in heaven*, which is   Mt 16:19
to say, 'I, God, and all the orders of the heavenly host, and all the saints in my glory praise with you and confirm those whom you bind and loose.' He did not say, 'whom you think to bind or loose,' but 'those in whom you exercise a work of justice or of mercy. Your other works in sinners, however, I do not acknowledge.'

"And therefore, let he who wants to confess his sins in order to find mercy seek out a priest who knows how to bind and loose, lest, if an ignorant priest lives around him, he be ignored by that kind of priest who could admonish and seek him compassionately, lest both fall into the snare which the fool refuses to avoid. So great

uis confessionis est, ut, si deest sacerdos, confiteatur proximo. Sepe
enim contingit quod penitens non potest uerecundari coram sacer-
Fs 302vb dote, | quem desideranti nec locus nec tempus offert. Et si ille cui
confitebitur potestatem soluendi non habeat, fit tamen dignus ue-
Aa 153v nia | ex desiderio sacerdotis qui ei confitetur turpitudinem criminis.
Mundati enim sunt leprosi dum ibant ostendere ora sacerdotibus
antequam ad eos peruenirent. Vnde patet, Deum ad cor respicere
Bi 300ra dum | ex necessitate prohibentur ad sacerdotes peruenire. Sepe qui-
Pf 108rb dem eos querunt, set, sani | et leti dum querunt, antequam perue-
niant moriuntur. Set misericordia est ubique, qui et iustis nouit
parcere, etsi non tam cito, sicut soluerentur a sacerdote. Qui ergo
omnino confitetur, et sacerdoti meliori, quam potest, confiteatur.

1125   "Si peccatum occultum est, sufficiat referre in notitiam sacerdo-
Sb 265vb tis ut grata sit oblatio muneris. | Nam in resurrectione filie principis
Fd 91ra pauci | interfuerunt qui uiderent. Nondum erat sepulta, nondum
extra portam ciuitatis delata, nondum extra domum in notitiam
portata. Intus resuscitauit quam intus inuenit, relictis solis Petro, et
1130   Iohanne et Iacobo, et patre et matre puelle, in quibus in figura continentur sacerdotes ecclesie. Quos autem extra inuenit animaduer-
tendum est quomodo suscitauit. Flebat enim turba post filium ui-
Mk 241va due. Fleuit Martha et Maria, supplicantes | pro fratre. Flebat et
turba, que Mariam fuerat secuta, lacrimis Marie admonita. In quo
1135   docemur publice peccantibus non proprium, set ecclesie sufficere
meritum."

1117 ei] socio *pos.* confitetur R2 (consocio *ant.* confitetur Sb)   **1122** ubique]
add. Dei R2 (*interlin.* Aa *pos.* misericordia Pf)   **1127** Nondum] *add.* enim R2 (*om.*
Pf)   **1130** in figura] figuraliter R2 (Fd_{pc}, in figura Sb)

1116 confitebitur] confitetur Aa confitebuntur Fd_{ac}   **1130** in figura] figurate Aa
1133 Fleuit] flebant Pf flebat Sb

is the power of confession, then, that, if a priest is not available, one may confess to a neighbor. For it often happens that a penitent cannot express his shame in the presence of a priest, for neither time nor place has offered a priest to the penitent desiring him. And if that person to whom he will confess does not possess the power to loose, the penitent who confesses the foulness of his evil deed to him[18] nevertheless becomes worthy of mercy because of his desire for a priest. For the lepers were cleansed while they went to show their mouths to the priests before they reached them. For this reason it is clear that the Lord looks at the heart when, by necessity, men are hindered from reaching priests. Indeed, oftentimes the healthy and happy seek out priests, but, while they are seeking, before they reach them, they die. But mercy,[19] which also knows how to spare the righteous, even if not as quickly as if they were loosed by a priest, is everywhere. Therefore, let he who confesses fully confess to as good a priest as he can.

"If the sin is secret, let it suffice to bring it to a priest's attention so that the giving of the offering may be acceptable. For in the resurrection of the daughter of the synagogue official, few were present who witnessed it. She had not yet been buried, not yet been removed outside the city gate, not yet been carried away outside the home in public view. The Lord revived inside her whom he found inside, and only Peter and John and James and the father and mother of the girl remained, in which persons priests of the church are figuratively[20] contained. But it should be taken note of how he raised those whom he found outside. For the crowd was weeping over the son of the widow. Martha and Mary wept, making supplication for their brother. The crowd which had followed Mary also wept, having been incited by her tears. In these examples we are taught that not one's own merit, but that of the church, suffices for those sinning publicly."

18. The second recension changed the pronoun to a noun, specifying that it is the penitent's "companion" or "friend" (*socius*) to whom he confesses instead of the priest.
19. Gratian seems to have left out the qualifier "of God." The second recension corrected the text in line with the original text of the *De vera et falsa penitentia* (although the word order differed), so that the final version reads, "But the mercy of God, who..., is everywhere."
20. The second recension made a change here from a prepositional phrase (*in figura*, which matches the material source) to an adverb (*figuraliter*). Both can be translated in English as "figuratively."

(FdB 161rb) | ITEM LEO PAPA:

Sufficit illa confessio, que primum Deo deinde sacerdoti offertur.

"Quamuis plenitudo fidei uideatur esse laudabilis, que propter Dei timorem   c.89
1140   apud omnes erubescere non ueretur, tamen, quia non omnium huiusmodi sunt
AaB 335r   peccata, ut ea, que penitentiam poscunt, | non timeant publicare, remoueatur inpro-
babilis consuetudo, ne multi a penitentie remediis arceantur dum aut erubescunt
aut timent inimicis suis sua facta reserare, quibus possint legum percelli constitutione. Sufficit enim illa confessio que primum Deo offertur, tunc etiam sacerdoti,
1145   qui pro delictis penitentium precator accedit. Tunc enim plures ad penitentiam po-
terunt prouocari, si populi auribus non publicetur conscientia confitentis."

Quibus auctoritatibus uel quibus rationum firmamentis utraque   d.p.c.89
Fs 303ra   sententia confessionis et satisfactionis nitatur in medium | breuiter
proposuimus. Cui autem harum potius adherendum sit lectoris iu-
1150   dicio reseruatur. Vtraque enim fautores habet sapientes et religio-
sos. VNDE THEODORUS CANTUARIENSIS ARCHIEPISCOPUS AIT IN
Pf 108va   PENITENTIALI SUO, "Quidam | Deo solummodo confiteri debere di-   c.90
cunt peccata, ut Greci. Quidam uero sacerdotibus confitenda esse
percensent, ut fere tota sancta ecclesia. Quod utrumque non sine
1155   magno fructu intra sanctam fit ecclesiam, ita dumtaxat, ut Deo, qui
Bi 300rb   remissor est peccatorum, | peccata nostra confiteamur, et hoc per-
fectorum est, et cum Dauid dicamus, *Delictum meum cognitum tibi feci,
et iniustitiam meam non abscondi. Dixi, confitebor aduersum me iniustitiam meam Domino, et tu remisisti inpietatem peccati mei.* Set tamen
1160   Apostoli institutio nobis sequenda est, ut confiteamur alterutrum
peccata nostra et oremus pro inuicem ut saluemur. Confessio ita-
Sb 266ra   que, que soli Deo fit, quod iustorum est, peccata purgat. | Ea uero,
que sacerdoti fit, docet qualiter ipsa purgentur peccata. Deus namque, salutis et sanctitatis auctor et largitor, plerumque prebet hanc

---

1139 Quamuis... **1146** confitentis] Leo I, *Epistola* 168 (PL 54:1211A–B) = JK
545   **1152** Quidam... **1166** operatione] Concilium Catalaunense (813) c.33
(MGH Conc. 2.1:280)

1150 religiosos] *add.* uiros R2 (*om.* Sb)

1138 Sufficit... offertur] *om.* Fs | deinde] et postea Bi   **1140** omnes] omnis Sb
homines Bipc EdF Fs Pf | omnium] hominum Pf   **1145** precator] procurator Fs
1151 Cantuariensis] cartuariensis Fd Sb cartagriensis Pf | Archiepiscopus] epi-
scopus Fdac

LIKEWISE, POPE LEO:

That confession which is offered first to God and then to a priest is sufficient.

c.89   "The fullness of faith which, because of the fear of God, is not afraid of blushing among men appears to be praiseworthy. Nevertheless, because not all the sins of men are of this kind, namely that they do not fear to publicize those sins that demand penance, let this objectionable custom be removed, lest many be scared away from the remedies of penance while they are either ashamed or afraid to disclose their deeds, for which they can be struck down by the order of laws, to their enemies. For that confession is sufficient which is first offered to God and then also to the priest, who approaches as the intercessor for the offences of the penitents.   cf. D.1 c.61 Then, if the conscience of the one confessing is not made public to the ears of the people, many will be able to be called to repentance."

d.p.c.89   We have briefly explained to all what authorities or what supporting arguments both opinions about confession and satisfaction rely upon. To which of these one should preferably adhere, however, is reserved to the judgment of the reader. For both have wise and religious supporters.[21] FOR THIS REASON THEODORE, ARCH-

c.90   BISHOP OF CANTERBURY, SAYS IN HIS PENITENTIAL, "Certain people, such as the Greeks, say that sins ought to be confessed to God alone. But others, such as almost the entire holy Church, agree that they are to be confessed to priests. Both of these are done with great fruit within the holy Church, to this extent, that we confess our sins to God, who is the forgiver of sins, and this practice belongs to the perfected, and let us say with David, *I have made my offence known to you, and I have not hidden my unrighteousness. I said, I will confess against myself my unrighteousness to the Lord, and you remitted the wickedness of my sin.* But the institution of the Apostle should   Ps 31:5 still be followed by us, namely that we confess our sins one to another and pray for one another so that we may be saved. Therefore,   cf. Jas 5:16 that confession which is made to God alone, the act of which belongs to the righteous, purges sins. But that confession which is made to a priest teaches how those very sins are purged. For God, the author and bestower of salvation and holiness, very often offers

---

21. R2 added an additional noun, "men," so that the English translation would read, "For both have wise and religious men as supporters."

1165 sue penitentie inuisibili administratione, plerumque medicorum
operatione."

1165 penitentie] *add.* medicinam R2 (Aa Fd$_{pc}$, *pos.* amministratione Pf)

this[22] by an invisible administration of his penance, and very often he does so by the operation of his doctors."

22. Gratian seems originally to have left this indefinite pronoun vague, just as did his probable formal source. Gratian himself or a later redactor then added the word "medicine," so that the second recension text would be translated, "very often offers this medicine of his penance by an invisible administration...."

Distinctio secunda

Quia uero de penitentia semel cepit sermo haberi, aliquantulum altius repetendum uidetur, diuersorum sententias certis auctoritatibus munitas in medium proponentes.

5 <Sententia prima>

Alii dicunt penitentiam semel tantum esse utilem. Unica enim est nec reiterari potest. Si uero reiteratur, | precedens penitentia non fuit. Et si de sententia iudicis eius merito peccata uidentur esse remissa, apud tamen eius prescientiam cui omnia futura presentia 10 sunt, numquam habentur remissa, quia non est seruata SENTENTIA ILLA UERI SACERDOTIS: *Vade, et amplius noli peccare*; item: *Ecce sanus factus es, iam amplius noli peccare, ne deterius tibi aliquid contingat.*

| ITEM EX VIII SINODO:

Primam uitii causam non penitus extinguit qui in idem postea recidit.

15 "Si quis semel notatus fuerit inuidie uel contemptionis uitio et rursum in hoc ipsum inciderit, sciat se primam causam, ex qua inuidia uel contemptio nascitur, in interioribus medullis habere reconditam. Oportet ergo eum per contraria atque aduersa curari, id est per humilitatis exercitium. Exercitia uero humilitatis sunt, si se uilioribus | offitiis subdat, et ministeriis indignioribus tradat. Ita namque arrogantie 20 et humane glorie uitium curari poterit, ut in consuetudine humilitatis affectus ultra iam non incidat arrogantie et uane glorie delictum. Set in singulis huiuscemodi uitiis cura similis adhibetur."

Item sine caritate nulli adulto peccatum | remittitur. Non autem habet caritatem qui aliquando peccaturus est criminaliter. VNDE 25 AUGUSTINUS AD IULIANUM COMITEM: "Caritas que deseri potest

Aa 154ʳ
Mk 241ᵛᵇ
(FdB 161ʳᵇ)
(AaB 335ʳ)
Fs 303ʳᵇ
Pf 108ᵛᵇ

pr.
d.a.c.1
c.1
d.p.c.1
c.2

2,15 Si…**22** adhibetur] Bas. Caes. (trans. Rufinus), *Regula* 22 (CSEL 86:71.7–72.11) **25** Caritas…**26** fuit] Paul. Aquil., *De salut. doc.* 7 (PL 99:202A)

2,9 prescientiam] presentiam R2

2,2 Quia…**4** proponentes] *om.* Aa *sed adest* AaB **12** amplius] *om.* Aa Pf **14** Primam…causam] Primas causas uitii FdB | Primam…recidit] *om.* Fs | penitus] plenius AaB Sb | postea] *om.* Bi **18** aduersa] diuersa FdB

Distinction 2

pr.　But since we have briefly begun to discuss penance, it seems that we should take up the issue again in somewhat greater depth, laying before all the opinions of various men defended by reliable authorities.

<First Position>

d.a.c.1　Some say that penance is beneficial only once. It is unique and cannot be reiterated. But if it is reiterated, the preceding act was not penance. Even if a person's sins seem from the sentence of his judge deservedly to have been remitted, nevertheless, according to the foreknowledge[1] of him to whom all future events are present, they are considered never to have been remitted, for THAT SEN-TENCE OF THE TRUE PRIEST has not been kept: *Go and sin no more,* Jn 8:11 and so also: *Behold, you have been healed, do not sin any longer, lest something worse befall you.* Jn 5:14

LIKEWISE FROM THE EIGHTH SYNOD:

He who afterward falls back on the same vice has not fully extinguished its first cause.

c.1　"If anyone has been censured once for the vice of envy or contentiousness and falls once again in this very vice, let him know that he holds concealed in his inner marrow that first cause from which envy or contentiousness are born. He should thus be cured through the contrary and opposite things, that is, through the exercise of humility. Now the exercises of humility are if he subjects himself to rather base duties and surrenders to rather shameful services. For the vice of arrogance and human vainglory can be cured in such a way that, having been affected by the custom of humility, he no longer falls into the transgression of arrogance and vainglory. And a similar remedy may be applied to each individual vice of this kind."

d.p.c.1　Likewise, no sin is remitted for any adult without love. But he who is going to sin mortally at some point does not have love.

c.2　THEREFORE AUGUSTINE WRITES TO JULIANUS COMES: "Love that

---

1. The second recension changed "foreknowledge" to "presence," so that the phrase would translate, "in the presence of him to whom all future events are present." Gratian's original rendering had terminological links to D.4 as well as a more logical connection to the following phrase ("to whom all future events are present"), and thus the second recension alteration was not a change for the better.

numquam uera fuit." IDEM SUPER EPISTOLAM IOHANNIS: "Radicata   c.3
est caritas? securus esto; nichil mali procedere potest." ITEM GRE-
GORIUS IN MORALIBUS: | *"Valida est, ut mors, dilectio.* Virtuti etenim   c.4
mortis dilectio conparatur quia nimirum mentem, quam semel ceperit, a delectatione mundi funditus occidit."

Bi 300va

30

ITEM PROSPER IN LIBRO DE CONTEMPLATIUA UITA: "Caritas est,   c.5
ut mihi uidetur, recta uoluntas, ab omnibus terrenis ac presentibus
prorsus auersa, iuncta Deo inseparabiliter et unita, igne quodam
Spiritus sancti a quo est et ad quem refertur incensa, inquinamenti
omnis extranea, | corrumpi nescia, nulli uitio mutabilitatis obnoxia,
supra omnia que carnaliter diliguntur excelsa, affectionum omnium
potentissima, diuine contemplationis auida, in omnibus semper in-
uicta, summa actionum bonarum, salus morum, finis celestium
preceptorum, mors criminum, uita uirtutum, uirtus pugnantium,
palma uictorum, anima sanctarum mentium, causa meritorum bonorum, premium perfectorum, sine qua nullus Deo placuit; cum
qua nec potuit aliquis peccare nec poterit, fructuosa in penitentibus, leta in proficientibus, gloriosa in perseuerantibus, uictoriosa in
martiribus, operosa in omnibus omnino fidelibus, ex qua quicquid
est boni operis uiuet."

Sb 266rb

40

45

Item: "Hec est caritas uera, germana, perfecta, quam excellen-
tiorem uiam nominat apostolus sanctus. Sicut enim sine uia nullus
peruenit quo tendit, ita sine caritate, que dicta est uia, ambulare
non possunt homines, set errare."
Item: "Ergo si caritatem Deo exhibeamus et proximo de corde |
puro et conscientia bona et fide non ficta, facile peccato resistimus,
bonis omnibus habundamus, seculi blandimenta contempnimus, et
omnia que difficilia sunt humane fragilitati, uel aspera etiam, cum

Fd 91rb

---

26 Radicata…**27** potest] Aug. Hipp., *In Ioh. epist. ad Parthos tract.* 8 (PL 35:2041)
28 Valida…**30** occidit] Greg. Magn., *Moralia in Iob* 10.21 (CSSL 143:565.22–25)
31 Caritas…**49** errare] Jul. Pom., *De vita contemplativa* 3.13 (PL 59:493B–D)
50 Ergo…**90** discedere] Ibid., 3.15.1–3 (PL 59:496B–497D)

---

35 corrumpi] corruptionis R2 (Fd_pc, corrumpi Sb)   **48** ambulare…**49** non] *tr.*
R2

---

30 delectatione] dilectione Mk delectione Bi_ac | occidit] cecidit Fd_ac   **33** auersa]
aduersa Fd_pc Bi Mk Sb | iuncta] *add.* uero Bi Fs Mk Pf | unita] *add.* deo Aa,
ignita Bi_pc iuncta Sb | igne] igni Bi Mk   **40** anima] *om.* Fd, arma Mk armatura Pf
42 nec potuit] non oportuit Aa_ac   **50** de] *interlin.* Bi *om.* Mk

can be abandoned was never true." THE SAME IN HIS COMMEN-

c.3 TARY ON JOHN'S EPISTLE: "Has love taken root? Be at peace; no

c.4 evil can go forth." LIKEWISE, GREGORY IN HIS *MORALIA*: "*Love, like death, is powerful.* Now love is compared to the power of death be-   Sg of Sol. 8:6
cause it undoubtedly utterly strikes down the mind, which it once
captured, from taking delight in the world."

    LIKEWISE, PROSPER IN THE BOOK OF *DE VITA CONTEMPLATIVA*:

c.5 "Love is, it seems to me, a right will, turned directly away from all
things earthly and present, inseparably joined and united to God,
inflamed by a certain fire of the Holy Spirit (by whom it exists and
to whom it is related), outside of all filth, unaware of how to be
corrupted,[2] beholden to no vice of mutability, elevated above
everything which is loved carnally, the most potent of all affections,
eager for divine contemplation, always unconquered in all things,
the highest of good actions, the health of character, the end goal of
celestial precepts, the death of wicked deeds, the life of virtues, the
power of fighters, the palm of victors, the soul of holy minds, the
cause of good merits, the reward of the perfected, without which
no one has pleased God, with which no one has been able to or will
be able to sin, fruitful in those who repent, propitious in those who
make progress, glorious in those who persevere, victorious in martyrs, operative in all who are entirely faithful, that from which
whatever good work there is lives."

    Likewise: "This is true, genuine, perfect love, which the holy
Apostle calls the more excellent path. Just as no one reaches where
he is going without a path, so, without love, which has been called
a path, people cannot walk straight but will wander off."

    Likewise: "Therefore, if we show love to God and neighbor from
a pure heart and a good conscience and unfeigned faith, we easily
resist sin, we abound in all good things, we despise the flatteries of
the world, and we perfect with love all the things which are diffi-

---

2. The second recension changed a passive infinitive to an abstract noun so that
the phrase would read, "unaware of corruption."

Fs 303va dilectione | perficimus, si tamen Deum caritate perfecta, que nobis
Mk 242ra ab illo est, ex toto corde et ex tota anima et ex totis uiribus | diliga-
mus. Ex ea enim parte quis peccat, ex qua minus diligit Deum.
Quem si ex toto corde diligamus, nichil erit in nobis unde peccati
Aa 154^v desideriis seruiamus. Et quid est Deum diligere, nisi occupari |
animo, concipere fruende uisionis eius effectum, peccati odium,
Pf 109ra mundi | fastidium, diligere etiam proximum, quem in se censuit di-
ligendum, in ipso amore seruare legitimum modum, nec peruertere
dilectionis ordinem constitutum? Ordinem dilectionis illi peruer-
tunt nec modum diligendi custodiunt, qui aut mundum qui con-
tempnendus est diligunt, aut corpora sua minus diligenda plus dili-
65 gunt, aut proximos non sicut se ipsos aut Deum plus quam se ipsos
forte non diligunt."

Item: "Corpus nostrum, quia pars nostri est, ad hoc nobis est di-
ligendum, ut saluti eius ac fragilitati naturaliter consulamus, et agamus quatinus spiritui ordinate subiectum ad eternam salutem ac-
70 cepta inmortalitate et incorruptione perueniat."

Bi 300vb Item: | "Proximos autem tunc diligimus sicut nos si non propter
aliquas utilitates nostras, non propter sperata beneficia uel accepta,
Sb 266va non propter affinitates uel consanguinitates, set propter hoc | tan-
tum, quod sunt nature nostre participes, diligamus." Item: "Non illi
75 tantum proximi nostri credendi sunt, quos nobis gradus sanguinis
iungit, set proximi nostri credendi sunt omnes homines nature nostre, sicut dixi, participes."
Item: "Proinde, secundum nos proximos omnes diligimus quando ad mores bonos et ad eternam uitam consequendam, sicut no-
80 bis, eorum saluti consulimus; quando nos in eorum peccatis ac periculis cogitamus et, sicut nobis subuenire optaremus, ita eis subue-
nimus aut, si facultas defuerit, uoluntatem subueniendi tenemus.

---

58 occupari] illi occupari *vel* illum occupare R2 (illi occupari Mk Sb EdF; illum
Deum occupare Bi, illum occupare Fs Pf; *add.* illi *interlin.* Aa_pc Fd_pc) **59** effec-
tum] affectum R2 (Fd_pc, effectum Sb) **72** sperata] speranda R2 (Aa_pc, sperata
Pf)

---

54 Deum] domini Fd *om.* Fs **55** ex³] *om.* Bi Fs Mk **59** peccati] *om.* Fd_ac, pec-
candi Fd_pc Pf **78** secundum] sicut Mk Pf | omnes] nostros Fs Pf **81** subuenire]
subueniri Bi Mk_pc EdF | subuenimus] subueniamus Pf

cult, or even hopeless, for human weakness, if we love God with a perfect love, which we have from him, with all our heart, all our soul, and all our strength. For someone sins with the same part with which he loves God less. If we were to love him with our whole heart, there will be nothing in us from which we would serve the desires of sin. And what is loving God if not being engrossed in the mind,[3] receiving the effect[4] of enjoying the vision of him, hating sin, having an aversion to the world, and also loving one's neighbor, whom God resolved was to be loved in himself, preserving in that very love the legitimate mode, and not perverting the established order of love? They pervert the order of love and do not guard the mode of loving who either love the world, which ought to be loathed, or love their own bodies more, which ought to be loved less, or happen not to love their neighbors as themselves or God more than themselves."

Likewise: "We ought to love our body, which is part of us, to the extent that we naturally take care of its health and weakness, and we should act in accord with the fact that, having been subject to a well-ordered spirit, it attains eternal salvation when immortality and incorruption has been received."

Likewise: "But then we love our neighbors as ourselves if we love them, not on account of some benefits to us, not on account of blessings hoped for[5] or received, not on account of kinship or consanguinity, but for this reason alone, that they are sharers in our nature." Likewise: "Not merely those of our neighbors whom the degree of blood joins to us are to be trusted, but our neighbors, all men as sharers in our nature, as I said, are to be trusted."

Likewise: "Accordingly, we love all our neighbors as ourselves when we have regard for their salvation, just as for ourselves, in order to attain a good character and eternal life, when we reflect on their sins and dangers, and when, just us we desire to be helped, so we help them, or, if an opportunity should fail to present itself, we possess a will for helping them. Therefore, dearly beloved, this is

---

3. The second recension had two ways to alter "being engrossed in the mind," but they both involved adding a pronoun to refer to God. This version would be translated, "being engrossed with God by the mind."

4. The second recension reads *affectum*, not *effectum*, meaning "receiving the desire to enjoy the vision of him."

5. The second recension changed the "hoped for" to "to be hoped for": "not on account of blessings to be hoped for or blessings received."

Quapropter carissime tota proximi dilectio est, ut bonum, quod tibi
conferri uis, uelis et proximo. Illi uero plus quam se diligunt Deum
85 qui pro eius amore sue ad tempus saluti non parcunt, se ipsos tri-
bulationibus ac periculis tradunt, nudari facultatibus propriis, patrie
sue extorres fieri, parentibus et uxoribus ac filiis renuntiare parati
sunt, et, ut totum dicam, ipsam mortem corporis non solum non
refugiunt set etiam libenter excipiunt, ambientes a corporis sui uita
90 magis quam a Deo uita uite sue discedere."

Fs 303ᵛᵇ   ITEM BEDA SUPER IOHANNEM: "Querendum est | interea quo-   c.6
modo spiritale filii Dei agnoscendi signum fuerit, quod super eum
descenderit et manserit Spiritus.... Quid magni est filio Dei, quod in
Pf 109ʳᵇ ipso manere Spiritus astruatur? Notandum quod semper | in Do-
95 mino manserit Spiritus sanctus; in sanctis autem hominibus, quamdiu mortale corpus gestauerint, partim maneat in eternum, partim rediturus secedat. Manet quippe apud eos ut bonis insistant ac-
tionibus, uoluntariam paupertatem diligant, mansuetudinem con-
Mk 242ʳᵇ sequantur, pro eterno desiderio lugeant, esuriant et sitiant | iusti-
Aa 155ʳ tiam, misericordiamque, munditiam | cordis, et tranquillitatem pa-
cis amplectantur; set et pro obseruatione iustitie persecutionem pati
non reuereantur, elemosinis, orationibus, ieiuniis, ceterisque Spiritus fructibus insistere desiderent. Recedit autem ad tempus, ne
semper infirmos curandi, mortuos suscitandi, demones eiciendi, uel
105 etiam prophetandi habeant facultatem. Manet semper ut possint
habere uirtutes ut mirabiliter ipsi uiuant. Venit ad tempus ut etiam
aliis per miraculorum signa, quales sint intus effulgeant."

---

91 Querendum...**107** effulgeant] Bed. Uen., *Hom. evang.* 1.15 (CCSL
122:109.167–110.190)

83 dilectio est] dilectione satage R2 (*cf. infra ad* Quapropter ... est)   **92** spiritale]
speciale R2 (Aa, spirituale Pf, spiritale Sb)   **97** actionibus] actibus R2

83 Quapropter...est] Quapropter carissime tota dilectio est Fd (*om.* est Fd_{ac})
Quapropter proximi tota dilectio est Sb Qua carissime propter tota dilectione sa-
tage Bi Quapropter carissime tota dilectione satage Fs Mk Pf | bonum] malum
Aa EdRom   **84** conferri] *add.* non *interlin.* Aa, nolis accidere EdRom | conferri
uis] *tr.* Sb, inferius Bi_{ac} Mk_{ac} | uelis] nolis Aa EdRom   **94** Notandum] *add.* quod
est Mk (est *interlin.*) *add.* quoque est Fs Pf   **96** gestauerint] gestauerit Fd gesta-
uit Sb   **97** insistant] consistant Fs Mk, *add.* uel in- *interlin.* Mk   **100** misericor-
diamque] misericordiam Aa Bi EdF Pf et misericordiam Fs   **102** reuereantur]
uereantur Bi EdF   **106** ut¹] et Fd_{ac} ac Pf

total love[6] of your neighbor, that you desire also for your neighbor the good that you want to be conferred on you. Now they love God more than themselves who, for the sake of their love of him, do not let their salvation alone for a time, surrender themselves to tribulations and dangers, are prepared to become naked by their own powers, to become exiles of their homeland, to renounce their parents and wives and sons, and, so that I may speak completely, not only do not shrink from the very death of the body but also gladly welcome it, wandering more away from the life of their body than they depart from God, the Life of their life."

c.6   LIKEWISE BEDE COMMENTING ON JOHN: "Meanwhile we should ask how the sign for acknowledging the son of God was of the Spirit[7]—the fact that the Spirit descended and remained upon him.... What great thing is it for the Son of God, that the Spirit is added to remain in him? We should note that the Holy Spirit always remained in the Lord; in holy persons, however, as long as they bear a mortal body, he partly remains forever and partly departs, ready to return. Indeed he remains among them so that they may persist in good actions,[8] love voluntary poverty, pursue gentleness, lament for the longing of eternal things, hunger and thirst for justice and mercy and pureness of heart, and embrace the tranquility of peace, but also so that they may not fear suffering persecution for the observance of justice, and so that they may desire to persist in almsgiving, prayers, fasting, and the other fruits of the Spirit. He temporarily withdraws, however, lest they always have the ability to heal the sick, to raise the dead, to cast out demons, or also to prophesy. He always remains so that they may be able to possess virtues and so that they themselves may live wondrously. He comes temporarily so that they may also radiate how they are inwardly out to others through miraculous signs."

---

6. The second recension changed the grammatical case of "love" and changed "is" to an imperative: "busy yourself with total love [in such a way] that...."
7. The second recension changed an adjective meaning "of the Spirit" or "spiritual" to "special."
8. The second recension changed "actions" to "acts."

ITEM APOSTOLUS: *Caritas numquam excidit.*   c.7

ITEM AUGUSTINUS SUPER EPISTOLAM IOHANNIS: "Vnctio inuisi-   c.8

Bi 301ra bilis Spiritus sanctus est; unctio | inuisibilis caritas est, que, in quo-

Sb 266vb cumque fuerit, tamquam radix illi erit. Quamuis ardente | sole are-
scere non potest, nutritur calore solis, non arescit."

ITEM GREGORIUS SUPER EZECHIELEM: "Pennata animalia mi-   c.9
nime reuertuntur cum incedunt quia predicatores sancti sic a terre-
115   nis actibus ad spiritualia transeunt, ut ad ea que reliquerant ulterius
nullatenus reflectantur." Et paulo post: "*Nemo mittens manum suam
in aratrum,* etc. Manum quippe in aratrum mittere est quasi per
quendam conpunctionis uomerem ad proferendos fructus terram
sui cordis aperire. Set retro post aratrum aspicit, qui post exordia
120   boni operis ad mala reuertitur que reliquit. Quod quia electis Dei
Fd 91va minime contingit, | recte nunc per Prophetam dicitur, *Non reuerte-
bantur cum incederent.*" Et paulo post: "Vnde et Paulus: *Vnum uero,
que retro sunt oblitus, in ea, que sunt ante, extendens me, sequor ad pal-
mam superne uocationis.* In anteriora etenim extentus, eorum que re-
125   tro sunt oblitus fuerat, quia temporalia despiciens que sola sunt
eterna requirebat."

Fs 304ra | IDEM IN EODEM, OMELIA V: "*Non reuertebantur cum incederent*   c.10
quia electi quique sic ad bona tendunt, ut ad mala perpetranda non
redeant. *Qui enim perseuerauerit usque in finem, hic saluus erit.* Et, sicut
Pf 109va per Salomonem | dicitur: *Iustorum semita quasi lux splendens procedit et
crescit usque ad perfectum diem.* In eorum namque animo bonum desiderium atque intellectus lucis intime iam pars diei est; set quia usque ad finem uite in uirtute proficiunt, ad perfectum diem tunc ue-
niunt quando ad regna celestia perducti, in ea luce quam deside-
135   rant iam minus aliquid non habebunt."

---

109 Vnctio...**112** arescit] Aug. Hipp., *In Ioh. epist. ad Parthos tract.* 3 (PL 35:2004)
113 Pennata...**126** requirebat] Greg. Magn., *Hom. in Hiezech. proph.* 1.3 (CCSL
142:42.311–315, 43.318–324, 43.330–334)   **127** Non...**135** habebunt] Ibid. 1.5
(CCSL 142:58.65–59.74)

116 suam...**117** aratrum[1]] *om.* Fs   **117** in[1]...etc] *om.* Fd | etc] *om.* Bi Mk Sb
122 Vnum] Vnde Mk_ac Enim Pf | uero] *interlin.* Aa   **123** ante] anteriora Fd_pc Fs
Mk Pf   **124** In anteriora] Interiora Bi_ac Mk_ac

c.7   LIKEWISE THE APOSTLE: *Love never dies.*   1 Cor 13:8

       LIKEWISE AUGUSTINE IN HIS COMMENTARY ON JOHN'S EPIS-
c.8   TLE: "The Spirit is an invisible anointing; the invisible anointing is
       love, which, in whomever it resides, will be like a root for him.
       However much it cannot dry up from the burning sun, it is nour-
       ished by its heat and does not dry up."

c.9   LIKEWISE GREGORY IN HIS HOMILIES ON EZEKIEL: "Winged an-
       imals do not turn back when they are moving forward because, as
       holy preachers, they pass over to spiritual things from earthly acts
       in such a way that they are in no wise brought back anymore to
       the things which they left behind." And a little later: "*No one putting
       his hand to the plough,* etc. Assuredly, to put his hand to the plough   Lk 9:62
       is, as it were, to uncover the earth of his heart through a certain
       ploughshare of compunction in order to produce fruits. But he
       looks back behind the plough who, after the beginnings of a good
       work, turns back to the evil things which he left behind. Because
       this is not suitable for the elect of God, it is correctly said here
       through the Prophet, *They did not turn back when they moved forward.*"   Ezek 1:9
       And a little later: "For this reason Paul says, *But one thing: having for-
       gotten what lies behind, reaching forward to what lies ahead, I strive for
       the crown of the highest calling.* Indeed, having been stretched toward   Phil 3:13
       the things in front of him, he had forgotten the things which are
       behind because, despising temporal things, he was seeking only
       those things that are eternal."

c.10   THE SAME IN THE SAME WORK, IN THE FIFTH HOMILY: "*They did
       not turn back when they moved forward,* because every one of the elect   Ezek 1:9
       tend toward the good in such a way that they do not return to
       committing evil. *Now he who perseveres to the end will be saved.* And, as   Mt 10:22
       is said through Solomon, *The path of the righteous goes forth like a shin-
       ing light and grows until the perfected day.* For in their souls, a good de-   Prv 4:18
       sire and an intellect of innermost light is already a large share of
       the day; but because they advance all the way to the end of life in
       virtue, they come to the perfected day at the time when they are
       led to the heavenly realms and they will no longer have anything
       less in that light than they desire."

IDEM IN EODEM OMELIA V: "Potest discursus atque mobilitas c.11
Spiritus sic intelligi: in sanctorum quippe cordibus iuxta quasdam
uirtutes semper manet; iuxta quasdam uero recessurus uenit et
uenturus recedit. In fide enim, spe atque caritate, et in bonis aliis,
140 sine quibus ad celestem patriam non potest perueniri (sicut est humilitas, castitas, iustitia atque misericordia), perfectorum corda non
Aa 155ᵛ deserit. In prophetie uero uirtute, doctrine facundia, | miraculorum
exhibitione, electis aliquando adest, aliquando se subtrahit." Et
Mk 242ᵛᵃ paulo post: "In his itaque | uirtutibus, sine quibus ad uitam minime
145 peruenitur, Spiritus sanctus in electorum suorum cordibus perma-
net; unde recte stabilis dicitur. In his uero per quas sanctitatis uirtus
Sb 267ʳᵃ ostenditur, aliquando misericorditer presto est, | aliquando miseri-
corditer recedit."

AMBROSIUS SUPER EPISTOLAM SECUNDAM AD CORINTHIOS:
150 "Ficta caritas est que deserit in aduersitate."   c.12
Ex premissis itaque apparet quod caritas semel habita ulterius d.p.c.12
non amittitur. Qui autem caritatem habuerit criminaliter peccare
Bi 301ʳᵇ non potest. Qui ergo caritatem semel habuerit criminaliter | ulterius
peccare non poterit, ut ad gratiam non ad naturam inpossibilitas re-
155 feratur.
Quod autem caritatem habens criminaliter peccare non possit,
testatur AUGUSTINUS IN OMELIA VIII dicens: "Quia *radix omnium* c.13
malorum est cupiditas, et radix omnium bonorum est caritas, et simul
ambe esse non possunt, nisi una radicitus euulsa fuerit, alia plantari
160 non potest. Sine causa aliquis conatur ramos incidere si radicem
non contendit euellere." Cum ergo qui criminaliter peccat caritatem d.p.c.13

---

136 Potest... **148** recedit] Ibid. (CCSL 142:62.170–179, 62.183–187)
150 Ficta... aduersitate] cf. Ambros., *In epist. B. Pauli ad Cor. secundam* 6.6 (PL
17:300B)   **157** Quia... **161** euellere] Caes. Arel., *Sermo* 182 (CCSL 104:739–40)

152 caritatem] *add.* semel R2 (*interlin.* Aa, *om.* Sb)

138 uero] *om.* Fs *interlin.* Bi Mk   **139** atque] et Aa Pf | bonis] multis Pf   **140** pa-
triam] gloriam Pf | sicut] sicuti Bi Pf   **141** misericordia] *add.* fecunda Fs | perfec-
torum] *add.* fecunda *interlin.* Bi Pf   **143** Et... **144** post] *interlin.* Fd   **147** est] *add.*
et Aa Fs Sb   **149** Ambrosius] *praem.* Item Pf Vnde EdF   **152** habuerit... **153** ca-
ritatem] *om.* EdF Fs Pf *exp.?* Bi   **154** poterit] potest Sb | referatur] inferatur Fd_{ac}
156 peccare] *pos.* possit Bi Fs Mk Sb   **157** in] *om.* Bi EdF Pf Sb

c.11   THE SAME IN THE SAME PLACE IN THE FIFTH HOMILY: "The wandering about and mobility of the Spirit can be understood in this way: certainly he persists in the hearts of the saints according to certain virtues; but according to certain things, he comes but will withdraw and withdraws but will come back. In faith, hope, and love and in the other good things without which there can be no coming to the celestial homeland (such as humility, chastity, justice, and mercy), he does not desert the hearts of the perfected. But in the virtue of prophecy, in the eloquence of teaching, in the producing of miracles, he is sometimes present to his elect and sometimes draws himself away." And a little later: "Therefore in these virtues, without which there is no attaining of life, the Holy Spirit persists in the hearts of his elect; whence he is rightly called stable. In these things, however, through which the virtue of sanctity is shown, sometimes in his mercy he is at hand, and sometimes in his mercy he withdraws."

c.12   AMBROSE SAYS IN HIS COMMENTARY ON 2 CORINTHIANS, "The love which abandons in adversity is feigned."

d.p.c.12   From the aforesaid, it is thus apparent that, once had, love is not lost anymore. But he who possesses love cannot sin mortally. Therefore, he who once has love can no longer sin mortally such that this impossibility may be attributed to grace, not to nature.

1 Tm 6:10
I Jn 4:13

But that the man possessing love cannot sin mortally is testified

c.13   to by AUGUSTINE, SAYING IN HOMILY 8: "Because *the love of money is a root of all evil* and love is the root of all good things, and both cannot exist simultaneously, if one is not utterly eradicated, the other cannot not be planted. Someone pointlessly tries to burn

1 Tm 6:10

Fs 304^{rv}   numquam habuisse probatur, euidenter colligitur penitentiam | non
agere qui quandoque criminaliter peccabit.

VNDE AUGUSTINUS: "Caritas est aqua de qua Dominus ait in   c.14
165   euangelio, *Qui biberit ex aqua quam ego dabo ei, non sitiet in eternum.*"
Reprobus ergo, cum eternis mancipatus incendiis in eternum sitiat,   d.p.c.14
quomodo bibet aquam uiuam aut quomodo potabit aquam salien-
Pf 109vb   tem | in uitam eternam, qui, quasi plumbeus demersus in ima, pe-
nas luit dampnationis eterne?

170   Item: Sine caritate quomodo ueram cordis contritionem quis
habere poterit? quomodo delictorum remissionem? que si non dimissa, quomodo non omnia prorsus ad penam exigenda? ITEM
DOMINUS: *Amen, amen dico uobis, qui credit in me habet uitam eternam.*
Qui ergo non habet uitam eternam in Christum non credit. In Chri-
175   stum uero credit qui caritatem habet. In Christum quippe credere
est amando in ipsum tendere. Hec est *fides*, UT DIFFINIT APOSTO-
LUS, *que per dilectionem operatur*; huic duntaxat delictorum remissio
promittitur. Quod si caritas a fide Christianorum seiungi nequit, cui
scilicet soli uenia promittitur, quomodo qui caritatem non habuerit
180   fidem Christianorum habuit, id est in Christum credidit? Quomodo
ergo ueniam delictorum accepit? Quam si non accepit, quomodo
non omnia prorsus eternis suppliciis ferienda? ITEM DOMINUS: *Ego*
Aa 156^r   *sum panis uiuus qui de celo descendi; si quis | manducauerit ex hoc pane*
uiuet in eternum. Qui ergo non uiuit in eternum non manducauit
185   panem uiuum, set qui non manducauit in eum non credidit. Hoc
Sb 267rb   est enim manducare | panem uiuum, quod credere in Christum, id
est amando tendere in ipsum. Cum igitur reprobus in eum non cre-
Fd 91vb   diderit, quem non manducauit, et ita fidem Christianorum (qua |
sola peccata laxantur) non habuerit, quomodo, si uiuit Dominus

---

164 Caritas…165 eternum] *fons materialis non invenitur*

171 quomodo] *add.* ergo R2 (*add.* ergo Aa Sb_{pc})   179 habuerit] habuit R2 (habuerit EdRom Fs)   182 omnia] *add.* opera R2 (*om.* Sb)   189 laxantur] relaxan-
tur R2 (Fd_{pc})

163 peccabit] peccauit EdF Fd Pf   164 ait] *om.* Bi Mk Sb *pos.* euangelio Fs
167 bibet] bibit Fd_{ac} bibat Aa Mk Pf   171 poterit] potuit Fd | que] qua Fd Fs *om.*
Bi Pf   175 uero] *om.* Fd | caritatem] ueritatem Fd | Christum] *add.* uero Aa Pf
quippe] *om.* Aa *pos.* credere Pf   177 delictorum] dilectorum Mk Pf_{ac}   183 de-
scendi] descendit Bi Mk Sb   185 credidit] credit Fd

d.p.c.13 branches if he does not strive to tear out the root." Therefore, since it is proven that he who sins mortally never had love, it is clearly gathered that he who will at some point sin mortally does not do penance.

c.14 AUGUSTINE THUS WRITES, "Love is the water of which the Lord says in the Gospel, *He who drinks from the water which I will give him* Jn 4:13

d.p.c.14 *will never thirst again.*" How, then, will the reprobate, when he thirsts eternally since he has been delivered up to the eternal fires, drink living water or lap up water flowing into eternal life when he suffers the punishment of eternal damnation as if a leaden man plunged into the deep?

Likewise: Without love, how can someone have true contrition of the heart? How[9] can he have remission of his transgressions? If they are not forgiven, how should not all of them be exacted instead for punishment? LIKEWISE, THE LORD SAYS, *Assuredly, assuredly I say to you, he who believes in me has eternal life.* Therefore, he Jn 6:47 who does not have eternal life does not believe in Christ. But he who has love believes in Christ. Indeed, to believe in Christ is to tend to him in love. This is *the faith,* AS THE APOSTLE DEFINES IT, Gal 5:6 *that works through love*; the remission of transgressions is to this extent promised to this faith. But if love cannot be disconnected from the faith of Christians, namely that to which alone mercy is promised, how did he who did not have love have the faith of Christians, that is, believe in Christ? How then has he received mercy for his transgressions? If he has not received mercy, how are they all[10] not instead to be struck with eternal torments? LIKEWISE THE LORD SAYS, *I am the living bread who has come down from heaven; if anyone eats of this bread, he will live forever.* Therefore he who does Jn 6:51 not live forever has not eaten the living bread, but he who has not eaten it has not believed in him. For to eat the living bread is this, to believe in Christ, that is, to tend to him in love. Therefore, since the reprobate does not believe in him whom he has not eaten and thus does not have the faith of Christians (by which alone sins are

---

9. Although it is possible that Gratian originally included a logical connector at this point, the manuscript evidence suggests he did not. If he did not, a "thereforc" sccms to have entered into the tradition quite early, making the sentence begin, "How, then, can he have...."

10. Gratian initially used simply *omnia*; its antecedent is the "transgressions." The second recension added a new word, *opera*, so that this question would read, "how are not all their works instead to be struck...?"

190 cui omne iudicium dedit Pater iudicium perpetue dampnationis effugiet omnium non solum actualium set et originalium?

<Responsio Gratiani>

Mk 242vb | Hec que de caritate dicuntur de perfecta intelligi possunt, que
semel habita numquam amittitur. Exordia uero caritatis enutriun-
195 tur ut crescant, et conculcantur ut deficiant. Nemo enim repente fit
summus, set in bona conuersatione, que sine caritate nulla est, a
Bi 301va minimis quisque inchoat | ut ad magna perueniat. Sunt itaque gra-
Fs 304va dus non solum inter uirtutem | et uirtutem set etiam in eadem uir-
tute.

200   VNDE GREGORIUS SUPER EZECHIELEM SCRIBIT, DICENS, "Dum   c.15
sanctam ecclesiam Dominus suscipit, in gradibus eius noscitur, quia
eius gloria per illius incrementa declaratur. Quantum enim sancta
ecclesia ascendendo profecerit, tantum Deus hominibus ex eius uirtute innotescit. De his quoque gradibus Beatus Iob loquitur, dicens,
Pf 110ra *Per singulos gradus meos pronunciabo illum.* Omnipotentem | quippe
Dominum per singulos gradus suos pronunciat, qui per incrementa
uirtutum que accipit ei semper laudem pietatis sue reddit. Si quidem gradus in cordis ascensione non essent, Psalmista non diceret,
Ambulabunt de uirtute in uirtutem. Nec mirum si de uirtute in uirtu-
210 tem gradus sunt, quando ipsa unaqueque uirtus quasi quibusdam
gradibus augetur et sic per incrementa meritorum ad summam perducitur.

"Alia namque sunt uirtutis exordia, aliud prouectus, aliud perfectio. Si enim et ipsa fides ad perfectionem suam non gradibus qui-
215 busdam duceretur, sancti Apostoli minime dixissent, *Auge nobis fidem.* Et quidam uenit ad Dominum, qui curare uoluit filium suum,
set requisitus an crederet, respondit, *Credo, Domine, adiuua increduli-*

---

200 Dum…**269** separatur] Greg. Magn., *Hom. in Hiezech. proph.* 2.3 (CCSL
142:238.57–241.131)

191 et] etiam R2 (*interlin.* Aa)   **201** noscitur] dinoscitur R2 (Aa$_{pc}$ Fd$_{pc}$, noscitur
Sb, dinoscetur Pf)   **207** quidem] quidam R2 (quidem Pf)

194 enutriuntur] et nutriuntur Aa Mk$_{pc}$ Sb   **202** gloria] ecclesia Fs Fd$_{pc}$ Pf
203 profecerit] proficit Aa EdF Fs Sb proficitur Bi$_{ac}$ Mk   **207** accipit] accepit Aa
Bi Mk | pietatis sue] *tr.* Aa EdF Sb   **213** perfectio] prouectio Fd   **216** curare] cu-
rari Aa EdF Pf

loosened), how, if the Lord to whom the Father has given all judgment lives, will he escape the judgment of perpetual damnation for all sins, not only actual, but also original?

<Gratian's Response>

These things which are said about love can be understood concerning perfected love, which is never lost once had. But the beginnings of love are nourished such that they grow, and they are trampled underfoot such that they fail. For no one suddenly becomes the best, but in a good way of life, which does not exist without love, each person starts out from the least things so that he may reach the great things. Therefore, there are degrees not only between one virtue and another but also within the same virtue.

c.15   AND SO GREGORY WRITES ON EZEKIEL, SAYING, "When the Lord welcomes his holy Church, it comes to be known[11] in its degrees, because his glory is declared through its increments. For the holy Church will have advanced in ascent to the extent that God is made known to men by its virtue. The blessed Job also speaks about these degrees, saying, *I will proclaim him through each individual degree of mine.* Certainly he who always renders the praise of his   Jb 31:37 piety to the omnipotent Lord through increments of the virtues which he receives proclaims him through his every individual degree. If indeed[12] there were not degrees in the ascent of the heart, the Psalmist would not say, *They will walk from virtue into virtue.* And   Ps 83:8 it is not wondrous if there are degrees from virtue into virtue when each individual virtue is enriched, as it were, in certain degrees, and is thus led through increments of merits to the highest virtue.

"For the beginnings of virtue are one thing, the progress of it another, and the perfection of it yet another. For if even faith itself were not being led in certain degrees to its perfection, the holy apostles would not have said, *Increase our faith.* And a certain man   Lk 17:5 who wanted the Lord to heal his son came to him, but when he

---

11. The second recension changes the verb so that the English translation would read, "it is distinguished in its degrees."
12. The second recension changed one letter, a *quidem* ("indeed") to a *quidam* ("certain"), thus rendering this phrase, "If there were not certain degrees in the ascent...."

tatem meam. Pensate, rogo, quod dicitur. Si credebat, cur incredulitatem dicebat? Si uero incredulitatem habere se nouerat, quomodo
220   credebat? Set quia per occultam inspirationem gratie meritorum
suorum gradibus fides crescit, uno eodemque tempore is qui ne-
cdum perfecte crediderat simul et credebat et incredulus erat.

"Hos nimirum gradus Dominus sub messis nomine describit, di-
cens, *Sic est regnum | Dei, quemadmodum | si iactet homo semen in terram,*
et dormiat, et exsurgat nocte ac die, et semen germinet, et crescat, dum nescit
ille. Vltro enim terra fructificat, primum herbam, deinde spicam, deinde
plenum frumentum in spica; et cum ex se produxerit fructus, statim mittit
falcem, quoniam adest tempus messis. Semen homo iactat in terram
cum cordi suo bonam intentionem inserit, et postquam semen iac-
230   tauerit, dormit quia iam in spe boni operis quiescit. Nocte uero surgit ac die, quia in aduersa et prospera proficit; et semen germinat et
crescit, dum nescit ille, quia et cum adhuc metiri incrementa sua
non ualet semel concepta uirtus ad prouectum ducitur; et ultro
terra | fructificat quia preueniente se gratia mens hominis sponta-
235   nea ad fructum boni operis assurgit. Set hec eadem terra primum
herbam, deinde spicam, deinde | plenum frumentum producit in
spica. Herbam quippe producere est inchoationis bone adhuc tene-
ritudinem habere. Ad spicam | uero herba uenit cum se uirtus
animo concepta ad prouectum boni operis pertrahit. Plenum uero
240   frumentum in spica fructificat quando iam tantum uirtus proficit ut
| esse robusti et perfecti operis possit. Set cum ex se produxerit fruc-
tus, statim mittit falcem quoniam adest tempus messis. Omnipotens
enim Deus producto fructu falcem mittit, et messem suam desecat
quia, cum unumquemque ad opera perfecta perduxerit, eius tem-
245   poralem uitam per emissam sententiam incidit ut granum suum ad
celestia horrea perducat. Cum igitur desideria bona concipimus, semen in terram mittimus. Cum uero operari recta incipimus, herba
sumus. Cum autem ad prouectum boni operis crescimus, ad spicam

Sb 267va | Aa
156^v

Fs 304vb

Mk 243ra

Bi 301vb

Pf 110rb

241 fructus] fructum R2 (fructus EdRom Sb)

218 rogo] *interlin.* Aa ergo Pf   **226** herbam] *add.* et Bi Mk   **227** fructus] fructum
Bi Mk Sb | mittit] mittet Fd_pc Bi Mk mittat Pf   **228** iactat] iacit Aa iactet Fs Sb
229 semen] semel Bi Fs Mk   **231** in] inter Aa_pc EdF Mk   **237** spica] spicam Bi
Mk   **238** herba] herbam Aa Mk   **243** suam] *om.* Fd Mk   **248** prouectum] pro-
fectum Mk Sb prospectum Fs

was asked if he believed, he answered, *I believe, Lord, help my unbe-*
lief. Think, I ask you, about what is being said. If he believed, why   Mk 9:23
was he talking about unbelief? Now if he knew that he had unbelief, in what way was he believing? But because faith grows in the
degrees of its merits through a hidden inspiration of grace, at one
and the same time, he who had not yet perfectly believed was simultaneously both believing and unbelieving.

"Indeed, the Lord describes these degrees in the terminology of
the harvest, saying, *The Kingdom of God is like if a man scatters seed on*
the ground, and he sleeps and then rises day and night, the seed both
sprouts and grows, while he does not know how. For on its own accord the
ground produces grain, first young shoots, then the head, then the full grain
in the head; and when it has produced the grains from itself, he immedi-
ately sends out the sickle since the time of harvest is at hand. A man   Mk 4:26–29
throws seed on the ground when he inserts a good intention into
his heart, and after he scatters the seed, he sleeps because he is already at rest in the hope of a good work. He rises night and day because he progresses between misfortunes and fortunes. And the
seed sprouts and grows while he does not know how because,
while he still cannot measure his increments, the virtue, once it has
been conceived, is led to completion. And the ground produces
grain on its own because, with grace coming before it, the mind of
the man of its own accord rises to the advance of the good work.
But this same ground produces first the young shoot, then the
head, then the full grain in the head. Certainly, producing the
young shoot is having as yet the softness of a good beginning. But
the young shoot grows into a head when the virtue conceived in
the mind draws itself to the advancement of the good work. But it
bears forth a full grain in the head when the virtue now advances
so much that it can be a strong and perfect work. But when the
grain produces from itself, the man immediately sends forth the
sickle since the time of harvest is at hand. For the omnipotent God
sends forth the sickle once the grain has been produced, and he
cuts away the harvest because, when he leads each individual to
perfect works, he kills his temporal life by the sentence that he ut-
ters so that he may lead his grain to his celestial storehouse. Therefore, when we conceive good desires, we send seed to the ground.
But when we begin to labor in righteous things, we are young

peruenimus, cumque in eiusdem operationis perfectione solidamur,
250 iam plenum frumentum in spica proferimus.

"Herba etenim Petrus fuerat qui, passionis tempore per amorem
Dominum sequens, hunc confiteri ante ancille uocem timebat. Erat

Fd 92ʳᵃ enim iam uiriditas in mente, quia credebat omnium redemptorem, |
set ualde adhuc flexibilis pede conculcabatur timoris. Iam in spica
255 surrexerat quando eum quem moriturum confiteri timuerat nuntiante angelo in Galilea uiuentem uidebat. Set ad plenum granum
in spica peruenerat, quando ueniente desuper Spiritu et suam men-

Sb 267ᵛᵇ | Aa tem in illius amore roborante, | ita solidatus est ut uires | perse-
157ʳ quentium cesus despiceret et redemptorem suum libere inter fla-
260 gella predicaret.

"Nullus itaque, qui ad bonum propositum adhuc in mentis tene-
ritudine esse conspicitur, despiciatur, quia frumentum Dei ab herba
incipit ut granum fiat. Vir ergo uenit ad portam quia Dominus ac
redemptor noster membris suis intrantibus perducit ad se, et ascen-
265 dit per gradus eius, quia nobis proficientibus eo nobis amplius exal-
tatur, quo altus et inconprehensibilis esse cognoscitur. In uirtutum
quippe nostrarum gradibus ipse ascendere dicitur, quia tanto ipse
nobis sublimior ostenditur, quanto noster animus a rebus infimis
separatur."

Fs 305ʳᵃ HINC ETIAM AUGUSTINUS AIT IN LIBRO DE LIBERO ARBITRIO, |
"Qui uult facere Dei mandata et non potest iam quidem habet bo- c.16
nam uoluntatem, set adhuc paruam et inualidam. Poterit autem
cum magnam habuerit et robustam. Quando enim martires illa
mandata magna fecerunt, magna utique uoluntate, id est magna
275 caritate fecerunt, de qua ipse Dominus ait, *Maiorem caritatem nemo
habet,*" etc. Et paulo post: "Ipsam caritatem apostolus Petrus non-

---

271 Qui... **279** ponam] Aug. Hipp., *De grat. et lib. arb.* 17 (PL 44:901)

251 etenim] enim Bi_ac Fs **257** suam mentem] sua mente Fs Sb **261** qui ad]
quia eius Bi Pf eius *interlin.* Bi **264** perducit] perducitur Aa Sb **265** nobis²] *interlin.* Bi, *om.* Mk Pf EdF **270** de] *add.* gratia et Pf Sb **274** mandata magna] *tr.*
Aa Sb

shoots. But when we grow to the advancement of a good work, we attain the status of a head, and when we are strengthened in the perfection of this same work, we bear forth now the full grain in the head.

"To be sure, Peter had been a young shoot when, at the time of the Passion, even though he followed the Lord out of love, he was afraid to confess him before the face of a maidservant. For there was already greenness in his mind, for he believed the Lord to be the Redeemer of all, but, still very much wavering, he was trampled upon by the foot of fear. He had already risen up into a head when, after an angel made the announcement, he saw alive in Galilee he whom he had been afraid to confess when he had been about to die. But he had reached a full grain in the head when, with the Spirit coming upon him and invigorating his mind in love for him, he was strengthened in such a way that, having been knocked down, he looked down upon the strength of his avengers and boldly proclaimed his redeemer among whips.

"Therefore, let no one who is observed to be still in the tenderness of mind with regard to a good intention be disdained, for the fruit of God begins as a young shoot so that it may become grain. A man thus comes to the gate dressed in linen because our Lord and Redeemer guides him to himself as his members enter in, and he ascends through his degrees, because, the more he is recognized to be high and incomprehensible, the more, as we are progressing, he is lifted up by us. Indeed, he is said to ascend in virtue by the degrees of our minds because, the more our mind is separated from the basest things, the more sublime he himself is shown to be by us."

FOR THIS REASON ALSO AUGUSTINE SAYS IN HIS BOOK ON FREE

c.16 WILL, "He who desires to do the commands of God and cannot surely has a good will already, but as yet a small and weak one. But he will be able when he has a great and robust one. For when the martyrs carried out those great commands, they undoubtedly did them with a great will, that is, with great love. The Lord himself speaks of this love: *Greater love hath no one than this*, etc. And a little   Jn 15:13

Pf 110ᵛᵃ dum | habebat quando timore ter Dominum negauit. Et tamen, quamuis parua et inperfecta, non deerat ei caritas quando dicebat, *Domine animam meam pro te ponam."*

280   IDEM SUPER EPISTOLAM IOHANNIS: "Si quis tantam habuerit
Mk 243ʳᵇ   caritatem ut paratus sit etiam pro fratribus | mori, perfecta est in illo
Bi 302ʳᵃ   caritas. Set numquid | mox, ut nascitur, iam prorsus perfecta est? Vt perficiatur, nascitur; cum fuerit nata, nutritur; cum fuerit nutrita, roboratur; cum fuerit roborata, perficitur; cum ad perfectum uene-
285   rit, quid dicis? *Mihi uiuere Christus est et mori lucrum."* In eadem: "Forte nata est in te caritas, set nondum perfecta. Noli desperare;   c.18 nutri eam ne forte suffocetur." In eadem: "Sicut seta introducit li-   c.17 num, ita timor caritatem; crescit caritas, minuitur timor, et e con- uerso." IDEM AD IERONIMUM: "Caritas in quibusdam perfecta, in   c.19
290   quibusdam inperfecta. Perfectissima autem in hac uita haberi non potest."

ITEM GREGORIUS: "Si sermo meus inuenerit in cordibus uestris   c.20 aliquam scintillam gratuiti amoris Dei, ipsam nutrite; ad hanc au- gendam uos aduocare studete." Et paulo post: "Flate, nutrite in uo-
295   bis ut, cum creuerit et flammam dignissimam fecerit, omnium cupi- ditatum ligna consumat."

Sb 268ʳᵃ   E contrario etiam gradus in uirtute | esse probantur quia et ipsius peccati gradus   d.p.c.20 euidenter apparent. Sicut enim nemo repente fit summus, ita nemo repente fit tur- pis.

300   HINC ETIAM AUGUSTINUS IN SERMONE HABITO IN MONTE: "Sicut tribus gra-   c.21
FdB 161ᵛᵃ   dibus | ad peccatum peruenitur: suggestione, delectatione, consensione; ita ipsius peccati tres sunt differentie: et in corde, et in facto, et in consuetudine, tamquam

---

280 Si…**285** lucrum] Aug. Hipp., *In Ioh. epist. ad Parthos tract.* 5 (PL 35:2014) **286** Forte…**287** suffocetur] Ibid. (PL 35:2018) **287** Sicut…**289** conuerso] Ibid. 9 (PL 35:2047–48) **289** Caritas…**291** potest] cf. Aug. Hipp., *Epistula* 167.4 (CSEL 44:602.12–14) **292** Si…**296** consumat] Aug. Hipp., *Sermo* 178.10 (PL 38:966) **300** Sicut…**307** agnoscit] Aug. Hipp., *De serm. Dom.* 1.12.35 (CCSL 35:38.823–31)

289 perfecta] *add. uel praem.* est R2 (Aaₚ꜀ Fdₚ꜀, *om.* Fs)

285 dicis] dices Biₚ꜀ Sb dicitur Pf **292** inuenerit] inuenit Aa Bi interuenerit Pf **293** scintillam] scintillulam Aa Pf **297** E] Ex AaB Bi Fs **300** habito] Domini Bi EdF Pf

later: "The apostle Peter did not yet have this very love when he denied the Lord three times on account of his fear. Nevertheless, although small and imperfect, love did not fail him when he said, *Lord, I will lay down my life for you.*"   Jn 13:37

THE SAME WRITES ON JOHN'S EPISTLE: "If anyone has so much love that he is ready to die for his brothers, his love has been perfected in him; but surely it has not been perfected already as soon as it is born, has it? It is born so that it may be perfected; when it has been born, it is nourished; when it has been nourished, it is strengthened; when it has been strengthened, it is perfected; when it has come to perfection, what does he say? *For me, to live is Christ,*
c.18 *and to die, gain.*" Likewise, in the same work:[13] "Love has perhaps   Phil 1:21
been born in you but has not yet been perfected. Do not despair;
c.17 nourish it, lest it by chance be suffocated." In the same work: "Just as a rope starts out from a bristle, so love starts out from fear; love grows as fear is lessened, and fear is lessened as love grows." THE
c.19 SAME IN A LETTER TO JEROME: "Love is[14] perfect in certain men, in certain men it is imperfect, but the most perfect love cannot be had in this life."

c.20   LIKEWISE, GREGORY: "If my sermon finds some spark of spontaneous love for God in your hearts, nourish it; be zealous to summon yourselves to increase it." And a little later: "Blow on it, nourish it in yourselves so that, when it grows and makes a most worthy flame, it will consume the wood of all carnal desires."

d.p.c.20   On the other hand, degrees in virtue are also proven to exist since degrees of sin itself are clearly apparent as well. For just as no one immediately becomes the best, so also no one immediately becomes foul.

FOR THIS REASON, AUGUSTINE ALSO SAYS IN HIS COMMENTARY ON THE
c.21 SERMON ON THE MOUNT: "Just as people reach sin in three stages: suggestion, delight, consent; so also are there three differences of the sin itself: in the heart, in the deed, and in habit, which are like three deaths: one as if in the home, that is, when

---

13. This edition produces the original order of the two texts that in later manuscripts and printed editions (including EdF) came to be called c.17 and c.18. I have followed the traditional numbering to avoid confusion in any literature referring to these texts, but I present the order of the texts (c.18 prior to c.17) as Gratian originally intended it.
14. This "is," implicit in the first recension, was made explicit in the second.

tres mortes: una quasi in domo, id est cum in corde consentitur libidini; altera, quasi prolata iam extra portam, cum in factum procedit assensio; tertia, cum in

Fs 305rb consuetudinis male tamquam mole terrena premitur | animus, quasi in sepulchro iam putens. Que tria genera mortuorum Dominum resuscitasse quisquis euangelium legit agnoscit."

ITEM GREGORIUS: "Sciendum quippe est quod peccatum tribus modis admitti- c.22
tur. Nam aut ignorantia, aut infirmitate, aut studio perpetratur, et grauius quidem

310 infirmitate quam ignorantia, set multo grauius studio quam infirmitate peccatur."

Pf 110vb Idem: "Inter hec | sciendum est, aliud esse quod animus de temptatione carnis pati- c.23
tur, aliud uero cum per consensum delectationibus obligatur. Plerumque enim cogitatione praua pulsatur, set renititur. Plerumque autem peruersum quid concipit intra semetipsum etiam per desiderium uoluit. Et nimirum mentem nequaquam cogi-

315 tatio inmunda inquinat cum pulsat, set cum hanc sibi per delectationem subiugat. Hinc etenim predicator egregius: *Temptatio uos non apprehendat nisi humana*. Humana quippe temptatio est qua plerumque in cogitatione tangimur etiam nolentes, quia, ut nonnumquam illicita ad animum ueniant, hoc utique in nobismetipsis ex

AaB 335^v humanitatis corruptibilis | pondere habemus. Iam uero demoniaca est et non hu-
Bi 302rb mana temptatio, cum ad hoc | quod carnis corruptibilitas suggerit per consensum se animus astringit."

ITEM IERONIMUS: "Super tribus sceleribus Damasci," etc., ut supra.   c.24

Mk 243va Non est mirum, si in uirtute gradus esse dicuntur, quandoquidem et peccati | d.p.c.24
gradus ita euidenter monstrantur.

Aa 157^v | Hec itaque caritas, que in Petro ante negationem herba fuit et in singulis nascitur antequam roboretur, ante sui perfectionem amittitur et reparatur. VNDE AUGUSTINUS IN LIBRO DE CORRECTIONE ET GRATIA: "Quicumque ab illa originali dampnatione ista diuine gratie largitate discreti sunt, non est dubium quin procuretur

330 eis euangelium, et, cum audiunt, credunt, et in fide que per dilec-

---

308 Sciendum…**310** peccatur] Greg. Magn., *Moralia in Iob* 25.11 (CCSL 143B:1253.2–5)   **311** Inter…**321** astringit] Ibid. 21.3 (CCSL 143A:1068.20–1069.34)   **328** Quicumque…**338** deputantur] Aug. Hipp., *De corr. et grat.* 7 (PL 44:924–25)

311 de temptatione] deceptione Sb   **313** pulsatur] prepulsatur FdB | renititur] remittitur FdB Fs Pf | peruersum] *add.* cor FdB   **322** sceleribus] generibus scelerum Bi Mk   **327** correctione] correptione Bi   **330** audiunt credunt] audierunt et crediderunt Pf | credunt] crediderint Fd_{pc}

one consents to lust in the heart; the second as if brought about already outside the door, when assent proceeds to deed; the third as if already rotting in the grave, when the mind is thrust forward in a mountain of evil habit. Whoever reads the gospel comes to know that the Lord has brought back to life these three types of the dead."

c.22   LIKEWISE GREGORY: "Surely it should be known that sin is committed in three ways. For it is perpetrated either out of ignorance or weakness or zealousness, and indeed the sinning which occurs out of weakness is more serious than that out of ignorance, but the sinning which occurs out of zealousness is much more serious

c.23   that that out of weakness." The same: "Among these things, it should be known that what the mind suffers from the temptation of the flesh is one thing, but it is another thing when it is bound through consent to pleasures. For very often it is struck with an improper thought but it resists. Very often, however, it desires even with longing within itself the perverse thing which it conceives. And doubtless an unclean thought in no way defiles the mind when it strikes, but when it subjugates it to itself with pleasure. Indeed for this reason the illustrious preacher says, *No temptation is to seize you other than what is human.* Surely human temptation is that with   1 Cor 10:13
which we are very often touched in our mind, even when we do not wish it, for we surely have this experience within ourselves as a result of the weight of corruptible humanity in such a way that illicit temptations never make it to the mind. For temptation is demonic and not human at the moment when the mind consensually strains itself to that which the corruptibility of the flesh suggests."

c.24   LIKEWISE JEROME: *"For three sins of Damascus,"* etc., as above.   cf. D.1 c.71

d.p.c.24   It is not wondrous if degrees in virtue are said to exist seeing that degrees of sin are also clearly shown in this way.

Therefore, this love, which was in Peter as a young shoot before his denial and is born in each individual person before it is strengthened, is lost and recovered before its perfection. AND SO AUGUSTINE IN HIS BOOK *DE CORREPTIONE ET GRATIA*: "Whatever persons have been distinguished from that original damnation by that abundance of divine grace, it is beyond doubt that the gospel, is procured for them, and, when they hear, they believe, and they

Sb 268rb

335

Fs 305va

340

Pf 111ra

tionem operatur usque in finem perseuerant, et, si quando exorbi-
tent, correcti | emendantur, et quidam eorum, etsi ab hominibus
non corripiantur, in uiam quam reliquerant redeunt," etc. In eodem: *Firmum fundamentum Dei stat habens signaculum hoc: Scit Domi-*   c.25
nus qui sunt eius. Horum fides, que per dilectionem operatur, profecto aut omnino non deficit, aut, si qui sunt quorum deficit, repa-
rantur antequam uita finiatur ista, | et deleta iniquitate que inter-
currerat usque in finem perseuerantia deputantur." In eodem:
"Nullus eorum ex bono in malum conmutatus finit hanc uitam." In   c.26
eodem: *"Talibus Deus diligentibus eum omnia cooperatur in bonum,* us-   c.27
que adeo prorsus omnia, ut etiam si qui eorum deuiant et exorbi-
tant, etiam hoc ipsum faciat eis | proficere in bonum."

345

Fd 92rb

ITEM APOSTOLUS AD GALATHAS: *Circumcisio non est aliquid, ne-*   c.28
que preputium, set fides que operatur per dilectionem. Et hoc olim in uobis,
quia currebatis bene per opera fidei et ex dilectione. ITEM AD EBREOS:
Non est tam iniustus Deus ut obliuiscatur operis uestri, etc.—operis: quod   c.29
| omnia sua fecerunt conmunia, et hoc ex dilectione, et hoc ad glo-
riam Dei. Ecce triplex bonum, quasi diceret, "Olim multa operati
estis, pro quibus, si penitetis de malis, benefaciet uobis Deus."

350

355

Romanos quoque et Galathas dum Apostolus redargueret, me-   d.p.c.29
rito fidei probat assecutos remissionem peccatorum, et sanctificationem in Spiritu sancto, et iustitiam bone operationis, que omnia aut
sine caritate numquam uere in eis fuerunt, aut ueram caritatem
habuerunt, a qua postea lapsi sunt qui de operibus legis gloriaban-
tur.

---

339 Nullus…342 bonum] Ibid. 9 (PL 44:929–30)

334 stat] *add.* inmobile R2 (Aa~pc~ Fd~pc~)   338 deputantur] deputatur R2 (deputantur Sb)   342 faciat] faciet R2 (Fd~pc~, faciat Pf Sb)   344 operatur] *pos.* dilectionem R2 (*pos.* que Pf)

332 correcti] correpti Bi Fs   334 Dominus] Deus Bi Fs Mk Sb   336 aut[1]] autem
Fd ut Bi~ac~   337 intercurrerat] intercucurrerat Fd Pf   338 perseuerantia] perse-
uerentie Pf Sb   340 Deus] *om.* Aa *exp.* Bi | cooperatur] cooperantur Aa Bi Fs Mk
Pf   346 quod] qui Aa quia Pf   353 ueram caritatem] ueritatem Fd~ac~

persevere all the way to the end in the faith which works through love. And if they get off track at times, after they are reproached, they are improved, and certain of them, even if they are not rebuked by men, return to the path which they had abandoned." In

c.25 the same place: "*The firm foundation of God stands,*[15] *having this seal: The Lord knows who are his.* Their faith, which works through love,   2 Tm 2:19 either does not entirely disappear from the one who has professed or, if there are some from whom it has disappeared, it is recovered before this life reaches its completion, and, since the iniquity which had interceded has been destroyed, they are considered[16] to stand

c.26 to the end in perseverance." In the same place: "Not one of them

c.27 ends this life changed from good to evil." In the same place: "*God works all things to the good for those who love him*, indeed all things in   Rom 8:28 such a way that, even if some of them deviate and turn aside, he also causes this very thing, for them to advance to good."

c.28   LIKEWISE THE APOSTLE TO THE GALATIANS: *Circumcision is not*   Gal 5:6–7 *anything, neither is uncircumcision, but faith that works through love. And this was formerly in you, for you were running well through works of faith*

c.29 *springing from love.* LIKEWISE TO THE HEBREWS: *God is not so unjust*   Heb 6:10 *as to forget your work,* etc.—the work: the fact that they had made all their things common, and this out of love, and this for the glory of God. Behold a threefold good, as if he were to say, "Formerly you labored in many things for which, if you were to repent of evil things, God would bless you."

d.p.c.29   When the Apostle speaks against the Romans as well as the Galatians,[17] he proves that, by the merit of faith, they have attained the remission of sins, sanctification in the Holy Spirit, and the righteousness of good work—all of which either, without love, were never truly in them, or they had true love, from which they who were boasting in the works of the law afterward fell away.

---

15. The second recension added "immobile": "The firm foundation of God stands immobile...."
16. The second recension changed the number of the verb, making it singular, and thus making either the perseverance or a single person the subject of the verb. It could be translated, "perseverance is considered to stand to the end."
17. Gratian is referring to the biblical texts (and surrounding passages) cited just previously in c.27 and c.28.

ITEM DE QUOLIBET ADULTO AUGUSTINUS AIT, "Tolle caritatem,   c.30
odium tenet." Item: "Omnis, *qui non diligit*, odit." ITEM IN EUANGE-   d.p.c.30
LIO: *Nemo potest duobus Dominis seruire; aut enim unum odio habebit, et
alterum diliget, aut unum sustinebit et alterum contempnet.* Adam ergo,
cum in uirili etate a Domino creatus sit, | antequam a diabolo temp-
taretur, dum de latere eius uxor formabatur, dum | in extasi raptus
angelice curie intererat, dum euigilans futura Christi et ecclesie sacramenta uaticinabatur, aut caritatem aut odium habebat. Si autem
odium habebat, non fuit diabolus auctor nostri peccati. Item, si sine
caritate a Deo creatus est, eius similitudinem nequaquam in sui
creatione accepit. Item, si sine caritate creatus est, iustus et innocens a Deo factus non est. Creatura namque, rationis capax et liberi
arbitrii, iustitie et innocentie sine caritate particeps | esse non po-
test. Colligitur ergo, quod Adam, antequam peccaret, caritatem habuit, sine qua iustus et innocens esse non potuit.

VNDE AUGUSTINUS IN GENESI | AD LITTERAM: "Quomodo | re-   c.31
nouari dicimur si non recipimus quod perdidit primus homo? ...
Hoc plane recipimus, quia iustitiam, ex qua per peccatum lapsus
est." Et paulo post: *"Expoliantes ueterem hominem, induite nouum, qui
renouatur in agnitione Dei secundum imaginem | eius qui creauit eum.*
Hanc imaginem in spiritu mentis inpressam perdidit Adam per peccatum." Et post pauca: "Stola illa prima ipsa iustitia est unde lapsus
est Adam." IDEM IN OMELIA XI: "Princeps uitiorum omnium, dum   c.32
uidit Adam ex limo terre ad imaginem Dei factum, pudicitia orna-
tum, temperantia conpositum, caritate splendidum, primos parentes a tantis bonis expoliauit, pariter ac peremit. Namque cum ho-

Margin left:
Bi 302va
Aa 158^r

365

Mk 243vb

370

Sb 268va |
Fs 305vb

Pf 111rb

380

---

356 Tolle…**357** tenet] Aug. Hipp., *In Ioh. epist. ad Parthos tract.* 7 (PL 35:2029)
357 Omnis…odit] cf. ibid. 5 (PL 35:2016)   **371** Quomodo…**374** est] Aug.
Hipp., *De Gen. ad litt.* 6.24 (CSEL 28.1:196.13–19)   **374** Expoliantes…**378**
Adam] Ibid. 6.27 (CSEL 28.1:198.25–199.2, 199.6–7)   **378** Princeps…**384** est²]
cf. Caes. Arel., *Sermo* 178 (CCSL 104:722)

381 a tantis] illis donis ac tantis R2 (arantis Sb)

358 enim] *om.* Bi Fd Fs Mk   **359** ergo] uero Aa EdF Fs Pf   **367** factus] *pos.* est Pf
om. Sb   **369** peccaret] peccare Fd_ac *add.* et Sb   **372** dicimur] dicuntur Mk_ac Pf
373 per] *om.* Fs Pf Sb   **374** Expoliantes] *add.* uos Aa EdF | hominem] *add.* et
Fd_pc Bi Fs Mk   **375** agnitione] agnitionem Fd Fs | Dei] fidei Aa_pc Bi EdF Fd Fs
Mk Pf (*mg.* Bi *interlin.* Mk)   **379** Dei] eius qui creauit eum Pf, *om.* Sb   **381** ac]
hos Aa

c.30   LIKEWISE, CONCERNING ANY ADULT, AUGUSTINE SAYS, "Take

d.p.c.30   up love, for otherwise hatred takes hold." Likewise: "Everyone *who does not love* hates." LIKEWISE IN THE GOSPEL: *No one can serve two*   1 Jn 3:10, 14 *masters; for either he will consider the one with hatred and love the other, or he will preserve the one and loathe the other.* Thus Adam, since he   Mt 6:24 was created by the Lord as a full-grown man, before he was tempted by the devil, while his wife was being formed from his side, while he was seized with ecstasy and attended the angelic court, while he was prophesying, watching carefully for the future things of Christ and the sacraments of the church, he possessed either love or hate. But if he possessed hate, the devil was not the author of our sin. Likewise, if he was created by God without love, in no way did he receive God's likeness in his creation. Likewise, if he was created without love, he was not made righteous and innocent by God. For a creature capable of reason and free will cannot be a participant of righteousness and innocence without love. Therefore it is gathered that, before he sinned, Adam possessed love, without which he could not be righteous and innocent.

c.31   AND THUS AUGUSTINE IN HIS *DE GENESI AD LITTERAM*, "How are we said to be renewed if we do not receive what the first man lost? ... We clearly do receive this, for we receive righteousness, from which he fell through sin." And a little later: "*Polishing the old man, put on the new one, who is renewed in the knowledge of God*[18] *according to the image of him who created him.* Adam lost this image impressed on   Col 3:9–10 the spirit of his mind through sin." And after a few lines: "That first robe is the very righteousness from which Adam fell." THE SAME IN

c.32   HOMILY 11: "When the prince of all vices saw Adam made in the image of God from the mire of the earth, adorned with virtue, ordered with temperance, shining with love, he ruined our first parents of good things[19] so great as these, and he moreover destroyed

---

18. Many manuscripts, including Fd, read "faith," not "God," but, based on the original reading in Aa and Sb, it seems that Gratian originally wrote "God."

19. The second recension made an addition so that the English translation would read, "ruined our first parents of those gifts and good things so great as these."

mini abstulisset pudicitiam, continentiam, suo dominio eum subiu-
gauit." Et paulo post: "Adam amissa temperantia intemperans factus est; perdita caritate malus inuentus est."

385   ITEM AMBROSIUS AD SABINUM: "Quando Adam solus erat, non   c.33
est preuaricatus quia mens eius adherebat Deo." Idem ad eundem:
"Primus homo recens Dei opus, confabulator assiduus, qui sancto-   c.34
rum conplantatus erat uirtutibus." IDEM IN EXAMERON: "Illa anima   c.35
a Deo pingitur que habet in se uirtutum gratiam renitentem, splen-
390   doremque pietatis. Illa anima bene picta est in qua elucet diuine
operationis effigies. Illa anima bene picta est in qua est splendor
glorie et paterne imago substantie. Secundum hanc imaginem, que
refulget, pictura preciosa est. Secundum hanc imaginem ante peccatum depictus fuit Adam; set ubi lapsus est, deposuit." IDEM DE
395   FUGA SECULI: "Similem esse Dei est habere iustitiam, sapientiam, et   c.36
Aa 158ᵛ   in uirtute esse perfectum." |

        IDEM DE UITA BEATA: "Sapiens numquam inanis est, set semper   c.37
in se habens amictum prudentie, qui potest dicere, *Iustitiam indue-*
bam, uestiebam iudicium. Mentis namque hec sunt interna uelamina
Bi 302ᵛᵇ   que nemo | alius potest auferre, nisi cum aliquem sua culpa despo-
liat. Denique sic spoliatus Adam nudus inuentus est." IDEM IN LI-
BRO DE YSAAC ET ANIMA: "Set nec Adam primus nudus erat, quem   c.38
innocentia uestiebat." IDEM IN LIBRO DE PARADYSO: "*Vt cognoue-*   c.39
runt quia nudi essent. Et ante quidem nudi erant, set non sine uirtu-
405   tum tegumento."

---

385 Quando...**386** Deo] Ambr. Med., *Epistula* 6.33.2 (CSEL 82.1:230.17–18)
387 Primus...**388** uirtutibus] Ibid., 6.34.16 (CSEL 82.1:237.111–113)
388 Illa...**394** deposuit] Ambr. Med., *Exameron* 6.7.42 (CSEL
32.1:233.26–234.6)   **395** Similem...**396** perfectum] Ambr. Med., *De fuga saeculi*
4.17 (CSEL 32.2:178.11–12)   **397** Sapiens...**401** est] Ambr. Med., *De Iacob et*
uita beata 2.5.22 (CSEL 32.2:44.11–16)   **402** Set...**403** uestiebat] Ambr. Med.,
De Is. uel an. 5.43 (CSEL 32.1:668.12–13)   **403** Vt...**405** tegumento] Ambr.
Med., *De paradiso* 13.63 (CSEL 32.1:322.20–22)

387 homo] *add.* quia Fd | recens] *pos.* opus Bi EdF   **389** renitentem] remitten-
tem Mk$_{ac}$ Sb   **392** que...**393** imaginem] *om.* Fs Sb   **404** erant] *add.* corpore Aa

them. For when he had snatched away the virtue, continence, love, and immortality of man, he bound him to his lordship." And a little later: "After his temperance was lost, Adam became intemperate; after his love was squandered, he was found to be evil."

c.33   LIKEWISE AMBROSE TO SABINUS: "When Adam was alone, he did not sin because his mind was clinging to God." The same to the

c.34   same recipient: "The first man was a fresh work of God, a perpetual conversant with him, and one who had been planted with the

c.35   virtues of the saints." THE SAME IN HIS *HEXAMERON*: "That soul is pictured by God which has in itself the resistant grace of virtues and the splendor of piety. That soul has been well pictured in which a likeness of the divine workings shines out. That soul has been well pictured in which there is a splendor of glory and an image of the paternal substance. In accordance with this image, which shines brilliantly, a picture is precious. Adam was represented before sin in accordance with this image, but when he fell, it was put

c.36   aside." THE SAME, IN HIS *DE FUGA SAECULI*: "To have righteousness, to have wisdom, and to be perfect in virtue is to be like God."

c.37   THE SAME ON THE BLESSED LIFE: "The wise man is never empty, always having in himself a mantle of prudence, and he is able to say, *I put on righteousness and I clothed myself with judgment.*   Jb 29:14 For these things are the internal clothes of the mind which no other person can take away except when he despoils someone with his guilt. And thereupon, having been spoiled in this way, Adam was found naked." THE SAME IN HIS BOOK ON ISAAC AND THE

c.38   SOUL: "But Adam was not naked at first, when innocence was

c.39   clothing him." THE SAME IN HIS BOOK *DE PARADISO*: "*When they recognized that they were naked.* And indeed they were naked before, but   Gn 3:7 not without the covering of virtues."

Fs 306ra | Opponitur etiam illud quod omnis clamat auctoritas: si sic   d.p.c.39
mansisset ut erat ante peccatum, esset translatus in gloriam, quam
habituri sunt sancti; set nemo adultus sine caritate intrat; caritatem
ergo habebat.

410   Item opponitur de Moyse, cuius fidem Apostolus in epistola ad
Ebreos conmendans, dignis preconiis eius merita predicauit, dum se
Pf 111va | Sb   negauit | esse filium filie Pharaonis, malens affligi cum | fratribus
268vb
Mk 244ra   quam perfrui | iocunditate temporalis peccati; dum fratri conpatiens
Egiptium sabulo obruit; dum ueritus animositatem regis Egiptum
Fd 92va   reliquit; dum diuino uallatus | auxilio regis furorem contempsit at-
que in uirtute signorum populum de Egipto eduxit. Que omnia
quibus laudibus sunt efferenda, si tunc caritas in eo non erat, cum
non habeat aliquid uiriditatis in se ramus boni operis, nisi procedat
ex radice caritatis? Quomodo autem caritatem non habebat, cui
420   Dominus facie ad faciem loquebatur sicut homo solet loqui cum
amico suo? Quomodo caritatem non habebat, qui pro populo supplicans dicebat, *Aut dimitte ei noxam hanc aut dele me de libro tuo?* An
non proximum diligebat, qui pro populo se obiciens, illum ab interitu liberauit? An non Deum diligebat, qui pro eo in uituli cultores
425   deseuiens, ipsius uituli caput in puluerem conminuit, atque, ut in
secessum proiceretur, aque inmixtum Israelitis bibendum dedit,
nonnullos ex eius cultoribus gladio feriri precipiens, ut populum,
cuius erat interitus maior futurus, Deo reconciliaret? An non caritatem habebat, de cuius spiritu Dominus accepit et super septuaginta
430   seniores Israelis posuit? Qui tamen ad aquam contradictionis de Dei
Aa 159^r | potentia siue de eius benignitate dubitans, cum cetera certa fide
promiserat, producturus aquam de petra, diffidenter excrepuit, di-
cens, *Numquid de petra hac potero uobis aquam educere?* Quod nulli
leue uideatur, cum in penam eius delicti sibi et Aaron a Domino

---

407 mansisset] permansisset R2   413 peccati] palatii R2 (*add.* peccati *sed exp.*
Mk, peccati Sb)   432 promiserat] promisissent R2 (Aa_{pc}, promiserat Sb)

410 epistola] *add.* sua Pf Sb EdF   412 filie] *interlin.* Aa *om.* Sb   413 perfrui] per-
flui Bi_{ac} Mk | temporalis] originalis Fd, *add.* uel temporalis *interlin.* Fd_{pc}   422 ei]
eis Aa Pf   433 educere] eicere Aa producere Pf

d.p.c.39   That which every authority proclaims is also propounded with the following argument: if he had remained thus, as he was before sin, he would have been translated into glory, which the saints are going to possess; but no adult enters without love; therefore he used to have love.

Likewise it is propounded with the example of Moses. Commending his faith in the epistle to the Hebrews, the Apostle preached his merits with worthy laudations: when he denied that he was the son of Pharaoh's daughter, preferring to be afflicted with his brothers rather than to enjoy thoroughly the delight of temporal sin;[20] when, suffering together with his brother, he covered over the Egyptian with gravel; when, fearful of the animosity of the king, he abandoned Egypt; when, protected with divine aid, he defied the king's rage and led the people out of Egypt in the power of signs. With what praises should all these things be proclaimed if there was no love in him at that time, since the branch of a good work has no life in it unless it proceeds from the root of love? But how did he, to whom the Lord spoke face to face just as a man is accustomed to speak with his friend, not have love? How did he not have love, who made supplication for the people, saying, *Either forgive them of this injury or erase me from your book*? Did he not love his neighbor, who offered himself for the people and freed them from annihilation? Did he not love God, who, raging on his behalf against the worshippers of the golden calf, crushed the head of that very calf to dust and, so that it might be given up for good, gave it mixed with water to be drunk by the Israelites, ordering some of its worshippers to be struck with the sword so that he might reconcile the people, whose very great annihilation was about to occur, to God? Did he not have love, from whose spirit the Lord took and placed upon the seventy elders of Israel? Nevertheless, at the waters of contention, doubting the power of God or his kindness, when he had put forth everything else with certain faith, when he was about to bring water forth from the rock, he spat out without confidence and said, *Will I be able to bring waters out of this rock for you?* Let this not appear trivial to anyone, because as a punishment for this offence, the Lord said to him and Aaron, *Because*

cf. Heb 11:23–29

Ex 32:32

Nm 20:10

---

20. The second recension (and Friedberg's edition) changed "sin" to "palace." Hebrews 11:25 reads as Gratian originally wrote, i.e. "sin," but the R2 version also makes historical sense since, as Gratian recalled, Moses was raised as Pharaoh's grandson.

435   dictum sit, *Quia non exaudistis uocem meam, ut glorificaretis me coram fi-*
      liis Israel, non introducetis populum hunc in terram quam dedi eis.

Bi 303ra   An non caritatem habebat Aaron quando fratri | coadiutor datus
      est ut esset os eius ad populum, ut per eum signa in Egipto fierent?
Fs 306rb   Qui tamen in cultura uituli postea populo consensum adhibuit. | An
440   non caritatem habebat quando ex omni multitudine filiorum Israel
      solus a Domino electus est ut pontificatu ante eum fungeretur? Si
      caritatem non habebat, bonus non erat; si autem bonus non erat,
      cur pre ceteris a Domino in pontificem electus est? An non carita-
      tem habebat quando pro populo cum thuribulo incendio se oppo-
445   suit et iram Domini placauit? Et tamen, ut premissum est, ad
Pf 111vb   aquam | contradictionis iram Domini aduersum se postea prouoca-
      uit.

      Numquid etiam Dauid caritatem non habuit, super quem spiri-
      tus Domini a die unctionis directus est? An forte dicetur esse direc-
450   tus super eum ut ex tunc gratiam prophetandi haberet, non ut ex
Sb 269ra   eo gratiam diuine dilectionis | acciperet? Quod absurdum plane ui-
      detur de eo sentire, de quo Dominus ait, *Inueni hominem secundum*
      cor meum. Quomodo etiam caritatem non habebat qui querenti ani-
      mam suam pepercit, et quia oram clamidis eius precidit, postea cor
Mk 244rb   suum grauiter percussit, clamans, *Quem persequeris rex Israel, canem* |
      mortuum et pulicem unum? Quomodo caritatem non habebat, qui
      mortem inimici sui tam grauissime tulit? Quomodo caritatem non
      habebat, qui aquam de cisterna Bethleem suorum periculo sibi ob-
      latam non bibit set coram Domino libauit? Quomodo caritatem non
460   habebat, qui irrisus a Michol, filia Saul, eo quod ante archam Do-
      mini cytharam et psalterium percutiens saltasset, ait, *Ludam, et uilior*
      fiam in oculis meis. Si caritatem non habebat, qua conscientia securus
      sibi ipsi inprecabatur, dicens, *Si reddidi retribuentibus mihi mala, deci-*
Aa 159^v   *dam merito ab inimicis meis inanis*? Si caritatem non habebat, qua | te-
465   meritate iuste se iudicari rogabat, dicens, *Iudica me, Domine, secun-*
      dum iustitiam meam et secundum innocentiam meam super me? Item: *Iu-*

---

456 pulicem] culicem R2 (pulicem Fs Pf Sb; *add.* uel c[ulicem] *interlin.* Pf)
466 Item] Idem R2 (Item Pf)

435 glorificaretis] sanctificaretis Aa   439 cultura] culpam Fs culturam Sb
443 electus est] factus est Aa   452 hominem] uirum Aa Pf   465 iudicari] iudi-
care Fd Fs Pf uindicare Sb | Domine] *om.* Pf Sb

you have not listened to my voice to glorify me before the sons of Israel, you will not lead this people into the land which I have given them. Nm 20:12

Did not Aaron have love, when he was given as an assistant to his brother so that he might be his mouth to the people, so that signs might be done in Egypt through him? Nevertheless, he afterward gave consent to the people in the worship of the calf. Did not he have love when he alone was chosen by the Lord from the whole multitude of the sons of Israel to execute the priesthood before him? If he did not have love, he was not good; but if he was not good, why was he chosen by the Lord before the rest as a priest? Did not he have love when he offered himself with the censer fire for the people and placated the wrath of God? And nevertheless, as has been mentioned, at the waters of contention he later provoked the wrath of the Lord against him.

Did not David also have love, upon whom the Spirit of the Lord was directed from the day of his anointing? Could it be that the Spirit would be said to have been directed upon him so that he might from that time on possess the grace to prophesy and not so that he might receive the grace of divine love from him? It is clearly absurd to think this about him concerning whom the Lord says, *I have found a man after my own heart.* How also did he not have love who spared the one seeking his life, who, because he cut off the edge of his cloak, afterward solemnly beat his breast, crying out, *Whom do you pursue, King of Israel, a dead dog and a flea?*[21] How did he not have love, who brought death to his enemy so very solemnly? How did he not have love, who did not drink the water from the cistern of Bethlehem offered to him because of the danger his men were in but poured it out as an offering before the Lord? How did he not have love, who, ridiculed by Michal the daughter of Saul because he had danced before the Ark of the Lord, playing a guitar and lute, said, *I will play, and I will become more lightly esteemed in my eyes.* If he did not have love, with what conscience did he fearlessly call down on himself, saying, *If I have returned evil to those giving it back to me, let me deservedly fall down lifeless by the hand of my enemies?* If he did not have love, with what foolhardiness did he ask that he be judged justly, saying, *Judge me, Lord, according to my right-* cf. 1 Sm 13:14; Acts 13:22

1 Sm 24:15

2 Sm 6:22

Ps 7:5

---

21. The second recension changed "flea" (*pulicem*) to "gnat" (*culicem*), but the original matched the Vulgate.

dica me, Domine, quoniam ego in innocentia mea ingressus sum? Et tamen post tot et innumera alia diuine et fraterne dilectionis indicia
quam grauiter deliquerit nullus ignorat qui Bethsabee adulterium
470 et Vrie homicidium audiuit. Cuius penitentiam si sine caritate Domino obtulit, ueram cordis contritionem non habuit. Quomodo
ergo sacrificium cordis contriti et spiritus contribulati Domino pro-
Fs 306ᵛᵃ mittere audebat, dicens, | *Si uoluisses sacrificium, dedissem utique; holo-
caustis non delectaberis. Sacrificium Deo spiritus contribulatus, etc.? Deni-
Fd 92ᵛᵇ que, cum false penitentie | nulla a Deo promittatur remissio, quo-
modo a Propheta audire meruit, *Dimissum est peccatum tuum,* si ueram contritionem cordis non habuit? Euidenter itaque apparet eum
Bi 303ʳᵇ tunc caritatem habuisse et ex caritate | sacrificium cordis contriti et
Pf 112ʳᵃ spiritus contribulati Domino obtulisse; alioquin temerarie | postu-
480 lasset, *Auerte faciem tuam a peccatis meis,* et cetera, que in eodem
Psalmo continentur, nisi odium mali et dilectio boni ad humilita-
tem penitentie illum prouocasset. De quo etiam SANCTUS AMBRO-
SIUS IN LIBRO DE ANIMA ET YSAAC SCRIBIT, dicens, "Fugerat sanctus Dauid odia Saul regis, non relinquens terras, set declinans con-
485 tagia regis inmitis et superbi, quia mens eius adherebat Deo," cui
sine caritate nullus adultus adherere potest. Et tamen, quam grauiter in populi dinumeratione postea deliquerit ipsius delicti pena in-
dicauit.

<Modus argumentationis secundus ex sententia
490 prima>

Item, secundum hanc sententiam qui criminaliter delinquit ueram peccatorum remissionem in baptismo consecutus non est, si

---

483 Fugerat…485 Deo] cf. Ambr. Med., *De Is. uel an.* 3.6 (CSEL 32.1:646.4–7)

468 fraterne] superne R2 (Aa, fraterne Pf Sb) | indicia] iudicia R2   484 Saul re-
gis] *tr.* R2   492 si…493 accessit] siue in annis infantie siue adultus ad baptisma
accessit R2 (*etiam in* Aa *sed praem.* si adultus ad baptisma accessit)

467 Domine] *om.* Aa Mk Sb   468 innumera alia] innumerabilia Aa Fs Pf
470 audiuit] addidit Bi audierit Pf   476 tuum] *om.* Bi Sb *interlin.* Mk
483 anima] Abraam Bi animabus Fs   485 cui] Qui Pf Sbₐ꜀   487 dinumeratione]
numeratione Biₚ꜀

eousness and according to my innocence upon me? Likewise[22]: *Judge me,* Ps 7:9
Lord, for I have entered into my innocence? And nevertheless, how Ps 25:1
gravely he offended after so many and innumerous other indications of divine and fraternal love[23] no one does not know who has
heard of the adultery with Bathsheba and the murder of Uriah. If
he offered his repentance to the Lord without love, he did not have
true contrition of the heart. Thus, how did he dare to promise the
Lord the sacrifice of a contrite heart and a crushed spirit, saying, *If*
you had wanted sacrifice, I would surely have given it; you will not delight
in sacrifices. A sacrifice to God is a crushed spirit, etc.? Finally, since no Ps 50:18–19
remission is promised by God for false repentance, how did he de-
serve to hear from the prophet, *Your sin has been forgiven,* if he did cf. 2 Sm
not have true contrition of the heart? It is clearly apparent, then, 12:13
that he had love at that time and that he offered to the Lord the
sacrifice of a contrite heart and a crushed spirit out of love; otherwise he would have rashly demanded, *Turn your face away from my*
sins, etc., which words are contained in the same Psalm, unless ha- Ps 50:11
tred for evil and love of good had called him forth to the humility
of repentance. SAINT AMBROSE ALSO WRITES OF THIS MATTER IN
HIS BOOK ON THE SOUL AND ISAAC, saying, "Holy David had fled
the hatred of King Saul, not leaving the land but avoiding the in-
fections of the fierce and proud king, because his mind clung to
God," to whom no adult can cling without love. And nevertheless,
afterward, in the enumeration of the people, how gravely he offended is indicated by the punishment of that very sin.

\<Second Mode of Argumentation from the First Po-
sition\>

Likewise, according to this opinion, he who offends with a mortal sin did not attain the true remission of sins in baptism, if he ap-

---

22. The second recension changed this connector, indicating similarity in content, to *Idem,* or "the same [author]."
23. Gratian was originally commenting on the "indications," or signs and
demonstrations, of David's love for both God ("divine") and his fellow man
("fraternal"), which the previous examples from David's life have most clearly
shown. Most later manuscripts (and Friedberg in his edition, although he
noted some original readings in a few of his manuscripts) changed "indications"
to "judgments" and "fraternal" to "supernal," so that the phrase would be translated, "after so many and innumerable other judgments of divine and supernal
love."

Sb 269rb adultus ad baptisma accessit, | quia Dei amorem non habuit, sine
quo nemo umquam gratiam inuenit, atque ita secundum heresim
495 Iouiniani, si uere ex aqua et Spiritu quis renatus est, ulterius criminaliter peccare non potest, uel, si criminaliter peccat, aqua tantum,
non Spiritu probatur esse renatus. Cui sentencie ILLUD EPISTOLE
IOHANNIS consentire uidetur: *Omnis qui natus est ex Deo peccatum non*

Aa 160^r *facit, quoniam semen ipsius in eo manet, et non | potest peccare quia ex Deo*
Mk 244va *natus est. In hoc manifesti sunt filii Dei, et filii diaboli.* | Et in fine epi-
stole: *Omnis qui natus est ex Deo non peccat, set generatio Dei conseruat*
eum, et malignus non tangit eum.

<Responsio Gratiani>

Verum hec auctoritas Apostoli quantum illi sentencie faueat at-
505 que illa secta erroris quam ueritati sit aduersa, IERONIMUS OSTEN-
DIT, SCRIBENS CONTRA IOUINIANUM, "Si enim," inquit, "omnis qui   c.40
natus est ex Deo non peccat et a diabolo temptari non potest, quomodo precipit ut caueant, ne temptentur, dicens, *Filioli, custodite uos*

Fs 306vb *a simulacris?* | Et in eadem rursus epistola: *Si dixerimus quia peccatum*
510 *non habemus, ipsi nos seducimus, et ueritas in nobis non est. Si confiteamur*
peccata nostra, fidelis est et iustus, ut remittat nobis peccata nostra et mun-
det nos ab omni iniquitate. Si dixerimus quoniam non peccamus, menda-
cem facimus eum, et uerbum eius non est in nobis. Estimo quod Iohannes baptizatus ad baptizatos scripserit et quod omne peccatum ex
515 diabolo sit. Ille peccatorem se confitetur, et sperat remissionem post
baptisma peccatorum. Et Iouinianus meus dicit, 'Ne tangas me,

Pf 112rb quoniam mundus sum.' Quid ergo? Contraria sibi Apostolus | lo-
quitur? Minime. In eodem quippe loco, cur hoc dixerit statim edi-

Bi 303va xit: *Filioli mei, hec scribo uobis ut non peccetis; set si quis peccauerit,* |
520 *aduocatum habemus apud Patrem, Iesum Christum iustum, et ipse est pro-*
pitiatio pro peccatis nostris—non pro nostris autem tantum, set etiam pro

---

506 Si … **700** nuptiarum] Hier., *Aduers. Jou.* 2.2–4 (PL 23:283A–289B)

500 hoc] *add.* enim R2 (*interlin.* Aa Sb)   **502** eum²] illum R2   **512** peccamus]
peccauimus R2   **513** quod] *add.* beatus R2 (*om.* Pf Sb)   **516** peccatorum] *pos.*
remissionem R2 (*pos.* baptisma *sicut in R1* Pf Sb)

493 habuit] habuerit Aa Fs   **501** generatio] gratia Aa   **508** caueant … temptentur] caueat ne temptaretur Bi   **509** simulacris] simulationibus Fd   **511** mundet]
emundet Aa_pc EdF emundabit Bi Fs Sb mundabit Mk emundabis Pf   **517** quoniam] quia Fs Mk Pf | mundus] *add.* ego Bi Fs Mk | ergo] igitur Bi Mk Sb
519 set] *add.* et Aa EdF   **520** habemus] habens Bi Sb (*ant.* aduocatum Bi)

proached baptism as an adult,[24] because he did not have love for God, without which no one ever finds grace. And therefore, according to the heresy of Jovinian, if anyone has truly been reborn by the water and the Spirit, he can no longer sin mortally, or, if he does sin mortally, it is proven that he was reborn by water alone, not by the Spirit. THAT TEXT OF THE EPISTLE OF JOHN seems to agree with this opinion: *Everyone who is born of God does not sin, because his seed remains in him; and he cannot sin because he is born of God. The*[25] *sons of God are made known in this, and the sons of the devil.* And, at the end of the epistle: *Everyone who is born of God does not sin, but the generation of God preserves him, and the evil one does not touch him.*

1 Jn 3:9

1 Jn 5:18

<Gratian's Response>

Nevertheless, how much this authority of the apostle favors that opinion, and how much those erroneous doctrines are adverse to the truth, JEROME SHOWS WHEN WRITING AGAINST JOVINIAN: "For if," he says, "everyone who is born of God does not sin and cannot be tempted by the devil, in what way does he command that they take care lest they be tempted, saying, *Little children, guard yourselves from idols?* And again in the same epistle: *If we should say that we do not have sin, we deceive ourselves, and the truth is not in us. If we should confess our sins, he is faithful and just to forgive us our sins and to cleanse us from all iniquity. If we should say that we do not sin,*[26] *we make him a liar, and his Word is not in us.* I think that John,[27] baptized himself, was writing to the baptized and that every sin is of the devil. He confesses that he is a sinner, and he hopes for the remission of sins after baptism. And my Jovinian says, 'Do not touch me, for I am clean.' What then? Does the apostle contradict himself? Hardly. For in the same place, he has immediately declared why he has said this: *My little children, I write these things to you so that you may not sin; but even if someone sins, we have an advocate with the Father, Jesus Christ the righteous, and he himself is the propitiation for our sins—but*

c.40

1 Jn 5:21

1 Jn 1:8–10

24. A very early alteration changed this clause to "whether he approached baptism in the years of infancy or adulthood." Fd has the original reading, Aa has the original reading preceded by the altered text, and the other collated manuscripts and Friedberg have merely the later text.
25. The second recension added a "for" at the beginning of this clause: "For the sons of God...."
26. The second recension changed the tense (in accordance with the Vulgate of 1 John): "that we have not sinned...."
27. The second recension calls John here "the blessed John."

totius mundi. Et in hoc scimus quoniam cognouimus eum, si mandata eius
obseruemus. Qui dicit se nosse eum, et mandata eius non custodit, mendax
est, et in eo ueritas non est. Qui autem seruat uerbum eius, uere in hoc per-
525 *fecta caritas Dei est. In hoc scimus quoniam in ipso sumus. Qui dicit se in*
ipso manere debet, sicut ille ambulauit, et ipse ambulare. Propterea scribo
uobis, filioli mei, *omnis qui natus est ex Deo non peccat.* Ideo dico uobis
ut non peccetis, et tamdiu uos sciatis in generatione Domini permanere, quamdiu non peccaueritis; immo, qui in generatione Domini
530 perseuerant peccare non possunt. Que enim conmunicatio luci et
Sb 269ᵛᵃ tenebris? | Christo et Belial? Quomodo dies et nox misceri ne-
queunt, sic iustitia et iniquitas, peccatum et bona opera, Christus et
antichristus. Si susceperimus Christum in hospitio pectoris nostri,
illico fugamus diabolum. Si peccauerimus et per peccati ianuam in-
Aa 160ᵛ gressus fuerit diabolus, protinus Christus | recedit. Vnde et Dauid
post peccatum: *Redde mihi,* ait, *letitiam salutaris tui,* scilicet quam
peccando amiserat. *Qui dicit se nosse Deum et mandata eius non custodit,*
mendax est, et in eo ueritas non est. Christus ueritas appellatur, immo
est: *Ego sum uia, ueritas, et uita.* Frustra in eo nobis applaudimus
Fs 307ʳᵃ cuius mandata | non facimus. *Scienti bonum, et non facienti illud, pecca-*
Fd 93ʳᵃ *tum* | *est. Quomodo enim corpus sine spiritu mortuum est, sic et fides sine*
operibus mortua est. Nec grande putemus unum Deum nosse, cum *et*
Mk 244ᵛᵇ *demones credant et contremiscant.* | *Qui dicit se in ipso manere debet, sicut*
ille ambulauit, et ipse ambulare.

545   "Eligat aduersarius quod uult e duobus, optionem damus: manet in Christo, an non manet? Si manet, ita ergo ambulet ut Christus. Si autem temerarium est similitudinem uirtutum Domini polliceri, non manet in Christo quia non ingreditur ut Christus. Ille
peccatum non fecit, nec inuentus est dolus in ore eius, qui cum
550 malediceretur non remaledicebat, et tamquam agnus coram ton-

---

523 eum] Deum R2   **539** sum] *add.* inquit R2 (inquam Sb)   **545** e duobus] *ant.*
quod R2   **550** remaledicebat] remaledixit R2 (maledixit Fs Pf) | tondente] *add.*
se R2 (*om.* Sb)

523 obseruemus] obseruamus Aa Pf Sb   **526** ipso] eo Bi Fs Mk   **532** sic] *add.* et
Fd | peccatum] peccata Fd   **533** susceperimus] suscepimus Bi Fs Mk Pf suscipi-
mus Sb   **540** illud] illi *pos.* est Aa Pf   **542** unum Deum] *praem.* esse Fs *add.* esse
Sb   **543** contremiscant] contremescant Bi Fs   **550** remaledicebat] maledixit Fd_{ac}
Pf

not only for us, but also for those of the whole world. And in this we know *that we have come to know him, if we observe his commands. He who says* *that he knows him*[28] *and does not keep his commandments is lying, and the* *truth is not in him. But in him who keeps his word, the love of God has* *truly been perfected. In this we know that we are in him. He who says that* *he abides in him ought himself also to walk just as he walked.* For this   1 Jn 2:1–6 reason, I write to you, *my little children, everyone who is born of God* *does not sin.* And thus I say to you, do not sin, and as long as you   1 Jn 5:18 know that you abide in the generation of the Lord, do not sin; nay rather, those who persevere in the generation of the Lord cannot sin. For what communication does light have with darkness? Christ with Belial? And therefore day and night are unable to mix, like righteousness and iniquity, sin and good works, Christ and the Antichrist. If we should welcome Christ into the chamber of our breast, we instantly cause the devil to flee. If we should sin and the devil should enter through the door of sin, Christ departs immediately. Thus, after his sin, David also said, *Restore unto me the joy of*   Ps 50:14 *your salvation,* which he had indeed lost by sinning. *He who says that* *he knows God and does not keep his commandments, is lying, and the truth* *is not in him.* Christ is called—nay rather, is—the Truth: *I am*[29] *the*   1 Jn 2:4 *Way, the Truth, and the Life.* In vain do we clap for ourselves in him   Jn 14:6 whose commandments we do not perform. *The person who knows the* *good but does not do it sins. For in the way that a body without a spirit is*   Jas 4:17 *dead, so also faith without works is dead.* And let us not think it grand   Jas 2:26 to know that there is one God, for *even the demons believe and trem-* *ble. He who says that he abides in him ought himself to walk also just as he*   Jas 2:19 *walked.*   1 Jn 2:6

"Let our opponent choose what he wants from two things; we give him the option: Does he abide in Christ or not? If he abides, then let him walk as Christ did. But if it is rash to promise an imitation of the Lord's virtues, he does not abide in Christ because he does not walk as Christ did. He did not sin, and no deceit was found in his mouth. When he was cursed, he did not curse back,

---

28. The second recension specified that this "him" is "God."
29. At this point, the second recension interjected a "he says": "I am," he says, "the Way...."

dente, sic non aperuit os suum; ad quem uenit princeps mundi

huius, et inuenit in eo nichil; qui cum peccatum I non fecisset, pro
nobis peccatum eum fecit Deus. Nos autem iuxta epistolam Iacobi
multa peccamus omnes, et nemo mundus a peccatis, nec infans, si
555 unius quidem diei fuerit uita eius. Quis enim gloriabitur castum se
habere cor, aut quis confidet mundum se a peccatis esse? tenemur-
que rei in similitudinem preuaricationis Ade. Vnde et Dauid: *Ecce*,
ait, *in iniquitatibus conceptus sum, et in delictis peperit me mater mea.* Et
Beatus Iob: *Si fuero iustus, os meum inpia loquetur, et si sine crimine,*
Bi 303vb *prauus inueniar, et si purificatus I in niue et lotus mundis manibus, satis*
me sorde tinxisti, et execratum est uestimentum meum.

"Verum, ne penitus desperemus, arbitrantes nos post peccata
baptismi non posse saluari, statim hoc ipsum temperat: *Et si quis pec-*
cauerit, aduocatum habemus apud Patrem Iesum Christum, et ipse est pro-
565 *pitiatio pro peccatis nostris; non pro nostris autem tantum, set etiam pro to-*
tius mundi. Hoc ad credentes post baptisma loquitur et aduocatum
pro delictis eorum Dominum pollicetur. Nec dicit, 'Si quid peccaue-
Sb 269vb ritis, aduocatum habetis apud Patrem I Iesum Christum, et ipse est
propitiatio pro peccatis uestris,' ne eos diceres non plena fide bapti-
570 sma consecutos; set, *aduocatum*, inquit, *habemus apud Patrem, et ipse*
Fs 307rb *est I propitiatio pro peccatis nostris*, et non solum pro Iohannis aliorum-
que peccatis, *set etiam pro totius mundi.* In toto autem mundo et Apo-
Aa 161^r stoli sunt omnesque credentes. Ex quibus I liquido conprobatur post
baptismo posse peccari. Frustra enim aduocatum habemus Iesum
575 Christum si peccari non potest. Petrus apostolus, ad quem dictum
fuerat, *Qui lotus est non habet necesse ut iterum lauet*; et, *Tu es Petrus, et*
super hanc petram edificabo ecclesiam meam, ab ancilla perterritus negat. Et ipse Dominus: *Simon, Simon, ecce*, inquit, *Sathanas postulauit*

---

564 Christum] *add.* iustum R2   **574** habemus] *add.* apud Patrem R2 (*om.* Sb)
578 Simon²] *om.* R2 (Aa_{ac})

552 huius] istius Bi EdF Mk Sb, *ant.* mundi Aa Pf   **553** eum] *om.* Bi Fs Mk Sb
eum fecit] factus est Aa I fecit Deus] factus est Fs   **555** quidem diei] *tr.* Mk EdF
Sb diei quid Fs   **557** Ade] Adam Bi Fd Fs   **558** in¹] *om.* Bi Sb   **560** prauus] par-
uus Fd_{ac} Sb I niue] nie? me? Fd nineue Sb   **562** post] propter Pf Sb   **563** sal-
uari] lauare Sb   **567** Dominum] Deum Bi Mk   **568** habetis] habemus Pf habentes Sb   **569** ne] nec Aa Sb I diceres] dicit Aa diceret Bi dicens Sb   **570** Patrem]
add. Iesum Christum Mk Pf EdF   **571** aliorumque] illorumque Fd EdRom
572 et] *om.* Bi   **574** baptismo] baptisma Aa Bi Mk I peccari] peccare EdF Fs Mk
578 Simon²] *interlin.* Aa

and like a lamb before its shearer, he did not open his mouth. The prince of this world came to him, and he effected nothing in him. Since he had not sinned, God made him sin on our behalf. According to the epistle of James, however, we all sin many times, and no one is untainted by sins, and neither is an infant, if his life should last but one day. For who will boast that he has a spotless heart? Or who has confidence that he is untainted by sins? And we are subject to this reality in the likeness of the transgression of Adam. And so also David says, *Behold, I was conceived in iniquity, and my mother bore me in sin.* And the blessed Job: *If I am righteous, my mouth will speak wicked things, and if I am without sin, I will be found depraved, and if I have been purified in snow and washed with clean hands, you have sufficiently bathed me with filth, and my clothing has been cut away.* Ps 50:7

Jb 9:28–31

"But, lest we despair completely, thinking that we cannot be saved after the sins of our baptism, John immediately tempers this very statement: *And if someone sins, we have an advocate with the Father, Jesus Christ,*[30] *and he is a propitiation for our sins—but not only for our sins, but also for those of the whole world.* He speaks this to believers after baptism and promises an advocate, the Lord, for their sins. He does not say, 'If you commit some sin, you will have an advocate before the Father, Jesus Christ, and he is a propitiation for your sins,' lest you say that they did not attain their baptism with full faith; but he said, *We have an advocate with the Father, Jesus Christ, and he is a propitiation for our sins,* and not only for the sins of John and the others, *but also for those of the whole world.* But even the apostles are in the whole world, and all believers. From these things it is clearly proven that, after baptism, sinning is possible. For in vain do we have an advocate with the Father, Jesus Christ, if there cannot be sinning. The apostle Peter, to whom it had been said, *He who has been washed does not have need to wash again,* and, *You are Peter, and on this rock I will build my church,* was frightened thoroughly by a maid-servant and denied Christ. And the Lord 1 Jn 2:1–2

Jn 13:10
Mt 16:18

---

30. The second recension adds, in accordance with the biblical text, "the Righteous."

uos ut cribraret quasi triticum; ego autem rogaui pro te ne deficeret fides
580 *tua."*

Et infra: "Si non peccamus post baptisma, cur nobis poscimus peccata dimitti, que in baptismate iam dimissa sunt? Aliud autem

Pf 112vb est si ad catecuminos hec oratio pertinet, *dimitte nobis debita | nostra sicut et nos dimittimus debitoribus nostris* et non conuenit fidelibus et
585 Christianis. Paulus electionis uas castigat corpus suum, et in seruitutem redigit, ne aliis predicans ipse reprobus inueniatur. Ad

Mk 245ra Ebreos quoque scribens | ait, *Inpossibile est enim eos, qui semel sunt illuminati et gustauerunt donum celeste et participes facti Spiritus sancti, gustauerunt nichilominus bonum Dei uerbum uirtutesque seculi futuri, et*
590 *prolapsi sunt, renouari iterum ad penitentiam, rursus crucifigentes sibimetipsis filium Dei et ostentui habentes.* Certe eos, qui illuminati sunt et gustauerunt donum celeste et participes facti sunt Spiritus sancti gustaueruntque bonum Dei uerbum, negare non possumus baptizatos. Si autem baptizati peccare non possunt, quomodo nunc Apo-
595 stolus dicit, *Et prolapsi sunt?* Verum ne Montanus et Nouatus hic redeant, qui contendunt non posse renouari per penitentiam eos, qui crucifixerunt sibimet filium Dei et ostentui habuerunt, consequenter hunc errorem soluit et ait, *Confidimus autem de uobis, dilectissimi, meliora et uiciniora saluti, tametsi ita loquimur. Non enim iniustus Deus ut*

Bi 304ra *obliuiscatur operis uestri | et dilectionis quam ostendistis in nomine ipsius, qui ministrastis sanctis et nunc ministratis.* Et reuera grandis iustitia Dei, si tantum peccata puniret et bona opera non susciperet? 'Locutus sum,' inquit Apostolus, 'ita, ut uos a peccatis retraherem et de-

Fs 307va sperationis | metu facerem cautiores. Ceterum confido de uobis ca-
605 rissimi, meliora et uiciniora saluti. Neque enim iustitie Dei est ut

---

582 autem…583 est] *tr.* R2   595 hic] hinc R2 (hic Sb)   599 Non…Deus] Non est iniustus Dominus R2   601 iustitia] iniustitia R2

579 quasi] sicut EdF Fs Pf Sb | deficeret] deficiat Pf Sb   584 et³] *interlin.* Aa *om.* Fs Pf   588 facti] *add.* sunt Aa Bi Mk EdF   593 gustaueruntque] -que *interlin.* Aa et gustauerunt Pf Sb | Dei] fidei Fd   599 saluti] salutis Fd   601 ministrastis] ministratis Fd Pf | sanctis…ministratis] *om.* Aa | ministratis] ministrate Fd   603 a peccatis] *pos.* retraherem Bi Fs Mk

himself said, *Simon, Simon,*[31] *behold, Satan has demanded to sift you like wheat; but I have pleaded for you that your faith might not fail."*   Lk 22:31

And below: "If we do not sin after baptism, why do we ask that our sins be forgiven us, which have already been forgiven in baptism? But it is one thing if this prayer pertains to catechumens, *Forgive us our debts as we forgive our debtors,* and does not apply to the   Mt 6:12
faithful and to Christians. Paul, a choice vessel, chastens his body and reduces it to servitude, lest, while preaching to others, he himself be found to be reprobate. Writing also to the Hebrews, he says, *For it is impossible for those who have once been enlightened and have tasted the heavenly gift and, having been made partakers of the Holy Spirit, have no less tasted the good Word of God and the powers of the age to come, and then have fallen away, to be renewed again to repentance, since they have crucified the Son of God again to themselves and made him a public spectacle.* Certainly we cannot deny that those who have been illu-   Heb 6:4–6
minated and tasted the heavenly gift and been made partakers of the Holy Spirit and have tasted the good Word of God are baptized. But if the baptized cannot sin, how does the apostle say next, *And they have fallen away?* But, lest Montanus and Novatus return at this juncture[32] and contend that those who have crucified the Son of God to themselves and made him a public spectacle cannot be renewed through repentance, he consequently removes this error and says, *But, dearly beloved, we have confidence in better things concerning you and things kindred to salvation, though we are speaking this way. For God is not unjust*[33] *that he would forget your work and the love which you have shown in his name as you have ministered to the saints and still do.* And how grand in fact would the justice[34] of God be, if he were   Heb 6:9–10
only to punish sins and were not to accept good works? 'I spoke in this way,' the apostle says, 'so that I might draw you back from sins and make you more careful with the fear of despair. Notwithstand-

---

31. The second recension removed this second "Simon."

32. The second recension changed a *hic* to a *hinc*, so that the phrase "at this juncture" would be rendered "on this account."

33. The second recension removed the "for," made the "is" explicit (originally it was simply implied), and changed "God" to "the Lord." The phrase as a whole would read, "The Lord is not unjust...."

34. Gratian originally wrote "justice," but the second recension corrected it to "injustice." In either formulation, the verb "to be" is gapped. Gratian's original rendering makes sense only if he understood the sentence to be a question, and so I have translated it as such. The second recension makes sense only if "to be" is a subjunctive, setting forth a hypothetical statement. That version would read, "And in fact it would be a grand injustice on the part of God...."

Fd 93rb obliuiscatur bonorum | operum et ministerii, quod propter nomen
eius exhibuistis et exhibetis in sanctos, et tantum meminerit peccatorum.'"

Sb 270ra Et paulo post: "Liberi | arbitrii nos condidit Deus, nec ad uirtu-
Aa 161^{v} tem | nec ad uitia necessitate trahimur; alioquin, ubi necessitas nec
corona est. Sicut in bonis operibus perfector est Deus (non est enim
uolentis, neque currentis, set miserentis et adiuuantis Dei, ut peruenire ualeamus ad calcem), sic in malis atque peccatis semina nostra sunt incentiua, et perfectio diaboli. Cum uiderit nos super fun-
615   damentum Christi edificasse fenum, ligna, stipulam, tunc supponit
Pf 113ra incendium. Edificemus aurum, | argentum, lapides pretiosos, et
temptare non audebit. Quamquam et in hoc non sit certa et secura
possessio. Sedet quippe leo in insidiis ut in occultis interficiat inno-
centem, et uasa figuli probat fornax, homines autem iustos tempta-
620   tio tribulationis. Et in alio loco scribitur, *Fili, accedens ad seruitutem*
Dei, prepara te ad temptationem. Rursus idem Iacobus loquitur, *Estote*
factores uerbi et non auditores tantum. Si quis auditor est uerbi et non fac-
tor, iste similis est uiro qui considerat uultum natiuitatis sue in speculo; con-
siderauit illud et statim recedens oblitus est qualis sit. Frustra monuit ut
625   iungerent opera fidei, si post baptisma peccare non poterant. *Qui to-*
tam, inquit, *legem seruauerit, et peccauerit in uno, factus est omnium reus.*
Mk 245rb Quis nostrum absque | peccato est? Conclusit Deus omnia sub de-
licto ut omnibus misereatur.

"Petrus quoque: *Nouit,* inquit, *Deus pios de temptatione eripere.* Et
630   de falsis doctoribus: *Hi sunt fontes sine aqua et nebule turbinibus exagi-*
tate, quibus caligo tenebrarum reseruatur. Superbia enim uanitatis loquen-
tes pellicent in desideriis carnis luxurie eos, qui paululum effugerant et ad
errorem conuersi sunt. Nonne tibi uidetur pinxisse sermo apostolicus
nouam imperitie factionem? Aperiunt enim quasi fontes scientie,

---

612 Dei] *pos.* miserentis R2   **621** loquitur] ait R2

617 et^2] *om.* Fd Fs Mk   **620** accedens] accede Fs Sb   **621** loquitur] *add.* dicens
Aa   **623** qui considerat] consideranti Aa   **624** est] sit Fd *om.* Fs | sit] fuerit Bi
Mk fuit Fs est Pf   **625** iungerent] iungerentur Bi Fs Mk Pf   **632** pellicent] pelli-
ciunt Bi EdF polliceret Fs$_{ac}$

ing, dearly beloved, I have confidence in better things concerning you and things kindred to salvation. For it does not belong to the justice of God to forget good works and the ministry which you have exhibited and do exhibit in his name toward the saints and to remember only your sins.'"

And a little later: "God made us with free will, and we are not drawn to either virtue or vices; moreover, where there is necessity, there is no crown. Just as God is the One who perfects in good works (for it is not about a person willing or running but God who has mercy and assists so that we may be able to reach the goal), so also in evil things and sins, our seeds are the inciters, and the completion belongs to the devil. When he sees that we have built with hay, wood, and straw upon the foundation of Christ, then he sets a fire. Let us build with gold, silver, and precious stones, and he will not dare to try, although even in this our possession is not safe and secure. Indeed, a lion lies in wait so that it may kill the innocent in secret, and the kiln of a potter makes his vessels usable, but the trials of tribulation prove men righteous. And in another place it is written, *My son, as you come to the service of God, prepare yourself for temptation.* Again, the same James says, *Be doers of the Word and not hearers only. If anyone is a hearer of the Word and not a doer, he is like the man who looks at the face of his birth in a mirror; having looked at it and withdrawn, he has immediately forgotten how it is.*[35] James has warned in vain to join works to faith if his addressees had been unable to sin after baptism. *He who keeps the whole law,* he says, *and sins in one thing has become guilty of all.* Which one of us is without sin? God has enclosed all things under sin so that he may have mercy on all.

"Also Peter says, *God knows how to snatch the pious out of temptation.* And, concerning false teachers: *These are fountains without water and a mist driven about by storms, for whom the shadowy darkness is reserved. For speaking proud words of vanity, with the desires of the flesh and of extravagance, they entice those who had escaped a little and turned them back to error.* It seems to you, does it not, that the words of the apos-

Ecclus 2:1

Jas 1:22–24

Jas 2:10

2 Pt 2:9

2 Pt 2:17–18

---

35. The second recension changed the tense of the final verb so that it would read "was."

Fs 307vb   qui non habent aquam | doctrinarum; promittunt imbrem uelut
nubes prophetice ad quas perueniat ueritas Dei, et turbinibus exigantur demonum atque uitiorum. Loquuntur grandia, et totus eo-
Bi 304rb   rum sermo | superbia est (inmundus est autem apud Deum omnis,
qui exaltat cor suum), ut qui paululum refugerant a peccatis ad
640   suum reuertantur errorem, et suadent in luxuria ciborum carnis-
que deliciis. Quis enim non libenter audiat, *Manducemus, et bibamus,*
et in eternum regnabimus? Sapientes et prudentes prauos uocant, eos
Aa 162^r   uero qui dulces sunt | in sermonibus plus audiunt.

"Iohannes apostolus, immo in Iohanne Saluator scribens Angelo
Sb 270rb   ecclesie Ephesi, *Scio,* inquit, *opera tua et laborem et patientiam | tuam,*
et quia sustinuisti propter nomen meum et non defecisti; set habeo aduer-
Pf 113rb   *sum te, | quod caritatem tuam primam reliquisti. Memor esto unde cecideris,*
et age penitentiam, et prima opera tua fac. Sin autem, uenio tibi, et mouebo
candelabrum tuum de loco, nisi penitentiam egeris. Similiter ceteras ec-
650   clesias, Smirnam, Pergamum, Thyatiram, Sardis, Philadelfiam, Lao-
diciam, ad penitentiam prouocat, et, nisi reuertantur ad opera pri-
stina, conminatur, et in Sardis paucos habere se dicit, qui non coin-
quinauerunt uestimenta sua et ambulaturi sunt cum eo in albis
quia digni sunt. Cui autem scribit, *Memento unde cecideris,* et, *Ecce,*
655   *missurus est diabolus ex uobis in carcerem ut temptemini,* et, *Scio ubi habi-*
tas, ubi sedes est Sathane, et, *In mente habe qualiter acceperis et audieris,*
et serua et penitentiam age, Et reliqua? Vtique dicit ei, qui credidit et
baptizatus est, et stans quondam corruit per delictum.

---

636 exigantur] exigitantur R2 (Aa, exagitantur Fs exigantur Sb)   649 loco] *add.*
suo R2 (*interlin.* Aa)

635 qui…aquam] quia quem non habent Aa Pf qui cum aquam non habent Bi
Fs Mk quia cum aquam non habent Sb | qui…promittunt] *add.* uel quia quam
non habent doctrinam promittunt *mg.* Fd | non] *interlin.* Fd_{pc}   638 autem] *inter-*
lin. Aa, *ant.* est Bi Mk EdF, *om.* Pf   644 Saluator] Dominus Aa *om.* Pf
646 meum] tuum Pf_{ac} Sb   647 te] *add.* pauca Bi Fs Pf Sb (*interlin.* Bi)   648 ue-
nio] ueniam Aa Pf   654 cecideris] excideris Aa ceciderit Pf   656 habe] habes Fs
Pf   657 ei] *om.* Mk EdF | credidit] crediderit Aa EdF Fs Mk Pf Sb   658 est] fuit
Bi fuerit EdF Fs Mk, *om.* Pf Sb

tle have portrayed a new order of ignorance? For the false teachers unveil fake fountains of knowledge, but they have no water of teaching; they promise rain like prophetic clouds which the truth of God reaches, and they are driven forth[36] by the storms of demons and vices. They speak grandiose things, and their whole manner of speaking is proud (but everyone who exalts his heart is unclean before God) so that those who had escaped a little from sins may be turned back to their error, and they urge them into the luxuries of food and the delights of the flesh. For who does not gladly hear, *Let us eat and drink, and we will reign forever*? They call the wise and prudent deformed, for they listen more to those who are sweet in their speech.

cf. Is 22:13, 1 Cor 15:32

"The apostle John, nay rather the Savior in John, writing to the Angel of the church of Ephesus, says, *I know your works and your labor and your endurance, and that you have maintained them for my name's sake and have not failed; but I have this against you, that you have abandoned your first love. Be mindful from where you have fallen, and repent and do your earlier works. If, however, I come to you, I will also move your lampstand from its place, unless you repent*. He similarly calls the remaining churches, Smyrna, Pergamum, Thyatira, Sardis, Philadelphia, and Laodicea, to repentance, and, unless they turn back to their former works, he threatens, and he says that he has few in Sardis who have not contaminated their garments and are ready to walk with him in white garments because they are worthy. But to this church he writes, *Remember from where you have fallen*, and, *Behold, Satan is ready to cast some of you into prison so that you may be tested*, and, *I know where you dwell, where Satan's throne is*, and, *Keep in mind how you received and listened, and keep that word and repent*. And the rest? Certainly he speaks to one who believed and was baptized and, though formerly standing, fell through sin.

Rv 2:2–5

Rv 2:10
I Rv 2:13
Rv 3:3

---

36. Gratian seems to have written *exigantur* (the reading of Fd and Sb), which would be "driven out" or "forth," while a later change made the verb match the verb in Peter's text, changing *exigantur* to *exigitantur*, or "driven about." The latter is an intensified version of the former.

"Paulisper de ueteri testamento exempla distuleram, quia so-
660 lent, ubicumque contra eos facit, dicere, *Lex et prophete usque ad Io-*
hannem. Ceterum quis ignoret sub altera dispensatione Dei omnes
retro sanctos eiusdem fuisse meriti, cuius nunc Christiani sunt?
Quomodo ante Abraham placuit in coniugio, sic nunc uirgines placent in perpetua castitate. Seruiuit ille legi et tempori suo, seruia-
665 mus et nos legi et tempori nostro, in quos fines seculorum deuene-
runt. Dauid electus secundum cor Domini, qui omnes eius faceret
Fs 308ʳᵃ uoluntates et qui in | quodam Psalmo dixerat, *Iudica me, Domine,*
quoniam ego in innocentia mea ingressus sum, et in Domino sperans non
Mk 245ᵛᵃ *infirmabor. Proba | me, Domine, et tempta me; ure renes meos et cor meum,*
670 postea temptatus a diabolo, et post peccatum penitens loquitur, *Mi-*
Fd 93ᵛᵃ *serere | mei, Deus, secundum magnam misericordiam tuam.* Magnum
peccatum magna uult deleri misericordia. Salomon, amabilis Domini et cui bis fuerat Deus reuelatus, quia amator mulierum fuit a
Dei amore discessit. Manassem inpiissimum regem post captiuita-
675 tem Babiloniam in pristinam dignitatem liber dierum restitutum re-
fert. Et Iosias uir sanctus in campo Mageddon ab Egiptio rege con-
foditur. Iesus quoque filius Iosedech sacerdos magnus, quamquam
Bi 304ᵛᵃ | Pf in | typo precesserit Saluatoris qui nostra peccata portauit | et alieni-
113ᵛᵃ genam sibi ex gentibus copulauit ecclesiam, tamen secundum litte-
680 ram post sacerdotium sordidatus inducitur, et stat diabolus a dextris
Aa 162ᵛ eius, et candida | illi deinceps uestimenta redduntur.

"Superfluum est de Moyse et Aaron scribere, quod ad aquam
contradictionis offenderint Deum et terram repromissionis non in-
Sb 270ᵛᵃ trauerint, cum Beatus | Iob angelos quoque et omnem creaturam
685 peccare posse conmemoret, dicens, *Quid enim? Numquid homo coram*
Deo mundus est? Aut ab operibus suis sine macula uir? Si contra seruos

---

661 altera] alta R2 (altera Fs altare Sb)   672 Domini] Domino R2   675 Babilo-
niam] Babilonicam R2 (Babilonia Mk_ac Babiloniam Fs Sb)

659 distuleram] distulerant Fd   660 facit] faciunt Fs Pf | Iohannem] *add.* pro-
phetauerunt Bi Fs Mk   661 dispensatione] dispositione Mk | dispensatione Dei]
dispositione Dei uel dispensatione Pf   664 Seruiuit] seruiunt Fd Pf   665 deue-
nerunt] decurrerunt Bi Mk Sb   667 dixerat] dixerant Fs diceret Pf   668 in¹...
mea] innocentiam meam Bi | innocentia mea] innocentiam meam Mk
683 Deum] Dominum Pf Sb   686 Deo] Domino Aa Bi Fs

"I have put off examples from the Old Testament for a while, because, whenever an example comes out against them, Jovinian and his supporters are accustomed to say, *The Law and prophets [prophesied] until John.* Yet, who does not know that, under the other[37]   Mt 11:13
dispensation of God, all the saints in past times were worthy of the very same thing that Christians now are? In the way that in earlier times Abraham was pleasing in his marriage, now virgins are pleasing in their perpetual chastity. He served the law and his time, and let us upon whom the ends of the ages will arrive serve the law and our time. David was chosen of the Lord according to his heart; he who did all the Lord's will and had said in a certain Psalm, *Judge me, o Lord, for I have walked in my innocence, and, hoping in the Lord, I will not grow weak. Test me, o Lord, and try me; burn my inner being and my heart,* afterward was tempted by the devil, and, after his sin, says   Ps 25:1–2
in repentance, *Have mercy on me, o God, according to your great loving-kindness.* He wants his great sin to be destroyed by great loving-   Ps 50:1
kindness. Solomon, worthy of the Lord's love and to whom God had been revealed twice, departed from the love of God because he was a lover of women. The book of days reports that Manasseh, a very wicked king, was restored to his former dignity after the Babylonian captivity. And Josiah, a holy man, is stabbed by the king of Egypt on the field of Mageddo. Moreover, Joshua the high priest, the son of Jehozadek, although he has gone before as a type of savior who has carried our sins and joined a foreign church to himself from the peoples, nevertheless literally is clothed in dirty robes and a demon stands at his right, and then the white garments are returned to him.

"It is superfluous to write about Moses and Aaron, that they offended God at the water of contention and did not enter into the land of promise, since the blessed Job recounts that angels as well as every creature are able to sin, saying, *What then? A man is not clean before God, is he, or without stain from his works? If he does not put*

---

37. The second recension changed the "other" (*altera*) to something like "great," "noble," or "deep/profound" (*alta*). The change is rather strange, but it is partially explained by, or itself caused a further change in, a few manuscripts (Mk and Pf from my selections), where "dispensation" reads "disposition."

suos non credit et aduersos angelos suos prauum quid repperit, quanto ma-
gis habitantes in domibus luteis? De quibus enim et nos ex eodem luto
sumus. Temptatio est uita hominis super terram.

690 "Et cecidit Lucifer, qui nitebat ad uniuersas nationes, et ille, qui
in paradyso deliciarum inter duodecim nutritus est lapides, uulne-
ratus a monte Domini ad inferna descendit. Vnde et Saluator in
euangelio: *Videbam*, inquit, *Sathanam quasi fulgur de celo cadentem.* Si
altissima illa sublimitas cecidit, quis cadere non possit? Si in celo
695 ruine, quanto magis in terra. Et tamen, cum ceciderit Lucifer, immo
post casum coluber antiquus, uirtus eius in lumbis est, et potestas
eius super umbilicum uentris. Obumbrantur in eo arbores magne,
et dormit iuxta iuncum, et calamum, et caricem. Ipse est rex om-
Fs 308ʳᵇ nium que in aquis sunt, ubi scilicet uoluptas | et luxuria et propago
700 et irrigatio nuptiarum."

Et infra: "Transiuimus ad secundam partitionem, in qua negat
eos qui tota fide baptisma consecuti sunt deinde posse peccare, et
docuimus quod excepto Deo omnis creatura sub uitio sit—non quo
uniuersi peccauerint, set quo peccare possint, et similium ruina
705 stantium metus sit."

Euidenter itaque ex premissis apparet, nonnullos caritatem ha- d.p.c.40
bere, quam postea criminaliter delinquendo amittunt. Quod si quis
contendat non de uirtute, set de uirtutis opere debere intelligi, deli-

---

701 Transiuimus… **705** sit] Ibid. 2.35 (PL 23:333B)

690 nitebat] mittebat (Bi EdF Sb) *vel* mittebatur (Fs Mk Pf) R2   **699** que] qui
R2 (Aa)   **703** quo] quod R2 (quo Fs)   **704** quo] quod R2 (quo Fs)

687 credit] credidit Pf Sb   **688** ex] de Bi Mk   **692** monte] morte Biₐᵧ Mk Sb
695 ceciderit] cecidit Bi Pf   **696** uirtus] si *praemit.* Bi Mk   **697** super umbilicum]
in umbilico Aa | umbilicum] *add.* est Pf Sb | uentris] *add.* eius Bi Mk Pf   **704** si-
milium] a simili Bi Mk

trust in his servants and discovers something distorted against his angels,
how much more in those living in clay houses? For, as regards these peo-   Jb 4:17–19
ple, we also are out of the same mire. Trial is the life of man on
earth.

"And Lucifer, who shone bright[38] to all the nations of the world,
fell, and he who was nourished in the paradise of delights amid the
twelve stones, having been wounded by the mountain of the Lord,
descended to the inferno. For this reason also the Savior in the
Gospel says, *I saw Satan falling from heaven like lightning.* If that high-   Lk 10:18
est sublimity fell, who would be able not to fall? If individuals come
crashing down in heaven, how much more so on earth? And nevertheless, when Lucifer fell, nay rather, after the fall, the ancient
serpent, his power is in the loins, and his might is upon the middle
of the belly. Great trees are obscured in him, and he sleeps next to
a rush, reed-grass, and cane. He is king of all the things that[39] are in
the waters, namely where there is pleasure and luxury and off-
spring and the watering of marriage."

And below: "We have crossed to the second partition, in which
Jovinian denies that those who have attained baptism with complete faith then can sin, and we have taught that, except for God,
every creature is under vice—not for the reason that all have
sinned, but for the reason that[40] they are able to sin, and the fall of
similar people still standing is a cause for fear."

d.p.c.40   It is clearly apparent from the preceding, therefore, that some
have love that they later lose by sinning mortally. But if anyone
should contend that this ought to be understood not concerning

---

38. Gratian seems to have written "shone bright" (*nitebat*). Either his text of
Jerome (a complete *Aduersus Jouinianum* or a florilegia with extensive patristic
texts) was faulty, or Gratian misread the text, mistaking an m for an n. Jerome's original and a later version of the Decretum, undoubtedly corrected
against another manuscript of Jerome, read *mittebat*. Many second-recension
manuscripts used the passive *mittebatur*, translated either "who sent to all the
nations" or "who was sent to all the nations." The former is difficult to make
sense of (since there is no direct object of "sent"), even though it is what
Jerome wrote. Probably because the "who sent" was difficult to understand,
some scribes preferred the passive form.
39. The second recension changed the "that" (*que*) to a humanized "who" (*qui*).
Only Fd has the former reading, which matches Jerome's original.
40. The second recension changed both instances of "for the reason that" to a
simple "that" parallel to the "that" following "we have taught," i.e., "we have
taught that, except for God, every creature is under vice—not that all have
sinned, but that they are able to sin...." The later version matches Jerome's
original.

beret quid respondeat de innocentia Ade, de iustitia Moysi, Dauid,
710   et ceterorum qui plena fide ad baptisma accedentes, licet postea
prolapsuri sint, tamen celestia dona degustant et Spiritus sancti
Mk 245vb fiunt participes, ut non solum | ante humanos, uerum etiam ante
Dei oculos ex aqua et Spiritu sancto inueniantur renati; qui, si cari-
Pf 113vb tatem | non haberent ante Dei oculos, aqua tantum regenerarentur,
715   non Spiritu. Opera enim seu sacramentorum participatio, nisi ex
caritate procedant, apud Deum nec iustitiam nec innocentiam pre-
stant. *Si enim,* INQUIT APOSTOLUS, *habuero omnem fidem, ita ut mon-*
Bi 304vb *tes transferam, et si distribuero | omnem facultatem in cibos pauperum, et si*
tradidero corpus meum ita, ut ardeam, caritatem autem non habuero, ni-
Aa 163^{r} *chil | mihi prodest.*

<Argumentum Gratiani de reprobis caritatem ha-
bentibus>

Sb 270vb Set quia de predestinatis ad uitam a nonnullis conceditur | quod
caritatem amittant et amissam recuperent, de reprobis etiam uiden-
725   dum est, an ipsi caritatem habeant qua amissa postea dampnentur.
De his ita scribit AUGUSTINUS IN LIBRO DE CORRECTIONE ET GRA-
TIA, "Apostolus, sciens nonnullos diligere Deum et in eo modo us-   c.41
que in finem non perseuerare, mox addidit, *his qui secundum proposi-*
tum uocati sunt sancti," etc. In eodem: "An adhuc et iste nolens cor-
730   ripi poterit dicere: 'Quid ego feci, quod non accepi?', quem constat
accepisse et sua culpa quod acceperat amisisse. 'Possum,' inquit,
'possum omnino quando me arguis dicere, quod ex bona uita in
malam mea uoluntate relapsus sum, adhuc: Quid ego feci quod non
accepi? Accepi enim fidem que per dilectionem operatur, set in illa
Fs 308va | Fd   usque in finem | perseuerantiam non accepi." In eodem: "In bono |
93vb illos uolebat proculdubio manere; erant utique in bono, set in eo
non permanserunt." In eodem: "Propter huius utilitatem secreti

---

727 Apostolus…**729** sancti" Aug. Hipp., *De corr. et grat.* 9 (PL 44:929)
729 An…**735** accepi] Ibid. 6 (PL 44:921)   **735** In²…**740** etc] Ibid. 9 (PL 44:928)

---

729 sancti"] *om.* R2 (sancti *adest* Fs)

714 haberent] habent Bi habet Fs   715 Spiritu] *add.* sancto Aa Bi Mk Sb (*inter-lin.* Aa)   718 omnem facultatem] omnes facultates meas Bi EdF, *add.* meam Pf Sb   719 habuero] habeam Aa EdF   726 correctione] correptione Bi   733 adhuc Quid] *tr.* Fd | Quid] quod Bi$_{ac}$Mk$_{ac}$ 736 uolebat] uolebam Bi EdF Fs Mk

virtue as a whole but concerning a particular work of virtue, let him think about what the writer to the Hebrews answers concerning the innocence of Adam, concerning the righteousness of David, of Moses, and of the others who came to baptism with full faith and who, although they afterward would fall, nevertheless taste celestial gifts and are made partakers of the Holy Spirit so that they may be found reborn of water and the Holy Spirit, not only before men but also before the eyes of God. If they did not have love in the eyes of God, they would be regenerated by water only, not by the Spirit. For works or participation in the sacraments, if they do not proceed from love, present neither righteousness nor innocence before God. *For if,* SAYS THE APOSTLE, *I have all the faith to move mountains, and if I give all my means in food to the poor, and if I hand over my body to burn, but I have not love, if profits me nothing.* 1 Cor 13:2–3

<Gratian's Argument about the Reprobate Having Love>

But, because it is granted by some concerning those predestined to life, that they may lose love and recover it once it has been lost, it should also be seen concerning the reprobate, whether they themselves have love and, after it has been lost, are afterward condemned. Concerning these things, AUGUSTINE WRITES IN THIS

c.41 WAY IN HIS BOOK *DE CORREPTIONE ET GRATIA*: "The apostle, knowing that some love God and do not persevere in this manner to the end, quickly added, *those who have been called saints*[41] *according to his purpose,*" etc. In the same work: "Or yet perhaps that man who does not want to be rebuked will be able to say, 'What have I done that I have not received?', since it is agreed that he received and by his guilt lost what he had received. 'I am able,' he says, 'I am entirely able to say, when you accuse me, saying that to this point I have fallen from a good life into an evil one by my will: What have I done that I have not received? For I received the faith that works through love, but I have not received perseverance in it all the way to the end.'" In the same work: "Without a doubt he wanted them to remain in the good; indeed they were in the good, but they did

Rom 8:28

cf. 1 Cor 4:7

41. The second recension removed this word.

credendum est, quosdam de filiis perditionis, non accepto dono
perseuerandi usque in finem, in fide que per dilectionem operatur,
740 incipere uiuere et postea cadere," etc.

Multa similia de reprobis DE EUANGELIO etiam: *Qui perseueraue-*   d.p.c.41
rit usque in finem, etc. ET ITERUM: *Homo iste incepit,* etc. ITEM IN EO-
DEM: "Mirandum est quare Deus quibusdam filiis perditionis det fi-   c.42
dem operantem per dilectionem nec det in ea perseuerantiam."
745 ITEM ILLUD EUANGELII: *Non qui ceperit, set qui perseuerauerit usque in*
finem, hic saluus erit. ITEM GREGORIUS: "Multi bene incipiunt qui in   c.43
malo uitam finiunt." Non autem bene incipit qui numquam ex cari-   d.p.c.43
tate operatur. Quod si aliquando ex caritate aliquid agit, et caritatem aliquando in ipso necesse est esse.

750 Illud autem Gregorii, "Qui seduci quandoque non reuersuri possunt," etc., non de omnibus generaliter reprobis, set de ypocritis
specialiter intelligendum est. Quod ex uerbis eiusdem euidenter da-
Pf 114ᵃ tur intelligi. Cum enim | questionem proponeret cur misericors
Deus ista fieri permittat, ut Leuiathan seu nunc per suggestiones
755 callidas siue per dampnatum illum, quem replet, hominem, uel solis sibi radios, id est doctos quosque sapientesque, subiciat, uel aurum, hoc est uiros sanctitatis claritate fulgentes, quasi lutum sibi ui-
tiis coinquinando substernat, mox IN EIUSDEM QUESTIONIS SOLU-
TIONE SUPPOSUIT, dicens, "Citius ad hoc respondemus, quia aurum   c.44
Mk 246ᵃ quod prauis eius persuasionibus | quasi lutum sterni potuerit, au-

---

743 Mirandum...**744** perseuerantiam] cf. Ibid. 8 (PL 44:926)   **746** Multi...**747**
finiunt] cf. *Gl. ord. in 2 Chr.* 9:29 (ed. Rusch, 2.236)   **759** Citius...**808** osten-
dunt] Greg. Magn., *Moralia in Iob* 34.15 (CCSL 143B:1754.84–1756.138)

739 in fide] in fidem Fd idem fidem Mk, *om.* Pf Sb   **742** etc¹] In eodem etc. Aa
Bi Fd Fs Mk Sb, etc. In eodem EdF | Et] *om.* Bi Mk EdF   **743** Deus] *add.* det Fd
Bi Mk | quibusdam] quibus Fd | det] *om.* Aa Bi Mk, *ant.* quibusdam Fs
744 operantem] *pos.* dilectionem Sb EdF | nec...perseuerantiam] non accepto
dono usque in finem perseuerandi Pf   **747** caritate] *add.* aliquid Aa Pf   **748** ali-
quando] *om.* Aa EdF   **750** autem] *interlin.* Fd Fs   **756** sapientesque] sapientes
Bi Sb   **757** fulgentes] fungentes Biₐc Mk   **759** hoc] hec Aa Mk

not persist in it." In the same work: "On account of the usefulness of this mystery, we should believe that, because they have not received the gift of persevering all the way to the end, certain of the sons of perdition begin to live in the faith that works through love and afterward fall," etc.

d.p.c.41   Many similar things are said concerning the reprobate, even FROM THE GOSPEL: *He who perseveres all the way to the end,* etc.[42]   Mt 10:22
LIKEWISE AGAIN: *That man began,* etc. LIKEWISE, IN THE SAME   Lk 14:30
c.42   WORK: "We should wonder at why God gives faith working through love to certain sons of perdition and does not give them perseverance in it." LIKEWISE, THAT STATEMENT OF THE GOSPEL: *Not he who begins, but he who perseveres all the way to the end, will be*
c.43   *saved.* LIKEWISE GREGORY: "Many begin well who finish life in   Mt 10:22
d.p.c.43   evil." But he who never works from love does not begin well. But if he ever does something out of love, it is necessary that love also be in him at some point.

But that statement of Gregory, "Those have been led astray at some point will not be able to turn back," etc., should be under-   cf. D.2 c.44
stood as referring not to all the reprobates generally but specifically to hypocrites. This is clearly given to be understood from the words of the same author. For when he put forward the question why a compassionate God allows these things to happen, that the Leviathan, either through clever suggestions or through that condemned man whom he fills, subjects to himself either the rays of the sun, that is, the learned as well as the wise, or gold, that is, men shining with the brightness of holiness, as if he is spreading mud on himself by polluting with vices, GREGORY SOON ADDED IN THE SO-
c.44   LUTION OF THE SAME QUESTION, saying, "We respond to this rather

42. Only Pf makes sense at this juncture. All other manuscripts have an "in the same work" (*in eodem*) before the "etc." (although Friedberg placed it after). Gratian probably included this phrase, but, because it cannot be made sense of in this location, I have chosen not to include it in the edition. Gratian probably copied the *in eodem* from his formal source, and that formal source may not have been clear on the precise location of the phrase (perhaps it was inserted in the margin). The treatise *Ut autem hoc euidenter* included the in eodem prior to the statement that "many similar things are said about the reprobate," which also does not make sense since that statement is not a quotation. Either *Ut autem* was Gratian's source, and he attempted (unsuccessfully) to put the *in eodem* in a more logical place, or *Ut autem* and Gratian shared a common formal source (my viewpoint), and each author dealt with the awkward *in eodem* in his own way. Only the Pf scribe made sense of the nonsense and excised what was out of place.

rum ante Dei oculos numquam fuit. Qui enim seduci quandoque
non reuersuri possunt, quasi | habitam sanctitatem ante oculos ho-
minum uidentur amittere, set eam ante Dei | oculos numquam |
habuerunt. Sepe namque homo multis occulte peccatis inuoluitur,
et in una aliqua uirtute magnus uidetur, que ipsa quoque uirtus
inanescens deficit, quia, dum innotescit hominibus, proculdubio
laudatur, eiusque fauor inhianter appetitur. Vnde fit ut et ipsa uirtus ante Dei oculos uirtus non sit dum abscondit quod displicet,
prodit | quod placet. Que itaque esse merita apud Deum possunt,
quando et mala occulta sunt, et bona publica? Plerumque enim, sicut diximus, latet superbia et castitas innotescit. Atque ideo ostensa
diu castitas circa finem uite perditur, quia cooperta superbia usque
ad finem incorrecta retinetur.

"Alius elemosinis uacat, propria distribuit, set tamen multis
iniustitiis seruit, uel fortasse linguam in detractionibus exerit, et fit
plerumque ut is qui misericors fuerat iuxta uite sue terminum ra-
pacitatis et crudelitatis stimulis inardescat. Quod ualde iudicio iusto
agitur, ut perdat et ante homines unde hominibus placuit, qui hoc
unde Deo displicuit corrigere numquam curauit. Alius patientie
studet, set inuidere aliis et seruare malitiam in corde non cauet; fit
quandoque inpatiens quia diu latuit dolens. Hi itaque et per aliquid
aurum sunt, et per aliquid lutum sunt. Atque hoc aurum quasi lutum sternitur quando occultis peccatis exigentibus etiam uirtus,
que publice claruerat, dissipatur.

"Set opere pretium credimus si in his uirtutem superni ordinis
subtilius | perpendamus. Sepe enim omnipotens Deus occulta eo-
rum mala diu tollerat, et aperta eorum bona electorum suorum usi-

Bi 305ᵃ

Aa 163ᵛ | Sb
271ᵃ

765

Fs 508ᵛᵇ
770

775

780

785
Pf 114ʳᵇ

---

761 Qui] Quod Fd   762 hominum…764 habuerunt] Dei numquam fuit erunt
habituri *sed exp. et add. interlin.* uel hominum numquam habuerunt Fd   767 fa-
uor] *om.* Fd | inhianter] inhiantur Biₐ𝚌 inaniter Aa Pf | et] *om.* Aa Pf   768 displi-
cet] displiceret Bi, *add.* et Aa Pf (*interlin.* Aa)   773 ad] in Aa Pf | incorrecta] in-
correpta Bi correcta Sb   775 exerit] exercet EdF Mk   777 iudicio iusto] *tr.* Aa
EdF Mk Pf Sb | iusto] *add.* Dei Aa Pf Sb (*pos.* iudicio Sb)   778 et] etiam Fs Mk

quickly that the gold which the depraved one was able to spread out like mud by his perverse persuasions was never gold in the eyes of God. For those who have been led astray at some point will not be able to turn back, and they seem to lose the holiness held, as it were, in the eyes of men, but they never had it in the eyes of God. For often a man is secretly enveloped by many sins, and in some one virtue he seems great, which itself also disappears as a virtue which grows empty, because, while it becomes known to men, it is undoubtedly praised, and its approbation is eagerly desired. And thus it happens that even the virtue itself is not a virtue in the eyes of God, so long as it hides what displeases and parades what pleases. Therefore what things can be worthy before God, when the evil things are secret while the good things are public? For, for the most part, as we have said, pride lies hidden while modesty becomes known. And for this reason modesty long shown is lost around the end of life, because the covered pride remains uncorrected to the end.

"The one man calls for alms, distributes his property, but nevertheless serves many injustices, or perhaps thrusts out his tongue in slanders, and, for the most part, it happens that he who had been compassionate burns with the spurs of rapacity and cruelty near the end of his life. By a most just judgment does it happen that he who never cared to correct that which caused God's displeasure loses before men that which caused their pleasure. The other man has zeal for patience but does not avoid envying others and storing up malice in his heart; eventually he becomes impatient because for a long time he has stayed hidden in his pain. These people, then, are gold according to one thing and mud according to another. And this gold is spread out like mud when even the virtue which they had shown forth publicly is squandered by driving secret sins.

"But we believe in a reward for work if we ponder rather keenly in these matters virtue of the highest order. For often the omnipotent God bears with their secret evil for a long time, and he manages their open good which is ready to benefit the practices of his

bus profutura dispensat. Nam nonnulli, mundum nequaquam funditus deserentes, non perseueraturi angustum iter arripiunt, set ad
790 querendam angustam uiam exemplo suo eos qui perseueraturi sunt
accendunt. Vnde plerumque contingit ut ipsum hoc quod bene uidentur uiuere, non sibi, set potius solis electis uiuant, dum exemplis suis ad bene uiuendi studia perseueraturos alios non perseueraturi prouocant. Sepe enim quosdam uidemus ad uiam ingredi, ad
795 locum propositum festinare, quos alii, quia euntes conspiciunt, secuntur, eundemque pariter locum petunt; set fit plerumque ut ir-
ruente aliquo inplicationis articulo post se redeant qui preibant, et
hi ad locum perueniant, qui sequebantur. Ita nimirum sunt qui

Fd 94ʳᵃ   non perseuerant et uiam sanctitatis arripiunt. Idcirco enim | uirtutis
Sb 271ʳᵇ   iter non peruenturi inchoant, ut eis, qui peruenturi | sunt, uiam
Fs 309ʳᵃ   qua gradiantur ostendant, quorum etiam casus | utilitate non mo-
dica electorum prouectibus seruit, quia illorum lapsum dum con-
Aa 164ʳ | Bi   spiciunt, | de suo statu | contremiscunt, | et ruina que illos dampnat
305ʳᵇ | Mk   istos humiliat. Discunt enim in superni adiutorii protectione confi-
246ʳᵇ   dere, dum plerosque conspiciunt de suis uiribus cecidisse. Quando
ergo bene agere uidentur reprobi, quasi planum iter electis sequen-
tibus monstrant. Quando uero in lapsum nequitie corruunt, electis
post se pergentibus quasi cauendam superbie foueam ostendunt."

Quod uero reprobi negantur comedere panem qui de celo de-   d.p.c.44
810 scendit uel bibere aquam uiuam non sic accipiendum est, ut a caritate penitus credantur alieni, set ut in caritate radicem figere non
intelligantur. Aliud est enim bibere uel manducare atque aliud de-
gustare. Vnde IN EUANGELIO de Christo legitur, *Et cum gustasset, nol-*
uit bibere. Bibit ergo aquam uiuam, manducat panem qui de celo
815 descendit, qui in caritate radicem figit; degustat, qui ea aliquatenus
conmunicat, a qua postea delinquendo recedit. De talibus APOSTO-

---

816 talibus] qualibus R2 (qua Fs)

790 suo] *interlin.* Fd *om.* Pf   800 peruenturi¹] perseueraturi Bi Pf | uiam] uia Fd
805 uiribus] uirtutibus Aa Pf   807 monstrant] demonstrant Aa Pf | uero] ergo
Fs   809 uero] ergo Aa Bi Pf autem Fs   811 caritate] *interlin.* Aa caritatem Mk

elect. For some, in no way completely abandoning the world, seize upon the narrow path although they will not persevere, but by their example they set those who will persevere aflame to seek the narrow way. And so it very often happens that they live the very thing that they seem to live well not for themselves but rather for the elect alone, as long as, by their examples, they who will not persevere provoke others who will persevere to the zeal for living well. For often we see that certain people enter the way and hasten to the intended place, and because other people, while going on their way, look to them, these others are follow along and seek the same place in the same way; but, for the most part, it happens that, because some moment of entanglement makes an attack, those who were setting the example, go back to their old selves and those who were following reach the place. Indeed in this way there are those who do not persevere and [yet] lay hold of the way of holiness. For they thus begin although they will not reach the path of virtue, so that they may show the way on which they walk to those who will reach it. Their case serves the progress of the elect with not a small benefit, because the elect tremble at the others' state when they gaze upon their fall, and the ruin which condemns them humbles the elect. For the elect learn to put their trust in the protection of the highest aid, when they observe that several have fallen from their strength. Therefore, when the reprobate seem to act well, they show a clear path, as it were, to the elect following them. But when they tumble down in the slide into wickedness, they show the pit of pride to be avoided, as it were, to the elect continuing after them."

d.p.c.44   But the fact that the reprobate are denied the eating of the bread which comes down from heaven or the drinking of the living water ought not to be understood in such a way that they are believed to be a complete stranger to love but that they are understood not to take root in love. For it is one thing to drink or to eat and another to taste. Whence we read IN THE GOSPEL concerning Christ, *And when he had tasted, he did not want to drink*. Therefore, he who takes   Mt 27:34 root in love drinks the living water and eats the bread which comes down from heaven; he who to a certain extent partakes of this,

LUS AIT, *Inpossibile est eos, qui semel illuminati sunt et gustauerunt celeste donum et post hec omnia prolapsi sunt, rursus renouari ad penitentiam.*

Pf 114ᵛᵃ   Hinc etiam diabolus in ueritate | stetisse, non in ea creatus esse
820   negatur. Fuit enim in ueritate conditus, set, dum de se superbiendo
presumpsit, ab ea alienus factus est. In ueritate autem quomodo
creatus perhibetur si sine dilectione sui conditoris creatus esse probatur? Aut quomodo bonus a Deo conditus asseritur si nichil diuine
dilectionis in sui creatione accepit? Quomodo ante superbie motum
825   sine uitio extitit si conditorem suum nullatenus dilexit? Aut quomodo par siue exellentior ceteris creatus dicitur si, nonnullis eorum
in Dei amore conditis, hic ab eius dilectione uacuus factus est?
Vnde autem hec distantia inter bonos et malos angelos processit? Si
ex creante, iniustus uidetur Deus, qui ante peccatum infert penam
830   uel qui hoc punit quod creando infudit. Si autem non ex creante,
cum non ex traduce, restat ut ex proprie libertatis arbitrio uitium
Fs 309ʳᵇ   superbie in angelicam naturam processerit. | Bona ergo condita est,
que suo uitio a bono in malum conmutata est. Set quomodo bona
esse potuit si dilectione penitus caruit? Neque enim angelus nobis
Sb 271ᵛᵃ   similis factus | est, quos usque ad certum tempus etatis infirmitas
grauat, ut neque uirtus neque uitium ullum locum in nobis obti-
neat. Accepit ergo dilectionem in sui creatione, sicut et ceteri, DE
QUIBUS DICITUR, "Angelice uirtutes, que in Dei amore perstite-
runt." Non ait, "que Deum diligere ceperunt," set, "que in eius
Aa 164ᵛ   amore perstiterunt," que ex creatione | diligere ceperant, ut princi-
pium diuine dilectionis omnibus credatur esse conmune, perseuerantia uero eorum tantummodo intelligatur qui in retributione hoc
accipere meruerunt, ut confirmati ulterius cadere non possent et
hoc de se certissime scirent. Vnde bene apud Moysem prius *celum,*
Bi 305ᵛᵃ | Mk   deinde | *firmamentum* factum esse dicitur, quia nimirum angelica |
246ᵛᵃ   natura prius equaliter subtilis in superioribus est condita, postea in
persistentibus in amore sui conditoris mirabiliter est confirmata.

---

838 Angelice…perstiterunt] *Gl. ord. in Gen.* 1:6 (ed. Rusch, 1.10b)   **844** Vnde…
847 confirmata] cf. ibid.

824 dilectionis] electionis Fd   **828** distantia] differentia Bi EdF Pf | angelos] *in-
terlin.* Aa *mg.* Bi Mk   **839** Deum] ex creatione Aa dominum Biₐ𝒸 *pos.* ceperunt Pf
847 est] *om.* EdF Fs Mk Pf

from which afterward he departs by sinning, merely tastes. Concerning such people THE APOSTLE SAYS, *It is impossible that those who have once been enlightened and tasted the heavenly gift and after all these things fallen to be renewed again to repentance.*

Heb 6:4–6

On this account the devil also is denied to have stood in truth, but not denied to have been created in it. For he was made in the truth, but, when he took it for granted by taking pride in himself, he became a stranger to it. But how is it claimed that he was created in the truth if it is proven that he was created without love for his Maker? Or how is it asserted that he was made good by God if he received nothing of divine love when he was created? How did he exist without vice before the movement of pride if he in no way loved his Maker? Or how is he said to have been created equal to or more excellent than the others if, when some of them were created in the love of God, he was made empty of the love of God? But from where did this disparity between good and evil angels proceed? If from the one creating, God, who inflicts punishment before sin or who punishes that which he infused in his creating, appears to be unjust. But if not from the one creating, since not from an inheritance, it remains that the vice of pride in the angelic nature proceeded from the will of its own liberty. It was thus made good and was changed from good to evil by its own vice. But how could it have been good if it entirely lacked love? For the angel was not made like us, whom weakness weighs down until a fixed age so that neither virtue nor any vice may obtain a place in us. Therefore, the devil received love at his creation, just as the others also did, CONCERNING WHOM IT IS SAID, "The angelic virtues, which persisted in the love of God." It does not say, "which began to love God," but, "which persisted in the love of God," which had begun to love from their creation, so it may be believed that the starting point of divine love is common to all, but perseverance may be understood to belong solely to those who were worthy to receive it as remuneration so that, having been confirmed, they might not be able to fall anymore and might know this concerning themselves with great certitude. For this reason it is well said in the works of Moses first that *heaven* and then that *the firmament* was made, because, to be sure, the angelic nature was first made equally acute in higher matters and afterward was wondrously confirmed in persisting in the love of its Maker.

Gn 1:1
I Gn 1:6

Hinc etiam GREGORIUS IN MORALIBUS, multa de perfectione
angelice creationis replicans, caritate repletum negat, non ea peni-
850 tus uacuum asserit, qua si penitus caruisset, numquam ea que de
eius excellentia dicuntur conuenienter de eo intelligi possent. *"Prin-*   c.45
cipium | enim,"* inquit Beatus Gregorius, *"uiarum Dei* Behemoth dici-
tur quia nimirum cum cuncta creans ageret, hunc primum condi-
dit, quem reliquis angelis eminentiorem fecit. Huius primatus emi-
855 nentiam conspicit Propheta, cum dicit, *Cedri non fuerunt altiores illo*
in paradyso Dei; abietes non adequauerunt summitatem eius; platani non
fuerunt equales frondibus illius; omne lignum pretiosum paradysi Dei non
est assimilatum illi et pulchritudini eius, quoniam | speciosum fecit eum in
multis condensisque frondibus. Quid namque accipi in cedris, abieti-
860 bus, et platanis possunt nisi illa uirtutum celestium procere celsitu-
dinis agmina, in eterna letitie uiriditate plantata? Que quamuis excelsa sint condita, huic tamen nec prelata sunt nec equata, qui *spe-*
ciosus factus in multis condensisque frondibus dicitur, quia prelatum ceteris legionibus tanta illum species pulchriorem reddidit, quanta et
supposita angelorum multitudo decorauit. Ista arbor in | paradyso
Dei tot quasi condensas frondes habuit, quot sub se positas supernorum spirituum legiones attendit.

"Qui et idcirco peccans sine uenia dampnatus est, quia magnus
sine conparatione fuerat creatus. Hinc ei rursum per eundem Pro-
870 phetam dicitur, *Tu signaculum similitudinis, plenus sapientia, et perfectus*
decore in deliciis paradysi Dei fuisti. Multa enim | de eius magnitudine
locuturus, primo uerbo cuncta conplexus est. Quid namque boni
non habuit si signaculum Dei similitudinis fuit? De sigillo quippe
annuli talis similitudo imaginaliter exprimitur, qualis in sigillo eo-
875 dem essentialiter habetur. Et licet homo ad similitudinem Dei crea-

Pf 144ᵛᵇ

Fd 94ʳᵇ

Fs 309ᵛᵃ

Sb 271ᵛᵇ

---

851 Principium... **928** prosternitur] Greg. Magn., *Moralia in Iob* 32.23 (CCSL
143B:1665.6–1667.88)

860 possunt] potest R2 (Aa_pc)   **861** eterna] eterne R2 (eterna Fs Sb)   **873** si]
qui R2 (Aa)

859 condensisque] *om.* -que Fd Bi Sb, condempsis Fs Mk   **860** celsitudinis] alti-
tudinis Aa   **862** qui] quod Bi_ac Fd Fs   **868** Qui] Quod Fd Quia Pf   **874** exprimi-
tur] exponitur Fd

For this reason, GREGORY TOO, IN HIS *MORALIA*, reflecting upon many things about the perfection of the angelic creation, denies that the angelic nature was filled full with love, but does not claim that it was entirely empty of it, for if it had entirely lacked love, the things which are said concerning the excellence of the angelic nature would never be able to be appropriately understood concern-

c.45 ing the devil. "For *the beginning of the ways of God*," says the blessed Gregory, "is called Behemoth, because indeed, when he acted creating all things, he made this one first, which he made more eminent than all the other angels. The prophet looks to the eminence of this primacy when he says, *The cedars were not taller than it in God's garden; silver-firs have not equaled its highest point; the plane-trees have not been equal to its boughs; no precious wood of God's garden is likened to it and its beauty, since he made it splendid with many and dense boughs*. For what can be understood in cedars, silver-firs, and plane-trees except those armies of heavenly virtues with a high title, planted in the eternal[43] verdure of happiness? Although these were made tall, they nevertheless have been placed neither before nor equal to that which is said to be *made splendid with many and dense boughs*, because, the more a multitude of angels adorns the things placed under it, the more its form renders it more beautiful when it has been placed before the other armies. That tree in God's garden has as many dense boughs, so to speak, as armies of supernal spirits placed under it to which it attends.

"The one sinning was condemned without mercy for this reason, that he had been created great without comparison. For this reason it is said again to him through the same prophet: *You were a sign of the likeness [of God], full of wisdom, and perfect in beauty in the delights of God's garden*. For God is ready to speak many things about this angel's greatness and expresses all things in the first word. For what did he not have of the good if[44] he was a sign of God's likeness? Indeed, what is possessed in terms of essence in this same seal is expressed for such a likeness in terms of images with the seal of a signet ring. And although man was created in the likeness of God,

Right margin references:
Jb 40:14

Ezek 31:8

Ezek 28:12

---

43. The second recension changed the "eternal" to modify "happiness" instead of "verdure," i.e., "planted in the verdure of eternal happiness."
44. An early modification changed the "if" to a relative pronoun, a *si* to a *qui*. The second recension version of the sentence (also found in Aa) would be translated: "For what did he who was a sign of God's likeness not have of the good?"

Aa 165ʳ tus sit, angelo tamen | quasi maius aliquid tribuens, non eum ad si-
militudinem Dei conditum, set ipsum signaculum Dei similitudinis
dicit, ut, quo subtilior est natura, eo in illum similitudo Dei plenius
credatur expressa.

880 "Hinc est, quod primatus eius potentiam adhuc insinuans idem
Propheta subiungit, *Omnis lapis pretiosus operimentum tuum, sardius et
topazius, iaspis, crisolitus et onix, et berillus, saphirus, carbunculus, et smaragdus*. Nouem dixit genera lapidum quia nimirum nouem sunt or-
Pf 115ʳᵃ dines angelorum. Nam cum per sacra | eloquia angeli, archangeli,
Bi 305ᵛᵇ throni et dominationes, uirtutes, principatus, | potestates, Cheru-
bim atque Seraphim aperta narratione memorantur, supernorum
ciuium quante sint distinctiones ostenditur. Quibus tamen Behe-
Mk 246ᵛᵇ moth | iste opertus fuisse describitur quia eos quasi uestem ad orna-
mentum suum habuit, quorum dum claritatem transcenderet, ex
890 eorum conparatione clarior fuit.

"De cuius illic adhuc descriptione subiungit, *Aurum, opus decoris
tui, et foramina tua in die, qua conditus es, preparata sunt*. Aurum opus
extitit decoris eius quia sapientie claritate canduit quam bene creatus accepit. Foramina uero idcirco in lapidibus fiunt, ut uinculati
895 auro in ornamenti conpositione iungantur, et nequaquam a se dis-
sideant, quos interfusum aurum repletis foraminibus ligat. Huius
ergo lapidis in die conditionis sue foramina preparata sunt, quia ui-
Fs 309ᵛᵇ delicet capax | caritatis est conditus, qua si repleri uoluisset, stanti-
bus angelis tamquam positis in regis ornamento lapidibus potuisset
900 inherere. Si enim caritatis auro sese penetrabilem prebuisset, sanctis angelis sociatus in ornamento, ut diximus, regio lapis fixus ma-
neret. Habuit ergo lapis iste foramina, set superbie uitio caritatis
auro non sunt repleta. Nam quia idcirco ligantur auro, ne cadant,

---

882 topazius] *add.* et R2 (*om.* Pf)   **891** illic] *om.* R2

881 subiungit] ait Aa Pf | et] *om.* Aa Bi   **882** crisolitus] *add.* et Fd Bi Mk Sb | et¹]
om. Aa EdF Pf | et³] *om.* Fd Pf   **886** atque] et Aa EdF Mk Sb   **888** opertus] ope-
ratus Biₐ꜀ Pf   **891** illic] *pos.* adhuc Aa   **895** dissideant] discedant Aa dissidet Sb
901 ut diximus] *pos.* regio Bi Fs Mk

nevertheless, giving something greater, as it were, to the angel, he says not that he was made in the likeness of God but that he himself was the sign of God's likeness, so that it may be believed that, the higher he is by nature, the more fully the likeness of God is expressed in him.

"On this account there is what the same prophet adds, making known at this point the power of his primacy, *Every precious stone was your covering: the carnelian and topaz,*[45] *jasper, chrysolite and onyx, and beryl, sapphire, ruby, and emerald.* He mentioned nine types of stones because, to be sure, there are nine orders of angels. For when through holy communications angels, archangels, thrones and dominions, heavenly powers, principalities, authorities, cherubim, and seraphim are mentioned explicitly, it is shown how many distinctions of the supernal citizens exist. Nevertheless, the Behemoth is described as having been covered by these because he had them as a garment, so to speak, for his adornment. As long as he transcended their splendor, he was more splendid as a result of the comparison with them. Ezek 28:13

"Concerning the description of him still in that place,[46] he adds, *Gold, the work of your embellishment, and apertures, were prepared on the day on which you were created.* The work of its embellishment was gold because he glistened with the brightness of wisdom which he received when he was created well. But the apertures are made in the stones for this reason, so that, joined to the gold, they may be worked into the composition of the crown and so that the parts, which the infused gold binds to the filled apertures, may in no way be separated from it. Therefore, on the day of its creation, the apertures of this stone were prepared, because, naturally, the capacity for love was made. If he had wanted to be filled up with this love, he would have been able to cleave to the angels standing like stones placed in the crown of a king. For if he had presented himself susceptible to the gold of love, he would have remained a fixed stone in the royal crown, as we have said, as one united to the holy angels. Thus, that stone had apertures, but they were not filled up with the gold of love because of the vice of pride. For because they are bound to the gold for the express purpose of not falling, he fell Ezek 28:13b

---

45. The second recension added an "and," which matches Gregory's original.
46. The second recension removed "in that place," probably because the word I have translated "still" could also be translated something like "at this point," making the two terms in Latin (*adhuc* and *illic*) seem redundant.

idcirco iste cecidit, quia etiam perforatus manu artificis amoris uin-
905 culis ligari contempsit. Nunc autem ceteri lapides, qui hic similiter
fuerant perforati, penetrantes se inuicem caritate ligati sunt, atque
hoc in munere, isto cadente, meruerunt, ut nequaquam iam de ornamento regio cadendo soluantur.

Sb 272ra   "Huius principatus | celsitudinem adhuc idem Propheta intuens
910 adiungit: *Tu Cherub extentus et protegens in monte sancto Dei; in medio
ignitorum lapidum perfectus ambulasti.* Cherub quippe plenitudo
scientie interpretatur, et idcirco iste Cherub dicitur, quia transcen-
Aa 165v disse cunctos scientia non dubitatur, qui in medio | lapidum ignito-
Pf 115rb rum perfectus ambulauit quia inter angelorum corda | caritatis igne
915 succensa clarus gloria conditionis extitit. Quem bene extentum ac
Fd 94va protegentem dicit. Omne enim quod extenti | protegimus obumbra-
mus, et quia conparatione claritatis sue obumbrasse ceterorum claritatem creditur, ipse fuisse extentus et protegens repperitur. Reli-
quos enim quasi obumbrando operuit, qui eorum magnitudinem
920 excellentia maiore transcendit.

    "Quod ergo illic *speciosus in multis frondibus*, quod illic *signaculum
similitudinis*, quod illic *Cherub*, quod illic *protegens* dicitur, hoc hic
uoce dominica Behemoth iste *uiarum Dei principium* uocatur. De
Bi 306ra quo idcirco tam mira, in quibus | fuit et que amisit, insinuat, ut ho-
925 mini ostendat quid ipse, si superbiat, de elationis sue culpa passurus
sit, si feriendo illi parcere noluit, quem creando in gloria tante claritatis eleuauit. Consideret ergo homo elatus quid in terra mereatur;
etsi angelis prelatus in celo prosternitur."

---

910 Dei] *add.* et R2 (*om.* Fs Mk)   917 et] *om.* R2

906 penetrantes] penetrante Aa Sb   916 protegimus] protegit Bi_ac progenitus Pf
925 si] *om.* Aa, in Pf | superbiat] superbia Mk Pf   926 quem] que Fd   928 etsi]
si etiam Aa si Fs Pf | angelis prelatus] *tr.* Aa Bi Fs Mk Sb

for the very reason that, although he too had been pierced by the hand of the Maker, he disdained being bound with the chains of love. Now the remaining stones, however, which had similarly been pierced for this reason, have penetrated each other and been bound by love, and, although that one has fallen, they have deserved this in their service, that they may not in any way now be loosened and fall from the royal crown.

"And now giving attention to the title of this principality, the same prophet adds, *You were stretched out as a cherub and were covering on the holy mountain of God;*[47] *you walked perfected in the midst of the kindled stones.* Surely a cherub is interpreted as the fullness of knowledge, and he is called a cherub for this reason, that it may not be doubted that he transcended all in knowledge, and he walked perfect in the midst of the kindled stones because he shone bright with the glory of his creation among the angels' hearts set aflame with the fire of love. He says that he was well stretched out and was covering, for we give shade to everything which we cover while stretched out. And[48] because it is believed that the brightness of the others was shaded over by comparison to his brightness, he is found to have been stretched out and covering. For he who transcended the greatness of the rest with a greater excellence covered over them as if by providing shade. Ezek 28:14

"Therefore what in one place is said to be *splendid in its many boughs* and, in another place, *the sign of God's likeness,* and, in another place, *a cherub,* and, in another place, a being *covering,* is here by the Lord's voice called Behemoth, that *beginning of the ways of God.* He introduces such wondrous things about this being—in what he existed and what he lost—for this reason, that he may show to man what he will suffer as a result of the guilt of his self-exaltation if he is proud, if he refuses to spare and kills him whom God lifted up by creating him in the glory of such great splendor. Therefore, let the proud man consider what he deserves on earth; even if he is placed before angels in heaven, he is cast down." Ezek 31:8
Ezek
28:12–14

Jb 40:14

---

47. The second recension added an "and" here.
48. The second recension omitted this "and."

<Responsio Gratiani ultima ad sententiam primam>

Fs 310ʳᵃ | Mk 247ʳᵃ | Caritas autem que in aduersitate deseritur | ficta, id est fictilis   d.p.c.45
et fragilis, esse perhibetur, sicut fides ex qua caritas procedit ficta, id
est fragilis, apud Apostolum esse negatur. Similiter caritas que in
aduersitate deseri potest dicitur numquam uera fuisse. SICUT ENIM
IERONIMUS CONTRA IOUINIANUM SCRIBIT, "Omnis creatura sub ui-
935   tio est, non quod omnis peccauerit, set quia nulla est que peccare
non possit." Posse autem peccare, UT AUGUSTINUS AIT, non est aliquid posse, immo aliquid non posse. Vnde ille solus uocatur omnipotens qui hoc non potest, qui omnia potest, que posse est aliquid
posse. Sicut ergo eius conparatione qui mutabilitatem nescit, omnis
940   creatura uitiosa dicitur quia mutabilitatis est capax, IUXTA ILLUD,
Non iustificabitur in conspectu tuo omnis uiuens, et, *Astra non sunt
munda in conspectu eius*, sic conparatione eius creature que mutatio-
nem non recipit, omnis creatura que permutatur non uera, set
uana esse probatur. Vnde omnis homo mendax dicitur et uanitati
Sb 272ʳᵇ   similis factus. HINC ETIAM ECCLESIASTES: Cuncta, que *sub sole* |
sunt, id est que temporum uicissitudinem recipiunt, non tantummodo uanitas, que omni creature ratione mutabilitatis inest, set
etiam *uanitas uanitatum*, uarietate permutationis quam recipiunt
Pf 115ᵛᵃ   esse | dicuntur.

Aa 166ʳ   Sic ergo conparatione diuine caritatis | nulla uirtus uera proba-
tur, aut conparatione eius que non deseritur, illa que amittitur uera
esse negatur. Sicut autem omnis creatura suo modo bona et uera
esse dicitur, sic et caritas que deseritur suo modo uera esse monstratur. Alioquin, a nullo desereretur si nullo modo in eo esset.
955   Quod enim nullo modo uere est nullo modo deseri potest. Quod si
aliquo modo uere deseritur, et aliquo modo id uere esse oportet.

---

936 Posse…**937** posse²] cf. Aug. Hipp., *De Trinitate* 15.5 (CCSL 50:498.20–22),
etiam translatio Iohannis Scoti Eriugenae *operis*: Ps.-Dionysius Areopagita, *De diuinis nominibus* (*Dionysiaca*, LLA 696, 428, l. E)

938 qui²] quia R2 (Fd_pc)

933 aduersitate] aduersitatibus Aa   **934** creatura] natura Aa   **938** que] quem
Aa, *interlin.* Fd   **943** recipit] *add.* comparata Aa   **944** uanitati] uanitatis Fs Pf
952 uera] uere Aa Fs   **956** id uere] uere adest et id Bi

<Gratian's Final Response to the First Position>

d.p.c.45 The love which is abandoned in adversity, however, is asserted
to be feigned, that is, fake and fragile, just as the faith from which   cf. c.12
love proceeds is denied to be feigned, that is fragile, in the works of
the apostle. Similarly, the love which can be abandoned in adversity is said to have never been true. For, JUST AS JEROME WRITES   cf. c.2
AGAINST JOVINIAN, "Every creature is under vice, not because
everyone sins, but because there is not one which is not able to
sin." But being able to sin, AS AUGUSTINE SAYS, is not being able to   cf. c.40
do something, but rather is not being able to do something. Thus
he alone is called all-powerful who is not able to do this, who[49] can
do all things, the being able to do which is a being able to do something. Therefore just as in comparison with him who knows no
mutability, every creature is called corrupt because every creature
is capable of mutability, ACCORDING TO THAT TEXT: *No living thing
will be justified in your sight*, and, *The stars are not pure in his sight*, so   Ps 143:2
also, in comparison with his creature that does not receive change, | Jb 15:15
every creature which is changed is proven to be not genuine but
empty. For this reason, every man is called a liar and has become
similar to vanity. ON THIS ACCOUNT ALSO ECCLESIASTES: All the   cf. Eccl 1:2–3
things which are *under the sun*, that is, which take in the changes of
the seasons, are not only called vanity, which enters into every
creature by reason of its mutability, but also *vanity of vanities* by reason of the variety of the complete change which they take in.

In this way, then, in comparison with divine love, no virtue is
proven to be genuine, or, in comparison with that which is not
abandoned, that which is lost is denied to be genuine. But, just as
every creature is said to be good and genuine in its own way, so
also the love which is abandoned is shown to be genuine in its own
way. Otherwise, it would not be abandoned by anyone if it did not
exist in him in some way, for what exists truly in no way can in no
way be abandoned. But if it is truly abandoned in some way, it
should also truly exist in some way.

---

49. The second recension changed the "who" (*qui*) to a "because [he]" (*quia*).

Distinctio tertia

Hec de caritate breuiter scripsimus propter eos qui penitentiam   pr.
negant reiterari posse, asserentes quod, sicut caritas semel habita
numquam amittitur, ita penitentia semel uere celebrata nulla se-
5 quenti culpa maculatur; si uero criminalis culpa illam aliquando sequitur, uera penitentia non fuit nec ueniam a Domino inpetrauit.

<Sententia prima>

Quod ex diffinitione ipsius penitentie et multorum auctoritati-   d.a.c.1
bus probare contendunt. Vt enim ait AMBROSIUS IN QUODAM SER-
10 MONE QUADRAGESIME, "Penitentia est et mala preterita plangere   c.1
et plangenda iterum non conmittere." IDEM IN LIBRO DE UNICA
Fs 310rb   PENITENTIA: "Repperiuntur qui sepius penitentiam | agendam pu-   c.2
Bi 306rb   tant, qui luxuriantur | in Christo. Nam si uere in Christo peniten-
tiam agerent, iterandam postea non putarent quia, sicut unum bap-
15 tisma, ita una est penitentia. Verum preteriti semper debet nos penitere peccati, set hec delictorum leuiorum. At ego facilius inueni
qui recte seruauerit innocentiam quam qui congrue egerit penitentiam." ITEM AUGUSTINUS: "Satisfactio penitentie est peccatorum   c.3
causas excidere nec earum suggestionibus aditum indulgere."

20   IDEM IN LIBRO DE PENITENTIA: "Penitentia est quedam dolentis   c.4
Mk 247rb   uindicta, puniens in se quod dolet conmisisse." | Et infra: "Continue
dolendum est de peccato quod declarat ipsa dictionis uirtus. 'Penitere' enim est 'penam tenere' ut semper puniat in se ulciscendo
quod conmisit peccando. Pena enim proprie dicitur lesio que punit
Fd 94vb   et uindicat quod quisque conmisit. Ille penam tenet qui semper |
uindicat quod commisisse dolet. Penitentia itaque est uindicta sem-

---

3,10 Penitentia…**11** conmittere] *Coll. sermonum ps.-Ambr.* 7 (ed. Mercier, SChr
161:186.14–16); *olim* Ambr. Med. (dub.), *Sermo* 25 (PL 17:655A–B)   **12** Reppe-
riuntur…**18** penitentiam] Ambr. Med., *De paenitentia* 2.10 (SChr
179:192.37–44)   **18** Satisfactio…**19** indulgere] Genn. Mass., *De eccles. dog.* 24
(PL 42:1218)   **20** Penitentia…**21** conmisisse] Ps.-Aug., *De uera* 8 (PL 40:1120;
ed. Wagner, 446–47)   **21** Continue…**27** conmisisse] Ibid. 19 (PL 40:1128; ed.
Wagner, 956–62)

3,3 semel] *add.* uere Aa *praem.* uere Pf   **15** una] unica Bi EdF   **16** hec] hoc Aa
20 Idem] Item Fs Mk   **22** dictionis] dilectionis Bi Fs Mk_ac Pf Sb   **25** uindicat]
uindicans Bi EdF Fd Fs Mk_ac Pf

Distinction 3

pr. We have briefly written these things about love on account of those who deny that penance can be repeated, asserting that, just as love, once it is had, is never lost, so also penance, once it is truly celebrated, is not tainted by any subsequent guilt; but if the guilt of a mortal sin follows that penance at some point, it was not true penance and did not obtain mercy from the Lord.

<First Position>

d.a.c.1 They make an effort to prove this from the definition of penance itself and from many authorities. For as AMBROSE SAYS IN A CER-

c.1 TAIN LENTEN SERMON: "Penance is both lamenting past evils and not committing again the evils to be lamented." THE SAME IN THE

cf. D.1 c.39

c.2 BOOK ON ONE-TIME PENANCE: "Those who think that penance should be done often, who are wanton in Christ, are found out. For if they were truly doing penance in Christ, they would think that it should not be repeated afterward, because, just as there is one baptism, so also is there one penance. We ought always to repent of a past sin, but this concerns lighter offences. But I have more easily found the person who rightly preserves his innocence than the per-

c.3 son who appropriately does penance." LIKEWISE AUGUSTINE: "The satisfaction of penance consists of cutting away the causes of sins and not allowing anything added to their instigating forces."

c.4 THE SAME IN THE BOOK ON PENANCE: "Penance is a certain punishment of the one grieving, punishing in himself what he grieves to have committed." And below: "There should be a continual grieving over sin. The very composition of the word makes this known, for 'to repent' is 'to hold punishment' so that one may always punish in oneself by avenging what one committed by sinning. For a punishment is properly called an injuring that punishes and avenges what each person has committed. That man holds punishment who is always punishing what he grieves to have com-

per puniens in se quod dolet conmisisse." In eodem: "Si Apostolus   c.5
etiam peccata per baptismum dimissa continue plorat, nobis super

Pf 115vb   fundamentum Apostolorum positis | quid preter plorare restat?
Sb 272va   Quid, nisi semper dolere in | uita? Vbi enim dolor finitur, deficit et
penitentia. Si autem penitentia finitur, quid relinquitur de uenia?
Tamdiu enim gaudeat et speret de gratia, quamdiu sustentatur a
Aa 166^v   penitentia. Dicit enim Dominus, *Vade et amplius noli peccare.* | Non
dixit, 'Ne pecces,' set, 'Nec uoluntas peccandi in te oriatur.' Quod
35   quomodo seruabitur nisi dolor in penitentia continue custodiatur?
Hic semper doleat et dolore gaudeat, et de doloris penitentia, si
contigerit, semper doleat, et non sit satis quod doleat, et ex fide doleat et non semper doluisse doleat."

ITEM GREGORIUS IN "ESTIUUM TEMPUS": "Penitentiam agere   c.6
40   digne non possumus nisi modum quoque eiusdem penitentie co-
gnoscamus. Penitentiam quippe agere est et perpetrata mala plangere et plangenda non perpetrare. Nam qui sic alia deplorat, ut tamen alia conmittat adhuc penitentiam agere aut ignorat aut dissi-
mulat. Quid enim prodest si peccata quis luxurie defleat et tamen
Fs 310va   adhuc | auaritie estibus anhelat?"

(AaB 335^v)   {| IDEM: "Si autem dicunt pauci temporis penitentiam contra peccatum debere
sufficere ut iterum liceat ad peccatum redire, recte hos pastoris primi sententia percutit, qui ait: *Canis reuersus ad suum uomitum, et sus lota in uolutabro luti.* Magna
est enim contra peccatum uirtus penitentie, set si quis in eadem penitentia perseue-
50   ret. Penitentiam uere agere est conmissa plangere set iterum plangenda declinare."
Bi 306va   IDEM: "Productior est pena quam culpa, ne parua putaretur culpa | si cum illa fini-   c.7
retur et pena. Ac per hoc, uel ad demonstrationem debite miserie uel ad emendatio-
nem labilis uite uel ad exercitationem necessarie patientie, temporaliter hominem

---

27 Si...38 doleat] Ibid. 13 (PL 40:1124; ed. Wagner, 667-79)   39 Penitentiam...45 anhelat] Greg. Magn., *Hom. in evang.* 2.34.15 (CCSL
141:314.417–315.423)   46 Si...50 declinare] Greg. Magn., *Reg. epist.* 11.27
(CCSL 140A:911.265–270)   51 Productior...56 constitutio] Aug. Hipp., *In Ioh.
evang. tract.* 124 (CCSL 36:684.17–22, 27–28)

3,36 et^1] *add.* de R2 (*om.* Sb)   37 et^2] sed R2

34 Nec] ne Fs Pf   35 continue] crimine Fd Sb   37 et^1...doleat^2] *rep. pos.* fide do-
leat Bi, *rep. pos.* semper doleat Pf | et^1...doleat^3] *rep. sed exp.* Mk   53 patientie]
penitentie AaB Pf potentie Sb

mitted. Penance is, therefore, a vengeance always punishing in

c.5 oneself what one grieves to have committed." In the same work: "If the apostle continuously weeps over even the sins forgiven through baptism, what besides weeping remains for us who have been placed on the foundation of the apostles? What except always grieving in this life? For where grief ends, penance is lacking as well. But if penance ends, what is left of mercy? For one may rejoice in and hope for grace as long as one is sustained by penance. The Lord says, *Go and sin no more*. He did not say, 'Do not sin,' but, Jn 8:11 'Let not the will to sin arise in you.' How will this be preserved unless grief in penance is continuously guarded? On this occasion, let one always grieve and rejoice in grief and always, if it is fitting, grieve in the penance of grief, and let it not be sufficient that one grieves, and[1] let one grieve out of faith and grieve to have not always grieved."

c.6 LIKEWISE GREGORY IN HIS HOMILY "ESTIUUM TEMPUS"[2]: "We cannot do penance worthily if we do not know the way of this same penance. To be sure, doing penance is both lamenting the evils committed and not committing the things to be lamented. For he who deplores some evils in such a way that he nevertheless commits others still either does not know how to do penance or is faking it. For what does it matter if someone weeps over sins of extravagance and nevertheless still pants with the fevers of greed?"

THE SAME: "But if they say that a short time of penance ought to suffice against a sin so that one may return to sin once more, the opinion of the first shepherd rightly strikes these when he says, *A dog returns to his own vomit and a sow, after having been washed, to the slough of mud*. For great is the power of penance against 2 Pt 2:22 sin, but [only] if someone perseveres in the same penance. Truly doing penance is cf. D.3 c.1 lamenting the things committed but also turning away from the things to be

c.7 lamented." THE SAME: "Punishment is prolonged more than the guilty act lest the guilty act be deemed a small thing if the punishment were also to be ended with it. And through this process, either to demonstrate the misery owed or to correct a wavering life or to set necessary suffering in motion, punishment temporarily detains

---

1. The second recension changed this "and" to "but."
2. "Estiuum tempus" is the Latin incipit, or beginning words, for the quoted homily by Gregory.

detinet pena quem iam ad dampnationem sempiternam reum non retinet culpa....
55 Ira Dei non est ut hominis, id est perturbatio concitati animi, set tranquilla iusti su-
plicii constitutio."}

ITEM IOHANNES OS AUREUM: "Perfecta penitentia cogit pecca-   c.8
torem omnia libenter sufferre." Et infra: "In corde eius contritio, in
Pf 116ra ore confessio, in opere tota humilitas: hec | est fructifera peniten-
60 tia." IDEM SMARAGDUS: "Ille penitentiam digne agit qui sic prete-   c.9
rita mala deplorat ut futura iterum non conmittat. Nam qui plangit
Mk 247va peccatum et iterum admittit peccatum, quasi quis lauet | laterem
crudum: quem quanto magis abluerit, tanto magis lutum facit."

Sb 272vb   ITEM AUGUSTINUS: "Penitentes | (si tamen estis penitentes, et   c.10
65 non estis irridentes) mutate uitam, reconciliamini, et uos cum catena pascetis. Qua, inquis, catena? *Que ligaueris in terra erunt ligata et
in celo.* Audis ligaturam, et Deo putas facere inposturam? penitentiam agis, genua figis, et rides, subsannas patientiam Dei? Si penitentiam agis, penitet; si non penitet, penitens non es. Si ergo peni-
70 tet, cur facis quod male fecisti? Si fecisse penitet, noli facere; si adhuc facis, certe non es penitens."

ITEM YSIDORUS DE SUMMO BONO: "Irrisor est, non penitens,   c.11
qui adhuc agit quod penitet, nec uidetur Deum poscere subditus set
subsannare superbus. Canis reuersus ad uomitum et penitens ad
75 peccatum. Multi enim lacrimas indesinenter fundunt, et peccare
non desinunt. Quosdam accipere lacrimas ad penitentiam cerno et
Fs 310vb affectum | penitentie non habere, quia inconstantia mentis nunc re-
cordatione peccati lacrimas fundunt, nunc uero reuiuiscente usu
ea, que fleuerunt iterando conmittunt. Ysaias de peccatoribus dicit,
80 *Lauamini, mundi estote.* Lauatur et mundus est qui et preterita plan-

---

57 Perfecta...60 penitentia] Haymo Halb., *De amore coelestis patriae* 2.64 (PL
118:929A)   60 Ille...63 facit] Isid. Hisp., *Sententiae* 2.13.7 (CCSL
111:121.25–29)   64 Penitentes...71 penitens] Aug. Hipp. (dub.), *Sermo* 393 (PL
39:1713)   72 Irrisor...83 repetit] Isid. Hisp., *Sententiae* 2.16.1–4a (CCSL
111:128.2–129.19)

60 Idem] Item R2 (Idem Sb)   65 reconciliamini] *add.* Deo R2 (*interlin.* Fd$_{pc}$)

60 agit] ait Bi$_{ac}$ ait Sb   63 crudum] crudrum Aa, *interlin.* Fd   64 Penitentes] *mg.*
Fd, *rep.* Mk Sb, penitens *praem. sed cancell.* Bi   66 ligaueris] ligaueritis EdF Pf Sb
68 agis] agere est Fd | figis] figere? Fd   69 es] est Fd   72 Irrisor] derisor Bi | est]
es Aa   77 nunc] non Bi$_{ac}$ Fd | recordatione] recordatio Fd$_{ac}$ 78 fundunt] fundit
Fd$_{ac}$

the person, whom, though guilty, the guilty act did not yet restrain for everlasting damnation.... The wrath of God is not like that of man, that is, the stirring up of an excited mind, but a quiet establishment of a just punishment."

c.8   LIKEWISE JOHN THE GOLDEN MOUTH: "Perfect penance compels the sinner to endure all things willingly." And below: "Contrition in his heart, confession in the mouth, humility in the whole

c.9   work: this is fruitful penance." LIKEWISE[3] SMARAGDUS: "He does penance worthily who deplores past evils in such a way that he does not again commit them in the future. For he who laments a sin and again commits the sin [is] like someone washing a bloody side: the more he washes it, the more he makes mud."

c.10   LIKEWISE AUGUSTINE: "Penitents (if you are penitents and not mockers), change your life, be reconciled,[4] and sustain yourselves with a chain. With what chain, you say? *What things you bind on earth will be bound also in heaven.* Do you listen to the bond and do   Mt 16:19 you think to deceive God? Do you do penance, do you plant your knees, and do you laugh and deride the patience of God? If you do penance, be repentant; if you are not repentant, you are not a penitent. Therefore, if you are repentant, why do you do what you wickedly did? If you are repentant for having done it, do not do it; if you still do it, you certainly are not a penitent."

c.11   LIKEWISE ISIDORE ON THE HIGHEST GOOD: "He is a mocker, not a penitent, who still does what he repents of, and he does not seem to ask God submissively but to deride him in pride. A dog returns to its vomit and a penitent to sin. For many unceasingly pour forth tears and do not cease sinning. I see that certain people undertake tears for penance and do not have a repentant disposition, for, as a result of an inconstancy of mind, they pour forth tears at one moment with the recollection of the sin, but, the next moment, with enjoyment coming alive again, they go out again and commit those things which they wept over. Isaiah talks about sinners, *Wash and be clean.* He is washed and clean who both laments past deeds and   Is 1:16

---

3. The first recension actually read "The same Smaragdus," but, since this does not make sense, I have chosen to go with the second recension correction at this point.
4. The second recension added "to God."

git, et flenda iterum non admittit. Lauatur et non est mundus qui
plangit que gessit nec deserit, et post lacrimas ea que fleuerat repetit."

Aa 167ʳ   ITEM | IN LIBRO SOLILOQUIORUM AUGUSTINUS: "Inanis est pe-   c.12
85   nitentia, quam sequens culpa coinquinat. Vulnus iteratum tardius
sanatur; frequenter peccans et lugens ueniam uix meretur. Nichil
prosunt lamenta si replicantur peccata. Nichil ualet ueniam a malis
poscere et mala denuo iterare. Persiste ergo in confessione; esto in
penitentia fortiter confirmatus; uitam bonam quam cepisti tenere
90   non deseras; propositum bone uite conserua iugiter."

ITEM GREGORIUS IN PASTORALI: "Qui admissa plangunt nec ta-   c.13
Bi 306ᵛᵇ   men deserunt, | considerare sollicite sciant quia flendo inaniter
mundant qui uiuendo se nequiter inquinant, cum idcirco se lacri-
Pf 116ʳᵇ   mis lauant, ut mundi | ad sordes redeant." Item: "Qui admissa plan-   c.14
95   git nec tamen deserit pene grauiori se subicit, quia ipsam quam
flendo inpetrare potuit ueniam contempnit." Item: "Lauamini,   c.15
mundi estote. Post lauacrum enim mundus esse negligit quisquis post
lacrimas uite innocentiam non custodit. Et lauantur ergo nec
mundi sunt qui conmissa flere non desinunt set rursus flenda con-
100   mittunt." Item: "Baptizatur quippe a mortuo qui mundat se fletibus   c.16
Fd 95ʳᵃ | Sb | a peccato; set post baptisma mortuum | tangit qui culpas post lacri-
273ʳᵃ   mas repetit." IDEM IN MORALIBUS: "Incassum quippe bonum agi-   c.17
tur si ante uite terminum deseratur, quia et frustra uelociter currit
qui priusquam ad metas ueniat deficit."

---

84 Inanis…90 iugiter] Isid. Hisp., Synon. 1.77–78 (PL 83:845A–846A)
91 Qui…102 repetit] Greg. Magn., Reg. past. 3.30 (SChr 382:476.6–10, 18–21,
27–31, 33–36) 102 Incassum…104 deficit] Greg. Magn., Moralia in Iob 1.37
(CCSL 143:57.1–4)

82 fleuerat] fleuerit Fs Pf 85 iteratum] in tantum Fd 87 ueniam] pos. malis Bi
EdF Mk 89 cepisti] accepisti Fs Pf 96 contempnit] contempsit Mk Sb 98 Et]
om. Aa Fs adest sed exp. Mk 100 mortuo] add. et Biₐc Fd Pf 102 Idem] Item Aa
EdF

does not again commit the deeds to be wept over. He is washed and not clean who laments what things he has done and does not give them up, and, after the tears, he repeats the things which he had wept over."

c.12   LIKEWISE AUGUSTINE IN HIS BOOK OF SOLILOQUIES: "Penance is empty which subsequent guilt wholly pollutes. A repeat wound is healed more slowly; the frequent sinner and lamenter hardly deserves mercy. Laments profit nothing if sins are repeated. None can demand mercy for evils and then repeat the evils. Therefore, persist in confession; be strengthened firmly in penance; do not abandon holding onto the good life which you began; perpetually preserve the intention of a good life."

c.13   LIKEWISE GREGORY IN HIS *REGULA PASTORALIS*: "Let those who lament the things they have committed and nevertheless not given up know to consider anxiously that, though weeping, they clean in vain who pollute themselves by living wretchedly, when they wash themselves with tears in order to return to the sordid things of the

c.14 world." Likewise: "He who laments the things which he has committed and nevertheless does not give them up subjects himself to very serious punishment because he shows contempt for the very

c.15 mercy which he was able to obtain by weeping." Likewise: "*Wash and be clean*. For whoever neglects being clean after washing does   Is 1:16 not guard the innocence of life after tears. And therefore they are not washed and are not clean who do not cease weeping over the deeds committed and yet commit again the deeds to be wept over."

c.16 Likewise: "Indeed he is baptized by a dead man who cleans himself of sin with weeping; but he touches a dead man after baptism who

c.17 repeats the guilty acts after tears." THE SAME IN THE *MORALIA*: "To be sure, a vain good is done if the good is abandoned before the end of life, because he also runs quickly in vain who stops short of the goal."

105 **<Responsio Gratiani>**

Set uerba diffinitionis non ad diuersa tempora set ad idem tem-   d.p.c.17
Mk 247vb pus | referuntur, uidelicet, ut tempore quo deflet mala que conmi-
sit, non conmittat quod adhuc eum flere oporteat. Quod ex subse-
quentibus uerbis eiusdem auctoritatis datur intelligi, dum dicitur,
110 "Nam qui sic alia deplorat, ut tamen alia conmittat, adhuc peniten-
Fs 311ra tiam | agere aut ignorat aut dissimulat."

(FdB 161va) | HINC AUGUSTINUS IN ENCHIRIDION: "Sane cauendum est, ne quisquam ex-   c.18
(AaB 335^v) istimet infanda illa crimina, qualia qui agunt regnum Dei non possidebunt, cottidie
perpetranda et elemosinis cottidie redimenda. In melius quippe est uita mutanda,
115 et per elemosinas de peccatis preteritis est propitiandus Deus, non ad hoc emen-
dus quodammodo, ut ea semper liceat inpune conmittere. Nemini enim dedit laxa-
mentum peccandi, quamuis miserando deleat iam facta peccata si non satisfactio
congrua negligatur." Idem: "Qui uult ordinate dare elemosinam a se ipso debet in-   c.19
cipere et eam sibi primum dare. Est enim elemosina opus misericordie uerissime
120 de qua dictum est: *Miserere anime tue placens Deo.* Propter hoc renascimur, ut Deo
placeamus." ITEM IOHANNES CRISOSTOMUS: "De cottidianis, breuibus, leuibus-   c.20
que peccatis, sine quibus hec uita non ducitur, cottidiana oratio fidelium satisfacit.
Eorum enim dicere est, *Pater noster, qui es in celis*, qui iam patri taliter regenerati
sunt ex aqua et Spiritu sancto. Delet omnino hec oratio minima cottidiana peccata.
Pf 116va Delet | et illa a quibus uita fidelium etiam scelerate gesta set penitendo in melius
mutata discedit. Sic quemadmodum ueraciter dicitur, *Dimitte nobis debita nostra*,
quoniam non desunt que dimittantur, ita ueracitur dicatur: *Sicut et nos dimittimus
debitoribus nostris*, id est, fiat quod dicitur, quia et ipsa elemosina est ueniam peten-
tibus omnino ignoscere." ITEM PIUS PAPA: "Nichil prodest homini ieiunare, et   c.21
130 orare, et alia religionis opera agere, nisi mens ab iniquitate reuocetur."

---

112 Sane...118 negligatur] Aug. Hipp., *Ench.* 19 (CCSL 46:87.1–8)   118 Qui...
121 placeamus] Ibid. 20 (CCSL 46:90.27–30)   121 De...129 ignoscere] Ibid. 19
(CCSL 46:88.9–19)   129 Nichil...130 reuocetur] Ps.-Pius, *Epistola* 1.6 (*Decr.
ps.-isid.*, ed. Hinschius, 117)

107 tempore] tempus Bi_ac Fs Mk   110 tamen] non Fd_ac iterum Pf   114 est] *om.*
Bi *ant.* quippe Fs Mk (*interlin.* Mk)   115 elemosinas] elemonisis Fs Pf_ac   123 ta-
liter] *om.* Pf   128 et] etiam AaB, in *sed exp.* Bi, *add.* in Pf

<Gratian's Response>

d.p.c.17   But the words of definition are not related to various times but to the same time, namely, so that in the time in which one is weeping over the evils which one has committed, one may not commit what one still ought to be weeping over. This is given to be understood from the subsequent words of the same authority when it is said, "For he who deplores some evils in such a way that he nevertheless commits others still either does not know how to do penance or is faking it." D.3 c.6

c.18   ON THIS ACCOUNT, AUGUSTINE IN THE *Enchiridion*: "Everyone would do well to guard against thinking that those unspeakable crimes, the kind which those who do them will not possess the kingdom of heaven, should be daily perpetrated and daily redeemed with alms. Life should certainly be changed for the better, and God should be propitiated for past sins through alms, not somehow bought off for the reason that one may always commit these things with impunity. For he gave a license to sin to no one, although he has compassion and erases sins already done if

c.19   a fitting satisfaction is not neglected." The same: "He who wants to give alms in an orderly manner ought to begin from himself and give alms first to himself. For alms is a work of the truest compassion, of which it is said, *Have mercy on your soul and please God*. We are born again for this reason: to please God." LIKEWISE JOHN   Ecclus 30:24

c.20   CHRYSOSTOM: "With respect to daily, brief, and light sins, without which this life is not led, the daily prayer of the faithful makes satisfaction. For to say, *Our Father, who art in heaven*, belongs to those who have already been regenerated unto the Fa-   Mt 6:9 ther in such a way by water and the Holy Spirit. This prayer entirely wipes out the smallest daily sins. It also wipes out those sins which the life of the faithful, carried out even wickedly but changed for the better through repentance, abandons. Just as how it is truly said, *Forgive us our debts*, since they are not lacking which may be forgiven, so also let it be truly said, *As we also forgive our debtors*, that is, let what is   Mt 6:12 said take place, because forgiving entirely those seeking mercy is also the essence of

c.21   almsgiving." LIKEWISE POPE PIUS: "Fasting and praying and doing other works of religious devotion profits man nothing unless his mind is called back from iniquity."

Bi 307ra   Ex persona huiuscemodi | penitentis etiam illud Smaragdi intelli-   d.p.c.21
gitur, "Ille penitentiam digne agit," etc., et illud Augustini, "Penitentes, penitentes," etc., et illud Ysidori: "Irrisor est, non penitens,"
et illud Ysaie, *Lauamini, mundi estote.* Idem illud Soliloquiorum,
135 "Inanis est penitentia." Similiter illud Gregorii, "Qui admissa plangunt," et, "Baptizatur a mortuo."

Sb 273rb | Illud autem Ambrosii, "Repperiuntur," etc., non secundum ge-
neralem, set secundum specialem consuetudinem ecclesie de solempni penitentia dictum intelligitur, que apud quosdam semel ce-
140 lebrata non reiteratur. VNDE AUGUSTINUS SCRIBIT AD MACEDO-
NIUM: "Quamuis caute et salubriter prouisum sit, ut locus illius hu-   c.22
Fs 311rb   millime penitentie | semel in ecclesia concedatur, ne medicina uilis
minus utilis esset egrotis, que tanto magis salubris est, quanto mi-
Aa 167v   nus | contemptibilis fuerit, quis tamen audeat Deo dicere, 'Quare
145 huic homini, qui post primam penitentiam rursus se laqueis iniqui-
Mk 248ra   tatis obstringit, adhuc | iterum parcis?'" Hac auctoritate et illud Am-   d.p.c.22
brosii determinatur, et iterum peccaturo per primam penitentiam
uenia dari monstratur; alioquin nequaquam iterum parceret Deus,
qui nec dum pepercisset.

150   "Satisfactio quoque penitentie," et, *Vade et amplius noli peccare*
eundem cum diffinitione intellectum habent.
Illud autem, quod in libro de penitentia dicitur, de perfecto intelligendum est. Sicut enim caritas alia est incipiens, alia proficiens,
alia perfecta; sic et penitentia alia est incipientium, alia proficien-
155 tium, alia perfectorum. Sicut autem caritati, licet nondum perfecte,

141 Quamuis... 146 parcis] Aug. Hipp., *Epistula* 153 (CSEL 44:403.5–11)

134 Idem] Item R2   140 reiteratur] iteratur R2 (reiteratur Pf recitatur Sb)
152 perfecto] perfecta R2 (perfecto Sb)   153 alia²] *add.* est R2 (*om.* Fs Pf Sb)

132 agit] ait Bi Fs | Penitentes...133 etc] *om.* Aa   133 penitentes] *om.* EdF Fs Pf
est] *add.* et Aa Mkpc EdF (*interlin.* Mk) | penitens] *om.* Bi Fs Mkac, *mg.* Mkpc
134 Idem] *add.* et Aa EdF   136 Baptizatur] baptizantur Bi Fs Mk Pf   148 ne-
quaquam] nequam Biac Mk   150 et¹] *om.* Aa Pf Sb   151 habent] non habent
Aa   153 proficiens] perficiens Fd *add.* uel pro-[ficiens] *interlin.* Fd

d.p.c.21   That statement of Smaragdus, "He does penance worthily," etc.,   D.3 c.9
is also understood from the viewpoint of the person of this kind of
penitent, as is that statement of Augustine: "Penitents," etc., and   D.3 c.10
that of Isidore: "He is a mocker and not a penitent," and that of Isa-   D.3 c.11
iah: *Wash, be clean.* Likewise[5] that sentence of the *Soliloquies*:   D.3 c.15
"Penance is empty." Similarly that statement of Gregory: "Let those   D.3 c.12
who lament the things they have committed," and: "He is baptized   D.3 c.13
by a dead man."   D.3 c.16

That statement of Ambrose, however: "They are found out,"
etc., is understood to be said not according to the general but ac-   D.3 c.2
cording to the special custom of the church concerning solemn
penance, which, according to certain people, is not repeated once it
has been celebrated. FOR THIS REASON AUGUSTINE WRITES TO
c.22   MACEDONIUS: "Although there is cautious and salubrious provi-
sion that the place of that most humble penance is granted one
time in the church, lest a weak medicine be less useful to the dis-
eased—a medicine, which, the more salubrious it is, the less it will
be able to be esteemed lightly—nevertheless, who would dare to
say to God: why are you yet sparing once more this person who
binds himself again with the chains of iniquity after a first
d.p.c.22   penance?" This authority both explains that of Ambrose and shows
that mercy is given through the first penance to the one who will
sin again; otherwise God, when he had not yet spared, would in no
way spare again.

Also the authorities, "The satisfaction of penance" and *Go and sin*   D.3 c.3
no more, have the same meaning as the texts of definition.[6]   D.3 c.5

But that which is said in the book about penance should be un-   D.3 cc.4–5
derstood as being about the perfected man.[7] For just as one love is
incipient, another progressing, and another perfected, so also one
penance is of those beginning, another of those progressing, and
another of the perfected. But just as mercy for sins is given in bap-

5. In a similar fashion to above at D.3 c.9, the second recension reads "Likewise" while the first recension has an incorrect "The same" (*idem*), which does
not make sense in the flow of the text or in relationship to the authors in the
order given.
6. In other words, these authorities should be interpreted just as he has interpreted cc. 6, 9–11, 15, 12–13, and 16 in the section just prior.
7. By the ending on the adjective "perfect," Gratian originally indicated that it
described a person, but the second recension changed the final letter and thus
the gender of the adjective, making it describe an assumed "penance," so the
English translation of the second recension would read, "...understood as being
about perfect penance."

in baptismo datur uenia peccatorum, ut quamuis postea grauiter
aliquis sit peccaturus, tamen tunc intelligatur esse renatus, non
aqua tantum (sicut Iouinianus tradidit), set aqua et spiritu (sicut Ieronimus contra eum scribit); sic et incipientium penitentie uenia
non negatur, | que quadam ratione perfecta dici potest, quia toto
corde gemit et dolet, licet alia ratione dicatur inperfecta, quia non
usque in finem duratura. Secundum primum modum perfectionis
intelligitur illud Iohannis Oris aurei, "Perfecta penitentia," etc.
Iuxta secundum modum perfectionis illud Augustini intelligitur,
"Penitentia est uindicta semper puniens in se quod dolet conmisisse."

Pf 116vb

165

Illud autem, "Si penitentia finitur, nichil de uenia relinquitur,"
dupliciter intelligi potest. Si enim iuxta quorumdam sententiam
peccata dimissa redeunt, facile est intelligere "nichil de uenia relinquitur," quoniam peccata que prius erant dimissa iterum replicantur. Sicut enim ille qui ex iusta seruitute in libertatem manumitti-
tur interim uere liber est, quamuis ob ingratitudinem in seruitutem
postea reuocetur, sic et penitenti peccata uere remittuntur, quamuis ob ingratitudinem uenie eisdem postea sit inplicandus. Si autem
peccata dimissa non redeunt, dicitur nichil relinqui de uenia quia
nichil sibi relinquitur de uite munditia | et spe eterne beatitudinis,
quam cum | uenia assecutus est. Sicut enim | argento perfecte pur-
gato nichil sui decoris relinquitur si sequenti erugine fedatur, non
tamen prima, set subsequenti sordidatur, sic expiato per penitentiam nichil de uenia dicitur relinqui, cum tamen non iam deletis,
set adhuc expiandis coinquinetur.

170

175

Sb 273va

Bi 307rb | Fs
311va

180

\<Sententia Gratiani\>

Aa 168^r

Quod autem per penitentiam non semel tantum | set sepissime
peccata remittantur multorum auctoritate probatur. AIT ENIM IE-

---

161 dicatur] potest dici R2 (dicatur Sb)

160 dici potest] *tr.* Bi Fs Mk Sb   **163** Oris] Os Bi Fs Mk Sb | Oris aurei] Os au-
reum Aa   **168** intelligi potest] intelligitur Aa   **170** iterum] *om.* Aa   **174** eisdem]
eis Bi eiusdem Mk_ac Pf   **184** auctoritate] auctoritatibus Sb

tism for love, although not yet perfected, so that, although someone may afterward sin gravely, nevertheless he may then be understood to have been reborn, not with water alone (as Jovinian hands
down), but with water and the Spirit (as Jerome writes against
him); so also mercy is not denied to the penance of those beginning, which, by a certain principle, can be said to be perfect because it groans and grieves with the whole heart, although, by another principle, it may be said[8] to be imperfect because it will not
last all the way to the end. That statement of John the Golden
Mouth, "Perfect penance," etc., is understood according to the first   D.3 c.8
mode of perfection. That statement of Augustine, "Penance is a
vengeance always punishing in oneself what one grieves to have
committed," is understood according to the second mode of perfec-   D.3 c.4
tion.

But that statement, "If penance ends, nothing is left of mercy,"   D.3 c.5
can be understood in two ways. For if, according to the opinion of
certain people, forgiven sins return, "nothing of mercy is left" is
easy to understand, since the sins which had previously been forgiven are repeated again. For just as he who is manumitted from a
just servitude into liberty is in the meantime truly free, although he
may afterward be called back into servitude on account of ingratitude, so also sins are truly remitted for the penitent, although he
may afterward have to be implicated by these same sins on account
of ingratitude for the mercy. But if forgiven sins do not return, that
"nothing of mercy is left" is said because nothing is left for him of
the purity of life and the hope of eternal beatitude which he obtained with mercy. For just as nothing of its beauty is left for perfectly polished silver if it should be marred with rust, but it would
nevertheless not be blemished by its first rust but a subsequent one,
so also nothing of mercy is said to be left for the person expiated
through penance, since he is nevertheless not polluted by sins already erased but by sins still to be expiated.

<Gratian's Position>

But that sins are remitted through penance not once only but
very often is proven by many authorities. FOR JEROME SAYS TO

---

8. The Latin present active subjunctive "may be said" (*dicatur*) became "can be
said" (*potest dici*) in the second recension, most likely in order to match the ver-
bal structure in the previous clause (*dici potest*).

185 RONIMUS AD RUSTICUM DE PENITENTIA, *"Septies cadit iustus et resur-*   c.23
Fd 95rb *git.* Si cadit, quomodo iustus? Si iustus, | quomodo cadit? Set iusti
uocabulum non amittit qui per penitentiam semper resurgit. Et non
solum septies set septuagies septies delinquenti, si conuertatur ad
penitentiam, peccata donantur. *Cui plus dimittitur, plus diligit."*

190   Dauid quoque per penitentiam adulterii simul et homicidii ue-   d.p.c.23
Mk 248rb niam inpetrauit. De cuius penitentia | in eodem libro Ieronimus
scribit, "Totam penitentiam peccatoris ostendit Psalmus quinquage-   c.24
simus, quando ingressus est Dauid ad Bersabee uxorem Urie, et,
Nathan prophetante correctus, respondit dicens, *Peccaui,* statimque
195 meruit audire, *et Dominus abstulit a te peccatum.* Adulterio enim iun-
xerat homicidium et tamen conuersus ad lacrimas: *Miserere,* ait, *mei,*
Deus, secundum magnam misericordiam tuam. Magnum enim pecca-
Pf 117ra tum magna | indigebat misericordia. Vnde iungit et dicit, *Multum*
laua me ab iniquitate mea et a peccato meo munda me, quoniam iniquita-
200 *tem meam ego cognosco, et peccatum meum contra me est semper. Tibi soli*
peccaui (rex enim, alium non timebat) *et malum coram te feci ut iustifi-*
ceris in sermonibus tuis et uincas cum iudicaris. Conclusit enim Deus omnia
sub 'peccato' ut omnibus misereatur. Tantumque profecit ut dudum
peccator et penitens transierit in magistrum: *Docebo iniquos uias tuas,*
205 *et inpii ad te conuertentur.* Confessio enim et pulchritudo coram eo,
ut qui fuerit sua peccata confessus et dixerit: *Corrupte sunt et conpu-*
truerunt cicatrices mee; feditatem uulnerum in sanitatis decorem con-
mutet."

ITEM AMBROSIUS IN APOLOGIA DAUID: "Ille rex tantus ac potens ne exiguo   c.25
210 quidem momento manere penes se delicti passus est conscientiam, set prematura
Fs 311vb confessione | atque inmenso dolore reddidit peccatum suum Domino." Et infra:

---

185 Septies...**189** diligit] Hier., *Epistula* 122 (CSEL 56:66.16–20)   **192** Totam...
208 conmutet] Ibid. 122 (CSEL 56:63.22–64.22)   **209** Ille...**223** lapsum] Ambr.
Med., *De apologia David* 2.5–6 (SChr 239:76.3–6, 11–15, 77.3–78.16)

189 dimittitur] donatur R2 (dimittitur Pf EdF)   **194** Nathan prophetante] a Nathan propheta R2 (Nathan prophetante Sb)   **198** indigebat] indiget R2 (indige-
bat Sb)   **200** cognosco] agnosco R2 (Aa, cognosco Pf)

192 scribit] ait Fd_ac Pf EdF   **193** quando] quoniam Fs Sb | Bersabee] *interlin. pos.*
Urie Mk_pc, *om.* Bi EdF Fs Pf   **194** correctus] correptus Aa_pc Bi EdF   **195** pecca-
tum] *add.* tuum Sb Pf, *ant.* a te Pf   **204** tuas] *om.* Mk Pf   **209** Dauid] *add.* De
eodem AaB

c.23 RUSTICUS ABOUT PENANCE: "*A righteous man falls seven times and gets back up*. If he falls, how is he righteous? If he is righteous, how does he fall? But he who always gets back up through penance does not lose the label of righteous. And not only seven times but seventy times seven times are sins forgiven for the offender if he should turn round to penance. *He who is forgiven*[9] *more loves more*." ⟨Prv 24:6⟩ ⟨cf. Lk 7:47⟩

d.p.c.23 David also obtained mercy for adultery and murder at the same time through penance. Concerning his penance, Jerome says in the

c.24 same book: "The fiftieth Psalm shows the whole penance of the sinner, when David entered into the wife of Uriah and, having been corrected by Nathan in his prophesying,[10] he answered, saying, *I have sinned*, and immediately he deserved to hear, *and the Lord has taken your sin away from you*. For he had added murder to adultery, and, nevertheless, he turned to tears and said, *Have mercy on me, o God, according to your great loving-kindness*. For his great sin required[11] great loving-kindness. For this reason he adds and says, *Wash me well from my iniquity and cleanse me of my sin, for I acknowledge my iniquity, and my sin is always in front of me. I have sinned against you alone* (for, as king, he did not fear any other) *and I have done evil in your sight so that you may be righteous in your words and overcome when you are judged*. For God has included all things under 'sin' so that he may have mercy on all. And David advanced so much that the recent sinner and penitent transitioned into a teacher: *I will teach your ways to the wicked, and the impious will be converted to you*. For confession is also beauty in his presence, as he who confessed his sins and said, '*My scars have grown worse and rotted*; let the foulness of my wound be exchanged for the beauty of health.'"

⟨2 Sm 12:13⟩
⟨Ps 50:1⟩
⟨Ps 50:2–4⟩
⟨Rom 11:32, Gal 3:22⟩
⟨Ps 50:13⟩
⟨Ps 37:6⟩

c.25 LIKEWISE AMBROSE IN *De apologia Dauid*: "He, so great and powerful a king, did not allow the conscience of his offence to remain in his power for even the slightest moment, but, with an early confession and immense grief, he related his sin to the Lord." And below: "Finally the grief of his innermost feelings moved the

---

9. The second recension reads "given" or "granted" (*donator*). All but one of Friedberg's manuscripts had this reading, but he nevertheless gave the reading of the one manuscript (Köln, Dombibliothek 127, which, like Pf and Sb, frequently also preserves first recension readings) since it matched Jerome's text.
10. The second recension simplified the phrase "by Nathan in his prophesying" to "by Nathan the prophet."
11. The second recension changed this verb to a present tense, "requires," rendering the sentence: "For a great sin requires great loving-kindness."

"Denique Dominum dolor intimi mouit affectus, ut Nathan diceret, *Quoniam peni-*

tuit | *te, et Dominus transtulit* | peccatum tuum. Maturitas itaque uenie profundam

regis fuisse penitentiam declarauit, que tanti erroris offensam transduxerit." Et infra:

"Sancti, qui consummare certamen pium gestiunt et currere cursum salutis, sic ubi

forte ut homines corruunt, nature magis fragilitate quam peccandi | libidine, acrio-

res ad currendum resurgunt, pudoris stimulo maiora reparantes certamina, ut non

solum nullum attulisse estimetur | lapsus inpedimentum, set etiam uelocitatis in-

centiua cumulasse. Ergo si currentium non soluitur cursus cum aliqui forte cecide-

runt, non luctantium contentio set inoffensa manent certamina, quin etiam plerique

post unum uel alterum lapsum gratia maiore uicerunt, quanto magis agonem pieta-

tis ingressi non debent unius prolapsionis offensione censeri, cum beatus sit qui se

potuit reparare post lapsum?" Et infra: "Quod peccauit, conditionis est; quod sup-

plicauit, correctionis. Lapsus conmunis, set specialis confessio. Culpam itaque inci-

disse nature est, diluisse | uirtutis." Et infra: "Peccatum aut donatur aut deletur aut

tegitur. Donatur per gratiam, deletur per sanguinem crucis, tegitur per caritatem; si-

militer et iniquitas que estimatur habitudo mentis iniuste, licet Iohannes in epistola

eum qui fecerit peccatum et iniquitatem fecisse dixerit. Peccatum est iniquitas, quia

in peccato ipso est iniquitas. Tamen, ut nobis uidetur, peccatum opus est | iniquita-

tis, iniquitas autem operatrix culpe atque delicti. Prius est ergo ut ipsa iniquitas de-

leatur, excidatur radix et seminarium peccatorum. Itaque quemadmodum intrans in

animam sapientis disciplina inprudentiam tollit et scientia ignorantiam, sic perfecta

uirtus iniquitatem et remissio peccatorum delet omne peccatum."

Item in eodem: "Illud uero quam admirabile est quod angelo ferienti plebem se   c.26

obtulit dicens, *Grex iste quid fecit? Fiat manus tua in* | *me et in domum patris mei.*

Quo facto statim sacrificio dignus iudicatus est qui absolutione estimabatur indi-

gnus. Nec mirum si tali sua oblatione pro populo peccati sui adeptus est ueniam,

---

223 Quod...**225** uirtutis] Ibid. 4.15 (SChr 239:92.12–15)   **225** Peccatum...**233**
peccatum] Ibid. 13.62–63 (SChr 239:164.1–13, 1–4)   **234** Illud...**251** errorem]
Ibid. 7.38–40 (SChr 239:120.1–122.8)

212 mouit] mouet AaB Bi EdF Fs moui Mkₐc monuit Pf   **213** transtulit] *add.* a
te Mk   **214** transduxerit] traduxerit AaB Mk   **215** gestiunt] contendunt FdB
216 corruunt] corruerint Sb   **217** reparantes] reputantes FdB   **218** uelocitatis]
uelocitas FdB Sb   **219** ceciderunt] ceciderint EdF Pf   **220** luctantium] lictan-
tium Biₐc Mkₐc   **223** conditionis] condicio Fs Mk Pf   **224** correctionis] correptio-
nis Pf | specialis] spiritualis Fs Pf   **234** plebem] *om.* FdB   **236** indignus] dignus
ant. estimabatur FdB   **237** tali] talis Bi talia Pf | sua] *add.* intentione Bi

Lord so that Nathan might say, *Since you have repented, the Lord has also removed your sin*. The completeness of mercy thus declared that the penance of the king, which removed the offense of so great an error, had been deep." And below: "The saints who long to consummate the pious struggle and run the race of salvation, wheresoever perchance they fall as men, more from the weakness of nature than from the desire to sin, they get back up to run more ardently, renewing the struggles greater than the pang of shame, not only so that it may not be thought that some-one caused an obstacle for the fall but also so that it may not be thought that some-one piled on incentives for speed. Therefore, if a runner's race is not cut short when certain of the runners happen to have fallen, if it is not a contest of wrestlers but un-obstructed struggles that remain, if indeed after one or another fall several runners also reach the finish line with greater grace, how much more ought they who have entered the contest of piety not be assessed by the offence of one lapse, since he is blessed who has been able to recover himself after a fall?" And below: "What one has sinned belongs to one's condition; what one has prayed belongs to correction. Falling is common, but confession is special. It is thus of nature that guilt has oc-curred but of virtue that it has washed away." And below: "Sin is either forgiven or erased or covered. It is forgiven through grace, it is erased through the blood of the cross, it is covered through love; similarly also the iniquity which is judged to be the habit of an unrighteous mind, although John in his epistle said that he who com-mits a sin has also committed injustice. Sin is injustice because injustice is in the sin itself. Nevertheless, as it seems to us, sin is a work of injustice, but injustice is the operator of guilt and offence. It is, therefore, preferable that the injustice itself be erased, that the root and nursery of sins be cut out. Therefore, in the way that learn-ing enters into the soul of the wise man and removes imprudence and knowledge removes ignorance, in this way perfect virtue destroys injustice and the remission of sins destroys every sin."

2 Sm 12:13

c.26   Likewise in the same book: "But how admirable is that which has offered itself as a nation to the angel who deceives, saying, *What did that crowd do? Let your hand be set against me and against my father's house*. By what sacrifice immediately made was he who was regarded as unworthy of absolution judged worthy? It is not wondrous if, when Moses, by offering himself to the Lord for the error of the com-

1 Chr 21:17

cum Moyses offerendo se Domino pro plebis errore peccata diluerit. Texit igitur
peccata sua, an non? Set quis hoc neget, cum ipse docuerit Propheta quod remit-
tantur iniquitates, tegantur peccata, non inputentur a Domino? | *Delictum meum*
agnosco, et iniustitiam meam non operui. Dixi, pronuntiabo iniustitiam meam Do-
mino, et tu remisisti inpietatem cordis mei. Si dixit, *pronuntiabo,* et ueniam meruit
antequam pronuntiaret, quanto magis ubi de se pronuntiauit dicens, *iniquitatem*
meam ego agnosco et delictum meum coram me est semper, remissum est ei omne
peccatum? Licet specialiter de hoc Nathan propheta responderit, *Et Dominus trans-*
tulit peccatum tuum. Ergo et remissionem meruit iniquitatis et texit caritate atque
operuit peccata sua, et texit operibus bonis, nec inputatum est ei peccatum, quia
non fuit in eo dolus malitie, set lapsus erroris; denique non fuit inprobitatis estus,
set umbra misterii, et tamen confessus est delictum suum, agnouit | iniquitatem, |
uidit lauacrum, et uidit et credidit. Dilexit multum | ut nimia caritate tegere quemuis
posset errorem."

Sb 274ra

245

Bi 307vb I AaB
336^v
Pf 117va

Ecce, cuius penitentia hic conmendatur, cui etiam uenia per Prophetam data monstratur, quam grauiter postea deliquerit, populi
multitudo prostrata ostendit.

d.p.c.26

255   Achab quoque (ut Ieronimus contra Iouinianum scribit) rex in-
piissimus, ut sententiam Dei subterfugeret et euersio domus eius
differretur in posteros, ieiunio inpetrauit et sacco. De quo ad eundem Rusticum scribit idem Ieronimus, dicens: "Achab rex in-
piissimus uineam Nabuthe cruore possedit, et, cum Iezabel, non
260   tam coniugio sibi quam crudelitate coniuncta, Elie increpatione
corripitur, hec dicit Dominus: *Occidisti et possedisti?* et iterum: *'In loco*
quo linxerunt canes sanguinem Nabuthe, ibi lingent sanguinem tuum.... Et
Iezabel canes comedent ante muros Iezrahel.' ... *Quod cum audisset Achab,*
scidit uestimenta sua et posuit saccum | super carnem suam, ieiunauitque et
265   *dormiuit in cilicio. Factusque est sermo Domini ad Eliam, dicens, 'Quoniam*
reueritus est Achab faciem meam, non inducam malum in | diebus eius.'
Vnum scelus et Achab et Iezabel conmiserunt; et tamen conuerso

c.27

Fs 312rb

Aa 168^v

258 Achab...269 iudicio] Hier., *Epistula* 122 (CSEL 56:64.23–65.13)

239 quis] Si FdB Pf   242 remisisti] dimisisti AaB EdF Fs Mk Pf   243 ubi] cum
FdB   245 responderit] respondit Bi Mk Pf | transtulit] traxit Sb   247 inputa-
tum] inputandum Sb EdRom   254 prostrata] monstrata Fd   262 lingent] lu-
gent Fd litigent Fs_ac

munity, washed away sins, he acquired mercy for his sin by such an offering as his
for the people. Therefore did he cover his sins or not? But who would deny this
when the prophet himself has taught that injustices are remitted, that sins are covered and are not imputed by the Lord? *I acknowledge my sin and I have not covered
up my unrighteousness. I said, I will declare my unrighteousness to the Lord and you
forgave the wickedness of my heart.* If he said, *I will declare*, and he deserved mercy   Ps 31:5
before he declared, how much more, when he declared and said concerning himself, *I acknowledge my injustice and my offence is always before me*, was every sin re-   Ps 50:5
mitted him? Indeed specifically concerning this the prophet Nathan responded, *And
the Lord has removed your sin.* Therefore he both deserved the remission of the in-   2 Sm 12:13
justice and covered and hid his sins with love, and he covered them with good
works, and his sin was not imputed to him, because the guile of malice was not in
him but a lapse of error; in the end, there was no burning desire for improbity, but
the shadow of a mystery, and he nevertheless confessed his offence, he acknowl-
edged his injustice, he saw a washing, and he saw and believed. He loved much so
that he might be able to cover any error whatsoever with excessive love."

d.p.c.26   Behold, commended here is the penance of him to whom mercy
is also shown to have been given through the prophet. How
gravely he afterward offended is shown by the ruined multitude of
the people.   cf. 2 Sm
     In addition, Ahab (as Jerome writes against Jovinian), a very   24:15–17
wicked king, through the means of fasting and sackcloth managed
to evade the judgment of God and delay to posterity the destruction of his house. JEROME WRITES ABOUT THIS TO THE SAME RUS-
c.27   TICUS, saying: "Ahab, a very wicked king, took possession of
Naboth's vineyard by bloodshed, and, when Jezebel, conjoined to
him not so much by marriage as by cruelty, is reproached by the
chiding of Elijah, the Lord says these things: *Have you killed and
taken possession?* and again, *'In the place in which dogs have licked the
blood of Naboth, they will lick your blood.... And dogs will eat Jezebel in
front of the walls of Jezreel.'...* When Ahab had heard this, he tore his
clothes and placed sackcloth on his flesh, and he fasted and slept in a hairshirt. The word of the Lord came to Elijah, saying, 'Since Ahab has revered
my face, I will not bring evil in his days.'* Ahab and Jezebel together   1 Kgs 21:19,
                                                                          23, 27–29

Mk 248vb Achab ad penitentiam pena differtur in posteros, | et Iezabel in sce-
lere perseuerans presenti condempnatur iudicio."

270   ITEM IOHANNES CRISOSTOMUS DE REPARATIONE LAPSI: "Talis,   c.28
mihi crede, talis est erga homines pietas Dei: talis nunquam spernit
penitentiam si ei simpliciter et sincere offeratur. Etiam si ad sum-
mum quis perueniat malorum et inde tamen reuerti uelit ad uirtutis uiam, suscipit, libenter amplectitur. Facit omnia quatinus ad
Sb 274rb priorem reuocet statum. Quodque est adhuc prestantius | et emi-
nentius, etiamsi non potuerit quis explere omnem satisfaciendi ordinem, quantulamcumque tamen et quamlibet breui tempore ge-
stam non respuit penitentiam. Suscipit etiam ipsam nec patitur
quamuis exigue conuersionis perdere mercedem. Hoc enim mihi
280   indicat Ysaias ubi de populo Iudeorum talia quedam dicit, *Propter*
peccatum modice conturbaui eum, et percussi eum, et auerti faciem meam
ab eo; et contristatus est, et ambulauit tristis, et sanaui eum, et consolatus
sum eum. Euidentius autem nobis testimonium dabit etiam rex ille
Pf 117vb inpius, qui cupiditatis quidem sue | predam uxoris nequitia quesi-
285   uit, set perturbatus ipsius sceleris inmanitate penituit et cilicio cir-
cumdatus facinus suum fleuit, atque ita erga se Dei misericordiam
prouocauit, ut a cunctis absolueretur peccatis. Sic enim ait Deus ad
Bi 308ra Eliam, *Vidisti quomodo conpunctus est Achab a | facie mea? Et quia fleuit*
in conspectu meo, non inducam mala in diebus eius."

(FdB 161vb) | ITEM GREGORIUS IN OMELIA X SUPER EZECHIELEM: "Sic Achab rex iniquus a   c.29
(AaB   Propheta reprehensus, cum contra se diuinam sententiam audisset, pertimuit, et
336^v)   magno merore deprehensus est, ita ut Prophete suo Dominus diceret, *Nonne uidisti*

---

270 Talis … **289** eius] Ioh. Chrys., *Ad Theodorum lapsum* 1.6 (PG 47:284)
290 Sic … **298** displicebat] Greg. Magn., *Hom. in Hiezech. proph.* 1.10 (CCSL
142:166.815–167.825)

287 absolueretur] eum absolueret R2

272 simpliciter … sincere] sincere et simpliciter Aa EdF Fs Pf   **282** ambulauit]
ambulaui Bi Fs Mk Pf   **285** ipsius] impius Aa | penituit] penitentie Fd   **286** Dei]
Domini Pf Sb EdF   **287** ut] et Fd_ac | absolueretur] absolueret Fd   **288** Et] *om.* Aa
289 mala] malum Aa   **290** in … Ezechielem] *om.* AaB | Sic] Sicut Pf EdF
291 et] in Bi EdF Mk Pf et in Fs   **292** magno] *add.* periculi Fs

committed one evil deed; and, nevertheless, after Ahab turned to penance, punishment is delayed to his posterity, while Jezebel, because she perseveres in the wicked deed, is condemned to present judgment."

LIKEWISE JOHN CHRYSOSTOM ON THE RECOVERY OF THE
c.28 FALLEN: "Such, believe me, such is the kindness of God toward men: it never spurns penance if it should be offered to him sincerely and simply. Even if someone should attain the highest of evils and then want to turn back to the way of virtue, God welcomes him and gladly embraces him. God does all things in order to call him back to his prior state. And, what is still more extraordinary and excellent, even if someone is not able to fulfill every step in making satisfaction, he does not reject however little and whatever penance done in a short time. He even accepts it and does not allow him to lose the reward of even so small a conversion. Isaiah indicates this to me when he says certain such things about the people of the Jews: *On account of sin I have stirred him up a little, and I struck him, and I turned my face away from him, and he was saddened and walked sadly, and I healed him and consoled him.* But even that   Is 57:17 wicked king, who sought the gain of his desire because of the wickedness of his wife, but who, being troubled by the monstrosity of this very crime, repented, donned a hairshirt, and wept over his wicked act, and called forth God's mercy to himself in such a way that he was absolved[12] of all his sins, will give clear testimony to us. For thus God says to Elijah, *Have you seen how Ahab has been stung by my face? And because he has wept in my presence, I will not bring evils upon him in his days.*"   1 Kgs 21:29

c.29   LIKEWISE GREGORY IN THE TENTH HOMILY ON EZEKIEL: "Just as the wicked king Ahab, having been reproached by the prophet, when he had heard the divine sentence against him, was greatly afraid and was overtaken with a great sorrow in such a way that the Lord said to his prophet, *Have you not seen Ahab's humility be-*

---

12. Gratian probably had this verb in the passive. That is the reading in Aa. Fd has an active verb form but no direct object; the active form (*absolueret*) instead of the passive (*absolueretur*) was likely a scribal mistake. That mistake in Fd or other early manuscripts may have caused later scribes to add a direct object while keeping the active verb form. Their later version would be translated, "in such a way that God absolved him of all his sins."

humiliatum Achab coram me? Quia ergo humiliatus est mei causa, non inducam ma-
lum in diebus eius. | In quibus Domini uerbis pensandum est, quomodo ei in electis
suis meror amaritudinis placeat, qui amittere timet Dominum, si sic ei et in | re-
probo penitentia placuit, qui timebat perdere presens seculum; aut quomodo ei
grata sit spontanea afflictio pro culpis in eis qui placent, si hec ad tempus placuit et
in illo, qui displicebat."

(Aa 168ᵛ)

Fs 312ᵛᵃ

Niniuite quoque, quos Dominus in euangelio conmendat, penitentiam egerunt in predicatione Ione, et ex misericordia Domini indulgentiam consecuti subuersionis interitum subterfugere meruerunt. Set qualis post acceptam ueniam Achab uixerit, textus libri
Regum declarat, DE QUO ETIAM | SCRIBIT AMBROSIUS quod Iezabel
uxor eius, "cuius inflammabatur arbitrio, cor eius conuertit, et ni-
miis sacrilegiis execrabilem fecit et hunc penitentie eius affectum
reuocauit." De Niniuitis autem IN PRINCIPIO IONE SCRIBIT IERONI-
MUS: "Sicut ait Herodotus, Niniue a rege Medorum subuersa est,
regnante apud Ebreos Iosia. Vnde patet, illam predicante Iona ex
penitentia ueniam meruisse, set quia post ad uomitum rediit, ex ira
Dei fuisse subuersa." ITEM | IN PRINCIPIO NAUM: | "Naum prophe-
tam ante aduentum | regis Assyriorum, qui populum Israel capti-
uum in suas regiones transtulerat, fuisse, Hebreorum traditio con-
firmat siquidem in fine huius lectionis predicti regis aduentum
idem Propheta annuntiare monstratur. Set cum habitatores | Ni-
niue, Iona interitum ciuitatis predicante, ne diuina ira denuntiatum
interitum sustinerent, peccatorum et inpietatis penitentiam egis-
sent, accepta Dei misericordia grauioribus se criminibus inplicue-
runt. Qua de re memoratus Propheta, Spiritu sancto plenus iudicium Dei annuntians, ita est elocutus: *Deus zelans et ulciscens Domi-*
nus."

d.p.c.29

300

Fd 95ᵛᵃ

305

c.30

Mk 249ʳᵃ | Aa
169ʳ
Sb 274ᵛᵃ

c.31

Pf 118ʳᵃ

315

320

---

304 cuius…**306** reuocauit] cf. Ambr. Med., *De Nabuthae* 17.71 (CSEL
32.2:514.15–17)   **307** Sicut…**310** subuersa] cf. Hier., *Comm. in prophetas mino-*
res, In Jonam, prol. (CCSL 76:378.54–379.60); *Gl. ord. in Jonam, Prol.* (München,
BSB lat. 16005, f. 61v)   **310** Naum²…**320** Dominus] *Gl. ord. in Naum, Prol.* (ed.
Rusch, 3.412b)

310 fuisse subuersa] subuersam fuisse R2   **318** re] causa R2

293 malum] mala Sb   **294** In…uerbis] Item Gregorius in omelia x Sb | In…**298**
displicebat] *adest in* Aa   **295** timet] timent *orig.* | Dominum] Deum Bi EdF Fs
Mk Pf | si…ei] *om.* FdB, si *om.* Pf_{ac}, ei *om.* Bi_{ac}   **297** placent] placeret Bi_{ac} placet
Sb   **299** quoque] *mg.* Fd   **310** Dei] *add.* dicitur Aa | subuersa] *sic!* Aa Fd | pro-
phetam] propheta Bi Mk   **315** predicante] predicare Fd   **319** elocutus] locutus
Fd_{ac} Sb

fore me? Thus, because he has been humbled for my sake, I will not bring evil upon *him in his days.* In these words of the Lord, one should contemplate how bitter sor-   1 Kgs 21:29
row pleases him in his elect, who are afraid to lose the Lord, if even penance in a
reprobate, who was afraid of losing this present world, pleased him in this way. Or
one should contemplate how a voluntary affliction for guilty acts in those who
please God is agreeable to him, if this voluntary affliction was pleasing for a time
and in him who was displeasing."

d.p.c.29   The Ninevites as well, whom the Lord commends in the Gospel,
did penance as a result of Jonah's preaching, and, having pursued
indulgence from the mercy of the Lord, they deserved to evade an
annihilating destruction. But how Ahab lived after he received
mercy the text of the Book of Kings declares, CONCERNING WHICH
AMBROSE ALSO WRITES that Jezebel, his wife, "by whose judgment
he was kindled, turned his heart, and he committed a detestable act
with excessive acts of sacrilege and revoked this state of his
penance." But concerning the Ninevites JEROME WRITES ON THE
c.30   BEGINNING OF JONAH: "Just as Herodotus says, Nineveh was overthrown by the king of the Medes when Josiah was ruling the Hebrews. From this it is clear that the city deserved mercy as a result
of its penance after Jonah preached, but, because it afterward returned to its own vomit, it was overthrown by the wrath of God."
c.31   Likewise on the beginning of Nahum: "The tradition of the Hebrews confirms that Nahum was a prophet before the coming of
the king of Assyrians, who had taken the people of Israel away captive into his realms, seeing that, at the end of this book, this same
prophet is shown to announce the coming of the aforementioned
king. But when, after Jonah had preached the destruction of the
city, the inhabitants of Nineveh had done penance for their sins
and wickedness so that they might not undergo the destruction declared by divine wrath, they received the mercy of God and then
entangled themselves in more serious crimes. For this reason, the
renowned prophet, filled with the Holy Spirit and announcing the
judgment of God, has spoken thus: *The Lord is a zealous and avenging*   Na 1:2
God."

Item, quod frequenter penitenti frequenter uenia prestetur te- d.p.c.31
statur Augustinus in libro de penitentia scribens contra quosdam
hereticos, qui peccantibus post baptismum semel tantum dicebant
utilem esse penitentiam, CONTRA QUOS AUGUSTINUS SCRIBIT di-
325 cens, "Adhuc instant perfidi, quoniam sapiunt plusquam oporteat, c.32
non sobrii, set excedentes mensuram. Dicunt enim, 'Etsi semel peccantibus post baptismum ualeat penitentia, non tamen sepe peccantibus proderit iterata; alioquin remissio ad peccatum esset inci-
tatio.' Dicunt enim, 'Quis non semper peccaret si redire semper
Fs 312ᵛᵇ   posset?' Dicunt Dominum incitatorem mali si semper penitentibus |
Bi 308ʳᵇ subuenit, et etiam ei placere | peccata, quibus semper presto est gra-
tia. Errant autem. Immo constat multum ei displicere peccata, qui
semper presto est ea destruere. Si enim ea amaret, non ita semper
destrueret set conseruaret atque ut sua munera foueret. Semper
335 destruit peccata que inuenit, ne soluatur quod creauit, ne corrum-
patur quod amauit. Sumunt occasionem ypocrite isti ex factis Domini: Quem enim bis illuminauit? Quem leprosum bis mundauit?
Quem mortuum bis suscitauit? Non Lazarum quem dilexit; non filium uidue quem misertus matri reddidit; non filium dissipatorem
340 legitur bis suscepisse; non filiam Abrahe bis a demonio liberasse. In
nulla persona iterauit factum, docens, ut aiunt, non sepe a Domino
fieri remedium. Dixit multis, *Vade et amplius noli peccare, ne deterius
tibi aliquid contingat*, promittens penam, non amplius ueniam.

"Quod autem multos cecos et in diuerso tempore illuminauit et
345 multos debiles confortauit ostendit in diuersis illis eadem sepe peccata dimitti, ut quem prius sanauit leprosum alio tempore illuminet

---

325 Adhuc...**390** deficere] Ps.-Aug., *De uera* 5 (PL 40:1116–18; ed. Wagner,
222–96)

330 Dicunt] *add.* enim R2 (*interlin.* Fd_pc)   **342** deterius...**343** aliquid] quod tibi
deterius R2

326 mensuram] *add.* fidei Aa | enim] esse Aa *om.* Bi Mk   **330** Dominum] Deum
EdF Fd Pf   **331** etiam] *om.* Mk Pf Sb   **336** factis] uerbis Aa_ac Fd_ac   **340** legitur]
legi Bi Fs   **345** eadem] eidem Aa | sepe] semper Aa   **346** illuminet] illuminauit
Bi EdF

d.p.c.31   Likewise, Augustine testifies that mercy is repeatedly offered to the repeated penitent in his book on penance, writing against certain heretics who were saying that penance is profitable only once for sinners after baptism. AUGUSTINE WRITES AGAINST THESE

c.32   HERETICS, saying, "The faithless are still insistent, for they understand more than is proper, not temperately but exceeding measure. For they say, 'Even if penance has power once for sinners after baptism, oft-repeated penance will not serve sinners; otherwise, remission would be a spur to sin.' For they say, 'Who would not always sin if he would always be able to return?' They say[13] that the Lord is an inciter of evil if he always comes to the aid of penitents, and also that sins for which grace is always ready please him. They are wrong, however, for it is instead greatly agreed that sins displease him who is always ready to destroy them. For if he were to love them, he would not always destroy them in this way but would preserve them and cherish them as his gifts. He has always destroyed the sins which he has found so that what he has created may not be consumed and what he has loved may not be corrupted. Those wretched hypocrites take advantage of the deeds of the Lord: For whom did he cause to see twice? What leper did he cleanse twice? What dead person did he enliven twice? Not Lazarus, whom he loved; not the son of the widow, whom, having compassion, he returned to his mother; we do not read that he welcomed the prodigal son home twice or that he freed the daughter of Abraham twice from a demon. He did not repeat his deed in any person, for he taught, or so they say, that a cure is not done by the Lord multiple times. He said to many, *Go and sin no more, lest something worse happen to you*, promising punishment, not more   Jn 8:11 mercy.

"But that he opened the eyes of many blind persons and at various times and that he strengthened many crippled shows that the same sins are forgiven many times in those various instances so that the Lord at one time may open the eyes of a blind man whom

---

13. The second recension reads, "For they say...."

cecum. Ideo enim tot sanauit claudos, cecos, et aridos, ne desperet
sepe peccator. Ideo non scribitur aliquem nisi semel sanatum, ut

Sb 274ᵛᵇ | Pf
118ʳᵇ
Aa 169ᵛ

quisque timeat | iungi peccato. | Videamus adhuc cotidie in ecclesia
sepe febricitantes, sepe languidos, sepe passionibus | captos sepe li-
berari, ut appareat totiens opus miserentis, quotiens confessio fit
penitentis. Quomodo enim corpus, quod uilius est, ab ipso dissimi-

Mk 249ʳᵇ

lius, sepe | sanaret, et animam digniorem et redemptam non totiens
liberaret? Medicum se uocat et non sanis, set male, habentibus

355 oportunum. Set qualis hic medicus, qui malum iteratum nesciret
curare? Medicorum enim est centies infirmum curare. Qui ceteris
minor esset si aliis possibilia ignoraret.

"Memor est sui qui promisit, *Nolo mortem peccatoris set ut conuerta-*
tur et uiuat. Quem enim peccatorem excludit? Quod omnibus pro-

360 misit indulgentiam, aliis promissionibus declarat, *Qui me confessus*
fuerit coram hominibus—omnis quantumcumque et quotiens peccator, cuiuscumque ordinis, etiamsi fuerit sacerdos—*confitebor et ego*

Fs 313ʳᵃ

eum. | Nam *qui inuocauerit nomen Domini* (id est secundum quod no-

Fd 95ᵛᵇ

minatur Dominus, id est qui | inuocauerit eum ad se seruiendo et

365 non contradicendo, ut forsitan sepe fecit), *omnis* (id est quicumque
sit ille peccator) *saluus erit.* Omnem enim animam iste promissor sa-
turauit bonis, etiam sedentem in tenebris et umbra mortis, nullam
excipiens animam. Hunc magistrum intellexit discipulus ille, qui
Corinthios per epistolas suas uoluit corrigere, et, ut ipse testatur, ter

370 in litteris eos correxit. Oportebat enim, ut quotiens eos uidebat ca-

349 Videamus] Videmus R2 (Aa Fd; Videamus Sb)   **356** infirmum] *add.* centies
R2 (Aa; *om.* Fs Pf)

348 sanatum] sanasse Aa   **352** est] *add.* et EdF Fd Sb   **353** totiens] totius Pfₐ꜀ Sb
356 centies] Fd_{pc}   **359** Quod] qui Pf EdF   **363** Nam] namque Mk Pf Sb | inuo-
cauerit] uocauerit Pf Sb | Domini] *add.* saluus erit Aa   **364** inuocauerit] uocaue-
rit Bi Fs Pf Sb   **365** forsitan] *interlin.* Fd   **366** enim] ergo Aa | iste promissor]
promissio ista Aa   **370** eos uidebat] *tr.* Fd EdF Pf (eos *interlin.* Pf)

he previously healed of leprosy. For he healed so many lame, blind, and shriveled people so that the sinner may not often despair. It is not written that someone has been healed only one time in such a way that every man may fear being bound to sin. We may see[14] that still daily in the church those often ill with fever, those often sick, and those often taken over by passions are liberated multiple times so that it may be apparent that, as many times as confession of a penitent is done, just as often is a work of the one having mercy done. For how would he heal the body, which is more vile, more dissimilar to himself, multiple times and not free so many times the more worthy and redeemed soul? He calls himself a physician and serviceable to those living badly, not well. For what kind of doctor would he be if he did not know how to heal a re- peated malady? For it is characteristic of doctors to heal the sick a hundred times.[15] He would be less than the rest if he were to ig- nore what is possible for others.

"He is mindful of himself when he promised, *I do not want the sin- ner to die but to convert and live.* What sinner does he exclude? Be- cause he promises indulgence to all, he declares with other promises: *He who confesses me before men*—every sinner, however great and however many times, of whatever order, even if he is a priest—*I will also confess him.* For *everyone* (that is, whoever that sin- ner may be) *who calls upon the name of the Lord* (that is, according to what the Lord is named, that is, he who calls him to himself by serving and not contradicting, as perhaps he often did) *will be saved.* For that maker of promises has saturated every soul with good things, even those sitting in the darkness and shadow of death, and has not excluded any soul. That disciple who wanted to correct the Corinthians through his epistles grasped this teaching and, as he himself testifies, he corrected them three times in his letters. For it

Ezek 18:32

Mt 10:32

Jl 2:32

14. Gratian's exemplar (the B-Vb tradition of *De uera et falsa penitentia*) has a subjunctive verb here. Sb retains that reading. Scribes, including those respon- sible for the early reading in Aa and Fd, exchanged the subjunctive for the in- dicative, which most manuscripts of *De uera et falsa* have, but, in this instance, the scribes' choice probably resulted more from intuition than from scholarship in checking other manuscripts. The later recension thus reads, "We see...."

15. The second recension added another "a hundred times" to the phrase "to heal the sick a hundred times." That version would be translated, "to heal one hundred times the man who was sick one hundred times." The original treatise read, "to visit the sick a hundred times and to heal a hundred times." The B-Vb tradition of *De uera et falsa*, and thus Gratian, removed both the verb "to visit" and one "a hundred times."

Bi 308ᵛᵃ dere, totiens iuuaret surgere. Memor enim erat illius, qui | dixerat, *Quorum remiseritis peccata, remittentur.*

"Scimus autem et primos patres et in omni tempore ecclesiam Dei semper usque in septuagies septies (quod est semper) peccata
375 remittere. Quam potestatem isti ab ecclesia auferre conantur. Oportet enim ecclesiam sic credere, que confitetur se peccare. Negant enim ueritatem seductis esse, qui se absque peccato audent iactare. In multis enim offendimus omnes nec infans unius diei absque peccato super terram esse potest. Quapropter eliminandus est ab eccle-
380 sia qui umquam penitentibus negat indulgentiam. Non enim inqui-
Pf 118ᵛᵃ rit quid Apostolus senserit, qui dixit, *Nichil mihi conscius | sum, set non in hoc iustificatus sum.* Sentiens etiam iustis peccata solere contingere, non se confirmabat absque peccato, qui se cognouit indissolubili uinculo caritatis coniunctum Christo. Nisi enim sciret iustos
385 sepe uenire ad ueniam, quomodo dubitaret se peccare, qui se sciebat spiritum Dei habere et intentione mundissima ei seruire? Cur
Sb 275ʳᵃ Dominus pedes Petri lauasset et ecclesiam | hoc idem docuisset, nisi
Aa 170ʳ (quoniam cotidiana est offensio) oportet ut cotidiana sit | remissio? Cur docuisset orantes dicere, *Dimitte nobis debita nostra,* nisi ipse mi-
390 sericors perseueraret, qui nos ab hac petitione non uult deficere?"

ITEM AUGUSTINUS AD MACEDONIUM: "In tantum autem ho- c.33 minum iniquitas aliquando progreditur, ut etiam post actam penitentiam, post altaris reconciliationem, uel similia uel grauiora committant. Et tamen Deus facit etiam super tales oriri solem suum,
395 nec minus tribuit quam ante tribuebat largissima munera uite ac
Fs 313ʳᵇ salutis. | Et quamuis eis in ecclesia locus ille penitentie non conce-
Mk 249ᵛᵃ datur, Deus tamen super eos sue patientie non obliuiscitur. | Ex quorum numero si quis nobis dicat, ... 'Dicite utrum mihi aliquid prosit ad uitam futuram, si in ista uita illecebrosissime uoluptatis

---

391 In...406 dementiam] Aug. Hipp., *Epistula* 153 (CSEL 44:401.20–403.5)

372 remittentur] remitti Fd Sb remittuntur eis Aa Fs remittentur eis Bi_pc (eis *interlin.* Bi)   382 etiam] autem Pf *om.* Sb | solere] *interlin.* Aa, soluere Sb
386 Cur] *add.* enim EdF Pf   387 lauasset] lauisset Aa EdF   389 nostra] *add.* a. Bi Mk   392 etiam] *om.* Bi *interlin.* Mk   395 tribuebat] tribuerat Bi EdF Pf Sb_pc? tribuatur Fs   399 in] *interlin.* Aa, *om.* Sb | uoluptatis] uoluntatis Bi Mk

was proper that he helped them rise as many times as he saw them fall. For he was mindful of him who had said, *The sins of those whom you forgive will be forgiven.*   Jn 20:23

"But we know that both the first fathers and the church of God in every time always forgives sins to seventy times seven times (that is, always). Those heretics try to remove this power from the church. For the church, which confesses that it sins, ought to believe such things. For those who dare to boast that they are without sin deny that truth is for those who have been led astray. For all people offend in many ways and the one-day-old infant cannot be on earth without sin. For this reason, he who ever denies indulgence to penitents should be eliminated from the church. He does not inquire into what the apostle means when he said: *I am aware of nothing against myself, but I am not justified because of this.* Believing   1 Cor 4:4 that sins customarily touch even the righteous, he was not confirming that he was without sin, even though he knew that he was bound to Christ with an indissoluble chain of love. For unless he knew that the righteous often come to mercy, how would he have doubts that he sins when he knows himself to have the Spirit of God and to serve him with the purest intention sins? Why would the Lord have washed Peter's feet and taught the church this same practice if it is not proper for remission to be daily (since transgression is daily)? Why would he have taught those who pray to say, *Forgive us our debts,* if he himself, who does not want us to fail in   Mt 6:12 this petition, would not persevere in mercy?"

c.33   LIKEWISE AUGUSTINE TO MACEDONIUS: "The iniquity of humans sometimes progresses to so great an extent that, even after penance has been done, after the reconciliation of the altar, they commit either similar or more grievous sins. And, nevertheless, God causes his sun to rise even upon such as these, and he has not given the very bountiful gifts of life and salvation less than he previously was giving. And although the place of penance may not be granted to them in the church, nevertheless God does not forget his patience with them. If anyone from among the number of these people should say to us, ... 'Tell me whether something may benefit me for the life to come, if I show contempt in this wretched life for

400 blandimenta contempsero, si me penitendo uehementius quam
prius excruciauero, si miserabilius ingemuero, si fleuero uberius, si
uixero melius, si pauperes sustentauero largius, si caritate que ope-
rit multitudinem peccatorum flagrauero ardentius,' quis nostrum
ita desipit, ut huic homini dicat, 'Nichil tibi ista in posterum prode-
405 runt; uade, saltem huius uite suauitate fruere'? Auertat Deus tam
inanem sacrilegamque dementiam!"

Siue autem quis dicat primam tantum penitentiam post bapti-   d.p.c.33
smum utilem esse, non sequentem, siue quis contendat ultime tantum ueniam dari, non precedenti. Semper tamen auctoritati aduer-
410 satur que sepissime penitenti ueniam repromittit.

\<Sententia Gratiani de uera penitentia\>

Que autem sit uera penitentia, cui numquam uenia negatur, et
Bi 308vb que sit falsa, | cui numquam indulgentia promittitur, Adamantius et
Esitius super Leuiticum testantur. ADAMANTIUS: "*Inter hec hyrcum*   c.34
Pf 118vb *qui oblatus fuerat,* etc. | Non peccare solius Dei est; emendare sapien-
tis. Set raro inuenias qui se corrigat. Rara confessio peccati; rara penitentia. Repugnat natura et uerecundia quia obnoxia est culpe
omnis caro, et quisque erubescit peccatum confiteri dum magis presentia cogitat quam futura. Vult Moyses peccati uacuam reperire
420 animam ut exuuias erroris deponat et culpe nuda sine pudore sui
discedat. Set irrationabilis inpetus preuenit et flamma celerrimi motus animam depascitur; exurit eius innocentiam. Preponderant
enim futuris presentia, seriis iocunda, et leta tristibus, et prepropera
Sb 275rb tardioribus. Velox enim iniquitas, que ad nocendum | occasionem
Fd 96ra suggerit; lenta uirtus. | Et cunctatrix ante iudicat, quam incipit quid
Aa 170^v decorum, quid honestum; iniquitas omnia precipitat. Pigra ergo et |
uerecunda penitentia quia presentium pudore premitur. Solis enim
intendit futuris, quorum spes sera, tardior fructus. Interim precurrit

---

414 Inter...**455** sincerum] *Gl. ord. in Lev.* 10:16 (ed. Rusch, 1.235); *in parte ex*
Orig.

421 Set] *add.* ubi R2 (*om.* Fs Sb)

402 uixero] dixero Fd Fs | sustentauero] suscitauero Fd_ac   **405** huius uite] *inter-
lin.* Aa, *tr.* Mk Sb | fruere] frueretur Fd   **416** inuenias] inuenies Aa Pf   **422** ex-
urit] esurit Fs Mk, *add.* enim Pf   **423** prepropera] prepara Fs propera Sb

the flatteries of the most enticing delight, if I crucify myself by repenting more vehemently than before, if I groan more miserably, if I weep more copiously, if I live better, if I support the poor more generously, if I burn more ardently with the love which covers a multitude of sins,' who among us is so foolish as to say to this person, 'Those things will profit you nothing in the future; go, at least enjoy the sweetness of this life'? May God turn away so empty and irreverent a madness!"

d.p.c.33   Or who should say that only the first penance after baptism is useful, not a subsequent one, or who should argue that mercy is given only for the last penance, not for an earlier one? Nevertheless one may always be directed to the authority which promises mercy again to the very frequent penitent.

<Gratian's Position on True Penance>

But what true penance is, for which mercy is never denied, and what false penance is, for which indulgence is never promised, Adamantius and Esitius testify in their commentaries on Leviticus.

c.34   ADAMANTIUS: "*Moses searched among these things for the goat which had been offered,* etc. Not sinning belongs to God alone; making improvements belongs to the wise man. But you may find he who corrects himself rarely. Confession of sin is rare; penance is rare. Nature and shame resist it because every flesh is beholden to guilt, and every person is ashamed to confess his sin as long as he thinks more about the present than the future. Moses wants to discover the empty soul of sin so that he may take off the clothing of error and depart without his shame, naked of guilt. But[16] an irrational impulse comes first and a very quick-moving flame consumes the soul; it burns up his innocence. For present things have more weight than future ones, delightful things than grave ones, and happy things than sad ones, and sudden things than delayed ones. For iniquity, which gives occasion to harm, is swift; virtue is slow. And it acts with deliberation and makes a decision before that which is noble and that which is honorable begins, but iniquity hastens everything along. Penance is, therefore, sluggish and bashful because it is weighed down with the shame of present things. For it extends to future things alone, whose hope comes late and

Lv 10:16

---

16. The second recension adds "where," thus turning an independent clause into a dependent one: "But where an irrational impulse comes first…, it burns up his innocence."

Fs 313va

430

435

inpudentia, et spe presentium penitentia excluditur, | et affectus
eius exuritur et aboletur. Querit eam lex et non inuenit, conbusta
est enim feruore et fumo iniquitatis. Inde irascitur et dicit, deuoran-
dam fuisse penitentiam in sanctis sanctorum; sacerdotes quasi se-
gnes increpat. Respondit Aaron prouidum debere esse sacerdotale
iudicium, nec male, sane conscientie facile esse credendum id muneris, ne fiat error deterior priore. Vase enim fetido uel oleum uel
uinum facile corrumpitur.

"Quomodo autem poterat, ubi ignis alienus erat, peccatum ex-
uri et in conspectu Domini, cui cuncta aperta, quasi non placet Deo
qui iniustitiam corde inclusam tenet, et se penitentiam agere perhi-
bet? Ignis alienus libido, auaritia, et omnis praua cupiditas. Hic ignis
exurit, non mundat. In quibus enim est, si offerant in conspectu
Domini, ignis eos celestis absumit, sicut Nadab et Abiud | cum his
que pro peccato fuerant oblata.

"Qui ergo uult mundari ignem alienum remoueat; illi igni se of-
ferat, qui culpam exurit, non hominem. Hic ignis siccauit | emo-
roisse sanguinem profluentem; hic siccauit culpam latronis. Ignis
enim consumens est; sanat simpliciter et pure confitentes. Iudas inquit, *Peccaui, tradens sanguinem iustum*; set in pectore habuit ignem
alienum, quo inflammante cucurrit ad laqueum. Indignus autem
remedio fuit quia non pura mente penituit. Culpam ergo eius non
auferunt | sacerdotes qui dolose offert, nec in eo possunt epulari
quorum cibus est peccatorum remissio. Vnde uerus sacerdos ait:
Meus cibus est ut faciam uoluntatem patris mei, id est, ut peccatores
conuersi et penitentes saluentur. Non est acceptum Deo sacrificium
nisi uerum et sincerum."

440

Mk 249vb

Pf 119ra

450

Bi 309ra

455

---

438 cuncta] *add.* sunt R2 (*om.* Fs Sb)   **444** illi] *praem.* et R2 (*om.* Sb; *interlin.* Aa)
451 dolose] *add.* se R2 (*om.* Fs Sb)

431 dicit] *add.* Moyses Fs   **433** Respondit] respondet Aa EdF Mk   **435** deterior]
peior Aa   **437** ubi] ut Aa Sb | erat...**438** et] peccatum exureret Aa   **438** non]
om. Aa | placet] conplaceat Aa, conplacet Fd_{pc} Bi_{ac} EdF Fs Mk Pf   **440** Ignis]
praem. ibi Fs *add.* ibi *interlin.* Mk   **448** pectore] peccatore Mk_{ac} Sb   **453** ut²] *interlin.* Bi *om.* Mk Sb   **454** conuersi] *add.* ad penitentiam Aa

whose profit come later. Meanwhile, shamelessness runs out front and penance is shut out by the hope of present things, and the desire for it is burned up and abolished. The law seeks it and does not find it, for it has been burnt up with the fervor and fume of iniquity. Then Moses grows angry and says that the penance was supposed to be eaten in the Holy of Holies; he chides the priests for being lazy, as it were. Aaron answered that priestly judgment ought to be wise and it ought to be believed to belong easily to the duty of a healthy conscience, not of an evil one, lest an error worse than the first be made. For either oil or wine is easily corrupted by a fetid vessel.

"But how had the sin [offering] been able to be burned up in the sight of God, to whom all things are clear, when the fire was strange, as if he who keeps unrighteousness enclosed in his heart and presents himself to do penance pleases God? The strange fire is lust, avarice, and every deprived desire. This fire burns up; it does not cleanse. For in whom it exists, if they should offer it in the sight of God, heavenly fire consumes them, just as it did Nadab and Abihu along with these things which had been offered for sin.

"Therefore, let he who wants to be cleansed remove the strange fire;[17] let him offer himself to that fire which burns up guilt, not the man. This fire dried up the flowing blood of the woman with the hemorrhage; it dried up the guilt of the thief. For it is a consuming fire; it heals directly and completely those who confess. Judas said, *I have sinned, betraying innocent blood*, but he possessed a strange fire   Mt 27:4 in his breast; when it was burning, he ran to the noose. But he was unworthy of a remedy because he did not repent with a pure mind. Therefore priests do not remove the guilt of him who makes an offering[18] deceitfully, and they whose food is the remission of sins cannot feast in him. For this reason, the true Priest says, *My food is that I do the will of my Father*, that is, that converted sinners and pen-   Jn 4:34 itents be saved. A sacrifice to God is not accepted if it is not genuine and sincere."

---

17. The second recension added an "and."
18. The second recension added a pronoun, making this verb reflexive. The phrase would be translated, "who offers himself deceitfully."

ITEM ESITIUS: *"Inter hec hyrcum qui offertur,* etc. Quia omne pec-   c.35
catum per penitentiam deletur, et qui predictum peccatum alterius
doctrine et blasphemie conmiserunt saluati non sunt, causam mortis eorum Legislator exponit: *Inter hec hyrcum qui oblatus fuerat,* etc.,
460 quia scilicet non comederunt filii Aaron qui pro peccato erat in loco
Sb 275ᵛᵃ sancto, id est, penitentiam | conmissi peccati in ecclesia peragi non
Fs 313ᵛᵇ fecerunt, quibus hoc preceptum est, quos Christus | uicarios suos in
ecclesia constituit. Ipse oblationis sue sanguinem, que pro nostro
sanguine oblata est, in sanctum, id est celum, in conspectu patris
465 obtulit. Debet autem comedi hoc sacrificium in loco sancto, scilicet
ecclesia, in propitiationem peccatorum. Vnde addit, *quemadmodum*
Aa 171ʳ *preceptum | est mihi,* sic precepi. Moyses ergo gerit personam Christi.
Exustum repperit, quia in Spiritum sanctum peccauerant. Ab intel-
ligibili igne Spiritus sancti oblatio pro penitentia ablata est; uolunta-
470 rie peccantibus non relinquitur hostia pro peccato. Nam sicut uera
penitentia ueniam promeretur, ita simulata Deum irritat, quia Spiritus sanctus discipline effugiet fictum. Hoc autem sancti Patres irre-
missibile peccatum et blasphemiam in Spiritum sanctum dixerunt:
in sceleribus usque ad finem uite perseuerare, de potentia et miseri-
475 cordia Dei et redemptoris diffidere."

[ITEM IOANNES OS AUREUM IN EPISTOLA AD EBREOS: "Iudas penituit, set   c.36
Pf 119ʳᵇ male; laqueo namque se suspendit. | Penituit etiam Esau, magis iste neque penituit.
Lacrime quippe non erant penitentie set animi uiolenti et indignationis inferne.
Quod eius operibus aperitur. Non igitur negemus peccata nostra, neque nos inpu-
480 dentia duros efficiat. Sponte nostra puniamus, ne pendamus non sponte supplicia.
Audiuit Cayn a Deo: *Vbi est Abel frater tuus?* et dixit, *Nescio, numquid custos fratris
mei sum?* Vides quomodo ex hoc peccatum amplius operatus est. Nonne et pater
eius similiter? Audiens enim et ipse, *Adam ubi es?* dixit, *Audiui uocem tuam, Domine, et timui quoniam nudus sum, et abscondi me.* Magnum est, ut quis peccata

---

456 Inter…**475** diffidere] Hesychius, *Comm. in Leviticum* 2 (PG 93:901A–D)
476 Iudas…**486** memoria] Ioh. Chrys., *Hom. in Heb.* 31 (PG 63:215–16)

460 qui] quod R2   **463** Ipse] *add.* autem R2   **464** est²] *add.* in R2 (*om.* Sb)
465 scilicet] *add.* in R2 (Aa; *om.* Fs Mk Sb)

456 hyrcum] ircus Fd hyrcus Sb   **457** qui] que Mk quia Pf   **459** hyrcum] hyrcus Bi Mk Pf   **460** quia] quem Aa   **461** penitentiam] penitentia Fd Sb   **466** ec-
clesia] ecclesiam Fs Mk_ac   **467** sic] sicut Fd Mk   **468** Exustum] et iustum Mk Sb
sanctum] *om.* Pf   **476** in…Ebreos] *om.* AaB

c.35   LIKEWISE ESITIUS: "*Moses searched among these things for the goat that is offered,* etc. Because every sin is erased through penance and   Lv 10:16
those who committed the aforementioned sin of another teaching and blasphemy were not saved, the Lawgiver explains the reason for their death: *[Moses searched] among these things for the goat which had been offered,* etc., because the sons of Aaron certainly did not eat [the goat] that[19] was in the holy place for sin, that is, they did not carry out in the church the penance for the sin committed. This was ordered them whom Christ established as his vicars in the church. He[20] offered the blood of his sacrifice, which was offered for our blood, in the holy place, that is, heaven,[21] in the sight of his Father. But this sacrifice ought to be eaten in a holy place, namely a church,[22] as a propitiation for sins. For this reason he adds, *how I was ordered,* thus I ordered. Moses thus bears the person of Christ.   Lv 10:18
He finds the sacrifice burned up, since they had sinned against the Holy Spirit. The sacrifice for penance was removed by the intelligible fire of the Holy Spirit, for the sacrifice for sin is not left for those who sin willingly. For just as true penance deserves mercy, so also feigned penance makes God angry, because the Holy Spirit flees from the deception of learning. The holy Fathers called this the unforgiveable sin and the blasphemy against the Holy Spirit: persevering in evil deeds all the way to the end of life, distrusting the power and mercy of God and the Redeemer."

c.36   [LIKEWISE JOHN CHRYSOSTOM ON THE EPISTLE TO THE HEBREWS: "Judas repented but badly; for he hung himself with a noose. Esau also repented, but he did not repent much. Indeed, the tears were not of penance but of a boisterous spirit and of an infernal displeasure. This is made apparent by his works. Let us thus not deny our sins, and let not impudence make us hard. Let us willingly punish our sins, lest we suffer punishments unwillingly. Cain heard from God, *Where is your brother, Abel?,* and he said, *I do not know; am I my brother's keeper?'* Do you see how, from   Gn 4:9
this, a more extensive sin took effect. And did not his father act similarly? For he also, upon hearing, *Adam, where are you?,* said, *I heard your voice, Lord, and I was*   Gn 3:9
afraid, for I am naked, and I hid myself. It is great for someone to acknowledge his   Gn 3:10

---

19. For this relative pronoun, the first recension read *qui,* having in mind the goat of Leviticus 10:16. The text does not explicitly say "goat," and the second recension changed the qui to the more generic *quod,* so that the phrase would read in English, "the sons of Aaron did not eat what was in the holy place."
20. The second recension added a "but" or "however" to start this sentence.
21. The second recension reads "in heaven."
22. The second recension reads "in a church."

Mk 250ra sua agnoscat | et memoriam eorum perseueranter retineat. Nullum inuenitur delic-
torum tale remedium, sicut eorum continuata memoria."

ITEM AMBROSIUS IN LIBRO DE PENITENTIA: *"In salicibus,* inquit, *in medio eius*   c.37
suspendimus organa nostra. Quomodo cantabimus canticum Domini in terra aliena?

Bi 309rb | Si enim caro menti repugnat nec subdita est animi gubernaculo et mentis inperio,
490   aliena est terra que non domatur exercitio cultoris; fructus non potest caritatis, peni-
Fs 314ra tentie, pacis afferre. Melius est ergo tunc quiescere quam | exercere non queras
opera penitentie, ne in ipsa penitentia fiat quod postea indigeat penitentia. Que si
semel fuerit usurpata nec iure celebrata, nec prioris fructum obtinet et aufert usum
Sb 275vb posterioris. | Sane et cum caro repugnat, mens ad Deum debet esse intenta, et, si
495   opera non secuntur, fides non deserat; et, si carnis inpugnant illecebre uel potesta-
tes aduersarie, maneat mens Deo dedita. Tunc enim maxime urgetur, cum caro non
cedit, et sunt qui uehementer incumbant, misere anime querentes omne auferre
presidium. Vnde illud est: *Exinanite, exinanite usque ad fundamentum in ea.* Quam
miseratus Dauid ait, *Filia Babylonis misera,* utique, Babylonis filia est, que Dei filia
500   esse desinit, cui tamen medicum inuitat, dicens, *Beatus, qui tenebit et allidet paruu-*
(*inc.* FdG *los suos ad petram,* hoc est qui infirmas et lubricas cogitationes | habet elidat ad
161^v) Christum, qui omnes irrationabiles motus sui reuerentia et discretione conminuat."

Pf 119va ITEM IERONIMUS SUPER MATTHEUM: "Nichil Iude profuit | egisse penitentiam,   c.38
per quam scelus corrigere non potuit. Si quando frater sic peccat in fratrem, ut
505   emendare ualeat quod peccauit, potest ei diuinitus dimitti; sin autem permanent
opera, frustra uoce assumitur penitentia. Hoc est quod de eo dicitur: *Et oratio eius*
fiat in peccatum, ut non solum emendare nequiuerit proditionis nefas, set proprii
homicidii scelus addiderit."

AaB 337^r | ITEM LEO PAPA IN SERMONE "INTER OMNIA": "Sceleratior omnibus, O Iuda,   c.39
510   et infelicior extitisti, quem non penitentia reuocauit ad Dominum set desperatio tra-

---

487 In...502 conminuat] Ambr. Med., *De paenitentia* 2.11 (SChr
179:198.49–73)   503 Nichil...508 addiderit] Hier., *Comm. in euang. Matt.* 4
(CCSL 77:263.1495–264.1501)   509 Sceleratior...512 distulisses] Leo I, *Sermo*
53.3 (PL 54:320A–B)

490 potest] *add.* enim Bi Fs Mk Pf (*pos.* fructus Pf) | penitentie] *add.* et Bi Mk Pf
491 quam...queras] cum exercere non queas *orig.*   495 illecebre] in celebre Bi
Fs   498 exinanite] *om.* Bi Fs Mk   510 Dominum] Deum Mk Pf

sins and perseveringly retain the memory of them. No cure for transgressions is found such as the continued memory of them."

c.37   LIKEWISE AMBROSE IN THE BOOK ON PENANCE: "*We hung our instruments*, he says, *in the willow-trees in the midst of [Babylon]. How will we sing the song of the Lord in a foreign land?* For if the flesh fights against the mind and is not subdued by the guidance of the spirit and the command of the mind, the land which is not conquered by the exercise of the worshipper is foreign. It cannot produce the fruits of love, penance, peace. Therefore it is better to stay still at the time when you cannot exercise works of penance,[23] lest in the penance itself it happen that one afterward requires penance. If penance is usurped once and is not celebrated rightly, it does not obtain the fruit of a previous penance and removes the benefit of a later penance. Certainly also when the flesh fights, the mind ought to be stretched to God, and, if works do not follow, faith might not give up, and, if the allurements and adversarial powers of the flesh attack, the mind remains given to God. Then, when the flesh does not yield, there is a maximum urging, and there are those who vehemently exert themselves, seeking to remove every aid to their wretched soul. For this reason there is that verse: *Raze it, raze it to its very foundation.* How compassionately David says, *Wretched daughter of Babylon*, assuredly she who stops being the daughter of God is a daughter of Babylon. Nevertheless, he invites a physician to her, saying, *Blessed is he who will hold your little ones and dash them against a rock*, that is, he strikes against Christ, who weakens anything irrational in his emotions with reverence and discretion, the person who has weak and deceitful thoughts."

Ps 137:2, 4

Ps 137:7
Ps 137:8

Ps 137:9

c.38   LIKEWISE JEROME ON MATTHEW: "To have done penance, through which he could not set his crime right, profited Judas nothing. If, when a brother sins against a brother in such a way that he has the power to amend his sin, he is able to be forgiven it from heaven; but if his works do not hold out, the penance is taken up by his voice in vain. This is what is said concerning him: *And let his prayer be made in sin*, so that, not only was he unable to amend the wickedness of his betrayal, but he added the crime of his own murder."

Ps 108:7

c.39   LIKEWISE POPE LEO IN HIS SERMON "INTER OMNIA": "O Judas, you have stood worse and less happy than all, you whom penance did not call back to the Lord but whom despair carried to the noose. Would that you had held off the con-

---

23. My overarching translation principle with regard to material sources is to translate the text as found in the *Decretum*, not the text of the material source itself. Nevertheless, in the case of this phrase, the Latin text in the *Decretum* is virtually impossible to make sense of and translate into English. The best rendition would be, "It is better to stay still at that time than not to seek works of penance," but the "not" reverses the meaning of the phrase (both of Ambrose's original and, more importantly for my purposes, of this text in the context in *De penitentia* D.3) and would need to be excised. Given the difficulty here, for this phrase alone, I have chosen to translate Ambrose's original.

xit ad laqueum. Expectasses consummationem criminis tui, et donec sanguis Christi pro peccatoribus funderetur, informis lethi suspendium distulisses."]

His auctoritatibus, que sit uera, que falsa penitentia ostenditur,   d.p.c.39
et false nulla indulgentia dari probatur.

515 <Sententia de uera penitentia contradicenda>

In quo illorum sententia destruitur, qua eum qui pluribus irretitus fuerit asseritur unius penitentia eiusdem ueniam a Domino
consequi sine alterius criminis penitentia. Quod etiam multorum
auctoritatibus probare conantur, quarum prima est ILLA NAUM
520 PROPHETHE: *Non iudicabit Deus bis in idipsum*. Set quem sacerdos iudicat Deus iudicat, cuius personam in ecclesia gerit. Qui ergo a sa-
Mk 250rb cerdote semel pro peccato punitur, non iterum pro eodem peccato |
Bi 309va a Deo iudicabitur. ITEM GREGORIUS SUPER EZECHIELEM: |"Pluit   c.40
Fs 314vb Dominus super unam ciuitatem, et super | alteram non pluit, et
525 eandem ciuitatem ex parte conpluit, et ex parte aridam relinquit.
Cum ille qui proximum odit ab aliis uiciis se corrigit, una eademque
ciuitas ex parte conpluitur, et ex parte arida manet, quia sunt, qui,
Fd 96rb | Sb cum uitia | quedam resecant, in aliis | grauiter perdurant." ITEM
276ra AMBROSIUS IN XVIII OCTONARIO: "Prima consolatio est quia non   c.41
530 obliuiscitur misereri Deus; secunda per punitionem ubi, etsi fides
desit, pena satisfacit et releuat."

Item opponitur de Ieronimo, qui super Naum sentire uidetur   d.p.c.41
quod, si infidelis adulterando interficeretur, de adulterio non amplius a Deo puniretur. Item, si illa satisfactio non fuit quam in adul-
535 terio uiuens pro homicidio obtulit, cum adulterii eum penituerit,

523 Pluit…**528** perdurant] Greg. Magn., *Hom. in Hiezech. proph.* 1.10 (CCSL
142:155.407–156.412)   **529** Prima…**531** releuat] *Gl. ord. in Ps.* 118:137 (*pars*
Sade; ed. Rusch, 2.618b)

517 unius] *add.* delicti R2   **528** uitia quedam] *tr.* R2

511 Expectasses] expectasset Pf   **512** distulisses] distulisset Pf   **516** eum qui]
cum Aa   **520** Deus] dominus Pf | idipsum] *add.* Item Iohannes Crisostomus:
Magnum est ut quis peccata sua agnoscat et in (*interlin.*) memoria perseueran-
ter retineat. Nullum inuenitur delictorum tale remedium, sicut eorum continuata memoria. Aa (cf. *supra in fine* c.36)   **527** sunt] *add.* quidam Aa   **531** sati-
sfacit] satisfecit Bi_ac Pf_ac | releuat] relauat Mk reuelat Fs Sb   **533** infidelis] fidelis
Aa

summation of your crime, and while the blood of Christ was being poured out for sinners, you would have delayed the horrid death of your hanging."]

d.p.c.39   By these authorities, what is true and what is false penance is shown, and it is proven that no indulgence is given to false penance.

<The Position on True Penance to be Countered>

In this position, their opinion, by which it is asserted that he who is ensnared by more than one sin acquires mercy for the one[24] from the Lord with penance for the same without penance for the second crime, is discredited. They attempt to prove this as well with many authorities, the first of which is THAT OF THE PROPHET NAHUM: *God will not judge the same thing twice.* But God judges him   Na 1:9 whom the priest, who bears God's person in the church, judges. Therefore, he who is punished once for sin by a priest will not be judged again for the same sin by God. LIKEWISE GREGORY ON

c.40   EZEKIEL: "The Lord caused it to rain over one city, and he caused it not to rain over the second one, and he caused it to rain upon part of the same city, and part of it he left dry. When he who hates his neighbor corrects himself in other vices, one and the same city is rained upon in part, and in part it remains dry, because there are those who hold out gravely in certain vices when they cut off others." LIKEWISE AMBROSE ON THE EIGHTEENTH IAMBIC VERSE:

c.41   "The first consolation is that God does not forget to have pity; the second is through punishment, where, even if faith is lacking, the penalty satisfies and lifts back up."

d.p.c.41   Likewise, this position is opposed with Jerome, who seems to feel in his thoughts on Nahum that, if an infidel in committing   cf. D.3 c.44 adultery were to be killed, he would not be punished additionally by God for the adultery. Likewise, if that which someone offered for a murder while living in adultery was not satisfaction, when he

---

24. The second recension added a clarifying "offence" (i.e. "...acquires mercy for the one offence from the Lord...."), while the first recension assumed a parallel with the later "crime."

Pf 119vb utriusque penitentia ei | inponenda erit; quod a ratione alienum ec-
clesiastica probatur consuetudine, que pro eodem peccato (nisi rei-
teratum fuerit) nulli bis penitentiam inponit.

\<Responsio Gratiani de uera penitentia\>

540   Set quod ei, qui crimen sibi reseruat, de alio uenia non prestetur, non solum premissis probatur auctoritatibus Esitii, Adamantii,
Smaragdi, Ysidori, Gregorii, Augustini, uerum etiam ALIA AUCTO-
Aa 171^v RITATE EIUSDEM AUGUSTINI IN LIBRO DE PENITENTIA. | Ait enim:
"Sunt plures, quos penitet peccasse, set non omnino, reseruantes   c.42
545   sibi quedam, in quibus delectentur, non animaduertentes, Dominum simul mutum et surdum et a demonio liberasse. Per hoc docet
nos numquam nisi de omnibus sanari. Si enim uellet peccata ex
parte reseruari, habentem septem demonia, perficere potuit sex ex-
pulsis. Expulit autem septem ut omnia crimina simul eicienda do-
550   ceret. Legionem autem ab alio eiciens, neminem reliquit de omnibus qui liberatum possideret, ostendens, si etiam peccata sint mille,
oportere de omnibus penitere. Laudatus est enim Dominus, quoniam eiecto demonio locutus est mutus. Numquam aliquem sanauit quem non omnino liberauit. Totum enim hominem sanauit in
555   sabbato, quia et corpus ab infirmitate et animam ab omni conta-
gione, indicans penitentes oportere simul dolere de omni crimine
ortum in anima et in corpore. Scio enim Dominum inimicum omni
criminoso. Quomodo ergo qui crimen reseruat de alio reciperet ueniam? Sine amore Dei consequeretur ueniam, sine quo nemo um-
560   quam inuenit gratiam. Hostis enim Dei est dum offendit perseue-
Fs 314va ranter. Quedam enim inpietas infidelitatis | est ab illo qui iustus et
iustitia est dimidiam sperare ueniam. Nam sine uera penitentia inueniret gratiam? Penitentia enim uera ad baptismi puritatem confi-
Bi 309vb tentem conatur ducere. | Recte enim penitens, quicquid sordis post
565   purificationem contraxit, oportet ut abluat, saltim lacrimis mentis.

---

544 Sunt… 571 peniteat] Ps.-Aug., *De uera* 9 (PL 40:1121–22; ed. Wagner, 506–38)

---

551 si etiam] quod si etiam R2 (quod si et Fs, quod etiamsi EdF, si etiam Sb)

542 Gregorii] *interlin.* Fd, *pos.* Augustini Pf | alia auctoritate] aliis auctoritatibus Bi 546 et²] *om.* Aa Mk EdF | docet] docens Sb 554 sanauit] sanum fecit Aa Fs 556 penitentes] penitentem Fd Bi Sb penitentie Fs 557 ortum] orto EdF Pf in¹] *praem.* et Pf Sb | in²] *om.* Fd Pf 558 reciperet] recipiet Aa 559 ueniam] *praem.* indulgentiam uel Sb 562 Nam] Nam enim Fs Non enim Sb | inueniret] inueniet Pf

repents of the adultery, penance for both sins will have to be imposed on him. This position is proven to be foreign to reason by ecclesiastical custom, which does not impose penance twice on anyone for the same sin (unless it were to be repeated).

<Gratian's Response about True Penance>

But that mercy is not presented for another crime to him who reserves a crime for himself, is proven not only by the aforementioned authorities of Esitius, Adamantius, Smaragdus, Isidore, Gregory, and Augustine but also by ANOTHER AUTHORITY OF THE SAME AUGUSTINE IN HIS BOOK ON PENANCE. For he says: "There are several people who repent of having sinned, but not entirely, reserving for themselves certain sins in which they were seduced, not noticing that the Lord freed a man, both mute and deaf, from a demon at the same time. Through this miracle he teaches that we are never healed unless from all things. For if he were to want sins to be reserved in part, he could have perfected the man having seven demons after he expelled six of them. But he expelled seven, so that he might teach that all wicked deeds have to be cast out together. But, casting out a legion from another, he left not one of all the demons who would take control of the freed man, showing that, if sins number even a thousand, one ought to repent of them all. For the Lord was praised, since the mute man spoke after the demon had been cast out. He never healed someone whom he did not entirely free. For he healed the entire man on the Sabbath, because he freed both his body from infirmity and his soul from every pollution, indicating that penitents ought to grieve the rise of every wicked deed in the soul and in the body at the same time. For I know that the Lord is an enemy to every criminal person. Therefore, how would he who reserves a wicked deed receive mercy for another one? He would be pursuing mercy, without which no one ever finds grace, without the love of God. For he is the enemy of God as long as he perseveres in his offence. For it is a certain impiety of the unfaithful to hope for a half-mercy from him who is just and Justice. For without true penance, would he find grace? For true penance attempts to lead the one confessing back to the purity of baptism. For the person repenting rightly, whatever filth he has

c.42

cf. D.3 c.35, c.34, c.9, c.11, c.6 (cc.13–15 for Gregory?), and c.10

Set satis durus est cuius mentis dolorem oculi carnis nequeunt de-
clarare; set sciat culpabiliter se durum, qui deflet dampna | temporis
uel mortem amici et dolorem peccati | non | ostendit in lacrimis.
Non itaque est ut quis excuset se non habere fontem lacrimarum,
qui umquam lacrimis ostendit dolorem temporalium. Quem ergo
penitet omnino peniteat," etc.

Auctoritas illa Naum prophete, *Non iudicabit Deus*, etc., non
ostendit omnia que temporaliter puniuntur non ulterius a Deo pu-
nienda. Quamquam enim Sodomitas, Egyptios, Israelitas in heremo
super eundem locum dicat Ieronimus temporaliter a Deo punitos,
ne in eternum punirentur, non tamen de omnibus generaliter hoc
intelligendum est. Alioquin cuique sceleroso optandum esset, ut,
celesti fulmine percussus aut aquis inmersus aut a serpentibus uul-
neratus pro peccatis suis, diuinitus interiret, ut eternos cruciatus
breuis et momentanea pena terminaret. ILLUD ETIAM APOSTOLI
falsum esset quod de prostratis in deserto IN EPISTOLA AD EBREOS
scribens ait: *Propter | incredulitatem suam non intrauerunt in terram pro-
missionis*. Vbi probatur, quod sicut merito sue infidelitatis requiem
illam amiserunt, ita propter eandem infidelitatem ueram requiem
eterne beatitudinis nullo modo intrauerunt.

Intelligitur ergo illud Ieronimi de his tantum qui inter ipsa flagella penitentiam egerunt, quam, etsi breuem et momentaneam,
tamen non respuit Deus. Sicut et illud Prophete, *Non iudicabit Deus
bis in idipsum*, de his tantum intelligi oportet quos presentia supplicia conmutant, super quos non consurget duplex tribulatio. Qui autem inter flagella duriores et deteriores fiunt, sicut Pharao, qui fla-
gellatus a Domino durior factus est, presentibus eterna connectunt,
ut temporale supplicium sit eis eterne dampnationis initium. VNDE

Pf 120ra
Sb 276rb | Mk 250va
570

d.p.c.42
575
580
Aa 172r
585
590

---

576 punirentur] cf. *Gl. ord. in Naum* 1:9 (ed. Rusch, 3.413b)

570 Quem...**571** etc] *om.* Aa   **572** iudicabit] iudicat Bi | Deus] *praem.* bis Bi *add.*
bis Pf EdF   **582** scribens] *om.* Aa   **584** infidelitatem] *add.* illam Bi Mk Pf
586 Intelligitur] intelligi Fd | ergo] *om.* Aa Bi *interlin.* Mk   **589** tantum] tamen
Fs Pf   **592** eterna] futura Aa

contracted after purification, ought to wash himself, at least with tears of the mind. But he is sufficiently hard whose physical eyes are unable to declare his mental grief; but let him know that he is hard to the point of culpability who weeps over temporal losses or the death of a friend and does not show grief for sin with tears. Thus it is that someone who shows grief at some point for temporal things with tears does not excuse himself for not having a fount of tears. Therefore let him who repents repent entirely," etc.

d.p.c.42   That authority of the prophet Nahum, *God will not judge twice,* Na 1:9 etc., does not show that all things which are punished temporally cf. D.3 must not be punished further by God. For, although Jerome says d.p.c.41 that Sodomites, the Egyptians, the Israelites in the desert were punished temporally by God upon the same place so that they might not be punished in eternity, this should not be understood concerning all persons generally. Otherwise each criminal person should wish that, by divine providence he might die after he was struck with the lightning of heaven or immersed in water or wounded by serpents for his sins so that the brief and momentary penalty might close off eternal torments. Also, THAT STATEMENT OF THE APOSTLE which he says when writing IN THE EPISTLE TO THE HEBREWS about those ruined in the desert would be false: *They did not enter the land of promise on account of their unbelief.* It is proven Heb 3:9 here that, just as they deservedly lost that rest by merit of their unfaithfulness, so also, on account of this same unfaithfulness, they in no way entered the true rest of eternal beatitude.

That statement of Jerome is thus understood only concerning these who did penance amid scourges. Even though brief and momentary, God did not reject this penance. In this way also that statement of the prophet, *God will not judge the same thing twice,* Na 1:9 ought to be understood only concerning these people whom present punishments change, upon whom a double tribulation will not arise. But those who become harder and worse amid scourges, just like Pharaoh, who became harder after being scourged by the Lord, adjoin eternal scourges to the present ones so that temporal punishment may be the beginning of eternal damnation for them.

Fd 96va AUGUSTINUS IN CANTICO DEUTERONOMII: | *"Ignis succensus est,* etc.   c.43
Fs 314vb Hoc est, uindicta hic | incipiet et ardebit usque ad eternam dampna-
tionem.*" Hoc contra illos notandum est qui dicunt *Non iudicabit*   d.p.c.43
Deus bis in id ipsum ad omnia pertinere flagella, quia quidam hic fla-
gellis emendantur, alii hic et in eternum puniuntur, sicut Antiochus et Herodes.

600   Quod autem super eundem locum de adultero infideli IERONI-
Pf 120rb MUS sentire uidetur | ex uerbis eiusdem falsum esse probatur. Ex-
emplo enim illius qui Israelite maledixerat et qui ligna in sabbato
Bi 310ra collegerat, ostendit parua peccata breuibus et temporalibus | suppli-
ciis purgari, magna uero diuturnis et eternis suppliciis reseruari.
605   AIT ENIM: "Querat hic aliquis, si infidelis deprehensus in adulterio   c.44
decolletur, quid de eo postea fiat. Aut enim punietur, et falsum est
hoc quod dicitur, *Non iudicabit Deus bis in idipsum in tribulatione,* aut
non punietur, et optandum est adulteris, ut in presentiarum breui
Sb 276va pena puniantur ut frustrentur | cruciatus eternos. Ad quod respon-
610   demus Deum, ut omnium rerum, ita suppliciorum quoque scire
mensuras, et non preueniri sententia iudicis nec illi in peccatorum
Mk 250vb exercende dehinc pene auferri potestatem; et magnum peccatum |
magnis diuturnisque lui cruciatibus; si quis autem punitus sit, ut
ille in lege qui Israelite maledixerat et qui in sabbato ligna college-
615   rat, tales postea non puniri, quia culpa leuis presenti supplicio con-
pensata sit."

Illud autem Gregorii, "Pluit Dominus super unam ciuitatem,"   d.p.c.44
etc., non ad criminis ueniam set ad eius detestationem referendum

---

594 Ignis...**596** dampnationem] cf. Greg. Magn., *Moralia in Iob* 18.22 (CCSL
143A:908.23–909.50), *Gl. ord. in Deut.* 32:22 (*interlin. et marg.*; ed. Rusch,
1.421a)   **605** Querat...**616** sit] Hier., *Comm. in prophetas minores, In Naum,* 1.9
(CCSL 76A:534.270–535.283)

595 eternam] extremam R2 (Aa_pc *add.* uel extremam *interlin.* Fd_pc)   **598** emen-
dantur] *add.* uel iudicantur R2 (*om.* Fs Sb; *ant.* emendantur *interlin. et mg.* Aa;
pos.? puniuntur *mg.* Bi)

596 iudicabit] iudicabis Bi_ac iudicat Pf   **605** infidelis] fidelis Bi EdF   **606** fiat]
fiet Aa   **609** respondemus] respondebimus Aa Sb respondendum est Pf
611 peccatorum] peccatorem Mk Pf   **615** conpensata] reconpensata Aa

FOR THIS REASON, AUGUSTINE ON THE SONG OF DEUTERONOMY:

c.43   *"The fire is kindled,* etc. That is, punishment will begin here and will   Dt 32:22

d.p.c.43   burn all the way to eternal[25] damnation." This should be noted against those who say that *God will not judge the same thing twice* pertains to all scourges, since certain people are amended[26] by scourges here, but others are punished here and in eternity, like Antiochus and Herod.

But what JEROME seems to think concerning the infidel adulterer is proven to be false by his own words in the same place. For, with the example of the man who had cursed the Israelites and the man who had collected wood on the Sabbath, he shows that small sins are purged with brief and temporal punishments, but great sins are reserved for lasting and eternal punishments. FOR HE SAYS,   cf. C.23 q.5

c.44   "Let someone ask here what afterward happens concerning an infi-   c.6
del if he should be caught in adultery and beheaded. For either he will be punished, and this is false which is said: *God will not judge the same thing twice in tribulation,* or he will not be punished, and adul-   Na 1:9
terers should wish to be punished with the brief penalty characteristic of present punishments so that they may make eternal torments useless. To this we answer that God, as he knows the measure of all things, also knows the measure of punishments and this measure of punishments is not prevented by the sentence of a judge, and it is not removed to God's disadvantage in the power of exercising a penalty for sins in the present. Moreover a great sin is paid for with great and lasting torments, but if someone has been punished, like the man in the Law who had cursed the Israelites and he who had collected wood on the Sabbath, such are not afterward punished, because light guilt is compensated for with punishment of the present world."

d.p.c.44   But that statement of Gregory, "The Lord caused it to rain upon one city," etc. is to be related not to mercy for a wicked deed but to   D.3 c.40

---

25. The second recension changed "eternal" to "the final."
26. A seeming very early gloss, "or judged," became a fairly standard intratextual addition at this point. It appears intralinearly and in the margin (prior to "amended") in Aa. The addition is in all but one of Friedberg's manuscripts. It was not included by the *Editores romani* in the 1582 edition. Somewhat surprisingly given its usual incorporation of second recension changes, Bi does not have the addition within the text but rather in the margin and seems to place it after the verb "are punished" in the following clause.

est, ut ideo pars ciuitatis dicatur esse conpluta, quia crimen quod
620 dilexerat detestari incipit, non quod eius ueniam consequatur. Cri-
Aa 172ᵛ minis autem detestatio pluuia uocatur ǀ quia ex fonte diuine gratie
cordi nostro instillatur, ut uel sic quisque ad ueram penitentiam
perueniat aut eo minus a Deo puniatur, quo diuturniori delectatione peccati maius sibi supplicium accumulasset. Si uero ad indul-
625 gentiam criminis pluuia referatur, euangelice sententie contraire
uidebitur. Si enim propter odium fraternum etiam que dimissa sunt
replicantur ad penam, multo magis que non sunt dimissa ad uindictam reseruari probantur.

Item, si secundum Augustinum arbiter sue uoluntatis non po-
630 test inchoare nouam uitam nisi peniteat eum ueteris uite, quomodo
ad nouitatis indulgentiam perueniet qui odii uetustatem non depo-
Fs 315ʳᵃ suit? Ad detestationem ergo criminis, ut dictum est, ǀ non ad eius
indulgentiam pluuia illa pertinere probatur.

Item illud Ambrosii, "Et si fides desit, pena satisfacit," non de ea
Pf 120ᵛᵃ fide intelligitur ǀ de qua dicitur, *fides sine operibus mortua est*, set de ea
de qua Apostolus ait, *Omne, quod non est ex fide*, id est omne, quod
contra conscientiam fit, *peccatum est*. Deest ergo fides cum non su-
best conscientia peccati. Set quia delicta omnia nullus intelligit, est
aliquando in homine peccatum cuius non habet conscientiam.
640 VNDE APOSTOLUS: *Nichil mihi conscius sum, set non in hoc iustificatus
sum*. Cuius ergo peccati deest conscientia, illius pena, si patienter
feratur, satisfacit et releuat grauatum.

Quod autem in fine obicitur: "Si satisfactio illa fuit, ueniam in-
Bi 310ʳᵇ petrauit; si autem ueniam non inpetrauit, satisfactio ǀ non fuit; si
645 autem satisfactio non fuit, adhuc sibi pena inponenda est," non
procedit argumentatione. Satisfactio namque est dum illius peccati
causa exciditur, et eius suggestionibus aditus non indulgetur, set

---

638 conscientia peccati] cf. *Gl. ord. in Ps.* 118:137 (ed. Rusch, 2.618b)

623 quo] quod R2

619 conpluta] copulata Mk_ac conpulta Pf   **620** dilexerat] dilexit Sb ǀ incipit] incepit Fd   **626** propter] per Aa ǀ etiam] et Aa   **627** non] nondum Aa Fd_pc Bi Fs
Mk   **631** perueniet] perueniret Fd_pc Fs   **646** argumentatione] argumentatio
codd. o. EdF

the detesting of it so that part of the city may be said to have been rained upon for this reason, that the wicked deed which it had loved begins to be detested, not that it obtains mercy for it. Detesting a wicked deed is called rain because it is instilled in our heart from the fount of divine grace so that either in this way each person may come to true penance or, the more he had piled up punishment for himself because of a rather long delight in the sin, the less he may be punished by God. But if the rain should be related to the indulgence for a wicked deed, this will seem contrary to evangelical opinion. For if, on account of hatred for one's brother, even those sins which have been forgiven are turned over for a penalty, much more so are those sins which have not been forgiven proven to be reserved for punishment.

Likewise, if according to Augustine the arbiter of one's own will cannot begin a new life unless he repents of his old life, how will cf. D.1 c.81 he who has not put away the oldness of hatred attain the mercy of newness? Therefore that rain is proven to pertain not to remission of a wicked deed, as has been said, but to the detesting of it.

Likewise, that statement of Ambrose, "Even if faith is lacking, the penalty satisfies," is not understood concerning that faith of D.3 c.41 which it is said, *Faith without works is dead,* but concerning that faith Jas 2:26 of which the Apostle says, *Everything which is not from faith,* that is, everything which is done against conscience, *is sin.* Therefore faith Rom 14:23 is lacking when an awareness of sin is not at hand. But because no one grasps all his offences, sometimes there is a sin in a person of which he has no awareness. AND SO THE APOSTLE: *I am aware of nothing against me, but I am not justified in this.* Therefore, if it is born 1 Cor 4:4 patiently, the penalty of him whose awareness of a sin is lacking makes satisfaction and lifts back up the one who is burdened.

But what is objected in the end: "If that was satisfaction, he obtained mercy; but if he did not obtain mercy, there was no satisfaction; but if there was no satisfaction, a penalty must still be imposed on him," does not proceed by argumentation. For there is cf. D.3 satisfaction when the cause of that sin is cut out and access to its d.p.c.41 instigating forces is not indulged, but the fruit of satisfaction is not

Sb 276vb

650

eius fructus non percipitur inpeditus peccato quod nondum deseri-
tur. Percipietur autem cum eius penitentia | fuerit subsecuta, sicut
ad lauacrum ficte accedens regenerationis sacramentum accipit,
non tamen in Christo renascitur; renascetur autem uirtute sacramenti quod perceperat cum fictio illa de corde eius recesserit ueraci
penitentia.

HINC ETIAM AUGUSTINUS IN LIBRO DE PENITENTIA SCRIBIT:

655   "Pium est credere, et nostra fides hoc expostulat, ut, cum gratia   c.45
Christi in homine destruxerit mala priora, etiam remuneret bona,
et, cum destruit quod suum non inuenit, amat et diligit bonum

Mk 251ra   quod in peccante plantauit." Ex hoc sensu | etiam ILLUD IERONIMI   d.p.c.45
Fd 96vb   DICTUM uidetur: "Si quando uideris inter multa opera peccatorum | c.46

660   facere quemquam aliqua que iusta sunt, non est tam iniustus Deus,
ut propter multa mala obliuiscatur paucorum bonorum."

Aa 173^r   Quamquam memoria bonorum ad presentem remunerationem | possit re-   d.p.c.46
ferri—sicut GREGORIUS IN OMELIA DE DIUITE ET LAZARO SCRIBIT: "Cauendum   c.47
nobis est, ut, si forte aliquod bonum agimus, in presenti seculo remunerationem

665   non accipiamus, ne forte dicatur nobis: *Receperunt mercedem suam.* Nisi enim diues iste aliquod bonum egisset, unde in presenti seculo remunerationem accepis-

(AaB 337^r)   set, nequaquam Abraham ei diceret, *Recepisti bona in uita tua.*"— | ITEM IOHAN-
Pf 120vb   NES CRISOSTOMUS: "Quid ergo turbamur? Nemo uidens malignos | prosperitatem   c.48
habere turbetur. Non est retributio malignitatis neque uirtutis; ac, si aliquando con-

Fs 315rb | FdB   tingit ut aliqua sit retributio uel malitie | uel uirtutis, | non tamen secundum quod
162ra   dignum est, set simpliciter ueluti quidam gustus iudicii, ut qui resurrectioni non
credunt talibus doceantur. Quando itaque uidemus malignum ditescere, non sub-
ruamur, et quando uidemus bonum mala pati, non turbemur. Illic corone; illic supplicia. Est et alia ratio, quia non potest uel malus in omnibus malus esse set habet

675   aliqua bona, neque bonus in omnibus bonus esse set habet aliqua peccata. Quando

---

655 Pium...**658** plantauit] Ps.-Aug., *De uera* 14 (PL 40:1125; ed. Wagner,
741–44)   **659** Si...**661** bonorum] Hier., *Comm. in prophetas minores, In Aggaeum*
1.6 (CCSL 76A, 720.244–247)   **663** Cauendum...**667**] cf. Greg. Magn., *Hom. in
evang.* 40.6 (CCSL 141:402.227–403.239)   **668** Quid...**677** punietur] Ioh.
Chrys., *Hom. in Heb.* 5 (PG 63:50–51)

651 renascetur] renascitur R2 (Aa; renascetur Pf Sb EdRom)   **665** non] *om.* R2
(*adest interlin.* Mk_pc)

649 Percipietur] percipitur Fd   **657** diligit] dirigit Fd_ac   **667** nequaquam] *add.* ab
Aa | diceret] diceretur Aa Bi_ac   **669** est] *add.* hic Fs Mk Pf (*interlin.* Pf)   **671** iudi-
cii] iustitie AaB *add.* uel iustitie *interlin.* Mk | resurrectioni] resurrectionem EdF
Mk Pf Sb   **673** corone] corona EdF FdB Fs Bi Mk Pf

received when it has been impeded by a sin which is not yet abandoned. But the fruit of the first satisfaction will be received when the penance for that sin ensues, just as a person insincerely approaching the wash-basin receives the sacrament of regeneration but is not reborn in Christ, but he will be reborn[27] by the power of the sacrament which he had received when that feigning withdraws from his heart because of genuine penance.

c.45 FOR THIS REASON AUGUSTINE ALSO WRITES IN HIS BOOK ON PENANCE: "It is pious to believe, and our faith requires this, that when the grace of Christ destroys prior evils in man, it also rewards good things, and, when it has destroyed what it does not find of its own, it loves and adores the good which it planted in the sinner."

d.p.c.45 | c.46 THAT STATEMENT OF JEROME also seems to have this sense: "If you see at any time that any person does some things that are righteous amid many works of sins, God is not so unjust as to forget the few good works on account of the many evil ones."

d.p.c.46 Although the memory of good works is able to be transferred into present remuneration,—as GREGORY WRITES IN HIS HOMILY ON THE RICH MAN AND
c.47 LAZARUS: "We should be on guard that, if we happen to do some good work, we do not[28] receive remuneration in the present world, lest by chance it be said of us, *They have received their reward.* For if that rich man had not done some good thing on   Mt 6:5 which count he had received remuneration in the present world, Abraham would by no means say to him, *You received good things in your life.*"—LIKEWISE JOHN   Lk 16:25
c.48 CHRYSOSTOM: "Why are we then agitated? Let no one seeing the malign prosper be agitated. It is not the retribution of wickedness and not of virtue; and, if at some point it happens that there is some retribution either of malice or of virtue, it is not nevertheless according to what is fitting, but simply like a certain taste of judgment so that those who do not believe in the resurrection may be taught by such things. Therefore, when we see the malignant grow rich, let us not be subverted, and when we see a good person suffer evil, let us not be agitated. Therein lie crowns; therein lie punishments. There is also another reason: because the evil person cannot be evil in all things but has some goodness, and the good person cannot be good in all things but has some sins. Therefore, when the evil person has prosperity, it is with

27. The second recension changed the verb to the present tense.
28. The second recension removed this "not," so the English translation of these phrases would have to read, "We should be wary, if we happen to do some good work, of accepting remuneration in the present world."

ergo prosperitatem habet malus, malo capitis sui. Cum enim pro illis paucis bonis retributionem hic accipit, illic iam plenius punietur."

—potest etiam referri memoria bonorum ad mitiorem penam d.p.c.48
habendam, ut bona que inter multa mala fiunt non proficiant ad
680 presentis uel future uite premium obtinendum set ad tollerabilius
extremi iudicii supplicium subeundum, sicut de fide et ceteris que
sine caritate habentur AUGUSTINUS SCRIBIT IN LIBRO DE PATIEN-
TIA dicens: "Si quis autem non habens caritatem, que pertinet ad c.49
unitatem spiritus et uinculum pacis, quo catholica ecclesia congre-
685 gata connectitur, in aliquo scismate constitutus, ne Christum neget,
Bi 310ᵛᵃ | patitur tribulationes, angustias, famem, nuditatem, persecutio-
Sb 277ʳᵃ nem, pericula, | carceres, uincula, tormenta, gladium, uel flammas,
uel bestias, uel ipsam crucem timore gehennarum et ignis eterni,
nullo modo ista culpanda sunt. Immo uero et hic laudanda patien-
690 tia est. Non enim dicere poterimus melius ei fuisse, ut Christum negando nichil eorum pateretur, que passus est confitendo, set esti-
mandum est fortasse tollerabilius ei futurum iudicium quam si
Christum negando nichil eorum pateretur, ut illud quod ait Apostolus, *Si tradidero corpus meum ita ut ardeam, caritatem autem non ha-*
695 *beam, nichil mihi prodest.* Nichil prodesse intelligatur ad regnum celorum obtinendum, non ad extremi iudicii tollerabilius supplicium
subeundum." Et infra: "Hec propter caritatem dicta sunt, sine qua
Mk 251ʳᵇ in | nobis non potest esse uera patientia, quoniam in bonis caritas
Dei est, que tollerat omnia."

Pf 121ʳᵃ   Penitentia ergo, ut ex premissis apparet, nulli in peccato | perse- d.p.c.49
ueranti utilis est; non tamen alicui deneganda est, quia sentiet fruc-
Fs 315ᵛᵃ tum eius cum | alterius criminis penitentiam egerit. Sic itaque peni-
tentie diffinitio et cetere auctoritates sibi consonantes negant eum

---

683 Si…**697** subeundum] Aug. Hipp., *De patientia* 26 (CSEL 41:687.22–688.13)
697 Hec…**699** omnia] Ibid. 23 (CSEL 41:685.3–5)

676 malo] *add.* est *interlin.* Bi, *add.* est *pos.* sui EdF   **680** uite] *pos.* presentis Bi Fs
Mk Pf   **682** scribit] *om.* Aa   **683** dicens] dicit Aa | habens] habet Aa Sb   **688** ge-
hennarum] gehenne Aa   **691** estimandum] existimandum Aa Sb   **692** quam]
quem Fd   **694** habeam] habuero Pf EdF   **697** sunt] sint Fd_{ac}   **698** patientia] penitentia Bi_{ac} EdF Fs Mk Pf

evil on his head. For when he receives retribution for those few good things here, he will forthwith be punished more fully in the hereafter."

d.p.c.48 —the memory of good things can also be transferred into having a lesser penalty such that the good things which were done amid many evil things advance not to obtain a reward of this present or the future life but to approach a more tolerable punishment at the Last Judgment, just as AUGUSTINE WRITES IN HIS BOOK ON SUF-FERING about that faith and the rest of the things that are possessed

c.49 without love, saying, "If someone does not have the love that belongs to the unity of the Spirit and the bond of peace, by which the catholic church gathered together is connected, and is established in some schism, and, lest he deny Christ, suffers tribulations, distress, hunger, nakedness, persecution, dangers, prisons, chains, torments, sword, or fires, or beasts, or the cross itself with the fear of hell and eternal fire, those things should not in any way be reproached. Nay rather, this suffering should even be praised. For we are not able to say that it would have been better for him if, for denying Christ, he were to suffer none of these things which he suffered for confessing him, but it should be considered that perhaps the future judgment will be more tolerable for him than if he were not to suffer any of these things for denying Christ, as that which the apostle says, *If I hand over my body in such a way that I burn but I do not have love, it profits me nothing.* It should be understood 1 Cor 13:3 that it profits nothing for obtaining the kingdom of heaven, not that it profits nothing for approaching a more tolerable punishment at the Last Judgment." And below: "These things have been said on account of that love without which true suffering cannot exist in us, since the love of God, which tolerates all things, exists in good people."

d.p.c.49 Therefore, as is clear from the preceding, penance is beneficial to no one persevering in sin; nevertheless if should not be denied to anyone because he will feel its fruit when he does penance for the other wicked deed. Therefore, the definition of penance and the remaining authorities agreeing with it in this way deny that he who

agere penitentiam qui perseuerat in crimine, utilem uidelicet sibi et
705 fructuosam.

ILLUD AUTEM AMBROSII, "Penitentia semel usurpata nec uere
celebrata, et fructum prioris aufert et usum sequentis amittit," de
solempni intelligitur, que, cum non uere celebrata fuerit, et fruc-
tum prioris, id est sui ipsius | secuturam precedentis, amittit (quia
710 ueniam quam inpetrare potuit contempsit), et usum sequentis aufert, secundum consuetudinem quarumdam ecclesiarum, apud
quas penitentie solempnitas non reiteratur. De hac eadem penitentia etiam illud intelligitur: "Non est secundus locus penitentie."

706 Penitentia...707 amittit] Ambr. Med., *De paenitentia* 2.11 (SChr
179:198.56–58)   713 Non...penitentie] *non Ambros. sed* cf. *Decretum, prima pars*
D.50 d.p.c.61

712 penitentie solempnitas] penitentia sollempnis Aa Bi$_{pc}$ Pf   713 etiam] et Bi
om. Fs

perseveres in a wicked deed does penance, specifically a penance which is beneficial to him and fruitful.

BUT THAT STATEMENT OF AMBROSE, "Penance which has been usurped once and not truly celebrated, both removes the fruit of a prior penance and loses the benefit of the subsequent one," is understood concerning solemn penance, which, when it is not truly celebrated, both loses the fruit of the prior penance, that is, of his very penance preceding the one about to follow (because he despised the mercy which he was able to obtain), and removes the benefit of the following penance, according to the custom of certain churches, in whose opinion the solemnity of penance is not repeated. This statement is also understood as being about this same penance: "There is no second place of penance."

cf. D.3 c.37
(R2 addition)

Distinctio quarta

<Quaestio>

Quia uero multorum auctoritatibus supra monstratum est peni-   pr.
tentiam uere celebrari et peccata uere dimitti ei qui aliquando in
5 crimen recasurus est, queritur an peccata dimissa redeant? Huius
questionis diuersorum uaria est sententia, aliis asserentibus, aliis
econtra negantibus, peccata semel dimissa ulterius replicari ad penam.

<Sententia prima>

10   Quod autem peccata dimissa redeant multorum probatur aucto-   d.a.c.1
ritatibus. Quarum prima est ILLA PROPHETE: *In memoriam redeat ini-*
quitas patrum eius, etc.; secunda ILLA EUANGELII: *Serue nequam, omne*
debitum dimisi tibi, etc.

    DEINDE AUGUSTINUS IN LIBRO PSALMORUM AIT, "Si Iudas te-   c.1
15 neret illud ad quod uocatus est, nullo modo ad eum uel sua preterita uel parentum iniquitas pertineret. Quia ergo non tenuit adoptionem in familia Dei set iniquitatem uetusti generis potius elegit,
rediit iniquitas | patrum in conspectu Domini ut in eo etiam ipsa |
puniretur."

20   ITEM RABANUS: "*Tradidit eum tortoribus*, etc. Considerandum est
quod dicit, *uniuersum debitum*, quia non solum peccata que post
baptismum homo egit reputabuntur ei ad penam, uerum etiam
peccata originalia que in baptismo ei dimissa sunt." ITEM GREGO-
RIUS: "Ex dictis euangelicis constat, quia, si in nos quod delinquitur   c.2
ex corde non dimittimus, et illud rursus exigitur, quod nobis | iam
per penitentiam dimissum | fuisse gaudebamus." ITEM AUGUSTI-
NUS IN OMELIA L: "Dicit Deus, *Dimitte et dimittetur tibi*; set ego prius   c.3
dimisi, dimitte uel postea. Nam si non dimiseris, reuocabo te, et
quicquid dimiseram replicabo tibi." ITEM: "Qui diuini beneficii obli-   c.4

Sb 277rb | Bi 310vb

Fd 97ra
Pf 121rb

4,14 Si...19 puniretur] Aug. Hipp., *Enarr.* 108.15 (CCSL 40:1591.19–23)
20 Tradidit...23 sunt] *fons materialis non inuenitur* 24 Ex...26 gaudebamus]
Greg. Magn., *Dial.* 4.62 (SChr 265:204.21–206.24) 27 Dicit...29 tibi] Aug.
Hipp., *Sermo* 83 (PL 38:518) 29 Qui...32 replicabuntur] Haymo Antis., *Homilia*
137 (*attribuatur* Haymo Halb., PL 118:732A)

4,28 non] nondum R2 (non EdF)

4,18 patrum] *add.* eius Aa 22 egit] gerit Fd Aa Sb 26 gaudebamus] gaudea-
mus Bi_ac gaudemus Pf_ac 27 Deus] Dominus Pf EdF | Dimitte] Dimittite Aa | tibi]
uobis Aa 29 dimiseram] dimiserim Pf Sb

Distinction 4

<Question>

pr.　But, because it has been shown above by many authorities that penance is truly celebrated and sins are truly forgiven for the person who at some time will fall back into a wicked deed, it is asked whether forgiven sins return. The opinion of diverse people on this question is varying, with some agreeing and others to the contrary denying that sins once forgiven are further turned back for penalty.

<First Position>

d.a.c.1　But that forgiven sins return is proven by many authorities, the first of which is THAT TEXT OF THE PROPHET: *Let the sin of his fathers*   Ps 108:14 *return to memory,* etc., and the second of which is THAT OF THE GOSPEL: *You wicked slave, I forgave you all your debt,* etc.   Mt 18:32

c.1　NEXT, AUGUSTINE IN HIS COMMENTARY ON THE BOOK OF PSALMS SAYS: "If Judas were to hold to that to which he was called, neither the iniquity of his past nor of his parents would in any way belong to him. Therefore, because he did not hold onto adoption in the family of God but chose instead the iniquity of his old people, the iniquity of the fathers returned in the sight of the Lord so that it might also be punished in him."

LIKEWISE RABANUS: "*He handed him over to his torturers,* etc. We   Mt 18:34 should consider that he says, *all his debt,* because, not only will the sins which a man performs after baptism be imputed to him for penalty, but also original sins which were forgiven him in baptism."

c.2　LIKEWISE GREGORY: "From the words of the gospel it is agreed that, if we do not forgive from our heart what is done wrongly against us, even that debt is again exacted which we were rejoicing had already been forgiven through penance." LIKEWISE AUGUS-

c.3　TINE IN HOMILY 50: "God says, *Forgive and it will be forgiven you,* but   Lk 6:37 I have forgiven before, so forgive afterward. For if you do not[1] forgive, I will call you back and whatever I had forgiven, I will turn

---

1. Many manuscripts of the second recension read "not yet" instead of simply "not."

Fs 315vb tus suas uult uindicare iniurias, | non solum de futuris peccatis ue-
niam non merebitur, set etiam preterita, que iam sibi dimissa crede-
bat, ad uindictam ei replicabuntur." ITEM BEDA SUPER LUCAM:
"*Reuertar in domum meam.* Timendus est iste uersiculus, non expo-   c.5
nendus, ne culpa quam in nobis exstinctam credebamus per incu-
Aa 174^r riam nos uacantes opprimat." ITEM: | "Quecumque enim post bapti-   c.6
Mk 251va sma siue | prauitas heretica seu mundana cupiditas arripuerit mox
omnium prosternet in ima uitiorum."

ITEM AUGUSTINUS IN LIBRO QUESTIONUM DEUTERONOMII:
"Peccatum quod ex Adam trahitur temporaliter redditur, quia om-   c.7
40 nes propter hoc moriuntur, non autem in eternum eis qui fuerint
per gratiam regenerati, si in ea usque in finem permanserint."

Horum uero qui hanc sententiam secuntur, alii dicunt quod   d.p.c.7
peccata reditura dimittuntur secundum iustitiam set non secundum
prescientiam, sicut nomina discipulorum qui retro abierunt erant
45 scripta in libro uite propter iustitiam cui deseruiebant, non secundum prescientiam, que in numero saluandorum eos non habebat.
Sic a latere Dei dicuntur mille casuri, et decem millia a dextris eius,
quos tamen diuina prescientia numquam suis annumerauerat.
HINC ETIAM DOMINUS AIT MOYSI, *Si quis peccauerit ante me, delebo*
50 *eum de libro uite,* ut secundum iustitiam iudicis ille peccando dicatur
deleri, qui secundum prescientiam numquam fuerat ascriptus.

33 Reuertar…**37** uitiorum] Bed. Uen., *In Luc. euang. expos.* 4.11 (CCSL
120:235.165–67, 177–79)   **39** Peccatum…**41** permanserint] Aug. Hipp., *Quaest.
in hept.* 5, *Quaestiones Deuteronomii* 42 (CCSL 33:297.817–298.820)   **43** secundum[1]…**51** ascriptus] cf. Ambros., *In epistolam ad Romanos* 9 (CSEL
81.1:315–319); Ans. Laud., *Sententia* 34 (ed. Lottin, 35) et *Gl. ord. in Rom.* 9:23
(ed. Rusch, 4.294b–295a)

31 sibi] *om.* Aa Sb   **32** ei] *interlin.* Fd, *ant.* ad Aa   **34** incuriam] iniuriam Fd
36 mundana] *interlin.* Bi, munda Mk_{ac} | arripuerit] arripiet Aa arripiunt Fs Pf
42 Horum] Eorum Sb EdF | Horum uero] Horum autem Fs, *add.* uel Eorum
uero *mg.* Fs   **44** prescientiam] presentiam Fd_{ac} Bi_{ac}   **46** prescientiam] presen-
tiam Mk_{ac}   **48** prescientia] presentia Bi_{ac} Mk_{ac}   **50** uite] uiuentium Bi Mk | iu-
stitiam] iudicium Aa   **51** prescientiam] presentiam Bi_{ac} Mk_{ac}

c.4 back to you." LIKEWISE: "Not only will he who forgets divine blessing and wants to claim wrongs as his own not deserve mercy for
future sins, but also his past sins, which he believed were already
forgiven him, will be turned back to him for punishment." LIKE-
c.5 WISE BEDE ON LUKE: "*I will return to my house.* That little verse   Lk 11:24
should be feared, not exposited, lest the guilt which we were thinking had been abolished in us oppress our unoccupied selves
c.6 through negligence." LIKEWISE: "Whatever either heretical per-
verseness or worldly desire takes hold after baptism will soon be
thrown headlong in the lowest of all vices."

LIKEWISE AUGUSTINE IN HIS BOOK OF QUESTIONS ON DEUTER-
c.7 ONOMY: "The sin which is handed down from Adam is temporarily
given back, because all die on account of this, but [it is not given
back] eternally to those who have been regenerated through grace,
if they persist in it all the way to the end."

d.p.c.7 But of these who follow this opinion, some say that sins which
will return are forgiven according to righteousness but not according to prescience, just as the names of the disciples who withdrew   cf. Jn 6:66
had been written in the Book of Life according to the righteousness   cf. Lk 10:20
to which they used to be devoted, not according to prescience,
which did not have them in the number of those to be saved. In
this way a thousand are said to be ready to fall from the side of God
and, from his right side, ten thousand, whom nevertheless divine   cf. Ps 91:7
prescience had never counted for its own. ON THIS ACCOUNT, THE
LORD ALSO SAYS TO MOSES: *If anyone sins before me, I will erase him*   Ex 32:33
from the Book of Life, so that, according to the justice of the Judge, he
who had never been written down according to prescience may be
said to be erased when he sins.

HINC AUGUSTINUS IN EPISTOLA AD CORINTHIOS: *"Set non in pluribus eorum beneplacitum est Deo,* etsi in aliquibus. Communia omnibus sacramenta, set non communis gratia."* Ita et nunc baptismus
55 communis est, set non uirtus baptismi. Verum hoc de ficte accedentibus, uel de his qui extra ecclesiam baptizantur intelligitur, qui sacramenti quidem integritatem accipiunt, uirtutem uero eius minime assecuntur. Paruulis uero, uel adultis plena fide accedentibus omnino peccata remittuntur, etsi aliquando a bono recessuri et in
60 malo uitam sint finituri.

Pf 121va

VNDE AUGUSTINUS | IN LIBRO DE CORRECTIONE ET GRATIA: *"Si   c.8
Bi 311ra Sb   ex bono in malum deficientes | bona uoluntate moriuntur, respon-
277va   deant, si possunt, cur illos Deus, cum fideliter et pie uiuerent, non
tunc de uite huius periculis rapuit, ne malitia mutaret intellectum
65 eorum et ne fictio deciperet animas eorum? Vtrum hoc in potestate
non habuit, an eorum mala futura nesciuit? Nempe nichil horum
Fs --   nisi peruersissime atque insanissime dicitur. Cur ergo | non fecit?
Respondeant qui nos irrident quando in rebus talibus exclamamus,
exclamamus, *Quam inscrutabilia sunt iudicia eius et inuestigabiles uie
70 eius.* Neque enim hoc non donat Deus quibus uoluerit, aut uero illa
scriptura mentitur, que de morte uelut inmatura hominis iusti ait,
Aa 174^v   *Raptus est ne malitia mutaret | intellectum eius et ne fictio deciperet animam eius.* Cur igitur hoc tam magnum beneficium aliis dat, aliis non
dat Deus, apud quem non est iniquitas nec acceptio personarum, et
75 in cuius potestate est, quamdiu quisque in hac uita maneat, que
temptatio dicta est *super terram?* Sicut ergo coguntur fateri donum
Dei esse ut finiat homo uitam istam antequam ex bono mutetur in

---

52 Set ... 54 gratia] cf. Aug. Hipp., *Enarr.* 77.2 (CCSL 39:1067.33–36)   61 Si ...
160 mali] Aug. Hipp., *De corr. et grat.* 8–9 (PL 44:927–929)

53 omnibus] omnia *uel* est omnia R2 (omnibus Sb EdRom, *om.* Fs)   59 et] *om.*
R2 (*adest* Fs Sb)   69 exclamamus] *om.* R2   70 illa ... 71 scriptura] *tr.* R2

53 beneplacitum] beneplacitendum? Fd   54 communis] conuersis Fd_{ac} *add.* est
Bi Mk Pf | baptismus] *pos.* est Aa Bi Mk   61 correctione] correptione Bi   66 habuit] habuerit Bi Fs Sb   70 uero] *om.* Bi Mk   71 uelut] aut Fd *om.* Aa

ON THIS ACCOUNT AUGUSTINE WRITES ON THE EPISTLE TO THE CORINTHIANS: *"But God did not take good pleasure in many of them,* 1 Cor 10:5 even if he did in some. Sacraments are common to all,[2] but grace is not common."* So also now baptism is common but not its power. This truth is understood concerning those who approach baptism insincerely or concerning those who are baptized outside of the church, who indeed receive the sacrament in its wholeness but do not obtain its power. But, both for small children and adults approaching the sacrament with full faith, sins are completely remitted, even if they will at some point withdraw from the good and[3] finish this life in evil.

AND THUS AUGUSTINE IN THE BOOK *DE CORREPTIONE ET GRATIA:*
c.8   "If those departing from good for evil die with a good will, let them answer, if they can, why God did not seize them from the perils of this life when they were living faithfully and piously, so that malice might not change their understanding and so that a fiction might not deceive their souls? Does he not have this in his power, or did he not know their evils to come? Surely none of these things is said except most perversely and unsoundly. Why, then, did he not do this? Let those who mock us answer when we exclaim in such circumstances—we exclaim,[4] *How inscrutable are his judgments and unfathomable his ways.* For either God gives this to those to whom he   Rom 11:33 desires, or truly that Scripture lies which says concerning the premature death, as it were, of a righteous man, *he was seized so that malice might not change his understanding and so that a fiction might not deceive his soul.* Therefore, why does God, in whom there is no iniq-   Wisdom 4:11 uity and no regarding of persons, and in whose power each person stands as long as he remains in this life (which has been called *temptation on earth*) give so great a blessing as this to some and not   cf. Jb 7:1 to others? Therefore, just as they are forced to confess that it is a gift of God that a man ends this wretched life before he is changed from good to evil, but they do not know why this gift is given to

---

2. The second recension changed the declension of the adjective "all," making it modify "sacraments" as opposed to standing on its own as a substantive adjective. The second recension would be translated, "All sacraments are common." The change made the text match more closely a sentence by Augustine in his *Enarratio* on Psalm 77.
3. The second recension removed this "and," effectively turning the verb "withdraw" into a pure future active participle.
4. The second recension removed this redundant "we exclaim," which also was absent from Augustine's original.

malum, cur autem id aliis donetur, aliis non donetur, ignorant, id
tantum donum Dei esse in bono perseuerantiam secundum scriptu-
80 ras (de quibus testimonia multa iam posui) fateantur nobiscum, et
cur aliis detur, aliis non detur, sine murmure aduersus Deum di-
gnentur ignorare nobiscum.

Mk 251vb "Nec | nos moueat quod filiis suis quibusdam Deus non dat
istam perseuerantiam. Absit enim ut ita sit, si de illis predestinatis
85 essent et secundum propositum uocatis, qui uere sunt filii promissionis. Nam isti, cum pie uiuunt, dicuntur filii Dei set quia uicturi
sunt inpie et in eadem inpietate morituri, non eos dicit filios prescientia Dei. Sunt enim filii Dei qui nondum sunt nobis et sunt iam
Fd 97rb Deo, de quibus euangelista ait Iohannes, *quia | Iesus erat moriturus*
90 *pro gente, nec tantum pro gente, set etiam ut filios Dei dispersos congregaret*
in unum, quod utique credendo futuri erant per euangelii predica-
tionem, et tamen antequam esset factum, iam filii Dei erant: in me-
Pf 121vb moriali patris sui inconcussa | stabilitate conscripti sunt.

"Et sunt rursus quidam qui filii Dei propter susceptam uel tem-
95 poraliter gratiam dicuntur a nobis, nec sunt tamen Dei. De quibus
ait idem Iohannes, *Exierunt ex nobis, set non erant ex nobis; quod si fuis-*
sent ex nobis, mansissent utique nobiscum. Non ait, 'Ex nobis exierunt,
set quia non manserunt nobiscum, iam non sunt ex nobis'; uerum
ait, *Ex nobis exierunt, set non erant ex nobis*, hoc est, 'et quando uide-
Sb 277vb bantur in nobis, non erant ex nobis.' Et tamquam ei diceretur, |
'Vnde id ostendis?', *Quod si fuissent*, inquit, *ex nobis, permansissent uti-*
que nobiscum. Filiorum Dei uox est; Iohannes loquitur in filiis Dei
Bi 311rb loco precipuo constitutus. Cum ergo filii Dei dicunt | de his qui per-

---

79 tantum] tamen R2   **85** uocatis] *add.* sanctis R2 (*om.* Sb)   **96** Exierunt] *pos.*
ex nobis R2

78 ignorant] ignoratur Bi Pf   **80** fateantur] fatentur Fd_{ac}   **90** nec... gente²] *mg.*
Fd *interlin.* Mk   **92** memoriali] memorialis Fd memoria enim Mk   **95** Dei] *prae-*
mitt. filii Aa, secundum (*interlin.*) Deum Bi   **103** dicunt] dicuntur Fd_{pc} Pf *om.* Sb

some and not to others, so also let them confess with us that perseverance in the good is purely[5] a gift of God according to the Scriptures (about whose testimony I have already posited many things), and, along with us, they deserve to be ignorant of why this is given to some and not to others without murmuring against God.

"And let it not disturb us that God does not give that perseverance to certain of his sons. For far be it that this be the case if they were to be from among those who have been predestined and called[6] according to his purpose, who truly are sons of promise. For those others, when they live piously, are called sons of God; but because they will live wickedly and will die in this same wickedness, the prescience of God does not call them sons. They are sons of God who do not yet belong to us and yet do already belong to God, concerning whom John the Evangelist says, *Jesus was going to die for the nation, and not only for the nation, but also so that he might gather into one the sons of God who are scattered*, because surely they were going   Jn 11:51–52 to be the sons of God by believing through the preaching of the gospel, and nevertheless, before this occurred, they were already the sons of God: they were inscribed in the remarkable unshaken firmness of their Father.

"And again, there are certain people who are called sons of God by us on account of at least temporarily received grace, and, nevertheless, they are not of God. The same John says about these people: *They departed from us, but they were not of us; but if they had been of us, they surely would have remained with us*. He does not say, 'They de-   1 Jn 2:19 parted from us, but because they did not remain with us, they are not now of us'; But he says, *They departed from us, but they were not of us*, that is, 'and when they seemed to be in us, they were not of us.' And as if it were to be said to him, 'From where do you show this?', he says, *But if they had been of us, they surely would have remained with us*. This is the voice of the sons of God; John speaks as one established in an especial place for the sons of God. Therefore,

---

5. Augustine did not originally have the word I have translated as "purely" (*tantum*). His text included a simple *ita*, or "so also," at the beginning of the second part of this complex sentence. Gratian originally wrote this as *id tantum*, and the second recension changed the *tantum* to *tamen*. These versions are difficult to translate. I have maintained a "so also" to connect the two main parts of the sentences. This is necessitated by the opening "just as" (*sicut*). The first-recension *tantum* I have translated as "purely"; the second-recension *tamen* gives the sense of "nevertheless," but it is difficult to work that into the sentence.
6. The second recension added "saints."

seuerantiam non habuerunt, *Ex nobis exierunt, set non erant ex nobis,*
105   et addunt, *quod si fuissent ex nobis, permansissent utique nobiscum,* quid
aliud dicunt, nisi non erant filii, etiam quando erant in professione
et nomine filiorum?—non quia iustitiam simulauerunt, set quia in
ea non permanserunt. Neque enim ait, 'Nam, si fuissent ex nobis,
ueram, non fictam, iustitiam tenuissent utique nobiscum.' In bono
110   illos uolebat proculdubio permanere; erant itaque in bono, set quia
in eo non permanserunt, id est non usque in finem perseueraue-
Aa 175ʳ   runt, 'non erant,' inquit, | 'ex nobis, et quando erant nobiscum';
hoc est, non erant ex numero filiorum, et quando erant in fide filiorum, quoniam qui uere filii sunt presciti et predestinati sunt con-
115   formes imaginis filii Dei et secundum propositum uocati sunt, ut
electi essent. Non enim perit filius promissionis, set filius perditionis.

"Fuerunt ergo isti ex multitudine uocatorum; ex electorum autem paucitate non fuerunt. Non igitur filiis suis predestinatis Deus
120   perseuerantiam non dedit. Haberent enim eam, si in eo filiorum
numero essent, et quid haberent, quod non accepissent secundum
apostolicam ueramque sententiam? Ac per hoc tales filii filio Christo dati essent, quemadmodum ipse dicit ad patrem, *Vt omne quod*
dedisti mihi non pereat set habeat uitam eternam. Hi ergo Christo intelli-
125   guntur dari, qui ordinati sunt in uitam eternam. Ipsi sunt illi predestinati et secundum propositum uocati, quorum nullus perit, ac per
Pf 122ʳᵃ   hoc nullus eorum | ex bono in malum mutatus finit hanc uitam,
quoniam sic est ordinatus et ideo Christo datus, ut non pereat set
Mk 252ʳᵃ   habeat | uitam eternam. Et rursus, quos dicimus inimicos eius, uel
130   paruulos filios inimicorum eius, quoscumque eorum sic regenera-
turus est ut in ea fide, que per dilectionem operatur, hanc uitam fi-
niant, iam et antequam hoc fiat, in illa predestinatione filii sunt

---

106 filii] *add.* Dei R2 (*interlin.* Fd$_{pc}$)   **109** nobiscum] *add.* set, 'Si fuissent,' inquit,
'ex nobis, permansissent utique nobiscum.' R2 (*mg.* Fd$_{pc}$)

104 Ex nobis] *pos.* exierunt Aa Pf   **105** quod] *om.* Bi Mk   **108** fuissent] essent Pf
fuerint Sb   **111** non²] *exp. et add. pos.* finem Bi; *pos.* finem EdF   **114** conformes]
add. fieri Aa   **115** imaginis] imagines Fd$_{ac}$ Bi | et] *om.* Aa sed Bi   **120** eo] *om.* Aa
eorum Pf   **123** ipse dicit] *tr.* Mk dicit esse ipse Bi, *pos.* patrem Pf

when the sons of God say concerning these who have not had perseverance, *They departed from us, but they were not of us*, and they add,
but if they had been of us, they surely would have persisted with us, what
else are they saying except that they were not sons,[7] even when
they were in the profession and name of sons?—not because they
simulated righteousness, but because they did not persist in it. For
he does not say, 'For, if they had been of us, they would surely
have held true, not fake, righteousness with us.'[8] Without a doubt,
he was wanting them to persist in the good; therefore they were in
the good; but because they did not persist in it, that is, they did not
persevere all the way to the end, 'they were not,' he says, 'of us,
even when they were with us'; that is, they were not among the
number of the sons, even when they were in the faith of the sons,
since those who truly are sons have been foreknown and predestined to be conformed to the image of the Son of God and have
been called according to his purpose, that they might be elect. For
the son of promise does not perish, but the son of perdition.

"Therefore, those were from the many who are called, but they
were not from the few who are chosen. Therefore, it is not that
God did not give perseverance to his predestined sons. For they
would have it if they were in that number of sons, and what would
they have, according to true and apostolic opinion, which they had
not received? And such sons would have been given to the Son,
Christ, in the way that he says to the Father, *So that all whom you
have given me may not perish but have eternal life*. Therefore these who   Jn 6:39
have been ordained to eternal life are understood to be given to
Christ. These very people are those predestined and called according to his purpose, of whom no one perishes, and through this not
one of them ends this life having changed from good to evil, since
he has been ordained in such a way and given to Christ for this reason, that he may not perish but have eternal life. And again, those
whom we call his enemies or the little sons of his enemies,
whomever of them he will regenerate in such a way that they end
this life in that faith which works through love, now and before

---

7. The second recension read "sons of God."

8. The second recension added, "but he says, 'If they had been of us, they
surely would have persisted with us.'" Whether Gratian originally omitted the
phrase on purpose or as the result of an error of homeoteleuton is unclear, but,
since both Fd and Aa omit this phrase, it does seem not to have been part of
Gratian's original text. A corrector later added it to Fd's margin.

eius et dati sunt Christo filio eius ut non pereant set habeant uitam eternam.

135 "Denique ipse Saluator: *Si manseritis,* inquit, *in uerbo meo, uere discipuli mei estis.* Numquid in his conputandi sunt illi, de quibus euangelium sic loquitur?—ubi Dominus, cum conmendasset manducandam carnem suam et bibendum sanguinem suum, ait Euangelista: *Hec dixit in synagoga docens in Capharnaum. Multi ergo audientes*
140 *ex discipulis eius dixerunt, 'Durus est hic sermo, quis potest eum audire?'*
Sb 278ra *Sciens autem Iesus apud | semetipsum, quia murmurabant de hoc discipuli eius, dixit eis, 'Hoc uos scandalizat? Si ergo uideritis filium hominis ascendentem, ubi prius erat? Spiritus est qui uiuificat, caro autem non prodest quicquam. Verba que ego locutus sum uobis Spiritus et uita sunt. Set sunt*
145 *quidam ex uobis qui non credunt.' Sciebat enim ab initio Iesus qui essent credentes et qui esset traditurus eum, et dicebat, 'Propterea dixi uobis, quia*
Bi 311va' *nemo | uenit ad me, nisi fuerit ei datum a patre meo.' Ex hoc multi discipulorum eius abierunt retro et iam cum illo non ambulabant.* Numquid non et isti discipuli appellati sunt, loquente euangelio? Et tamen non
150 erant uere discipuli quia non manserunt in uerbo eius, secundum
Aa 175v id quod ait, *Si manseritis in uerbo meo, uere | discipuli mei eritis.* Quia ergo non habuerunt perseuerantiam, sicut non uere discipuli Christi, ita nec filii Dei uere fuerunt, etiam quando esse uidebantur et ita uocabantur. Appellamus ergo nos et electos et Christi discipulos,
155 et Dei filios, quia appellandi sunt quos regeneratos pie uiuere cerni-
Fd 97va mus. | Set tunc uere sunt quod appellantur, si manserint in eo quod sic appellantur. Si autem perseuerantiam non habent, id est in eo quod ceperunt esse non manent, non uere appellantur propter
Pf 122rb quod appellantur, et non sunt. Apud eum enim hoc non sunt, | cui
160 notum est quod futuri sunt, id est ex bonis mali."

---

156 eo] *add.* propter R2 (*interlin.* Fdpc)

135 Saluator] *add.* ait Aa Pf   142 uideritis] uidebitis Fdpc Mk Sb | ascendentem] *interlin.* Bi Mk   145 Iesus] *ant.* ab initio Aa EdF   146 qui] quis Aa Pf EdF
147 datum] *add.* de supra Bi Mk   153 uere] *ant.* filii Aa Pf   154 nos] *add.* et Fd Aa Bi Sb | et¹] *om.* Mk Pf EdF   156 manserint] permanserint Bi Mk Pf
159 eum] deum Aa Pf

this happens, they are his sons in that predestination and have been given to Christ, his Son, so that they may not perish but may have eternal life.

"Finally, the Savior himself says, *If you remain in my word, you will* Jn 8:31 *truly be my disciples.* Those concerning whom the gospel speaks in the following text are not to be reckoned in these, are they?— when the Lord, when he had commended the eating of his flesh and the drinking of his blood, said in the gospel, *He said these things in the synagogue, teaching in Capernaum. Therefore, many among his disciples who were listening said, 'This word is hard; who is able to listen to it?' But Jesus, knowing in himself that his disciples were muttering about this, said to them, 'Does this cause you to stumble? If, then, you see the Son of Man ascending, where was he before? The Spirit is the one who vivifies, but the flesh profits nothing. The words which I have spoken to you are the Spirit and life. But there are certain ones of you who do not believe.' For Jesus knew from the beginning who were believing and who would betray him, and he said, 'Moreover I have said to you that no one comes to me except he be given to him by my Father.' As a result of this, many of his disciples withdrew and were not walking with him anymore.* By the word of Jn 6:59–66 the gospel, were not even these called disciples? And nevertheless, they were not truly disciples, because they did not remain in his Word, according to that which he says, *If you remain in my word, you will truly be my disciples.* Therefore, because they did not have perseverance, just as they were not truly disciples of Christ, so also they were not truly sons of God, even when they seemed to be and were called such. Therefore we call ourselves both the elect and disciples of Christ, and sons of God, because they should be called such whom we discern to be regenerate and to live piously. But they are truly then what they are called if they remain in that on account of[9] which they are thus called. But if they do not have perseverance, that is, they do not remain in that which they began to be, they are not truly called and are not truly that on account of which they are called. For in his opinion, they are not now that to which it has been noted that they are going to be, that is, evil people from good."

---

9. Gratian seems originally to have left out this crucial preposition, translated "on account of" (*propter*). Aa and Fd omit it, although a corrector later added it above the line in Fd. Because the original rendering does not make sense, I have translated the second-recension version.

Finis huius auctoritatis eorum sententie concordat, qui peccata   d.p.c.8
dicunt remitti secundum iustitiam, non secundum prescientiam.
Alii uero, quamuis fateantur peccata redire, tamen seu per baptisma seu per penitentiam asserunt omnino peccata remitti, et plena
165 fide accedentem ad lauacrum renasci non aqua tantum, set etiam
Spiritu sancto, et, si postea peccaturus sit, deinde penitentem, etsi
aliquando recasurus sit, tamen tempore sue penitentie ita perfecte
expiatum affirmant, ut, si tunc moreretur, salutem inueniret eternam. Quorum sententie eiusdem auctoritatis principium consentit.
170 Cum enim questionem proponat, quare prescitos ad mortem cum
fideliter et pie uiuerent non tunc de uite huius periculis Deus rapuit, ne malitia mutaret intellectum eorum et ne fictio deciperet
Mk 252ʳᵇ animas eorum, cum de | inmatura morte predestinati SCRIPTURA
DICAT: *Raptus est ne malitia mutaret intellectum eius et ne fictio deciperet*
175 *animam illius,* euidenter ostendit illos tales fuisse, qui, si fatali necessitate huius uite subducti essent periculis, profecto uitam consecuti essent eternam.

Vt ergo finis principio conueniat, et ne sibi ipsi contraire uidea-
Sb 278ʳᵇ tur, diffiniendum est quid sit scribi in libro | uite uel de eodem de-
180 leri secundum iustitiam, quid secundum prescientiam. Secundum
prescientiam scribi est ad uitam preordinari quod ab eterno factum
est. VNDE APOSTOLUS IN EPISTOLA AD EPHESIOS: *Benedictus Deus et*   c.9
pater Domini nostri Iesu Christi, qui benedixit nos in omni benedictione spi-
rituali in celestibus in Christo Iesu, sicut elegit nos in ipso ante mundi con-
185 *stitutionem mundi, ut essemus sancti et inmaculati in conspectu eius in cari-*
tate; qui predestinauit nos in adoptionem filiorum per Iesum Christum.

Aa 176ʳ   Similiter secundum prescientiam | deleri est ad mortem, non ad   d.p.c.9
Bi 311ᵛᵇ uitam presciri, quod | et ipsum ab eterno factum est. VNDE DOMI-
NUS IN EUANGELIO: *Qui credit in me habet uitam eternam; qui autem*

---

162 iustitiam] *add.* et R2 (*om.* Sb)

164 omnino] omnia Aa   **170** questionem] *add.* eius Aa Bi Mk (*interlin.* Aa)
174 dicat] dicit Pf EdF   **175** illius] eius Aa Pf   **176** consecuti] consecuturi Fd
178 et] *om.* Aa Bi

d.p.c.8   The end of this authority agrees with the opinion of those who say that sins are remitted according to righteousness,[10] not according to prescience. But others, although they confess that sins return, nevertheless assert that sins are entirely remitted either through baptism or through penance, and the person approaching the wash basin with full faith is reborn not only by water but also by the Holy Spirit, and, if he is going to sin afterward, they affirm that, even if he is going to fall again at some point, then he, as a penitent, has nevertheless been expiated completely at the time of his penance in such a way that, if he were to die at that moment, he would find eternal salvation. The beginning of this same authority consents to their opinion. For when Augustine proposes the question why God did not seize those foreknown for death from the perils of this life at the time when they were living faithfully and piously, so that malice might not change their understanding and so that a fiction might not deceive their souls, when SCRIPTURE SPEAKS of the premature death of the predestined: *He was seized so that malice might not change his understanding and so that a fiction might not deceive his soul*, it clearly shows that such were those   Wisdom 4:11
who, if they had been removed from perils by the fatal necessity of this life, surely they would have attained eternal life.

Therefore, so that the end of this authority may correspond to the beginning, and lest it seem to contradict itself, we should define what it is to be written in the Book of Life or to be erased from it according to righteousness, and what it is to be written or erased according to prescience. To be written according to prescience is to be foreordained to life, which was done from eternity. AND THUS
c.9   THE APOSTLE IN HIS EPISTLE TO THE EPHESIANS: *Blessed be the God and Father of our Lord Jesus Christ, who has blessed us in every spiritual blessing in the heavenly places in Christ Jesus, just as he chose us in him before the foundation of the world so that we might be holy and pure in his sight in love, who has predestined us in the adoption of sons through Jesus*   Eph 1:3–5
Christ.

d.p.c.9   Similarly, to be erased according to prescience is to be foreknown to death not to life, which very thing has also been done from eternity. AND THUS THE LORD IN THE GOSPEL: *He who believes in me has eternal life, but he who does not believe has already been judged.*   Jn 3:18

---

10. The second recension added a conjoining "and."

190   *non credit iam iudicatus est.* HINC ETIAM AUGUSTINUS AIT, *"Nouit Do-*   c.10
      minus qui sunt eius. Ex his nemo seducitur. Nondum apparuit iudi-
      cium, set iam factum est."

      Porro secundum iustitiam scribi est Deo auctore ea operari quo-   d.p.c.10
Pf 122ᵛᵃ rum merito sit dignus eterna salute. Hunc duplicem modo | scri-
195   bendi IN EUANGELIO DEUS ASSIGNAUIT, dicens discipulis, *In domo*
      patris mei mansiones multe sunt; si quo minus, dixissem uobis, quia uado
      parare uobis locum; et si abiero et preparauero uobis locum, iterum uenio,
      et accipiam uos ad me ipsum, ut ubi sum ego et uos sitis. Dicens, *In domo*
      patris mei mansiones multe sunt; si quo minus, dixissem uobis, quia uado
200   *parare uobis locum,* ostendit eos quibus loquebatur scriptos in libro
      uite predestinatione. Subiciens, *si abiero, et preparauero uobis locum,*
      etc., ostendit illos adhuc esse scribendos operatione.

      HINC ETIAM AUGUSTINUS IN EIUSDEM LOCI EXPLANATIONE
      AIT: "*In domo patris mei mansiones multe sunt.* Domus Dei, templum   c.11
205   Dei, regnum celorum sunt homines iusti in quibus sunt multe diffe-
      rentie, et hee sunt mansiones ipsius domus. Hee autem iam parate
      sunt in predestinatione, sicut ait apostolus, *Qui elegit nos ante consti-*
      tutionem mundi, predestinando. Parando autem in operatione. Vnde:
      Quos predestinauit, hos et uocauit, secundum hoc dicitur: *Fecit Deus que*
210   *futura sunt,* id est que facturus erat." Et infra: "*Si quo minus* confir-
      mat esse, quia, si non essent, dixisset, 'Ibo et parabo,' id est, 'Prede-
      stinabo.' Set quia ibi sunt, non est opus aliqua parare. Quia uero
      nondum sunt in operatione, addit, *Et si abiero et preparauero.* Abiens,
      set non relinquens, parat, quia subtrahit se et latet ut sit fides, que
215   non est de uisa re, et inde est meritum fidei. Ex hac uiuit iustus, et
      mundatur ei cor, dum peregrinatur, et in ea desideratur quod non-
      dum habetur. Et hec est preparatio mansionis quia sic parat nos sibi

---

190 Nouit...**191** seducitur] Aug. Hipp., *In Ioh. evang. tract.* 12.12 (CCSL
36:127.10–12)   **191** Nondum...**192** est] cf. *Gl. ord. in* 2 Tim 2:19 (ed. Rusch,
4.415a)   **204** In...**220** mansionum] cf. Aug. Hipp., *In Ioh. evang. tract.* 68.1–2
(CCSL 36:497.10–498.30, 498.2–10); *Gl. ord. in* Ioh. 14:2–3 (ed. Rusch, 4.257b)

194 modo] modum R2 (Aa; modo Mkₐ꜀ Sb)   **217** Et] *om.* R2 (*adest* Sb)

195 discipulis] *add.* suis Aa Pf   **208** Parando] parande Aa Bi | autem] *add.* sunt
interlin. Bi   **211** quia] qua Mk Sb   **213** sunt] *pos.* operatione Aa *om.* Sb   **216** ei
cor] cor eius Aa

c.10 ON THIS POINT, AUGUSTINE ALSO SAYS: "*The Lord knows who are his.* From these words, no one is led astray. The judgment has not 2 Tm 2:19
yet appeared, but it has already been done."

d.p.c.10 Indeed, to be written according to righteousness is, with God as the author, to perform the things on account of which a person is worthy of eternal salvation. GOD HAS MARKED OUT IN THE GOSPEL this double reality in the mode[11] of writing, saying to his disciples, *In the house of my Father are many mansions; if it were not so, I would have told you, for I am going to prepare a place for you; and if I leave and prepare a place for you, I am coming again, and I will welcome you to myself, so that, where I am, you may also be.* Saying, *In the house of my Fa- Jn 14:2–3
ther are many mansions; if it were not so, I would have told you, for I am going to prepare a place for you,* he shows that those to whom he was speaking were written in the Book of Life by predestination. Adding, *If I leave and prepare a place for you,* etc., he shows that these still had to be written in the Book of Life by their works.

ON THIS POINT, AUGUSTINE ALSO SAYS IN THE EXPLANATION
c.11 OF THIS SAME TEXT: "*In the house of my Father are many mansions.* Jn 14:2
The house of God, the temple of God, the kingdom of heaven are righteous men in whom are many differences, and these are mansions of the same house. But these have already been prepared in predestination, just as the apostle says, *who chose us before the foundation of the world* by predestining us. But he chose them by preparing Eph 1:4
them in works. And thus: *Those whom he predestined he also called*; ac- Rom 8:30
cording to this it is said, *God did what things are going to be,* that is, Eccl 3:15
what things he was going to do." And below: "*If it were not so* confirms the mansions' existence, because, if they did not exist, he would have said, 'I *will* go and I *will* prepare,' that is, 'I *will* predestine.' But because they are already there, it is no work to prepare some things. But because they do not yet exist in works, he adds, *And if I leave and prepare.* Leaving, but not abandoning, he prepares, Jn 14:3
because he withdraws and remains hidden so that faith, which is not of visible things, may exist, and then there is the merit of faith. The righteous person lives from this faith, and his heart is cleansed for him while he is a pilgrim, and in this faith, what is not yet had

---

11. The second recension appears to have changed the case of "mode" so that the adjective "double" modified it. Gratian seems initially (the version in Fd and Sb) to have used "double" substantively, and I have added the noun "reality" to give the sense of the original. The second recension would be translated, "God has marked out in the Gospel this double mode of writing."

Sb 278ᵛᵃ   et se nobis, ut maneat in | nobis et nos in eo, quantum quisque erit
Aa 176ᵛ   particeps eius plus uel minus pro | diuersitate meritorum. Et hec est
220   multitudo mansionum."

Mk 252ᵛᵃ | Fd | Secundum | iustitiam deletur qui gratia subtracta ea operari   d.p.c.11
97ᵛᵇ   permittitur quibus eternam dampnationem meretur. HINC PRO-
PHETA LOQUENS EX PERSONA CHRISTI AIT: *Deleantur de libro uiuen-*
tium, hoc est, subtrahatur eis gratia, qua subtracta hi in profundum
225   uitiorum, deinde in eternam dampnationem precipitentur, *et cum*
iustis non scribantur, id est, non apponatur eis gratia, qua fiant digni
eterna salute.

Pf 122ᵛᵇ   Sic itaque peccata secundum prescientiam remittuntur | cum ab
eterno gratia preparatur, qua uocatus iustificetur, iustificatus tan-
230   dem eternaliter glorificetur. Secundum iustitiam uero peccata re-
Bi 312ʳᵃ   mittuntur cum uel | baptisma plena fide accipitur uel penitentia
toto corde celebratur, que remissio et ipsa secundum prescientiam
non inconuenienter fieri dicitur.

Vt enim ex premissa auctoritate Apostoli datur intelligi, due
235   sunt preordinationes: una qua quisque preordinatur hic ad iustitiam et remissionem peccatorum percipiendam; altera qua aliquis
predestinatur ad uitam eternam in futuro obtinendam. Harum effectus sunt presens iustificatio et futura glorificatio, que omnia in
premissa auctoritate conuenienter distinguuntur. Prima enim pre-
240   destinatio, qua preordinantur ad presentem iustitiam, designatur
dum dicitur, *Sicut elegit nos in ipso ante mundi constitutionem,* etc.,
cuius effectus infra supponitur: *in qua gratificauit nos in dilecto filio*
suo, etc. Secunda preordinatio ibi ostenditur: *qui predestinauit nos in*

---

234 Vt...245 etc] cf. Ans. Laud., *Sententia* 11 (ed. Lottin, 22) et *Gl. ord. in Eph.*
1:3–6 (*interlin. et marg.,* ed. Rusch, 4.369)

221 qui] quia R2 (Fd_pc)   224 profundum] profundo R2 (profundum EdF)

224 hi] hic Aa Bi Mk   243 preordinatio] predestinatio Aa ordinatio Bi Mk_ac

is desired. And[12] this is a preparation of a mansion because God prepares us for himself and himself for us in such a way that he remains in us and us in him, as much as each person will more or less participate in him as a result of the variety of merits. And this is the multitude of mansions."

d.p.c.11   He is erased from the Book of Life according to righteousness who,[13] when grace has been removed, is allowed to work those things by which he deserves eternal damnation. SPEAKING IN THE PERSONA OF CHRIST, THE PROPHET THUS SAYS, *May they be erased from the book of the living,* that is, may grace be removed from them, Ps 68:29 for, when it is removed, these may be hurled down into the depth[14] of vices and then into eternal damnation, *and may they not be written down with the righteous,* that is, let grace, by which they may be made worthy of salvation, not be placed on them.

Therefore, in this way sins are remitted according to prescience, when grace is prepared from eternity, by which the person, having been called, may be justified, and, having been justified, may in the end be eternally glorified. But sins are remitted according to righteousness when either baptism is received with full faith or penance is celebrated with the whole heart, but this very remission also is not unsuitably said to occur according to prescience.

For, as is given to be understood from the preceding authority of the apostle, there are two fore-ordinations: one by which each person is foreordained here for receiving righteousness and the remission of sins; the second by which someone is predestined for obtaining eternal life in the future. The effects of these are present justification and future glorification, all of which are suitably distinguished in the preceding authority. For the first predestination, by which people are foreordained for present righteousness, is designated when it is said, *Just as he chose us in him before the foundation of the world,* etc., the effect of which is added below: *according to which* Eph 1:4 *he gave us a present in his beloved Son,* etc. The second fore-ordination Eph 1:6 is shown here: *who predestined us in the adoption of sons,* etc. The ef- Eph 1:5

12. The second recension omitted this "And."
13. The second recension changed the "who" (*qui*) to a "because" (*quia*). The sentence would then have to be translated, "[A person] is erased from the Book of Life according to righteousness, because, when grace has been removed, he is allowed to work those things by which he deserves eternal damnation."
14. Although Friedberg reads this way, all four manuscripts of the second recension collated at this point changed the case of "depth," thus rendering the phrase, "in the depth of vices."

adoptionem filiorum, etc. Eius effectus premittitur dum dicitur, *qui be-*
245 *nedixit nos in omni benedictione*, etc.

He due preordinationes et earum effectus ita se habent ut prima
et eius effectus natura precedant, lege consequendi inferantur. Si
enim est aliquis preordinatus ad uitam, consequenter infertur, ergo
est predestinatus ad iustitiam, et, si consequitur uitam eternam,
250 ergo est consecutus iustitiam; set non conuertitur. Vnde multi sunt
participes prime preordinationis et eius effectus, ad quos secunda
uel eius effectus minime pertinere probantur.

Iuxta hanc distinctionem intelligenda est auctoritas illa Iohannis:
Ex nobis exierunt; set non erant ex nobis. Nam si fuissent ex nobis, mansis-
255 *sent utique nobiscum. Ex nobis*, inquit, *exierunt*—id est, a nostra socie-
Aa 177ʳ tate recesserunt, qua prime preordinationis | et eius effectus nobi-
scum participes erant. *Set non erant ex nobis*—id est, secunde preordinationis et eius effectus societatem nobiscum non inierant. Quod
Pf 123ʳᵃ ex eo uideri potest, | quia, si fuissent ex nobis, id est, si illius preor-
260 dinationis nobiscum participes essent, mansissent utique nobiscum,
Sb 278ᵛᵇ id est, a societate effectus illius preordinationis, quam | nobiscum
contraxerant, non recessissent. Si enim ad secundam preordinatio-
nem utrumque referretur, non conuenienter illud inferretur, *man-*
sissent; immo cepissent utique esse nobiscum. Si uero ad primam,
265 falsa esset propositio, *si fuissent ex nobis*, etc. Multi enim presentis iustitie et sanctitatis participes fiunt qui tamen in ea non perseuerant.
Vɴᴅᴇ Dᴏᴍɪɴᴜs ɪɴ ᴇᴜᴀɴɢᴇʟɪᴏ ᴀɪᴛ: *Non qui ceperit, set qui perseuera-*
Mk 252ᵛᵇ *uerit usque in finem, hic | saluus erit.*

Hanc societatem si quis solo nomine et professione, non autem   (c.12)
270 rei ueritate a dampnandis dicat contrahi, eiusdem auctoritatis testi-
monio conuincitur. De his enim qui prime, non secunde, preordinationis sunt participes, ait, "Nec nos moueat, quod filiis suis quibusdam Deus non dat istam perseuerantiam. Absit enim, ut ita sit,

---

248 infertur] inferatur Aa   **249** et…**250** iustitiam] *mg.* Bi *om.* Sb   **251** eius ef-
fectus] *om.* Aa   **253** distinctionem] auctoritatem Aa diffinitionem Sb   **261** il-
lius] eius Pf EdF   **262** recessissent] recesserunt Pf_ac excessissent Sb   **267** Non]
om. Sb

fect of this is put forward when it is said, *who blessed us in every blessing,* etc.   Eph 1:3

These two fore-ordinations and their effects are constituted in
such a way that the first and its effect come first by nature and are
occasioned by the law of the thing to be attained. For if someone is
foreordained for life, he is consequently brought forward and
therefore has been foreordained for righteousness, and, if he attains
eternal life, he therefore has attained righteousness; but the con-
verse is not true. Whence there are many participants of the first
fore-ordination and its effect, to whom the second and its effect are
proven not to belong.

That authority of John, *They departed from us but they were not of
us. For if they had been of us, they surely would have remained with us,*   1 Jn 2:19
should be understood according to this distinction. He says, *They departed from us*—that is, they withdrew from our fellowship, by
which they were participants of the first fore-ordination and its effects with us. *But they were not of us*—that is, they had not entered
into the fellowship of the second fore-ordination and its effect with
us. This is able to be seen from this, because, if they had been of us,
that is, if they were participants in that fore-ordination with us,
they surely would have remained with us, that is, they would not
have withdrawn from the fellowship of the effect of that fore-ordination, which they had contracted with us. For if both texts were
to be related to the second fore-ordination, that statement, *they
would have remained,* would not be suitably introduced; no, they
surely had begun being with us. But if both texts were to be related
to the first fore-ordination, the proposition, *if they had been of us,* etc.
would be false. For many become participants in present righteousness and holiness who nevertheless do not persevere in them. AND
SO THE LORD SAYS IN THE GOSPEL, *Not he who begins, but he who
perseveres all the way to the end will be saved.*   Mt 10:22

(c.12)   If someone should say that this fellowship is contracted by the
damned in name and profession only, but not with the truth of the
thing, he is refuted by the testimony of this same authority. For
concerning those who are participants of the first and not the second fore-ordination, Augustine says, "And let it not disturb us that   cf. D.4 c.8
God does not give that perseverance to certain of his sons. For far

si de predestinatis essent," et cetera, que in eadem auctoritate supra
Bi 312rb continentur. Oues, | namque de quibus Dominus IN EUANGELIO
AIT, *Et alias oues habeo que non sunt ex hoc ouili*, et filii, de quibus IO-
HANNES AIT, *ut filios Dei qui erant dispersi congregaret in unum*, ita prescientia erant oues et filii ut qualitate presentie, non specie tantum,
set etiam ante Dei oculos, essent filii ire et perditionis eterne. Vnde
280 APOSTOLUS non ait, "Videbamur esse," set, *eramus*, INQUIT, *et nos
natura filii ire*. Nec ait: "Reputabamini ab hominibus," set, *Fuistis aliquando tenebre, nunc autem lux in Domino*. De se quoque SCRIBENS
AD TIMOTHEUM non ait, *Videbar*, set, *Fui persecutor, blasphemus, et
contumeliosus, nunc autem sum misericordiam consecutus*. Omnes quo-
285 que qui in Christo renascuntur et qui ex eius sanguine a diabolo re-
Fd 98ra dimuntur prius | ex Adam peccatores nascuntur et diabolice serui-
tuti obnoxii. Sicut ergo isti, quamuis sint filii futuri Dei, tamen
prius sunt filii diaboli, sic hi, de quibus sermo habetur, quamuis re-
Pf 123rb cedendo a iustitia sint filii futuri perditionis eterne, | tamen cum pie
290 et fideliter uiuunt, uere sunt filii Dei et iusti et eterna beatitudine
digni. Vnde auctoritas non ait, "Cum uiderentur pie et fideliter uiuere," set, "Cum pie et fideliter uiuerent." Nec ueraciter a bono in
malum conmutarentur qui numquam ueraciter boni fuerunt. DO-
MINUS quoque non ait PER EZECHIELEM, *Si auerterit se iustus a iusti-
295 tia*, "quam uidebatur habere," set, *sua*, quam scilicet ueraciter habet.

Aa 177^v   Quod autem | in eadem auctoritate sequitur: "Non erant in nu-
mero filiorum quando erant in professione filiorum," ita intelligen-
Sb 279ra dum est: filii Dei duobus modis appellantur. | Dicuntur filii Dei par-
300 ticipatione hereditatis eterne, sicut IOHANNES AIT IN EUANGELIO,
Quotquot crediderunt in eum, dedit eis potestatem filios Dei fieri. ET APO-
STOLUS IN EPISTOLA AD ROMANOS: *Expectatio creature reuelationem*

---

285 ex] *om.* R2 (*adest interlin.* Bi)   **287** filii futuri] *tr.* R2 (Aa; *non tr.* Sb)

274 de] *om.* Bi Mk   **277** congregaret] congregarent Bi_{ac} Mk_{ac} Sb   **278** presentie]
prescientie Aa Bi presentium Mk Pf EdF | specie] spe Aa Bi   **280** esse] *interlin.
ant.* uidebamur Bi *om.* Mk   **283** persecutor] *add.* et Aa_{pc} Fd Pf EdF   **289** futuri]
om. Aa Bi Mk, *pos.* iustitia Pf   **291** digni] digni sunt *mg.* Bi *interlin.* Mk
292 Nec] Ne Fd Bi Mk EdF

be it that this be the case if they were to be from among those who have been predestined," etc., which words are contained in the same authority above. For the sheep, of which the LORD SAYS IN THE GOSPEL, *And I have other sheep who are not of this fold,* and the sons, of which JOHN SAYS, *so that he might gather into one the sons of God who had been scattered,* were sheep and sons by prescience in such a way that they were sons of wrath and of eternal perdition by the quality of the present life, not just in appearance, but also in the eyes of God. And so the APOSTLE does not say, "We seemed to be," but he SAYS, *We also were sons of wrath by nature.* He does not say, "You were thought by men to be," but, *You were formerly darkness, but now you are light in the Lord.* Also, WRITING ABOUT HIMSELF TO TIMOTHY, he does not say, "I seemed to be," but, *I was a persecutor, blasphemer, and insolent, but now I have attained mercy.* Also, all who are reborn in Christ and who are redeemed from the devil by his blood, first were born sinners from Adam and beholden to the devil's servitude. Therefore, just as those, although they will be sons of God, are nevertheless first sons of the devil, so also these, concerning whom this discourse is being held, although by withdrawing from righteousness they are future sons of eternal perdition, nevertheless, when they live piously and faithfully, they truly are sons of God and righteous and worthy of eternal beatitude. And so the authority does not say, "When they seemed to live piously and faithfully," but, "When they lived piously and faithfully." And those who were never truly good could not truly be changed from good to evil. Also, THE LORD does not say THROUGH EZEKIEL, *If a righteous man turns away from* "the righteousness which he seemed to have," but *his righteousness,* which surely he truly has.

But that which follows in the same authority: "They were not in the number of the sons when they were in the profession of the sons," ought to be understood thus: they are called sons of God in two ways. They are said to be sons of God by participation in the eternal inheritance, as JOHN SAYS IN HIS GOSPEL, *However many have believed in him, he gave to them the power to become sons of God.* AND THE APOSTLE IN THE EPISTLE TO THE ROMANS: *The anxious waiting of the creature awaits the revelation of the sons of God.* And be-

Jn 10:16

Jn 11:52

Eph 2:3

Eph 5:8

1 Tm 1:13

cf. D.4 c.8

Ezek 18:24

cf. D.4 c.8

Jn 1:12

Rom 8:19

filiorum Dei expectat. Et infra: *Ipsa creatura liberabitur a seruitute corrup-*
tionis in libertatem glorie filiorum Dei. Et infra: *Ipsi intra nos gemimus,*
305 *adoptionem filiorum Dei expectantes.* HINC ETIAM AUGUSTINUS, eadem
uerba Apostoli exponens, ait, "Modo tantum creatura, cum nondum filiorum forma perfecta." Hoc ergo modo non sunt filii, nisi
participes beatitudinis eterne.

In presenti etiam dicuntur filii tribus modis: uel predestinatione
310 tantum (sicut hi de quibus IOHANNES AIT, *ut filios Dei, qui erant di-*
spersi, etc.), uel predestinatione et spe eterne beatitudinis (sicut illi
quibus DOMINUS AIT, *Filioli, adhuc modicum uobiscum sum*), uel me-
Mk 253ʳᵃ rito fidei et presentis iustitie, non autem predestinatione | claritatis
eterne (sicut hi de quibus DOMINUS AIT, *Si dereliquerint filii eius le-*
315 *gem meam et in iudiciis meis non ambulauerint,* etc.). Hi ergo, de quibus
in presenti agitur, filii sunt merito fidei et presentis iustitie, non autem sunt filii adoptionis eterne. Qui ergo peccata dimissa redire fa-
Pf 123ᵛᵃ tentur, secundum iustitiam, et non secundum | prescientiam ea di-
mitti—necesse est ut confiteantur, sicut saluandis peccata secun-
Bi 312ᵛᵃ dum iustitiam ad eternam | dampnationem inputantur, non secun-
dum prescientiam, quia et illis a bono in malum deficientibus singula replicabuntur ad supplicium, et his usque in finem in bono
perseuerantibus nulla inputabuntur ad penam.

<Expositio sententiae secundae>

325   Qui autem dicunt quod peccata dimissa non redeant auctoritate   d.a.c.13
Gregorii et Prosperi sententiam suam affirmare conantur. AIT ENIM
GREGORIUS IN MORALIBUS, LIBRO XXV: "Quid est quod dicitur: c.13
Qui reddis iniquitatem filiis ac nepotibus? Peccatum scilicet originale a
patribus trahimus, et, nisi per gratiam baptismi saluamur, etiam pa-
330 rentum culpam portamus, quia unum cum illis sumus. Reddet iniquitatem patrum in filiis, dum pro culpa parentis ex originali pec-

---

306 Modo…**307** perfecta] Aug. Hipp., *83 quaest.* 67 (CCSL 44A:167.69–70)
327 Quid…**335** habemus] Greg. Magn., *Moralia in Iob* 15.51 (CCSL
143A:785.12–20)

318 et non] non etiam R2 (Aa; et non Pf)   **327** XXV] *recte* XV

329 patribus] parentibus Aa | saluamur] soluamur Aa Bi Mk Pf

low: *The creature itself will be freed from the slavery of corruption in the liberty of the glory of the sons of God.* And below: *We ourselves groan within ourselves, waiting for the adoption of the sons of God.* ON THIS POINT, AUGUSTINE ALSO SAYS in explaining these same words of the apostle, "Now only a creature, although not yet the perfected form of sons." Therefore in this way they are not sons unless they are participants in eternal beatitude. Rom 8:21
Rom 8:23

In the present life, people are also said to be sons in three ways: either by predestination only (like those of whom JOHN SAYS, *so that he might gather the sons of God,* etc.), or by predestination and hope of eternal beatitude (like those to whom THE LORD SAYS, *My little children, I am still with you for a little while*) or by virtue of faith and present righteousness, but not by the predestination of eternal splendor (like those of whom THE LORD SAYS, *If his sons forsake my law and do not walk in my judgments,* etc.). Therefore, these concerning whom it is a matter of the present life are sons by virtue of their faith and present righteousness, but they are not sons of eternal adoption. Therefore, those who profess that sins which have been forgiven return, that these sins are forgiven according to righteousness and not according to prescience—it is necessary that they confess, just as sins are imputed for eternal damnation according to righteousness, not according to prescience, for those to be saved, both that for those deserting the good for evil, every single sin will be turned back for punishment, and that for these persevering all the way to the end in the good, no sin will be imputed for penalty. Jn 11:52

Jn 13:33

Ps 88:31

\<Explanation of the Second Position\>

d.a.c.13   But those who say that forgiven sins do not return attempt to bolster their opinion with the authority of Gregory and Prosper.

c.13   FOR GREGORY SAYS IN THE *MORALIA*, BOOK 15:[15] "What is it that is said: *You who return iniquity to sons and grandsons*? We indeed draw original sin from our fathers, and, if we are not saved through the grace of baptism, we also carry the guilt of our parents, because we are one with them. He will return the iniquity of the fathers on the Ex 34:7

---

15. The manuscripts all cite book 25 of Gregory's *Moralia*, but the text in fact comes from book 15.

cato anima polluitur prolis. Et rursus non reddit iniquitatem patrum in filiis, quia, cum ab originali culpa per baptismum libera-
mur, non iam parentum culpas set quas ipsi conmittimus habe-
mus." ITEM IN RESPONSIONIBUS PROSPERI: "Qui recedit | a Christo   c.14
et alienus a gratia finit hanc uitam, | quid nisi in perditionem uadit?
Set non in id, quod remissum est, recidit nec in originali peccato
dampnabitur, qui tamen ea morte afficitur, que ei propter dimissa,
debebatur."

Aa 178ʳ

Sb 279ʳᵇ

340   Finis huius auctoritatis principio contraire uidetur. Neque enim   d.p.c.14
aliud est peccata dimissa redire uel in originali peccato dampnari
quam penam peccato debitam post eiusdem remissionem excipere.
Auctoritates uero sibi contrarias assertores huius sententie ita de-
terminant: peccata dimissa redire dicuntur, quia quisquis post ac-
345   ceptam remissionem ad uomitum redierit—tanto grauius punietur,
quanto magis benignitate Dei abusus singulorum remissionis accepte ingratus extitit.

\<Responsio Gratiani pro sententia prima\>

Verum illa sententia fauorabilior uidetur, quia pluribus robora-
350   tur auctoritatibus et euidentiori ratione firmatur.

VT ENIM DOMINUS AIT PER EZECHIELEM: *Si auerterit | se iustus a*   c.15
iustitia sua et fecerit iniquitatem secundum omnes abominationes | quas
operari solet inpius, numquid uiuet? Omnes iustitie eius quas fecerat non
recordabuntur; in peccato suo morietur, et non erunt in memoria iustitie
355   *eius, quas fecit.* ITEM GREGORIUS IN EIUSDEM LOCI EXPLANATIONE:
"Hoc nobis maxime considerandum est, quia, cum mala conmitti-   c.16
mus, sine causa bona nostra transacta reuocamus, quoniam in per-
petratione malorum nulla debet esse fiducia bonorum preteritorum." Idem: "De pertuso quippe sacculo aliunde exit quod aliunde   c.17

Pf 123ᵛᵇ

Fd 98ʳᵇ

---

335 Qui…**339** debebatur] Prosp. Aquit., *Pro Aug. respons.* 1 (PL 45:1834)
356 Hoc…**359** preteritorum] Greg. Magn., *Hom. in Hiezech. proph.* 1.11 (CCSL
142:178.370–373)   **359** De…**361** perdatur] Ibid. 1.4 (CCSL 142:55.271–274)

332 reddit] reddet Aa   **333** filiis] filios Aa   **345** remissionem] *add.* peccatorum
Bi Pf   **346** remissionis] remissioni Aa Bi Mk   **359** Idem] Item Aa | sacculo]
sacco Aa sacculi Sb

sons when the soul of the progeny is polluted from original sin for the guilt of the parent. And, again, he does not return the iniquity of the fathers on the sons, because, when we are liberated from original guilt through baptism, we do not now have the guilty acts of our parents but those which we ourselves commit." LIKEWISE,

c.14   IN THE RESPONSES OF PROSPER: "He who departs from Christ and ends this life a stranger to grace, where does he go but into perdition? But he who nevertheless is afflicted with that death which was owed him on account of the sins which were forgiven does not fall back into that which was remitted, and he will not be damned for original sin."

d.p.c.14   The end of this authority seems contrary to the beginning. For forgiven sins returning or being damned for original sin is not different from receiving a penalty owed for a sin after its remission. But the proponents of this opinion settle the inwardly contrary authorities in this way: forgiven sins are said to return because, whoever returns to his vomit after remission has been received—the more he has abused the kindness of God and the more he shows himself to be ungrateful for the remission received for each individual sin, the more severely will he be punished.

<Gratian's Response in Favor of the First Position>

But the former opinion seems more viable, because it is strengthened by more authorities and is firmed up with clearer reasoning.

c.15   FOR AS THE LORD SAYS THROUGH EZEKIEL: *If a righteous man turns away from his righteousness and does iniquity according to all the abominations which the wicked are accustomed to do, he will not live, will he? All his righteous deeds which he had done will not be remembered; he will die in his sin, and his righteous deeds which he did will not be in memory.* LIKEWISE GREGORY IN HIS EXPLANATION OF THE SAME TEXT: Ezek 18:24, 3:20

c.16   "We should consider this to the fullest, that, when we commit evil deeds, we revoke without cause the good deeds which we had carried out, since no assurance of past goods is obligated to exist when

c.17   evils are perpetrated." The same: "What is put into a small, holey

Mk 253rb mittitur, | quia indiscrete mentes mercedem, que ex bono opere ac-
quiritur, non aspiciunt, quomodo ex malo opere perdatur."

Bi 312vb ITEM PETRUS IN | EPISTOLA SECUNDA: *Si refugientes coinquinationes*   c.18
mundi in cognitione Domini nostri et saluatoris Iesu Christi, his rursus in-
plicati superantur, facta sunt eis posteriora deteriora prioribus. Melius enim
365 *erat illis non cognoscere uiam iustitie, quam post cognitionem retrorsum*
conuerti ab eo quod illis traditum est sancto mandato.

PAULUS QUOQUE SCRIBENS AD EBREOS AIT, *Intermittentes sermo-*   c.19
nem inchoationis Christi feramur ad eius perfectionem, non rursus iacientes
fundamentum penitentie ab operibus mortuis. Dicens *opera mortua,*   d.p.c.19
370 priora bona significat, que per sequens peccatum erant mortua,
quia hi peccando priora bona irrita fecerunt. Hec, sicut peccando
Aa 178^v fiunt irrita, ita per penitentiam reuiuiscunt, et ad meritum | eterne
beatitudinis singula prodesse incipiunt etiam illa, que peccatis inue-
niuntur admixta. VNDE AUGUSTINUS: "Pium est credere," etc., ET
375 IERONIMUS: "Non est iniustus Deus," etc. Apostolus etiam scribens
Sb 279va ad Ebreos, cum fidem et dilectionem et bona opera | eorum breuiter
conmemorasset, horum omnium mercedem, quam peccando ami-
serant, post penitentiam a Domino eos recepturos ostendit. Porro,
QUI PER PROPHETAM DIXIT: *Si auerterit se iustus a iustitia sua,* etc.,
380 IPSE PER EUNDEM PROPHETAM promisit dicens: *Si inpius egerit peni-*
Pf 124ra *tentiam ab omnibus peccatis | suis que operatus est, et custodierit uniuersa*
precepta mea, et fecerit iudicium et iustitiam, uita uiuet et non morietur.
Omnium iniquitatum eius quas operatus est non recordabor; in iustitia sua,
quam operatus est, uiuet.

385 Filiis quoque Israel per Assyrios captiuandis ueteris ydolatrie
peccatum PER OSEE DOMINUS inproperat, et peccatum quod
Moyse supplicante patribus fuerat dimissum hoc in filiis reuixisse
ostendit, dicens: *Ve eis quoniam recesserunt a me; uastabuntur quia pre-*   c.20
uaricati sunt in me. Ego tamen redemi eos, et ipsi locuti sunt contra me
390 *mendacia, et non clamauerunt ad me in corde suo, set ululabant in cubili-*
bus suis; super triticum et uinum ruminabant, et recesserunt a me. Et ego

---

360 mittitur] inmittitur Aa Pf EdF | opere] *om.* Fd Pf   367 scribens] *om.* Bi Mk
Sb   370 erant] erat Fd Pf Sb   381 suis] *om.* Bi Mk Sb   386 et] ut Fd Pf, *add.* per
Bi   387 hoc] nec Fd

sack in one place surely exits from it in another, for indiscreet minds do not look at the reward which is acquired from a good work and how it is lost from an evil work."

c.18   LIKEWISE PETER IN HIS SECOND EPISTLE: *If those who escape the defilements of the world in the knowledge of our Lord and Savior Jesus Christ are entangled again and overcome by them, the later things have become worse for them than the former. For it was better for them not to know the way of righteousness than to turn back away from that which was handed down to them by holy command after knowing it.*   2 Pt 2:20–21

c.19   PAUL, ALSO, WRITING TO THE HEBREWS, SAYS: *Leaving the inchoate teaching of Christ, let us be carried to its perfection, not laying again*
d.p.c.19   *a foundation of penance from dead works.* Saying *dead works,* he means   Heb 6:1
prior good works, which, through subsequent sin, had died, because in their sin these people made their prior good works null and void. These good works, just as they become void by sinning, so they become alive again through penance, and even those individual good works which are found to be mixed up with sins begin to be beneficial for the meriting of eternal beatitude. AND THUS AUGUSTINE: "To believe is pious, etc.," AND JEROME: "God is not   D.3 c.45
unjust," etc. Also, the apostle, writing to the Hebrews, after he had | D.3 c.46
briefly reminded them of their faith and love and good works, shows that they will receive from the Lord the reward of all these things, which they had lost by sinning, after penance. Surely HE WHO SAID THROUGH THE PROPHET, *If the righteous man turns away from his righteousness,* etc., himself makes a promise THROUGH THE   Ezek 18:24
SAME PROPHET, saying, *If a wicked man does penance from all the sins which he committed, and keeps all my precepts and exercises judgment and righteousness, he will live with life and will not die. I will not remember all his iniquities which he did; in his righteousness which he exercises will he   Ezek
live.*   18:21–22

Also, when the sons of Israel were to be taken into captivity by the Assyrians, THE LORD THROUGH HOSEA reproaches the sin of old idolatry, and he shows that this sin, which had been forgiven their fathers through Moses' supplication, became alive again in the
c.20   sons, saying: *Woe to them since they have departed from me; they will be laid waste, for they have sinned against me. I redeemed them, and they spoke lies against me, and they did not cry out to me in their heart but they kept howling in their beds; they were ruminating upon wheat and wine,*

erudiui eos, et confortaui brachia eorum, et in me cogitauerunt malitiam.
Reuersi sunt ut essent absque iugo; facti sunt quasi arcus dolosus; cadent in
gladio principes eorum a furore lingue sue. Antiqua peccata parentum   d.p.c.20
395 filiis inproperat sermo diuinus, et propterea principes eorum in gladio casuros predicit. Set PER EUNDEM PROPHETAM contra DOMI-
NUS se facere ostendit, dicens: *Ne forte dicant in cordibus suis omnem*   c.21
malitiam eorum me recordatum; nunc circumdederunt eos adinuentiones
Bi 313ʳᵃ *sue; coram | facie mea facte sunt.*

400   IERONIMUS: "Cum ita puniantur, ne cogitent quod pro ueteri-   c.22
bus peccatis patrum puniam eos, quia nunc, id est in presenti, pro
malitiis suis quas inuenerunt circumdati sunt pena, et mala eorum,
Mk 253ᵛᵃ sicut putant, non possunt me | latere; set potius ipse adinuentiones
aperte sunt coram facie mea, que omnia clare uidet." Idem: "Here-   c.23
405 tici non possunt uetera peccata contra Deum causari, cum antiquis
operibus nouam addant inpietatem, et suis ligentur peccatis, et,
Aa 179ʳ cum Deum se celare putant, oculos eius uitare non | possunt, quia
uultus Domini super facientes mala."

{ITEM GELASIUS: "Diuina clementia dimissa peccata in ultionem ulterius redire   c.24
410 non patitur."}

Pf 124ʳᵇ   Set his auctoritatibus docentur filii, ab originali peccato | expiati,   d.p.c.24
non ideo puniendi quia patres peccauerunt, set ideo peccata pa-
Sb 279ᵛᵇ trum in eos redire quia eorum | culpam sequuntur. Sic et bona que
peccato moriuntur non proficient ad premium quia facta sunt, set
Fd 98ᵛᵃ quia per penitentiam | reuiuiscunt. Tale est et illud Augustini in li-
bro Psalmorum, "Si Iudas teneret adoptionem," etc. Sic etiam illud
Gregorii in Moralibus intelligitur: "Quid est quod dicitur: *Reddis ini-*
quitatem patrum," etc. Illis namque parentum iniquitas redditur qui

---

400 Cum...**404** uidet] cf. Hier., *Comm. in proph. min.*, *In Osee* 2.7 (CCSL
76:71.40–53); *Gl. ord. in Hos.* 7:2 (*interlin.*, ed. Rusch, 3.362b)   **404** Heretici...
408 mala] cf. Hier., *Comm. in proph. min.*, *In Osee* 2.7 (CCSL 76:71.60–72.63); *Gl.*
ord. in Hos. 7:2 (*marg.*, ed. Rusch, 3.362b)   **409** Diuina...**410** patitur] Gelasius,
Epistola ad Gerontium, Johannem, Germanum, et Petrum episcopum (*Fragmentum* 44,
ed. Thiel, 706)

392 eos] *add.* et confortaui eos Pf | confortaui] *add.* eos Bi_ac   **396** Dominus...
397 se] *tr.* Aa Mk Pf EdF   **414** premium] meritum Aa   **416** Psalmorum] sermonum Fd Mk_pc

and they departed from me. I both instructed them and strengthened their
arms, and they plotted malice against me; they have turned round so that
they might be without a yoke; they have become like a deceitful bow; their

d.p.c.20   *princes will fall by the sword because of the raving of their tongue.* The di-   Hos 7:13–16
vine Word reproaches the sons for the ancient sins of their parents
and predicts that for this reason their princes will fall by the sword.
But THROUGH THE SAME PROPHET, THE LORD shows that [they] do

c.21   [these things] against themselves: *Let them not happen to say in their*
hearts that I remember all their evil; now their inventions surround them;
they have been done in my presence.   Hos 7:2

c.22   JEROME: "When they are punished in such a way, let them not
think that I am punishing them for the old sins of their fathers, because now, that is, in the present time, they are surrounded by the
penalty for their evil deeds which they devised, and their evils cannot lie hidden from me as they think; but rather, their inventions
themselves have been laid open before my face, which sees all

c.23   things clearly." The same: "Heretics cannot debate old sins against
God, since they add new wickedness to the old works, and they are
bound to their sins, and, although they think that they hide [them]
from God, they cannot avoid his eyes, for *the face of the Lord is upon*
those doing evil."   Ps 33:17

c.24   {LIKEWISE GELASIUS: "Divine clemency does not allow forgiven sins to return   C.23 q.4 c.29
further in vengeance."}

d.p.c.24   But by these authorities the sons, having been expiated from
original sin, are taught that they are not to be punished for the reason that their fathers sinned, but that the sins of their fathers do return to them for the reason that they follow their guilt. So also,
good works which die as the result of sin will be useful for a reward, not because they were done but because they become alive
again through penance. Such is also the meaning of that statement
of Augustine on the book of Psalms, "If Judas were to hold onto   D.4 c.1
adoption," etc. That statement of Gregory in the *Moralia* is also understood in this way: "What is it that is said: *You return the iniquity of*   D.4 c.13
the fathers," etc. For the iniquity of the parents is returned to those
who are punished for the reason that they have drawn along in

propterea puniuntur quia in radice traxerunt amaritudinem pec-
420 cati. Illis autem non reddi dicitur in quibus merito sue iniquitatis
reuiuiscunt peccata parentis.

Sicut ergo bona que peccato moriuntur per penitentiam reuiuiscunt ad premium, sic et mala que per penitentiam delentur reuiuiscunt ad supplicium. VNDE PROPHETA ex persona penitentis DE-
425 PLORAT, dicens, *Putruerunt et corrupte sunt cicatrices mee,* id est plage
per baptismum sanate. Hinc etiam IDEM PROPHETA, quamuis fide et
sacramento circumcisionis ab originali peccato se mundatum co-
gnosceret, tamen adulterio et homicidio quod conmiserat illud reuixisse intelligens, non sine causa inter cetera ipsum confitetur, et di-
430 cit, *Ecce enim in iniquitatibus conceptus sum,* etc.

---

420 iniquitatis] *add.* non Mk EdF

their root the bitterness of sin. But the iniquity of the parents is not said to return to those in whom the sins of the parent come alive again[16] by virtue of their own iniquity.

Therefore, just as good works that die as the result of sin come alive again through penance, so also evil works that are destroyed through penance come alive again for punishment. AND SO THE PROPHET WEEPS in the persona of a penitent, saying, *My wounds*— that is, afflictions healed through baptism—*have grown rotten and worsened*. On this account THE SAME PROPHET also, although he recognizes that he has been cleansed from original sin with faith and the sacrament of circumcision, nevertheless, understanding that the original sin had become alive again by the adultery and murder that he had committed, not without reason confesses the original sin itself among other things, and says, *For behold, I was conceived in iniquities*. Ps 37:6

Ps 51:5

16. Some manuscripts, but only Mk of those collated here, and Friedberg's edition read "do not come alive again." For a discussion of this variant and rather difficult passage, which I do not directly address in my *Master of Penance*, see Appendix B.

Distinctio quinta

In penitentia autem que peccatorem considerare oporteat, AU- d.a.c.1
GUSTINUS IN LIBRO DE PENITENTIA DOCET, dicens: "Consideret c.1
qualitatem criminis: in loco, in tempore, in perseuerantia, in uarie-
5 tate persone, et quali hoc fecerit temptatione, et in ipsius uitii multiplici executione. Oportet enim penitere fornicantem secundum
excellentiam sui status aut officii aut secundum modum meretricis
et in modo operis sui, et qualiter turpitudinem suam peregit—si in
loco sacrato, aut cui debuit excellentiam fidei (ut sunt domus domi-
10 norum et aliorum multorum), si in tempore orationi constituto (ut
festiuitates sanctorum et tempora ieiunii). Consideret quantum
Bi 313ʳᵇ perseuerauerit, | et defleat quod perseueranter peccauit, et quanta
fuerit uictus inpugnatione. Sunt qui non solum non uincuntur set
ultro se peccato offerunt, nec expectant temptationem set preue-
15 niunt uoluptatem. Et pertractet secum quam multiplici actione uitii
Aa 179ᵛ delectabiliter peccauit. Omnis ista uarietas confitenda est | et de-
Pf 124ᵛᵃ flenda, | ut, cum cognouerit quod peccatum est multum, cito inue-
niat Deum propitium.

"In cognoscendo augmentum peccati, inueniat se: cuius etatis
Mk 253ᵛᵇ fuerit, cuius sapientie, et ordinis, et statum | omnem alterius non
peccantis. Inmoretur in singulis istis, et sentiat modum criminis,
Sb 280ʳᵃ purgans lacrimis omnem qualitatem | uitii.

"Defleat uirtutem qua interim caruit. Dolendum enim est et dolore purgandum, non solum quia peccauit, set quod se uirtute pri-
25 uauit. Nam, licet speret se consecuturum ueniam, dolere tamen potest quia non promeruit unde remunerari confidat. Anxietur et doleat quod, modo effugiens de preteritis penam, miser non inde ex-

---

5,3 Consideret... 107 uitam] Ps.-Aug., De uera 14–15 (PL 40:1124–26; ed. Wagner, 682–798)

5,13 fuerit uictus] tr. R2   27 exspectat] exspectet R2 (Fd; expectat Biₐc Sb)

5,2 oporteat] oportet Pf EdF   13 fuerit] om. Fd   15 pertractet] pertracteret Pf,
add. ergo Aa   24 purgandum] add. est Bi Pf   25 se] om. Fd interlin. Bi

Distinction 5

d.a.c.1   But what things it would be proper for the sinner to think about in penance AUGUSTINE TEACHES IN HIS BOOK ON PENANCE, say-

c.1   ing, "Let him consider the nature of his wicked deed: in what place, at what time, with what perseverance, with what specific circumstances of his person, and with what kind of temptation he did this, and how many times he executed this very vice. For the fornicator ought to repent according to the eminence of his state or office, or according to the manner of the whore and in the manner of her work, and how he carried out his foul act—whether in a sanctified place, or in a place to which he owed the highest level of trustworthiness (as are the houses of one's lords and of many others), whether at a time established for prayer (such as feast days of the saints and times of fasting). Let him consider how much he persisted, and let him weep over what he persistently sinned, and let him consider with how great of an assault he was conquered. There are those who are not only conquered but, beyond this, offer themselves to sin, and they do not wait for temptation but anticipate the delight. And this sinner churns over in his mind how delightfully he sinned in the multiple doing of the vice. Every specific circumstance must be confessed and wept over so that, when the sinner recognizes that his sin is great, he may quickly find God to be propitious.

"In recognizing the growth of his sin, let him find himself: of what age he is, of what level of wisdom, and of what order, and let him find out every condition of the other person who is not sinning. Let him linger in each of these matters for consideration individually, and let him perceive the effects of the manner of his wicked deed, purging every quality of the vice with tears.

"Let him weep over the virtue which he has been missing in the meantime. For there should be a great grieving and a great purging with grief, not only because he sinned, but because he deprived himself of virtue. For, although he hopes that he will attain mercy, nevertheless, he is able to grieve because he has not earned a reason to be confident that he will be rewarded. Let him be distressed and grieve that, although escaping a penalty for past sins now, the

spectat gloriam, cuius omne tempus, quoniam tempus breuissimum est, debuit decertauisse ad consequendum premium.

30 "Defleat etiam quoniam offendens in uno factus est omnium reus. Ingratus enim extitit qui plenus uirtutibus Deum non omnino timuit. In hoc enim quisque peccator fit culpabilior, quo est Deo acceptior. Ideo enim Adam plus peccauit quia omni bono habundauit. Etiam alio modo offendens in uno reus est omnium, quia omnis 35 uirtus patitur detrimentum ab uno uitio. Nam si quis cadit in auaritiam, largitatem destruit et etiam castitatem minorauit. Amore enim pecunie uel uiolaret castitatem uel saltim minus amaret. Si enim tanta propter Deum adhuc castitas inest, ut nolit eandem perdere, tamen saltim minori gaudio, minori affectione tuetur eam, 40 ubi uidet inde procedere dampnum pecunie. Sicque et in aliis, que, etsi non expellantur, tamen perceptione unius uitii uel satis uel parum minuuntur, uel intentione deteriorantur. Vnde omnis uirtus cuicumque crimini est deflenda et de omnibus indulgentia est petenda.

45 "Animaduertere etiam oportet et animaduertendo deflere animam proximi, quam fornicator Deo eripuit uel ereptam in malo confirmauit; etiam quod exemplum extitit mali in operatione sui criminis; cui magis profuisset si aliis causa fuisset conuersionis. Gemat itaque aliorum uitam in sua corruptam, uel corruptam conser-
50 uatam, et commodum proximi quod dedisset exemplum boni. Do-
Fd 98vb leat de tristitia quam bonis peccando intulit et de letitia | quam eis
Pf 124vb non adhibuit. Et non | solum cogitet quid et qualiter fecerit set quam iniuste Deum, ut diximus, peccando offenderit. Timeat illam
Bi 313va ueritatis sententiam: *Non potestis duobus dominis seruire.* Timeat |
55 ergo, ne omnia bona que fecit, dum in uno peccato perseuerauerit, excommunicatione mali perdiderit, ut qui seruiuit diabolo per cri-

---

28 tempus²] *om.* R2 *orig.* (*adest* Pf; omnium tempus Bi)   **50** exemplum] exemplo R2 (Fd) | Doleat] *pos.* tristitia R2

34 reus] *pos.* omnium Fd EdF   **39** tuetur] tueatur Aa   **41** etsi] etiamsi Aa Pf EdF   **48** Gemat] emat Fd Bi Sb   **49** uel corruptam] uel corrupte Aa, uel incorruptam Bi EdF (*interlin.* Bi), uel in-[corruptam] non *interlin.* Mk$_{pc}$, non Pf **52** cogitet] coegit Sb, *add.* et Pf Sb

wretch may not for this reason expect glory, for he ought to have determined every moment of time, since time is very brief, for attaining the reward of glory.

"Also, let him weep, because in his one offense he has become guilty of all. For he who, although full of virtues, does not entirely fear God, has been ungrateful. For in that by which he is more acceptable to God does each sinner become more guilty. For Adam sinned more because he abounded with every good thing. Also in another way, when he offends in one thing, he is guilty of all, because every virtue suffers loss from one vice. For if someone falls into greed, he has destroyed generosity and has even lessened chastity. For by the love of money, he either would injure chastity or at least would love it less. For if so great a chastity still is in him on account of God that he does not want to lose it, he at least guards it with less joy and less affection, when he sees the damage of money proceed from there. And so also in other virtues, which, even if they are not driven out, nevertheless are lessened either substantially or a little bit by the taking on of a vice, or are deteriorated intentionally. For this reason, for whatever wicked deed, we should weep over every virtue and seek indulgence for all.

"The fornicator should also notice, and, in noticing, weep over the soul of his neighbor which he tore away from God or which, already torn away, he confirmed in its evil; he should also notice and weep over what example of evil existed in the working out of his wicked deed, and whom he would have greatly profited if he had been the cause of conversion for others. Therefore, let him bemoan the life of others corrupted in his life, or the life preserved in its corruption, and the favorable opportunity for the neighbor which he could have given with an example of good. Let him grieve about the sadness which he inflicted on the good by sinning and about the happiness which he failed to bring upon them. And let him not only think about what he did and in what manner he did it but how unjustly he offended God, as we have said, by sinning. Let him fear that statement of truth: *You cannot serve two masters*. Let him fear that, as long as he perseveres in one sin, through evil's excommunication[1] he has lost all the good things which he has done, Mt 6:24

---

1. The text is difficult to understand and translate at this point. The original text of *De uera et falsa penitentia* reads "through the contamination of evil." The family of *De uera* manuscripts (B and Vb), to which Gratian's manuscript belonged, read "excommunication" instead of "contamination."

Aa 180ʳ men | Deo quas obtulit amiserit uirtutes. Pium tamen est credere ut
recepta gratia Dei, que in eo destruit mala priora, etiam remuneret
Sb 280ʳᵇ bona, ut, cum destruxerit quod suum non inuenit, | amet et diligat
60 bonum quod etiam in peccante plantauit.

"In omnibus dolens aut seculum derelinquat aut saltim illa que
sine ammixtione mali non sunt amministrata, ut mercatura et mili-
tia et alia, que utentibus sunt nociua, ut amministrationes secula-
rium potestatum, nisi his utatur ex obedientie licentia. Ponat se
Mk 254ʳᵃ omnino in potestate iudicis, in | iudicio sacerdotis, nichil sibi reser-
uans sui, ut omnia eo iubente paratus sit facere pro recipienda uita
anime, quecumque faceret pro euitanda corporis morte, et hoc cum
desiderio, quia uitam recuperat infinitam, ut Deus. Cum gaudio
enim facere debet immortalis futurus que faceret pro differenda
70 morte moriturus. Semper deprecetur Deum, certus de uenia, qui
omnibus modis et sine tedio dubius rogaret potestatem terrenam.
Abstineat a multis licitis qui in libertate arbitrii conmisit illicita.
Semper offerat Deo mentem et cordis contritionem, deinde et quod
potest de possessione. Tunc quod offerat securus offerat. *Respexit*
75 *enim Dominus ad Abel et munera.* Set prius dicit ad Abel, quam ad
munera. Sumens enim mentem, quam cognouit humilem et pu-
ram, remunerauit eius largitatis munera. Ad Cayn uero non respexit neque ad eius munera. Mentem eius, quam uiderat, quoniam
non cognouit, eius munera non recepit. In iudicio itaque cordis
80 consideranda est elemosina tribuentis, nec iam considerandum est
quantum set qua mente, qua affectione dat quod potest. Vidua
enim duobus que habuerat minutis larga plus omnibus posuit. Qui
Pf 125ʳᵃ igitur peccata sua redimere uult temporalium oblatione caueat ut |
prius offerat mentem.

---

75 munera] *add.* eius R2 (Aa Fd_pc)   83 ut] *om.* R2 (Fd)

58 destruit] *add.* omnia Bi Mk   61 derelinquat] relinquat Bi Pf Sb   75 et] *add.*
ad Aa Mk_pc Pf EdF, *add.* a Mk_ac Sb | dicit] dicat Fd Mk_ac   77 eius] ei Pf eis Sb
78 Mentem] *add.* enim Pf EdF   80 consideranda] conferenda Bi Mk | iam] ta-
men Bi Mk Pf

considering as he who has served the devil through a wicked deed has lost the virtues which he offered to God. Nevertheless, it is pious to believe that the received grace of God, which has destroyed the prior evils in the sinner, may also reward good things, so that, when it has destroyed what it does not find of its own, the sinner may love and adore the good that grace also planted in him.

"In all things, let the one grieving abandon either the world or at least those things that are not administered without an admixture of evil, such as the mercantile trade and the military and other activities which are harmful to those who exercise them, such as the managing of worldly powers, unless he exercises these things with the permission of obedience. Let him place himself entirely in the power of the judge, in the judgment of the priest, reserving nothing of himself for himself, so that, when the priest gives his command, he may be prepared to do all things to receive the life of the soul, that he might do whatever it takes to avoid the death of the body, and that he might do this with this desire, that he recover infinite life, as God possesses. Ready to be immortal, he ought joyfully to do whatever he would do when he was ready to die in order to delay death. Let him who asked dubiously in all ways and without disgust for worldly power always plead with God, certain of mercy. Let he who committed illicit acts in his free will abstain from many licit acts. Let him offer to God his mind and contrition of the heart, then also what he can of his possessions. Then he may securely offer what he offers. *For the Lord looked at Abel and his offerings.* But he Gn 4:4 spoke to Abel before his offerings. For taking up his mind, which he knew to be humble and pure, he rewarded his generous offerings. But he did not look at Cain or at his offerings. Since he did not recognize his mind, which he had seen, he did not receive his offerings. Therefore, in the judgment of the heart, the alms of the giver should be considered, and not how much ought to be considered now but with what mindset, with what disposition the giver gives what he can. For the widow, who was liberal with the two small coins which she had, gave more than all the rest. Therefore, he who wants to redeem his sins with the offering of temporal things should be careful to offer his mind first.

85   "Cautus sit ne uerecundia ductus diuidat apud se confessionem
ut diuersa diuersis uelit sacerdotibus manifestare. Quedam enim
uni celant que alii manifestanda conseruant, quod est se laudare et
ad ypocrisim tendere et semper uenia carere, quam per frusta totam putat peruenire.

90   "Paueat preterea quem uera delectat penitentia; non prius ad
Domini corpus accedat quam confortet bona conscientia. Set in hac
separatione tremendum iudicium cogitet ubi maius et terribilius in-
penitentes separabit in ignem. Doleat quod nondum audet sumere,
quem multum desiderat, cibum salutarem. Isti sunt digni fructus
95   penitentie, animam captiuam elaqueantes et in libertate seruantes.

Aa 180ᵛ | "Cohibeat se preterea a ludis, a spectaculis seculi, qui perfec-
Bi 313ᵛᵇ | Sb   tam uult consequi gratiam remissionis. | Nam Dina, | si se cohibuis-
280ᵛᵃ   set, si inter suos remansisset, ab extraneo raptore corrupta non esset. Tanto itaque magis sibi caueat et cohibeat se anima que sepe
100   uel semel rapta est et corrupta. Timeat iam docta experimento quod
ignorauit uirgo; eligat quem imitetur; non sequatur quem animus
suus dampnat. Se enim iudicat qui penitentie fructus non habentem a se non elongat. Laudat enim et amat quos digne fructificare
non ignorat; querat fructus dignos, etsi non dignos penitentie. Sunt
105   enim digni fructus uirtutum fructus, qui non sufficiunt penitentibus. Penitentia enim grauiores expostulat ut sic pacetur ecclesia ut,
pacata dolore et gemitibus, mortuis inpetret uitam."

88 quam] a qua Bi_ac, ad quam Bi_pc Pf EdF | totam] *om.* Bi Pf, *interlin. pos.* putat
Mk   89 putat] putant Aa | peruenire] inuenire Fd Aa Mk   90 Paueat] caueat Sb
91 confortet] *add.* illum Bi Pf   92 iudicium] *om.* Aa Sb   97 Dina] digna Pf_ac diuina Sb   106 pacetur] pacificetur Aa_ac placetur Bi Mk_ac pascetur Pf

"Let him be careful that, led by shame, he does not divide his confession in his own mind so that he may want to show different sins to different priests. For some people conceal certain things from one priest which they reserve to be shown to another. This activity amounts to praising oneself and tending to hypocrisy and always lacking mercy, which he thinks to attain in its entirety through bits.

"Moreover, let he whom true penance delights quake in fear; he is not to approach the body of the Lord before he is strengthened by a good conscience. But let him think the judgment tremendous in this separation, when a greater and more terrible judgment will separate the impenitent in the fire. Let him grieve that he does not yet dare to partake of the salutary food which he had greatly desired. These are the worthy fruits of penance which disentangle the captive soul and preserve it in liberty.

"Moreover, let he who wants to attain the complete grace of remission restrain himself from the games and spectacles of the world. For Dinah, if she had restrained herself, if she had remained with her family, would not have been corrupted by a foreign ravisher. Therefore, let the soul which has been either often or once ravished and corrupted be careful for itself and restrain itself so much more. Having been taught by experience, let it now fear what the virgin did not know; let it choose whom it may imitate; let it not follow he whom its intellect condemns. For he passes judgment on himself who does not keep aloof from himself the person who does not have the fruits of penance. For let it praise and love those fruits which it does not know how to produce worthily; let it seek the worthy fruits, even if they are not worthy of penance. For worthy fruits are fruits of the virtues, which are not sufficient for penitents. For penance requires more important fruits, so the church may be pacified in such a way that, after the grief and the groans have been subdued, it may obtain life for the dead."

ITEM LEO PAPA:

Mk 254rb | Penitens negotiationis lucra abiciat.

110   "Qualitas lucri negotiantem aut accusat aut arguit, quia et est honestus questus   c.2
et turpis. Verumtamen penitenti utilius est dispendia pati quam periculis negotiationis astringi, quia difficile est inter ementis uendentisque commercium non interue-
nire peccatum."
Idem:

115   Post penitentiam ad militiam secularem redire non licet.

"Contrarium omnino est ecclesiasticis regulis post penitentie actionem redire ad   c.3
militiam secularem, cum Apostolus dicat: *Nemo militans Deo inplicat se negociis se-*
Pf 125rb   *cularibus.* Vnde non est liber a laqueis diaboli | qui se militie mundane uoluerit im-
plicare."

120   ITEM EX NICENO CONCILIO:

Decennio peniteant qui post penitentiam ad secularem militiam redeunt.

"Si qui uero per Dei gratiam uocati primo quidem ostenderunt fidem suam de-   c.4
posito militie cingulo, post hec autem ad proprium uomitum reuersi sunt, ut et pe-
cunias darent et ambirent rursus ad militiam, isti decem annis sint inter penitentes
125   post primum triennium quo fuerint inter audientes. Ab omnibus uero illud precipue
obseruetur ut animus eorum et fructus penitentie attendatur. Quicumque enim
cum omni timore et lacrimis perseuerantibus et operibus bonis conuersationem
suam, non uerbis solis set opere et ueritate, demonstrant, cum tempus statutum a
his fuerit inpletum et orationibus iam ceperint conmunicare, licebit episcopo etiam
130   humanius circa eos aliquid cogitare. Qui uero indifferentem habuerint lapsum et
sufficere sibi, quod ecclesiam introierint, arbitrantur, isti omnimodo tempora statuta conplebunt."

110 Qualitas … **113** peccatum] Leo I, *Epistola* 167, *Ad Rusticum* (PL 54:1206B) =
JK 544   **116** Contrarium … **119** implicare] Ibid. (PL 54:1206C–1207A)
122 Si … **132** conplebunt] Concilium Nicenum (325), c.12 (COGD 1:26.245–54)

110 et] *mg.* Aa *om.* Mk   **112** commercium] consortium Sb   **118** militie mun-
dane] malitie seculari FdB   **121** secularem] *om.* Aa | secularem militiam] secula-
ria Mk Sb   **122** qui uero] *om.* Aa | ostenderunt] ostenderint Aa   **129** iam cepe-
rint] *om.* Aa   **131** arbitrantur] arbitrentur Aa | omnimodo] omnino Aa
132 conplebunt] conplebuntur Bi$_{ac}$ Mk$_{ac}$

The penitent is to give up the profits of business.

c.2   "The nature of profit either accuses or denounces the businessman, because, having been examined, he is both honorable and dishonorable. Notwithstanding, it is more useful for the penitent to suffer expenses than to be tied to the dangers of business, because it is difficult not to find sin among the trade of buyer and seller."

The same:

He is not permitted to return to the secular military after penance.

c.3   "It is entirely contrary to ecclesiastical rules to return to the secular military after the act of penance, since the Apostle says, *No one fighting for God entangles himself in secular affairs*. And thus he who wants to entangle himself in the worldly military   2 Tm 2:4 is not free from the nooses of the devil."

LIKEWISE, FROM THE COUNCIL OF NICAEA:

**Those who return to the secular military after penance are to do penance for
ten years.**

c.4   "But if any called through the grace of God indeed first demonstrated their faith by putting down their military belt, but after these things they returned to their own vomit so that they might both make money and go round to the military again, these are to spend ten years among penitents after the first three-year period in which they will have been among the hearers. But let that be especially observed by all so that their mind and the fruit of penance may be attended to. For whatever people demonstrate their way of life with all fear and persisting tears and good works, not in words alone but in deed and truth, when the proper period established by them is fulfilled and they begin forthwith to communicate in prayers, the bishop will be permitted also to think something more humane about them. But those who have a careless lapse and judge it sufficient for themselves to enter a church, these shall fulfill the established proper periods in every way."

ITEM EX CONCILIO AURELIANENSI:

Aa 181ʳ | A conmunione suspendantur qui post penitentiam ad secularia redeunt.

135   "De his qui suscepta penitentia religionem sue professionis obliti ad secularia   c.5
Bi 314ʳᵃ   relabuntur, placuit eos et a conmunione suspendi et ab omnium | catholicorum
Sb 280ᵛᵇ   conuiuiis | separari. Quod si post interdictum cum eis quisque presumpserit man-
ducare, et ipse conmunione priuetur."

ITEM GREGORIUS:

140   **Que sit falsa penitentia.**

"Falsas penitentias dicimus que non secundum auctoritatem sanctorum Patrum   c.6
pro qualitate criminum inponuntur. Ideoque miles uel negotiator uel alicui offitio
deditus quod sine peccato exerceri non possit, si culpis grauioribus irretitus ad penitentiam uenerit, uel qui bona alterius iniuste detinet uel qui odium in corde gerit,
145   recognoscat se ueram penitentiam non posse peragere per quam ad eternam uitam
peruenire ualeat, nisi negotium relinquat uel offitium deserat, et odium ex corde dimittat, bona quidem que iniuste abstulit restituat, arma deponat ulteriusque non fe-
rat, nisi consilio religiosorum episcoporum pro defendenda iustitia. Ne tamen desperet, interim quicquid boni facere poterit hortamur ut faciat ut omnipotens Deus
150   cor illius illustret ad penitentiam."

ITEM GREGORIUS IN OMELIA XXIV:

Mk 254ᵛᵃ   **Post conuersionem ad negotium | redire non licet quod sine peccato agi non
potest.**

Pf 125ᵛᵃ | "Negotium, quod ante conuersionem sine peccato extitit, hoc etiam post con-   c.7
155   uersionem repetere culpa non fuit.... Sunt enim pleraque negotia que sine peccatis
exhiberi aut uix aut nullatenus possunt. Que ergo ad peccatum inplicant ad hec necesse est ut post conuersionem animus non recurrat."

135 De…138 priuetur] Concilium Aurelianense (511), c.11 (CCSL
148A:8.93–97)   141 Falsas…150 penitentiam] Greg. VII, *Das Register Gregors VII*
6.6 (MGH Epp. sel. 2.2:404.4–17)   154 Negotium…157 recurrat] Greg. Magn.,
Hom. in euang. 2.24 (CCSL 141:197.8–9, 13–16)

137 quisque] quisquam Aa   140 Que sit] De Aa   142 miles…negotiator] milites uel negotiatores Aa   143 exerceri] exercere Bi Mk   144 bona…detinet] *mg.*
Aa | gerit] egit Biₐc egerit Mk   145 peragere] agere FdB   148 consilio] concilio
Bi | Ne] nec Aa Bi   149 boni] *add.* fecerit uel Aa Bi Mk   155 repetere] repente
Aaₐc repetende FdB Biₐc Mkₐc

Those who return to worldly things after penance are to be suspended from communion.

c.5   "Concerning those who, after they have undergone penance, forget the religion of their profession and fall back to worldly things, it has been resolved that they both be suspended from communion and be separated from the feasts of all catholics. But if someone presumes to eat with them after this prohibition, he himself is also to be deprived of communion."

LIKEWISE GREGORY:

What false penance is.

c.6   "We call penances false which are not imposed in accord with the authority of the holy Fathers for the nature of the wicked deeds. And for this reason, if a soldier or a trader or someone devoted to some office that cannot be exercised without sin, after being ensnared in rather serious guilty acts, who either unjustly detains the goods of another or bears hatred in his heart, should come to penance, let him recognize that he cannot carry out true penance through which he may be able to attain eternal life unless he gives up his business or leaves his office and dismisses the hatred from his heart, restores the goods which he formerly unjustly took, puts down his arms and does not bear them again, unless for defending righteousness by the counsel of religious bishops. Nevertheless, lest he despair, we encourage him to do whatever good he can do in the meantime so that the omnipotent God may illuminate his heart for penance."

LIKEWISE GREGORY IN HOMILY 24:

After conversion, [the convert] is not allowed to return to a business that cannot be done without sin.

c.7   "To seek again that business that existed without sin before conversion was also not a source of guilt after conversion.... But there are several businesses that can be exercised either hardly or not at all without sin. Therefore it is necessary that, after conversion, the spirit not run back to these things which involve sin."

ITEM INNOCENTIUS II:

"Fratres nostros et presbiteros ammonemus ne falsis penitentiis laicorum ani-   c.8

FdB 162rb   mas decipi et in infernum | pertrahi patiantur. Falsam autem penitentiam esse constat cum spretis pluribus de uno solo penitentia agitur aut cum sic agitur de uno ut non discedatur ab alio. Vnde scriptum est: *Qui totam legem obseruauerit, offendat autem in uno, factus est omnium reus*, scilicet quantum ad uitam eternam. Sicut enim si peccatis omnibus esset inuolutus, ita si in uno tantum maneat, eterne uite

165   ianuam non intrabit. Falsa est etiam penitentia cum penitens ab offitio uel curiali uel negotiali non recedit quod sine peccatis agi nullatenus preualet; aut si odium in corde gesserit aut si offenso cuilibet non satisfaciat aut si offendenti offensus non indulgeat, aut si arma quis contra iustitiam gerat."

---

159 Fratres ... **168** gerat] Concilium Lateranense II (1139), c.22 (COGD 2.1:111.153–112.164)

158 Item] *om.* Aa | Innocentius II] *in rubr.* Aa   **159** Fratres] *praem.* Que sit falsa penitentia Bi De eodem Pf EdF | et] *om.* Aa   **160** in] *interlin.* Bi Mk, ad Pf **161** spretis] pretis Bi_{ac} spetis Mk_{ac}   **162** obseruauerit] seruauerit Aa | offendat] offendit Aa offendi Pf   **164** tantum] *om.* Aa   **165** etiam] *om.* Aa enim Pf

c.8   "We admonish our brothers and priests not to allow the souls of the laity to be deceived with false penances and to be led away to the inferno. But it is agreed that there is false penance when penance is done for one sin only while many have been disregarded or when penance is done for one sin in such a way that the penitent does not abandon another. Thus it is written: *He who observes the whole law but offends in one thing has become guilty of all*, namely, to what extent is necessary for   Jas 2:10 eternal life. For just as if he would be enveloped by all sins, so also if he should remain in one only, he will not enter the gate of eternal life. There is also false penance when the penitent does not withdraw from either an office or a court or business post that cannot in any way be done without sin. There is also false penance if someone either bears hatred in his heart or does not make satisfaction to whatever person he has wronged or, after he is wronged, does not show kindness to the offender, or if anyone bears arms against justice."

Distinctio sexta

Cui autem debeat fieri confessio uel qualem illum oporteat esse d.a.c.1
qui aliorum crimina iudicat EX EODEM LIBRO docetur, dum dicitur:
Aa 181ᵛ "Qui uult confiteri peccata | ut inueniat gratiam querat sacerdotem c.1
5 scientem ligare et soluere, ne, cum negligens circa se extiterit, ne-
Sb 281ʳᵃ gligatur ab illo qui eum misericorditer monet et petit, | ne ambo in
Bi 314ʳᵇ foueam cadant quam stultus euitare noluit. | Tanta itaque uis con-
Fd 99ʳᵃ fessionis est | ut, si deest sacerdos, confiteatur proximo. Sepe enim
contingit quod penitens non potest uerecundari coram sacerdote,
10 quem desideranti nec locus nec tempus offert, et, si ille cui confite-
Pf 125ᵛᵇ bitur | potestatem soluendi non habeat fit tamen dignus uenia ex
desiderio sacerdotis qui socio confitetur turpitudinem criminis.
Mundati enim sunt leprosi dum ibant ostendere ora sacerdotibus,
antequam ad eos peruenirent. Vnde patet Deum ad cor respicere,
15 dum ex necessitate prohibentur ad sacerdotes peruenire. Sepe quidem eos querunt; set sani et leti dum querunt, antequam perueniant, moriuntur. Set misericordia Dei est ubique, qui et iustis nouit parcere, etsi non tam cito ut soluerentur a sacerdote. Qui ergo
omnino confitetur, et sacerdoti meliori, quam potest, confiteatur.

20 "Si peccatum occultum est, sufficiat referre in notitiam sacerdotis ut grata sit oblatio muneris."

Et infra: "Laboret itaque penitens in ecclesia esse et ad ecclesie
unitatem tendere. Nisi enim unitas ecclesie succurrat, nisi quod
deest peccatori sua operatione conpleat, de manibus inimici non

---

6,4 Qui … 88 Pontifice] Ps.-Aug., *De uera* 10–12, 20 (PL 40:1122–24, 1129–30;
ed. Wagner, 579–99, 628–49, 969–1022)

6,7 Tanta] *praem.* Et infra R2 (*om.* Sb EdRom) 13 ora] se R2 (Aa EdRom, *interlin.* Bi Mk; ora EdF)

6,2 debeat] debebat Bi Mk 8 proximo] *add.* et infra Bi Mk Pf 10 locus … tem-
pus] t. nec l. Fd 13 ibant] irent Aa 17 misericordia] in his ecclesia Biₐc Mk Sb
18 ut] sicut Aa Pf 19 confitetur] confiteatur Biₐc Sb | sacerdoti … confiteatur]
mg. Bi *om.* Sb

Distinction 6

d.a.c.1 But to whom confession ought to be made or of what kind of character he ought to be who judges the wicked deeds of others is

c.1 taught IN THE SAME BOOK, when it is said: "Let he who wants to cf. D.1 c.88 confess his sins in order to find grace seek out a priest who knows how to bind and loose, lest, when a careless priest lives in his area, he fail to be attended to by a priest who mercifully warns and seeks after him, and lest both fall into a pit that the foolish priest did not have the will to avoid.[1] So great, then, is the power of confession, that, if a priest is unavailable, one may confess to a neighbor. For it often happens that a penitent cannot express their shame in the presence of a priest, whom neither place nor time offers to the one desiring him, and, if he to whom one will confess does not have the power of loosing, the one who confesses the foulness of his wicked deed to a companion nevertheless becomes worthy of mercy[2] because of his desire for a priest. For the lepers were cleansed while they were going to show their mouths[3] to the priests, before they reached them. And thus it is clear that God looks at the heart as long as people are necessarily hindered from reaching priests. Indeed, oftentimes people seek them, but, though healthy and happy while they are seeking, they die before they reach them. But the mercy of God is everywhere, and he also knows how to spare the righteous, even if not as quickly as if they were loosened by a priest. Therefore, let he who confesses completely also confess to the best priest he can.

"If the sin is secret, let it suffice to relate it to the notice of a priest so that the offering of a gift may be acceptable."[4]

And below: "Therefore, let the penitent labor to be in the church and to strive for the unity of the church. For unless the unity of the church comes to the sinner's assistance, unless the unity of the

---

1. The second recension inserted an "And below," indicating a break in the text of *De uera et falsa penitentia* quoted by Gratian. In fact, there is no break in *De uera*.

2. Gratian seems to have added this Latin word (*uenia*) himself. It appears in no manuscript of *De uera* collated by Wagner, only in Migne's edition, which collated the *Decretum* texts of *De uera* in the relevant sections.

3. The second recension reads "themselves" instead of "their mouths." All earlier editions also read "themselves," but Friedberg chose the original reading of "their mouths" based solely on his manuscript A (Köln, Dombibliothek 127), an early manuscript that occasionally preserves first-recension readings.

4. The overlap with D.1 c.88 ends at this point.

25 eripietur anima mortui. Credendum est enim, et pietas fidei expostulat credere, quod omnes elemosine totius ecclesie et orationes et
Mk 254vb opera iustitie et misericordie succurrant recognoscenti | mortem
suam ad conuersionem. Ideoque nemo penitere digne potest quem
non sustineat unitas ecclesie, ideoque non petat sacerdotes per ali-
30 quam culpam ab unitate ecclesie diuisos. Iudas enim qui penitens
iuit ad Phariseos, relinquens Apostolos, nichil inuenit auxilii nisi
augmentum desperationis. Dixerunt enim, *Quid ad nos? Tu uide-*
ris—'Si peccasti, tibi sit; non tibi succurrimus, non peccata tua cari-
tatiue suscipimus, non conportanda promittimus, non qualiter de-
35 ponas onus docemus. Quid enim nobis et misericordie qui nec
Pf 126ra opera sequimur iustitie?' | Isset ad fratres! Isset ad illos qui oraue-
rant pro socru Petri febricitante, qui Cananeam inprobam misericordie obtulerant! Interrogaret Petrum pro se effundentem lacrimas! Non fugisset Mariam et Martham que uitam Lazaro inpetra-
Fs 320ra uerant, non turbam plorantem que unicum | filium acquisierat ui-
Aa 182^r due! | Iuit ad diuisos, et diuisus periit."

Et infra: "Sacerdos itaque, cui omnis offertur peccator, ante
quem statuitur omnis languor, in nullo eorum sit iudicandus que in
alio iudicare est promptus. Iudicans enim alium, qui est iudicandus,
45 condempnat se ipsum. Cognoscat igitur se et purget in se quod alios
uidet sibi offerre. Caueat ut a se proiecerit quicquid in alio dampno-
sum repperit. Animaduertat quod, *qui sine peccato est primus in illam*
Sb 281rb *lapidem* | *mittat.* Ideo enim liberauit peccatricem, quia non erat qui
Bi 314va iuste | proiceret lapidem. Quomodo lapidaret qui se lapidandum co-
50 gnosceret? Nullus enim erat *sine peccato,* in quo intelligitur, omnes
fuisse reos. Nam uenialia semper remittebantur per ceremonias. Si
quod ergo in eis peccatum erat, criminale erat. Deteriores itaque in

---

28 penitere digne] *tr.* R2 **38** Interrogaret] Interrogasset R2 (Interrogaret Mk
Sb)

---

29 petat] petant Mk Sb **31** Phariseos] sacerdotes Aa **34** non²] nec Pf Sb
39 fugisset] fuisset Fd Bi_ac Mk_ac Sb_ac **46** alio] aliquo Bi Mk alium Fs **47** pri-
mus] prius Bi Fs Pf **50** omnes] *add.* criminaliter Aa **51** per] pro Fs propter Sb
ceremonias] ceremoniis Fs **52** quod] quid Mk Pf

church in its operating fills in what is missing from the sinner, the soul of the dead would not be snatched away from the hands of the enemy. For it should be believed, and the piety of faith demands one to believe, that all the alms of the whole church and its prayers and works of justice and mercy assist the person recognizing his death to convert. Therefore, no one can worthily repent whom the unity of the church does not support, and for this reason let him not seek priests divided from the unity of the church through some guilty act. For Judas, who went to the Pharisees as a penitent, deserting the apostles, found no help but the increase of despair. For they said, *What is that to us? You are found out*—'If you have sinned,   Mt 27:4 may it be on you; we do not help you, we do not lovingly welcome your sins, we do not promise that they are to be borne together; we do not teach how you may put down your burden. For what even of mercy is there in us who do not follow works of justice?' Would that he had gone to his brothers! Would that he had gone to those who had prayed for Peter's mother-in-law who had a fever, who had brought the wicked Canaanite woman to mercy! Would that he ask[5] Peter, who poured out tears for himself! Would that he had not shunned Mary and Martha, who obtained life for Lazarus, or the weeping crowd that had secured the only son of the widow! He went to those cut off, and he died cut off."

And below: "Therefore, the priest before whom every sinner is brought, in front of whom every faintness takes root, must not need to be judged for any of the things that he is ready to judge in another. For he who, while judging another, has to be judged condemns himself. Therefore, let him know himself and purge in himself what he sees others expose to him. Let him be careful to cast out from himself whatever damnable thing he finds in another; let him heed that verse: *Let he who is without sin throw the first stone at her.* For, for this reason did he free the sinning woman, because   Jn 8:7 there was no one who could justly throw a stone. How would he who recognizes that he himself should be stoned stone somebody else? For there was no one who was *without sin*, in which it is understood that all were guilty. Now venial sins have always been remitted through ceremonies. Thus, if there was some sin in them, it was mortal. Priests who do not first build themselves up are worse

---

5. The second recension changed the tense of this subjunctive verb to make it parallel to the others in the series. It would be translated, "Would that he had asked...."

hoc sacerdotes sunt, se prius non edificantes, illis qui Dominum ob-
seruabant insidiis. In hoc itaque patentissimum est crimen sacerdo-
55 tum et ultra modum detestabile, qui non prius se iudicant et alios
alligant. Deberent enim timere crimen, quod timuerunt et detestabile esse senserunt. Hi qui adeo erant ceci, quod summam sapientiam sperabant capere suis insidiis. Quod illis patuit, quod tunc
quisque uitauit, uitet sacerdos qui in hoc peior illis Iudeis extitit.

Pf 126ʳᵇ   "Caueat spiritualis iudex: sicut | non conmisit crimen nequitie,
ita non careat munere scientie. Oportet ut sciat cognoscere quicquid debet iudicare. Iudiciaria enim potestas hoc expostulat, ut
quod debet iudicare discernat. Diligens igitur inquisitor, subtilis in-
uestigator, sapienter et quasi astute interroget a peccatore quod for-
65 sitan ignoret uel uerecundia uelit occultare. Cognito itaque crimine
uarietates eius non dubitet inuestigare, et locum, et tempus, et cetera, que supra diximus in exponenda eorum qualitate. Quibus co-
Mk 255ʳᵃ gnitis adsit beniuolus, paratus erigere et secum onus portare. | Ha-
beat dulcedinem in affectione, pietatem in alterius crimine, discre-
Fd 99ʳᵇ   tionem in uarietate. Adiuuet | confitentem orando, elemosinas fa-
ciendo, et cetera bona pro eo faciendo. Semper enim iuuet le-
niendo, consolando, spem promittendo, et, cum opus fuerit, etiam
Fs 320ʳᵇ increpando. Doleat | loquendo, instruat operando. Sit particeps la-
boris qui particeps uult fieri gaudii; doceat perseuerantiam.

75   "Caueat, ne corruat, ne iuste perdat potestatem iudiciariam. Sic
et enim penitentia ei possit acquirere gratiam, non tamen mox re-
stituit in potestatem primam. Sic et enim Petrus post lapsum resti-

---

75 Sic...76 et] Etsi R2 (Aa; et sic Biₐc Mkₐc)   77 Sic et] Etsi R2

56 Deberent] deberet Fs Sb   59 uitauit] mutauit Fs iurauit? Sb | uitet] Nitet Fs
Mk Sb | hoc] *add.* errore Pf EdF   71 leniendo] liniendo Fdₚc Bi Mk   73 Doleat]
doceat Aaₚc EdF   76 enim] *om.* Aa Biₚc   77 Sic et] Si Aa

in this regard than those who were watching the Lord with plots. In this it is thus very clear that the wicked deed of priests who do not first judge themselves and yet bind others is even beyond a detestable state. For they were supposed to fear the wicked deed that they have feared and have perceived to be detestable.[6] Those were so blind that they were hoping to capture the highest Wisdom by their plots. What was apparent to them, what each person at that time avoided, let the priest who has stood worse than those Jews in this avoid.

"Let a spiritual judge take care: just as he has not committed a deed of great evil, so let him not lack the gift of knowledge. It is proper for him to know how to recognize whatever he ought to judge. For judiciary power demands this, that he discern what he ought to judge. Therefore, let him as a diligent inquisitor, a subtle investigator, wisely and, as it were, cunningly question from the sinner that which he perhaps does not know or wants to hide due to shame. Thus, when the wicked deed has become known, let him not hesitate to investigate its various aspects, both time and place, etc., which we have said above in explaining the nature of wicked deeds. After these things have become known, let him be benevolent, prepared to encourage and bear the burden with him. Let him have sweetness in his disposition, kindness toward the wicked deed of the other, discretion in its various aspects. Let him assist the one confessing by praying, giving alms, and doing all other good things for him. For let him always help by soothing, consoling, promising hope, and, when there is need, alo by reproaching. Let him grieve with his words, instruct with his deeds. Let him be a participant of the penitent's labor as one who desires to become a participant of his joy; let him teach perseverance.

cf. D.5 c.1

"Let him be careful not to fall down, lest he justly lose his judiciary power. And so penance may obtain grace for him; nevertheless it will not soon restore him to his former power.[7] And so[8] Peter

---

6. The sentence is obtuse in Gratian's version. His manuscript of *De uera et falsa penitentia*, just like manuscripts B and Vb, omitted two key phrases. The treatise reads, "For they were supposed to fear in themselves the wicked deed that they have feared and have perceived to be detestable in others."

7. The second recension changed the opening of this sentence to "Even if": "Even if penance may obtain grace for him, it will nevertheless not soon...."

8. As in previous sentence, the second recension changed the opening of this sentence to "Even if."

tutus fuerat, et sepe lapsis sacerdotibus reddita sit dignitatis potestas, non tamen est necesse, ut omnibus concedatur quasi ex aucto-
80 ritate. Inuenitur auctoritas que concedit et quasi inperat; inuenitur
alia que minime concedit Set uetat. Que scripture non pugnant Set
concordant, si tempus et locus et modus penitentie pacem adhi-
Aa 182ᵛ beant. Cum enim tot sunt qui labuntur, ut pristinam | dignitatem
ex auctoritate defendant et quasi usum peccandi sibi faciant, reci-
Sb 281ᵛᵃ | Pf denda | est | spes ista. Si uero locus est ubi ista non concurrant, re-
126ᵛᵃ
Bi 314ᵛᵇ stitui possunt qui peccant. Itaque pontifex iustus atque discretus |
non cogitur suos sacerdotes semper abicere nec mox restituere, nisi
statutum fuerit a Romano Pontifice."

(FdB 162ʳᵇ) | Caueat sacerdos ne peccata penitentium aliis manifestet. Quod si fecerit, depo-   d.p.c.1
90 natur. Vnde Gregorius:

Deponatur sacerdos qui peccata penitentis publicare presumit.

"Sacerdos ante omnia caueat, ne de his qui ei confitentur peccata sua alicui reci-   c.2
tet quod ea confessus est, non propinquis, non extraneis, neque—quod absit!—pro
aliquo scandalo. Nam si hoc fecerit, deponatur, et omnibus diebus uite sue ignomi-
95 niosus peregrinando pergat."

Quod autem dicitur, ut penitens eligat sacerdotem scientem li-   d.p.c.2
gare et soluere, uidetur esse contrarium ei quod in canonibus inuenitur, ut nemo uidelicet alterius parrochianum iudicare presumat.
Set aliud est fauore uel odio proprium sacerdotem contempnere,
100 quod sacris canonibus prohibetur; aliud cecum uitare, quod hac
auctoritate quisque facere monetur, ne, si cecus ceco ducatum pre-
beat, ambo in foueam cadant.

---

92 Sacerdos…95 pergat] *possibiliter Gregorius I uel Gregorius II; similis canoni poeni-
tentiali in: Poenitentiale Casinense n.105* (ed. H. J. Schmitz, *Die Bussbücher und die
Bussdisciplin der Kirche*, 1.428).

78 fuerat] fuerit R2 | sit dignitatis] *tr.* R2 (s.d. EdF)

81 pugnant] repugnant Pf EdF   89 penitentium] penitentis Aa   90 Vnde…91
presumit] *om.* FdB   95 pergat] peragat Aa   101 prebeat] prestet Pf EdF

had been restored[9] after his lapse, and the power of dignity may often return to lapsed priests; nevertheless, it is not necessary that it be granted to all as if the authorities demand it. An authority is found that allows and as it were commands it; another is found that does not allow it in the least but forbids it. These Scriptures do not oppose each other but agree, if time and place and the manner of penance should bring peace. For when there are so many who fall that some priests defend their former dignity with authorities and use it as an excuse, as it were, to sin themselves, that hope must be cut down. But if there is a place where those things do not occur, those who sin can be restored. Therefore, a righteous and discrete bishop is not compelled always to get rid of his priests and not soon restore them, unless it has been established by the Roman pontiff."

d.p.c.1   Let a priest be careful not to make the sins of penitents known to others. But if he does, he is to be deposed. THUS GREGORY:

A priest who dares to make public the sins of a penitent is to be deposed.

c.2   "Above all, a priest should take care not to repeat to anyone, neither to relatives nor to strangers nor—may it be never be!—to create some scandal, what was confessed from those who confess their sins to him. For if he should do this, he is to be deposed and is to go on living the life of a wanderer in shame for all the days of his life."

d.p.c.2   But what is said, that a penitent should select a priest who knows how to bind and loose, seems to be contrary to that which is found in the canons, that no one indeed should presume to judge the parishioner of another priest. But it is one thing to reject one's own priest because of partiality or hatred, which is prohibited by the holy canons; it is another to avoid a blind priest, which by this authority each person is advised to do, lest, if a blind man offer to lead the blind, both fall into a pit.

---

9. To coordinate with the change to "even if" (*erit*), the second recension altered the mood of the verb to make it subjunctive (*fuerit* instead of *fuerat*). It would be translated, "Even if Peter was restored after his lapse...."

Vnde Vrbanus II:

Cuilibet sacerdoti conmissum, nisi pro eius ignorantia, alter sacerdos ad
105   penitentiam non suscipiat.

"Placuit, ut deinceps nulli sacerdotum liceat quemlibet conmissum alteri sacer-   c.3
doti ad penitentiam suscipere sine eius consensu cui se prius conmisit, nisi pro
Fs 320va ignorantia | illius cui penitens prius confessus est. Qui uero contra hec statuta fa-
cere temptauerit gradus sui periculo subiacebit."

110

---

106 Placuit… **109** subiacebit] *fons materialis non invenitur; cf. canonem similem ex
Concilio Claromontense (1095) in codice* Oxford, Bodleian Library, Selden supra 90
(ed. Somerville, *Councils of Urban II*, 113).

104 Cuilibet… **105** suscipiat] *om.* FdB | alter] aliter Aa Sb

Thus Urban II:

Another priest is not to receive to penance a person committed to any other priest, except on account of that priest's ignorance.

c.3   "It is resolved that no priest is allowed in turn under any circumstances to receive to penance anyone committed to another priest without the consent of that priest to whom he was first committed, except on account of the ignorance of that priest to whom the penitent first confessed. But he who attempts to act against these statutes will be subject to the loss of his office."

Distinctio septima

Mk 255rb Tempus uero penitentie est usque in ultimum | articulum uite, d.a.c.1

(FdB 162rb) | VNDE LEO PAPA: "Nemo desperandus est dum in hoc corpore constitutus est, c.1
quia nonnumquam quod diffidentia etatis differtur consilio maturiore perficitur."

5 <R1 c.2>

quamquam de differentibus penitentiam AUGUSTINUS SCRIBAT:
"Si quis positus in ultima necessitate sue egritudinis uoluerit acci- c.2
pere penitentiam, et accipit, et mox reconciliabitur et hinc uadit, fateor uobis, non illi negamus quod petit, set non presumimus quia
10 bene hinc exit.... Nam si tunc uis agere penitentiam quando iam
peccare non potes, peccata te dimiserunt, non tu illa."

<R2a cc.2–4>

Quamquam de differentibus penitentiam AUGUSTINUS SCRI-
BAT:

(FdB 162rb) | (IDEM:) "Qui egerit penitentiam ueraciter et solutus fuerit a ligamento, quo c.3
erat obstrictus et a Christi corpore separatus, et bene post penitentiam uixerit, sicut
ante penitentiam uiuere debuit, post reconciliationem quandocumque defunctus
fuerit, ad Deum uadit, ad requiem uadit; regno Dei non priuabitur, a populo diaboli
separabitur."

20 "Si quis positus in ultima necessitate sue egritudinis uoluerit ac- c.2
cipere penitentiam, et accipit, et mox reconciliabitur et hinc uadit,
fateor uobis, non illi negamus quod petit, set non presumimus quia
bene hinc exit. Nam si tunc uis agere penitentiam quando iam peccare non potes, peccata te dimiserunt, non tu illa."

25 Et infra: "Baptizatus ad horam securus hinc exit; fidelis bene uiuens securus c.4
hinc exit; agens penitentiam et reconciliatus cum sanus est et postea bene uiuens
hinc securus exit. Agens penitentiam ad ultimum et reconciliatus—si securus hinc

---

7,3 Nemo...**4** perficitur] Leo I, *Epistola* 167, *Ad Rusticum* (PL 54:1205B) = JL 544
7 Si...**11** illa] Caes. Arel., *Sermo* 63.1, 3 (CCSL 103:273–74); *olim* Aug. Hipp.
(dub.), *Sermo* 393 (PL 39:1714–15) **13** Quamquam...**24** illa] Ibid.

7,4 diffidentia] differentia Aa Bi_{ac} Mk_{ac}

Distinction 7

d.a.c.1 But the time for penance extends to the last moment of life,

c.1   AND THUS POPE LEO: "No one should despair while he is constituted in this body, because sometimes what is put off by the defiance of young age is perfected by more mature counsel."

<R1 c.2>

c.2   even though AUGUSTINE WRITES about those putting off penance, "If anyone positioned in the last dire stage of his illness should want to undertake penance, and he undertakes it and is quickly reconciled and passes on from this place, I profess to you, we do not deny to him what he seeks, but we do not presume that he departs from this place well.... For if you want to do penance at the time when you cannot now sin, your sins have sent you away, not you those sins."

<R2a cc.2–4>

Although AUGUSTINE WRITES about those putting off penance,

c.3   (The same:) "He who truly does penance, and is loosened from the bond by which he had been tied down and separated from the body of Christ, and lives well after penance as he ought to have lived before penance, whenever he dies after reconciliation, he goes to God, he goes to rest; he will not be deprived of the Kingdom of God, he will be separated out from the people of the devil."

c.2   "If anyone positioned in the last dire stage of his illness should want to undertake penance, and he undertakes it and is quickly reconciled and passes on from this place, I profess to you, we do not deny to him what he seeks, but we do not presume that he departs from this place well. For if you want to do penance at the time when you cannot now sin, your sins have sent you away, not you those sins."

c.4   And below: "He who has been baptized in time departs from this place secure; the faithful living well depart from this place secure; he who does penance and has been reconciled while he is healthy and afterward is living well departs from this place secure. He who does penance at the end of life and has been reconciled—I

exit, ego non sum securus. Vnde sum securus, dico, et do securitatem; unde non
sum securus, penitentiam dare possum, securitatem dare non possum." Et post
30   pauca: "'Set unde scis,' inquid, 'ne forte Deus dimittat mihi? Verum dicis, "Illud
scio; hoc nescio".' Nam ideo do tibi penitentiam: quia nescio. Nam si scirem nichil
tibi prodesse, non tibi darem. Item si scirem tibi prodesse, non te ammonerem,
non te terrerem. Due sunt res: aut ignoscitur tibi aut non ignoscitur. Quid horum
tibi futurum sit, nescio. Ergo tene certum, et dimitte incertum."

35   <R2b cc.2–4>

Quamquam de differentibus penitentiam AUGUSTINUS SCRI-
BAT: "Si quis positus in ultima necessitate sue egritudinis uoluerit   c.2
accipere penitentiam, et accipit, et mox reconciliabitur et hinc ua-
Pf 126vb   dit, fateor uobis, non illi negamus | quod petit, set non presumimus
40   quia bene hinc exit.

(FdG 162rb)   [| Si securus hinc exierit, ego nescio. Penitentiam dare possumus, securitatem
(AaB 337^r)   autem dare non possumus. Numquid dico, 'Dampnabitur'? Set nec dico, 'Liberabitur.' Vis ergo a dubio liberari? Vis quod incertum est euadere? Age penitentiam dum
sanus es. Si sic agis, dico tibi quia securus es, quia penitentiam egisti eo tempore,
45   quo peccare potuisti. Si autem]

uis agere penitentiam quando iam peccare non potes, peccata te
dimiserunt, non tu illa."

Sb 281vb | Idem: "Qui egerit ueraciter penitentiam et solutus fuerit a ligamento, quo erat   c.3
obstrictus et a Christi corpore separatus, et bene post penitentiam uixerit, sicut ante
50   penitentiam uiuere debuit, post reconciliationem quandocumque defunctus fuerit,
ad Deum uadit, ad requiem uadit; regno Dei non priuabitur, a populo diaboli separabitur."

Bi 315ra   "Si quis autem," | etc. Et infra: "Baptizatus ad horam securus hinc exit; fidelis   c.4
bene uiuens securus hinc exit; agens penitentiam et reconciliatus cum sanus est et
55   postea bene uiuens securus hinc exit. Agens penitentiam ad ultimum et reconcilia-

---

37 Si…62 incertum] Caes. Arel., *Sermo* 63.1, 3 (CCSL 103:272–74); *olim* Aug.
Hipp. (dub.), *Sermo* 393 (PL 39:1714–15)

41 exierit] *add.* qui in extremis suis penitentiam egerit AaB   43 dubio] diabolo
FdG Sb   44 eo…45 quo] quando AaB   53 fidelis…54 exit] *om.* AaB FdB *mg.* Pf
55 reconciliatussi] *interlin.* Mk *om.* FdB Pf

am not sure if he departs from this place secure. Of what I am sure, I say, and I give surety; of what I am not sure, I can give penance, but I cannot give surety." And after a few words: "'But from where do you know,' he says, 'that God may not perchance forgive me?' But you say, "I know that; I do not know this."' For I give penance to you for this reason: because I do not know. For if I were to know that it profits you nothing, I would not give it to you. Likewise, if I were to know that it profits you, I would not admonish you, and I would not scare you. There are two possibilities: either you are forgiven or you are not. Which of these possibilities will belong to you I do not know. Therefore, hold onto what is certain and let go of what is uncertain."

<R2b cc.2–4>

Although AUGUSTINE WRITES about those putting off penance,
c.2 "If anyone positioned in the last dire stage of his illness should want to undertake penance, and he undertakes it and is quickly reconciled and passes on from this place, I profess to you, we do not deny to him what he seeks, but we do not presume that he departs from this place well.

[If he has departed from here secure, I do not know; we can give penance, but we cannot give security. I did not say, 'He will be damned,' did I? But I do not say, 'He will be liberated.' Do you want to be liberated from doubt? Do you want to avoid what is uncertain? Do penance while you are healthy. If you act in this way, I say to you that you are secure because you have done penance in that time in which you could have sinned. But if]

you want to do penance when you cannot now sin, your sins have sent you away, not you those sins."

c.3 The same: "He who truly does penance, and is loosened from the bond by which he had been tied down and separated from the body of Christ, and lives well after penance as he ought to have lived before penance, whenever he dies after reconciliation, he goes to God, he goes to rest, he will not be deprived of the Kingdom of God, he will be separated out from the people of the devil."

c.4 "But if anyone," etc.[1] And below: "He who has been baptized in time departs   cf. D.7 c.2
from this place secure; the faithful living well depart from this place secure; he who does penance and has been reconciled while he is healthy and afterward is living well departs from this place secure. He who does penance at the end of life and has

---

1. These few words comprise the first words of a section of text which Gratian had copied in D.7 c.2. Gratian's original opening words were slightly different, namely *Si quis positus,* or "If anyone positioned." The reference to this incipit was meant to direct the reader to read the content of D.7 c.2 at this juncture.

tus—si securus hinc exit, ego non sum securus. Vnde securus sum, dico, et do securitatem; unde securus non sum, penitentiam dare possum, securitatem dare non
possum." Et post pauca: "'Set unde scis,' inquid, 'ne forte Deus dimittat mihi? Verum dicis, "Illud scio; hoc nescio".' Nam ideo do tibi penitentiam: quia nescio. Nam
60 si scirem nichil tibi prodesse, non tibi darem. Item si scirem, tibi prodesse, non te
ammonerem, non te terrerem. Due sunt res: aut ignoscitur tibi, aut non ignoscitur.
Quid horum tibi futurum sit, nescio. Ergo tene certum, et dimitte incertum."

Fs 320ᵛᵇ | Hoc autem quare Augustinus dixerit, CIPRIANUS OSTENDIT, di-
Pf 127ʳᵃ cens: | "Idcirco, frater carissime, penitentiam non agentes nec in do-   c.5
65 lore delictorum suorum toto corde manifestam lamentationis sue
professionem testantes, prohibendos omnino censuimus a spe conmunionis et pacis si in infirmitate atque periculo ceperint deprecari,
Aa 183ʳ quia rogare illos | non delicti penitentia, set mortis urgentis ammo-
nitio conpellit, nec dignus est in morte accipere solatium qui se non
70 cogitauit moriturum."

ITEM AUGUSTINUS IN LIBRO DE PENITENTIA: "Nullus expectet   c.6
quando peccare non potest. Arbitrii enim querit libertatem, ut delere possit conmissa, non necessitatem. Qui prius itaque a peccatis
Mk 255ᵛᵃ relinquitur | quam ipse relinquat, ea non libere set quasi necessitate
75 condempnat. Licet enim latro ueniam meruisset in fine de omni
crimine, non tamen dedit baptizatis peccandi et perseuerandi auctoritatem. Tunc enim baptizatus est qui tunc primum in cruce Christum confessus est. Penitentia enim, si in extremo hiatu uite adue-
nerit, sanat et liberat in ablutione baptismi ita quod nec purgato-
80 rium sentiunt qui in fine baptizantur, set ipsi ditati bonis sancte
Pf 127ʳᵇ matris ecclesie recepturi sunt multiplex bonum | in uera beatitu-
dine.

64 Idcirco ... 70 moriturum] Cypr. Carth., *Epistola* 55.23 (CCSL
3B:284.409–285.416)   71 Nullus ... 129 fine] Ps.-Aug., *De uera* 17–18 (PL
40:1127–28; ed. Wagner, 887–952)

60 tibi² ... non²] *mg.* FdB | tibi³] *add.* non AaB Bi Pf (*interlin.* Bi)   64 frater caris-
sime] fratres carissime Fs Sb   67 atque] *add.* in *vel* im- Bi Mk Pf | ceperint] cepe-
rim Fd_ac Mk ceperit Fs Sb   68 urgentis] urguentis Bi Mk Sb | ammonitio] a-
mono Bi_ac anmotio Mk_ac   78 enim] *om.* Aa uero Pf   80 sancte] *add.* Dei Bi Mk
Pf   81 bonum] donum Fd

been reconciled—I am not sure if he departs from this place secure. Of what I am sure, I say, and I give surety; of what I am not sure, I can give penance, but I cannot give surety." And after a few words: "'But from where do you know,' he says, 'that God may not perchance forgive me? But you say, "I know that; I do not know this".' For I give penance to you for this reason: because I do not know; for if I were to know that it profits you nothing, I would not give it to you. Likewise, if I were to know that it profits you, I would not admonish you, and I would not scare you. There are two possibilities: either you are forgiven or you are not. Which of these possibilities will belong to you I do not know. Therefore, hold onto what is certain and let go of what is uncertain."

c.5   But why Augustine said this CYPRIAN SHOWS, saying, "For this reason, dearest brother, we have resolved that those who do not do penance and do not demonstrate a clear profession of their lamentation in grief for their offences with their whole heart ought to be fully held back from the hope of communion and of peace if they should begin to pray earnestly in times of illness and danger, because it was not penance for the offence but the suggestion of imminent death which compelled these to make their request, and he who did not think that he was going to die [and repent] is not worthy of receiving comfort in death."

c.6   LIKEWISE AUGUSTINE IN HIS BOOK ON PENANCE: "Let no one wait for when he cannot sin. For he seeks freedom of judgment, not urgent necessity, so that he may be able to wipe out the things he has committed. Thus he who is abandoned by sins before he himself abandons them condemns them not freely but as if by necessity. For although the thief had merited mercy for every one of his wicked deeds at the end, nevertheless he did not grant authority to the baptized to sin and persevere [in that sin]. For he who first confessed Christ at that moment on the cross was baptized at that moment. For penance, if it arrives in the last opening of life, heals and liberates in the washing of baptism in such a way that those who are baptized at the end do not experience purgatory, but those enriched by the goods of the holy mother church will receive a multivalent good in true beatitude.

"Illi autem, qui cum potuerunt numquam conuerti uoluerunt, confitentes cum iam peccare nequeunt nec sic facile acquirunt
85   quod uolunt. Oportet enim ut penitentia fructificet, ut uitam mortuo inpetret. Scriptum est sine caritate neminem saluum esse. Non

Sb 282ra   itaque in solo timore uiuit homo. Quem ergo sero penitet | oportet non solum timere Deum iudicem, set iustum diligere; non tantum penam timeat set anxietur pro gloria. Debet enim dolere de crimine
90   et de omni eius predicta uarietate. Quod quoniam uix licet, de eius salute Augustinus potuit dubitare. Credo quidem illi, qui dixit, *Quacumque hora ingemuerit et conuersus fuerit, uita uiuet.* Dixit conuersum,

Fd 99va   non tantum uersum uiuere. Versum | quidem puto qui dolet de cri-
Bi 315rb   mine, | conuersum qui dolet de omni eius, quam exposuimus, ua-
95   rietate. Vertitur a peccato qui iam uult dimittere peccatum; conuertitur id est totus et omnino uertitur, qui iam non penas tantum timet set ad bonum Deum festinat tendere. Que conuersio si contigerit alicui etiam in fine, desperandum non est de eius remissione. Set quoniam uix uel raro est tam iusta conuersio, timendum est de pe-
100   nitente sero.

Fs 321ra   "Quem enim morbus urget et pena | terret ad ueram uix ueniet satisfactionem, maxime cum filii quos illicite dilexit sint presentes, uxor et mundus ad se uocet. Multos solet serotina penitentia decipere. Set quoniam Deus semper potens est, semper, etiam in morte,
105   iuuare ualet quibus placet. Cum itaque opus sit non hominis set Dei fructifera penitentia, inspirare eam potest quandocumque uult sua misericordia et remunerare ex misericordia quos dampnare potest ex iustitia. Set quoniam multa sunt que inpediunt et languen-
Aa 183v   tem retrahunt, periculosissimum | est et interitui uicinum ad mor-
110   tem protrahere penitentie remedium. Set magnum est cui Deus

88 tantum] tamen Aa Pf Sb_ac   **90** quoniam uix] quamuis Fs Sb quoniam uis Mk
92 hora] *add.* peccator Pf EdF   **93** qui] quod Fs Sb   **94** omni eius] homini eius
Fs hominibus Sb   **97** Deum] domini Bi Mk Sb   **101** et] *om.* Aa Bi Mk Pf
102 dilexit] dilexerit Aa Bi Fs Mk   **103** serotina] sera Fd *add.* uel serotina *interlin.* Fd   **109** interitui] interitu Fd Pf_ac Sb interitum Fs

"But those who never wanted to convert when they could and confess when they are no longer able to sin do not easily acquire in this fashion what they want. For penance should produce fruit in order to obtain life for the dead. It is written that no one is saved without love. Man does not thus live in fear alone. Therefore, he who repents at a late hour should not only fear God the Judge but love God the just; let him not only fear punishment but be anxious for glory. For he ought to grieve for his wicked deed and its every aforementioned aspect. Since this is only very narrowly permissible, Augustine was able to doubt the salvation of such a man.[2] Indeed, I believe him who said, *In whatever hour [the sinner] cries out and converts, he will live with life.* He said that he who converted, or turned round, not just turned, lives. Indeed, I regard the turned man as one who grieves for a wicked deed, the converted man as one who grieves for its every aspect, which we have explained. He is turned from sin who now wants to send his sin away; he is converted, that is, turned wholly and completely, who now not only fears punishments but hastens to strive for the Good, which is God. If this conversion happens to someone even at the end, there should be no despair about his remission. But since such a righteous conversion hardly or rarely exists, there should be fear concerning the one who repents in the last hour.

"For he whom sickness pushes and punishment terrifies will hardly come to true satisfaction, especially when the sons whom he has illicitly loved are present, when his wife and the world call to him. Last-minute penance has the habit of deceiving many. But since God is always powerful, he is always able, even in death, to help those whom it pleases him to help. Therefore, since fruitful penance is the work not of man but of God, by his mercy he is able to inspire it whenever he wants and to reward mercifully those whom he can damn justly. But since there are many things that impede and draw back the one who lingers, it is very dangerous and nigh near self-destruction to defer the cure of penance to death. But it is great for whom God inspires true penance at that

Ezek 33:12

cf. D.5 c.1

---

2. In this sentence, a text supposedly by Augustine refers to Augustine in the third person. This reference caused Renaissance humanists to question the authenticity of the text, and it has since that time been identified as an anonymous work. Scholars refer to the author(s) as Pseudo-Augustine simply because the work was throughout the Middle Ages attributed to Augustine.

Pf 127va   tunc inspirat—siquis | est—ueram penitentiam, quod exspectat Dei
clementiam, maiorem sentiens Dei bonitatem sua nequitia.

"Set si etiam sic conuersus uita uiuat et non moriatur, non promittimus quod euadat omnem penam. Nam prius purgandus est
115   igne purgationis qui in aliud seculum distulit fructum conuersionis.
Hic autem ignis, etsi eternus non sit, miro modo est grauis. Excellit
enim omnem penam quam umquam passus est in hac uita. Num-
Mk 255vb   quam in carne tanta inuenta est pena, | licet mirabilia martires passi
sint tormenta, et multi nequiter quanta sepe sustinuerunt supplicia.

120   "Studeat ergo quisque sic delicta corrigere ut post mortem non
oporteat penam tollerare. Quedam enim peccata sunt, que morta-
lia, in penitentia sunt uitalia, non tamen statim sanata: Sepe enim
est quod moreretur nisi medicaretur. Non statim sanatur; languet
uicturus qui prius erat moriturus. Qui autem inpenitens moritur
125   omnino moritur et eternaliter cruciatur. Qui enim inpenitens fini-
Sb 282rb   tur, si semper iuueret, | semper peccaret. At Dei est miserentis quod
operatur finem peccanti. Ob hoc etiam sine fine torquetur, quia
numquam uirtute ditatur. Semper plenus iniquitate, semper sine
caritate, torquetur sine fine."

---

111 inspiratsiquis estueram] quidem Sb *om.* EdF | quod] quem Pf qui EdF
113 conuersus] *add.* fuerit EdF Fs   **115** qui] quod Fs Pf   **116** Hic] Sic Fd Hinc
Mk_ac   **117** est] *add.* aliquis Aa_pc EdF   **119** sint] sunt Fs Sb   **129** fine] *add. in*
rubr. Finit de penitentia Aa

time—if there are any—because he waits on the clemency of God, perceiving that the goodness of God is greater than his wickedness.

"But if a man converted even in this way were to live with life and not die, we do not promise that he avoids all punishment. For he who delayed the fruit of penance in the other world must first be purged with the fire of purgation. This fire, however, even if it is not eternal, is severe in an astonishing way. For it exceeds every punishment that has ever been suffered in this life. Never has so great a punishment been found in the flesh, although marvelous martyrs have suffered torments, and many have often wickedly undergone punishments as great.

"Therefore, let each person make an effort to correct their offences in such a way that they do not have to tolerate punishment after death. For there are certain sins which, though mortal, become vital in penance, but are not immediately cleansed. For it is often the case that a person would die if he were not treated. He is not immediately healed; he who before was about to die is languid but will live. But he who dies impenitent dies completely and is eternally tormented. For if he who finishes his life impenitent were to live always, he would sin always. But it belongs to the compassion of God that he bring about the end of the sinner. He is also tortured without end on this account, because he is never enriched with virtue. Always full of iniquity, always lacking love, he is tortured without end."

Appendix A: C.30 q.3 in Sg

What follows is a transcription of the text of C.33 q.3 in Sg (Sankt Gall, Stiftsbibliothek 673). In this manuscript, the *causa* is numbered C.30. The text appears on pp. 183a–184b. In my "Evolution of Gratian's *Tractatus de penitentia*," I argued that this section of text provides evidence for the theory that Sg presents an earlier (pre-R1) redaction of Gratian's work and not an abbreviation of the "first recension."[1] John Wei's article on *De penitentia* DD.5–7 makes such a position, in its simplest form, untenable.[2] Nevertheless, what Wei proved was that D.7 c.2 in Sg must derive from the "second recension," not that Sg does not in some sense in a majority of its parts represent an earlier redaction. In other words, the story could be as simple as the theory put forward by Wei, namely that Sg is an abbreviation of the "first recension" with interpolations from the "second recension." The story could also be far more complex. Scholars such as Larrainzar, Pennington, and Viejo-Ximénez, who have defended the priority of Sg, have never claimed that Sg is simply an earlier version of the *Decretum* from which the first recension was directly derived.[3] Even if the manuscript's version of the *Decretum* con-

1. "The Evolution of Gratian's *Tractatus de penitentia*," BMCL 26 (2004–6): 59–123.

2. John Wei, "A Reconsideration of St. Gall, Stiftsbibliothek 673 (Sg) in Light of the Sources of Distinctions 5–7 of the *De penitentia*," BMCL 27 (2007): 141–80.

3. José Miguel Viejo-Ximénez, "*An inter uouentes possit esse matrimonium*: El texto de C.27 q.1 en los manuscritos antiguos del Decreto de Graciano," *Initium* 9 (2004): 77; idem, "La composición del Decreto de Graciano," *Ius Canonicum* 45, no. 90 (2005): 442; Carlos Larrainzar, "La investigación actual sobre el Decreto de Graciano," ZRG Kan. Abt. 90 (2004): 53; Kenneth Pennington, "Gratian, Causa 19, and the Birth of Canonical Jurisprudence," in *"Panta rei": Studi dedicati a Manlio Bellomo*, ed. Orazio Condorelli (Rome, 2004), 4:339–55.

tains texts from later stages and a stage approximating a fina ized
R2, it may still, in the majority of its parts, be a witness to an earlier,
pre-R1 stage of text. These R2 interpolations appear only after C.27.[4]
It is clear that, from that point on, Sg has a redacted text, so it seems
appropriate to print a separate transcription of the text of C.30 q.3
rather than incorporating its readings into the main edition.

If the scholarly community is ever to reach consensus on the nature of this manuscript, it must be comprehensively studied side-by-
side with early abbreviations of the *Decretum*.[5] Collations with other
twelfth-century manuscripts, not just Aa, Bc, Fd, and P, might also
provide some clarity.[6]

The transcription follows normalization principles outlined above
(pp. xl–xliii). In brackets are the canon or *capitulum* numbers from
Friedberg's edition and preserved in the inner margin of my edition.
As in the edition, R2 *additiones* (from D.6 and D.7) are in a smaller,
Scala typeface.

C.30 q.3 in Sg

[D.1 pr.] His decursis ad tertiam questionem accedamus, qua
quaesitum est si sola cordis contritione ac secreta satisfactione sine
oris confessione ecclesie et sacerdotali officio quisque Deo satisfacere possit.

[d.a.c.1] Et sunt nonnulli qui hoc asseuarent SECUNDUM ILLUD
LEONIS PAPE, [c.1] "Lacrimas Petri lego, satisfactio non lego." ITEM
CRISOSTOMUS, [c.2] "Lacrime lauant quod pudor est confiteri." ITEM
PROPHETA, [c.3] *Sacrifitiu deo spiritus contribulatus, etc.* Item, [c.4] *Dixi
confitebo aduersum me*, quod AUGUSTINUS EXPONIT, [c.5] "Magna pietas Domini ut ad solam promissionem peccata dimiserit. Nondum
pronuntiat ore et tamen Deus iam audit in corde, quia ipsum dicere quam si quoddam pronuntiare est, votum enim pro opere reputatur."

4. Pennington, "The Biography of Gratian," 689, 695.
5. Melodie H. Eichbauer's study of rubrics was a start ("St. Gall Stiftsbibliothek 673 and the Early Redactions of Gratian's *Decretum*," BMCL 27 [2007]: 105–
40), but see my reservations about comparing Sg with the later abbreviations she
does in *Master of Penance*, 19n44.
6. See my latest comments on Sg and recounting of the arguments about this
section in "Gratian's *De penitentia* in Twelfth-Century Manuscripts," 101–6.

[(c.30b)] Item sicut auctoritas testatur, uoluntas remuneratur, et non opus. Voluntas autem in cordis contritione est, opus uero in oris confessione. Liquido patet cordis contritione non oris confessione peccata dimitti—et multa alia in hoc modo.

[d.p.c.37] Fit ergo confessio in signum penitentie, non ad inpetrationem uenie, sicut et circumcisio data est Abrae in signum iustitie, non in causam iustificationis. Confessio sacerdoti offertur in signum uenie accepte, non in causam remissionis accipiende.

Alii contradicunt sine confessione oris et satisfactione operis neminem a peccato posse mundari, si tempus habeat satisfaciendi. Vnde et DOMINUS PER PROPHETAM, *Dic tu iniquitates tuas ut iustificeri* .

ITEM AMBROSIUS IN LIBER DE PARADISO, [c.38] "Non potest quisque iustificari a peccato ante confessionem." IDEM IN SERMONE QUADRAGESIMAE, [c.39] "Ecce nunc tempus adest[7] in quo confessio anima a morte liberat. Confessio aperit paradisum; confessio spem saluandi tribuit. Vnde *dic tu iniquitates tuas ut iustificeri* . His uerbum ostenditur quod non meretur iustificari qui in uita sua peccatum non uult confiteri. Illa confessio nos liberat quae fit cum penitentia. Penitentia uera est dolor cordis et amaritudo animae pro malis quae quis commisit. Penitentia est et mala preterita plangere et plangenda iterum non committere. ITEM IOHANNES OS AUREUM, [c.40] "Perfecta penitentia cogit peccatorem omnia libenter suffere. In corde eius est contritio, in ore confessio, in opere tota humilitas: hec est fructifera penitentia."

ITEM AUGUSTINUS, [c.42] "Nullus debite grauioris pene accipit ueniam nisi qualemcumque, etsi longe minorem quam debeat, soluerit penam. Ita enim inpertitur a deo largitas misericordie, ut non relinquatur iustitia disciplinae."

IDEM DE PENITENTIA: [c.44] "Agite penitentiam qualis agitur in ecclesia ut oret pro uobis ecclesia. Nemo dicat sibi, 'Occulte ago; nouit Deus, qui mihi ignoscit, quia in corde ago.' Ergo sine causa dictum est, *Quae solueritis in terra soluta erunt et in celo*. Ergo sine causa claues datae sunt ecclesiae dei frustramus euangelium Dei, frustramus uerba Christi, promittimus uobis quod ille negat. Nonne uos decipimus. Iob dicit, *Si erubui in conspectu populi peccata mea confiter* , etc."

7. All the manuscript gives is .a. The problem is that the text reads *acceptabile adest*, so it is impossible to determine which of the two words the scribe intended, but many manuscripts of the source read *adest* without *acceptabile*, and I take that reading here.

[D.6 d.p.c.1] Caueat sacerdos ne peccata penitentium aliis manifestet. Quod si fecerit, deponatur. Vnde Gregorius: [c.2] "Sacerdos ante omnia caueat, ne de his qui ei confitentur peccata sua alicui recitet quod ea confessus est, non propinquis, non extraneis, neque—quod absit!—pro aliquo scandalo. Nam si hoc fecerit, deponatur, et omnibus diebus uite sue ignominiosus peregrinando pergat."

[d.p.c.2] Quod autem dicitur, ut penitens eligat sacerdotem scientem ligare et soluere, uidetur esse contrarium ei quod in canonibus inuenitur, ut nemo uidelicet alterius parrochianum iudicare presumat. Sed aliud est fauore uel odio proprium sacerdotem contempnere, quod sacris canonibus prohibetur; aliud cecum uitare, quod ab hac auctoritate quisque facere monetur, ne, si cecus ceco ducatum prestet, ambo in foueam cadant.

Vnde Vrbanus II:

Cuilibet sacerdoti conmissum, nisi pro eius ignorantia, alter sacerdos ad penitentiam non suscipiat.

[c.3] "Placuit, ut deinceps nulli sacerdotum liceat quelibet conmissum alteri sacerdoti ad penitentiam suscipere sine eius consensu cui se prius conmisit, nisi pro illius ignorantia cui penitens prius confessus est. Qui uero contra hec statuta facere temptauerit gradus sui periculo subiacebit."

[D.7 d.a.c.1] Tempus uero penitentie est usque in ultimum articulum uite.

Vnde Leo papa, [c.1] "Nemo desperandus est dum in hoc corpore constitutus est quia nonnumquam quod diffidentia etatis differtur consilio maturiore perfic   ."

Quamquam de differentibus penitentiam Augustinus scribat, [c.2] "Si quis positus in ultima necessitate sue egritudinis uoluerit accipere penitentiam, et accipit, et mox reconciliabitur et hinc uadit, fateor uobis, non illi negamus quod petit, sed non presumimus quia bene hinc exit.

[Si[8] securus hinc exierit, ego nescio. Penitentiam dare possumus, securitatem autem dare non possumus. Numquid dico, 'Dampnabitur'? Sed nec dico, 'Liberabitur.' Vis ergo a dubio liberari? Vis quod incertum est euadere? Age penitentiam dum sanus es, etc."]

---

8. "Si securus hinc ... dum sanus es" is the section derived from what I have labeled in my edition R2b, that is, a late stage in the development of the "second recension."

Appendix B: Note on the Key Variant in D.4 d.p.c.24

As noted in the *apparatus* on the fourth distinction above (p. 245), the discussion of what I call the "intergenerational return of sins" (the sins of the fathers returning to the sons to be punished in them) in D.4 d.p.c.24 contains a significant variant in the manuscripts. I do not discuss the sentence or variant in question in my *Master of Penance*, so some commentary is in order here. Gratian argued in favor of the intergenerational return of sins in this sense, namely that sons who repeat or imitate their fathers' offences will be punished for the same offences. The sons are not punished for their fathers' sins but for their own sins in imitation of their fathers' sins. And, in this sense, the sons of the fathers become alive for punishment in the sons, and one can speak of the sins of the fathers returning to the sons.

In D.4 d.p.c.24, when Gratian turned to explain the passage from Gregory the Great (D.4 c.13) used to support the idea that forgiven sins do *not* return, he wrote a sentence reading, "But the iniquity of the parents is *not* said to return to those in whom the sins of the parent come alive again by virtue of their own iniquity." This would seem to be a very strange sentence coming from the pen of someone defending the idea that the sins of parents *do* return in some sense to the sons. After all, just a few sentences earlier, Gratian had written, "By these authorities the sons, having been expiated from original sin, are taught that they are not to be punished for the reason that their fathers sinned, but that the sins of their fathers *do return to them* for the reason that they follow their guilt." Nevertheless, for the later sentence, Fd, Aa, Bi, Pf, and Sb all read, "But the iniquity of the parents is *not* said to return..." In order to rectify an apparent contradiction, some later scribes (including the scribe of Mk) and later editions (including Friedberg's), added a second "not" to the second half of the sentence: "But the iniquity of the parents is *not* said to return to those in whom the sins of the parent do *not* come alive again by virtue of their own iniquity." That change would seem to make the sentence congruent with Gratian's opening sentence of the paragraph. It is not, however, what Gratian originally wrote.

So how should scholars understand Gratian's original? In short, it was part of a concise exercise in the *concordia* of discordant *auctoritates*. He was teaching his students how one could explain Gregory's text so that it would not stand opposed to his position. The two sentences in d.p.c.24 following his citation to Gregory's text (D.4 c.13) followed Gregory's text quite closely. Gregory had written, "[God] will return the iniquity of the fathers on the sons when the soul of the progeny is polluted from original sin for the guilt of the parent. And, again, he does not return the iniquity of the fathers on the sons, because, when we are liberated from original guilt through baptism, we do not now have the guilty acts of our parents but those which we ourselves commit." Gratian wanted to use the text to say that, yes, the sins of the fathers do become alive again for punishment in the sons, just as one's own personal sins become alive again for punishment, after someone commits further sins without repentance. The person is punished for his own sin, or, as Gratian phrases it here, the punishment will come "based on the merit of his own iniquity" (equivalent to Gregory's emphasis that we are punished for the guilty acts that "we ourselves commit"). To reconcile Gregory's text to his position, however, Gratian was suggesting that one could read Yahweh's Exodus warning "to return the iniquity of the fathers on the sons and grandsons" as referring to original sin that is never eradicated in the son through baptism (i.e., in the case where a son is never baptized). Gregory had explicitly connected the Exodus text to original sin. Gratian followed that train of thought, affirming that, for those who have not been baptized and thus not been cleansed from original sin, they will be punished in eternity for that original sin and thus for the sins of their parents, to whom they are united (Gregory said that the sons "are one" with the parents). As Gratian put it, the unbaptized sons "draw along in their root [or at their core] the bitterness of sin"—a poetic rendering of the concept of original sin. In other words, Gratian was saying that one could read the Exodus text about the iniquity of the fathers returning on future generations purely in terms of original sin, as applying to those who have not been baptized. In this sense, then, for anyone who has been baptized (i.e., anyone in the visible church), the iniquity of the fathers is not returned on them; rather, if they sin in the future without repentance, they will be punished for their sins alone. The iniquity of the fathers is *not returned* to them, but it does *"become alive in them again* by virtue of their own iniquity."

In the next and final paragraph of the distinction, Gratian argued that even original sin will be punished in those who return unrepentantly to sin, for David confessed his original sin along with his actual sins after his adultery with Bathsheba and his murder of Uriah. Perhaps Gratian was being less than consistent. The most charitable reading of Gratian in this section would view him as expressing a preference for what language should be used to describe the spiritual realities at issue. Based on his reading of Gregory's passage, which was fairly straightforward, he saw the Exodus language of "the iniquity of fathers returning on the sons" as referring to the case of unbelievers who have never been cleansed of original sin; the language should not be (or at least could be read as not being) applied to the apostate who face God's wrath for their own sins and ultimate lack of repentance. If one wanted to speak about how sins from one generation return for punishment in the succeeding generations, Gratian preferred the language of the sins of the fathers "becoming alive again." Actual sins of the fathers become alive again when their sons imitate those transgressions, and even original sin becomes alive again, meriting punishment, when humans commit offences against God here and now and do not repent of them. All in all, given the nuanced reading of Gratian I am suggesting, one cannot be surprised that many scribes and editors added an additional *non* to Gratian's text in D.4 d.p.c.24.

Appendix C: Possible Formal Sources and Other Related Texts

The following table presents important texts with which scholars might fruitfully compare individual sections of *De penitentia*. John Wei laid the groundwork for this table in his dissertation and subsequent articles. I disagree with several of Wei's identifications of Gratian's formal sources (that is, collections from which Gratian directly copied his *auctoritates*), and so I have made some alterations. I have also added several items, including sources or similar contemporary texts for sections identified as Gratian's *dicta*, some of which are all Gratian's own words and some of which include quotations from other authors. References in **bold** indicate texts that I am confident did serve as Gratian's formal source. All other references (preceded by "cf.") should be considered (1) a possible formal source, (2) a text that shared a common source with Gratian's *De penitentia*, or (3) a text that drew on *De penitentia* (i.e., for which *De penitentia* served as its formal source). This table should not be considered definitive; future research will undoubtedly uncover additional near-contemporary texts that overlap with *De penitentia* as well as possibly more certainty about his formal sources.

Each text is identified as belonging to stage R1, R2a (i.e., present in FdB, or the *additiones bononienses*), [post-R2a] (i.e., present in FdG, the margins of Fd or FdB), or {post-R2a} (i.e., not present anywhere in Fd).

Table C–1. Possible Formal Sources and Related Texts

De penitentia Text	Recension	Related Texts
D.1 c.5	R1	cf. *Gl. Ord. in* Ps. 31:6 (ed. Rusch, 2.490–91)[1]
D.1 c.23	R2a	cf. Ans. 11.38
D.1 c.24	R2a	cf. Ans. 11.36, 3L 3.13.2, 9L 8.4.2[2]
D.1 c.25	R2a	**3L 3.13.12**; cf. 9L 8.4.12
D.1 c.26	R2a	**3L 3.13.16**; cf. 9L 8.4.15
D.1 c.27	R2a	**3L 3.13.17**; cf. 9L 8.4.16
D.1 c.28	R2a	**3L 3.13.18**; cf. 9L 8.4.17
D.1 c.29	R2a	cf. 3L 3.15.17, 9L 9.1.14
D.1 cc.31–32	R1	directly from material source (Jul. Pom.)
D.1 c.35	R1	***Gl. ord. in* Ps. 70:17** (ed. Rusch, 2.542)
D.1 c.39	R1	directly from material source (*Coll. Sermonum ps.-Ambr.*)
D.1 c.41	{post-R2a}	cf. 3L 3.7.66, 9L 7.6.45, *De cons.* D.4 c.4
D.1 c.42	R1	cf. Ans. 11.124
D.1 c.43	R1	cf. Ans. 11.148
D.1 c.44	R1	cf. 3L 3.19.82
D.1 c.45	R2a	cf. 3L A40.29
D.1 c.46	R2a	cf. 3L A40.41
D.1 c.47 … noluit flagellari	R2a	cf. 3L A40.43
D.1 c.47 Nam pastor … futurum?	R2a	cf. 3L A40.44
D.1 c.48	R2a	cf. 3L A40.45
D.1 c.49	R1	**Ans. 11.11**
D.1 c.50	R1	**Ans. 11.152**
D.1 c.51 Verbum Dei … iudex.	[post-R2a]	cf. within Bh 7
D.1 c.51 Dominus par … c.52	R1	**Ans. 11.152**
D.1 c.53	R2a	**3L 3.19.89**
D.1 cc.54–56 esse debere.	R1	**Ans. 11.152**
D.1 c.56 Nam si … absoluere	R2a	**3L 3.19.95**
D.1 c.56 Nichil est … defluxerit	R1	**Ans. 11.152**
D.1 c.57	R2a	**3L 3.19.114**
D.1 c.58	R2a	**3L 3.19.116**
D.1 c.59 … orabit pro eo?	R2a	cf. D.50 c.67, Trip. 1.45.9
D.1 d.p.c.60 Puteus est … perit confessio. (Aug. Hipp.)	R1	***Gl. ord. in* Ps. 68:16** (*interlin. et marg.*, ed. Rusch, 2.538b)

1. For most works, texts are easy to locate in their edition (see bibliography) using the standard numbering; this is not always so in the edition of the *Glossa ordinaria*, and therefore for these references the page and sometimes column number in the edition are cited.

2. 9L, or the *Collectio nouum librorum* (in Città del Vaticana, Archivio S. Pietro C.118 and Berlin, Staatsbibliothek lat. fol. 552), has not been edited but is known to derive from 3L; the numbering here follows the numbering of 9L texts utilized by Giuseppe Motta in his edition of 3L. On 9L, see Kéry, *Canonical Collections of the Early Middle Ages*, 271–72.

D.1 c.61	R1	cf. within 3L 3.19.19, 9L 9.5.18
D.1 c.62	R1	**3L 3.19.21**; cf. 9L 9.5.20
D.1 c.63	R1	cf. 3L 3.19.99, 9L 9.5.87
D.1 c.64	R1	**3L 3.19.41**; cf. 9L 9.5.40
D.1 c.65	R1	**3L 3.19.50**; cf. 9L 9.5.49
D.1 c.66	R1	**3L 3.19.59**; cf. 9L 9.5.57
D.1 c.67	R1	**3L 3.19.61**; cf. 9L 9.5.59
D.1 c.68	R1	**3L 3.19.86**; cf. 9L 9.5.76
D.1 c.69	R2a	**3L 3.19.110**; cf. 9L 9.5.98
D.1 c.70	R2a	**3L 3.19.103**; cf. 9L 9.5.91
D.1 c.71	R2a	**3L 3.19.80**; cf. 9L 9.5.71
D.1 c.72	R2a	**3L 3.19.81**; cf. 9L 9.5.72
D.1 c.73	R2a	**3L 3.19.55**; cf. 9L 9.5.54
D.1 c.74	R2a	**3L 3.19.58**; cf. 9L 9.5.56
D.1 c.75	R2a	cf. 3L 3.19.87
D.1 c.77	R2a	**3L 3.19.100**; cf. 9L 9.5.88
D.1 c.78	R1	**3L 3.19.88**; cf. 9L 9.5.77
D.1 c.79	R1	**3L 3.19.91**; cf. 9L 9.5.81
D.1 c.80	R1	**3L 3.19.93**; cf. 9L 9.5.82
D.1 c.81 … non iudicaremur.	R1	**3L 3.19.98**; cf. 9L 9.5.86
D.1 c.81 Est etiam … cessamus.	R2a	cf. Ans. 11.1
D.1 c.82	R2a	cf. 3L 3.19.28, 9L 9.5.27
D.1 c.83	R2a	cf. Ans. 11.140
D.1 cc.84–85	R2a	cf. Trip. 3.28.3–4
D.1 c.86	R2a	cf. 3L 3.19.16, 9L 9.5.15
D.1 c.87	R1	**3L 3.19.97**; cf. 9L 9.5.85
D.1 d.p.c.87 Est enim penitentia alia interior … gratis condonat. (Gratian, Acts 2:38, Ambr. Med.)	R1	cf. *Summa sententiarum* 5.5, *Gl. ord. in* Rom. 11:29 (*interlin.*, ed. Rusch, 4.298b)
D.1 d.p.c.87 Gratia Dei … gratis condonat. (Ambr. Med.)	R1	**Gl. ord. in Rom. 11:29** (ed. Rusch, 4.298b)
D.1 d.p.c.87 Quoniam iniqui-tatem … non dissimulo. (Aug. Hipp.)	R1	**Gl. ord. in Ps. 50:5** (*interlin. et marg.*, ed. Rusch, 2.515b)
D.1 d.p.c.87 Sic Deus … punitur. (Aug. Hipp.)	R1	**Gl. ord. in Ps. 50:8** (ed. Rusch, 2.516a)
D.1 d.p.c.87 Veritas de terra … penitenti. (Aug. Hipp.)	R1	**Gl. ord. in Ps. 84:12** (ed. Rusch, 2.564b)
D.1 d.p.c.87 Et publica noxa … remedio. (Aug. Hipp.)	R1	**Gl. ord. in Marcum 5** (ed. Rusch, 4.153a)
D.1 c.88	R1	directly from material source (*De uera*)
D.1 c.89	R2a	**Trip. 1.43.42**
D.1 c.90	R2a	**Trip. 3.28.12**
D.2 c.1	R2a	cf. Trip. 2.17.12

D.2 c.2	R1	cf. F38
D.2 c.4	R1	directly from material source? (Greg. Magn.)
D.2 c.5	R1	directly from material source (Jul. Pom.)
D.2 c.7	R1	cf. *Vt autem* l.38
D.2 c.12	R1	**Gl. ord. in 2 Cor 6:6** (ed. Rusch, 4.345)
D.2 c.13	R1	cf. F21
D.2 c.14	R1	cf. F16b
D.2 c.15	R1	directly from material source? (Greg. Magn.)
D.2 c.16	R1	cf. *Vt autem* ll.278–92
D.2 c.18	R1	cf. F56, *Vt autem* ll.292–94
D.2 c.17 crescit … conuerso.	R1	cf. *Vt autem* l.294
D.2 cc.19–20	R1	cf. *Vt autem* ll.294–300
D.2 c.21	R2a	**3L 3.19.63**
D.2 c.22	R2a	**3L 3.19.78**
D.2 c.23	R2a	**3L 3.19.79**
D.2 d.p.c.24 Quicumque ab illa –D.2 c.29	R1	cf. *Vt autem* ll.108–113
D.2 c.30	R1	cf. *Vt autem* l.16
D.2 c.31	R1	cf. *Vt autem* ll.45–57
D.2 c.33	R1	cf. F88, *Vt autem* ll.61–62
D.2 c.34	R1	cf. F89, *Vt autem* ll.63–64
D.2 c.35	R1	cf. F91, *Vt autem* ll.65–70
D.2 c.36	R1	cf. F94, *Vt autem* ll.71–72
D.2 c.37	R1	cf. F94, *Vt autem* ll.73–77
D.2 c.38	R1	cf. F96, *Vt autem* ll.78–79
D.2 c.39	R1	cf. F98, *Vt autem* ll.80–81
D.2 d.p.c.39 Qui tamen ad aquam … leue uideatur (Gratian)	R1	cf. *Vt autem* ll.90–92
D.2 d.p.c.39 Fugerat sanctus … adherebat Deo (Ambr. Med.)	R1	cf. *Vt autem* ll.93–95
D.2 c.40	R1	directly from material source (Hier.)
D.2 c.41	R1	cf. *Vt autem* ll.138–51
D.2 d.p.c.41	R1	cf. *Vt autem* ll.152–54
D.2 c.42 Mirandum … perseuerantiam.	R1	cf. *Vt autem* ll. 311–12, 351–52
D.2 c.42 Non qui … saluus erit.	R1	cf. *Vt autem* l.357
D.2 c.43	R1	cf. *Gl. ord. in* 2 Chr. 9:29 (ed. Rusch, 2.234b), *Vt autem* l.358
D.2 c.44	R1	directly from material source (Greg. Magn.)
D.2 d.p.c.44 Angelice … perstiterunt; Vnde bene … est confirmat	R1	**Gl. ord. in Gen. 1:6** (ed. Rusch, 1.10b)
D.2 c.45	R1	directly from material source (Greg. Magn.)
D.3 c.1	R1	directly from material source (*Coll. sermonum ps.-Ambr.*)

D.3 c.2	R1	cf. F107, Bh 16
D.3 c.3	R1	cf. F16
D.3 cc.4–5	R1	directly from material source (*De uera*)
D.3 c.6 … estibus anhelat?	R1	cf. F119, Bh 13
D.3 c.7	{post-R2a}	cf. 3L A40.26
D.3 c.8	R1	cf. F129
D.3 c.9	R1	cf. F130
D.3 c.10	R1	cf. F116, Bh 11
D.3 c.11	R1	cf. F126
D.3 c.12	R1	cf. F127, Bh 12
D.3 c.13	R1	cf. F122, Bh 14
D.3 cc.14–16	R1	cf. F122
D.3 c.17	R1	cf. F123
D.3 d.p.c.17 … flere oporteat	R1	cf. Bh 33–34
D.3 c.18	R2a	cf. Ans. 11.28, 3L 3.19.104, 9L 9.5.92
D.3 c.19	R2a	cf. 3L 3.19.106, 9L 9.5.94
D.3 c.20	R2a	cf. 3L 3.19.105, 9L 9.5.93
D.3 c.21	R2a	cf. Ans. 11.6, 3L 3.8.22, 9L 7.7.16
D.3 d.p.c.21 Illud autem … non reiteratur.	R1	cf. Bh 36
D.3 c.22	R1	cf. F111
D.3 c.30	R1	*Gl. ord. in Jonam, Prol.* (München, Bayerische Staatsbibliothek lat. 16005, f.61v)
D.3 c.31	R1	*Gl. ord. in Naum, Prol.* (ed. Rusch, 3.412b)
D.3 c.32	R1	directly from material source (*De uera*)
D.3 c.33	R1	cf. F111
D.3 cc.34–35	R1	*Gl. ord. in* Lev. 10:16 (ed. Rusch, 1.235a)
D.3 c.36	[post-R2a]	cf. 3L 3.19.109, 9L 9.5.97
D.3 c.37	[post-R2a]	cf. 3L 3.19.94, 9L 9.5.83
D.3 c.40	R1	cf. F102, Bh 18
D.3 c.41	R1	*Gl. ord. in* Ps. 118:137 (ed. Rusch, 2.618b)
D.3 d.p.c.41	R1	cf. Bh 25, Bh 24
D.3 c.42	R1	directly from material source (*De uera*)
D.3 d.p.c.42 … eternum punirentur	R1	cf. *Gl. ord. in* Naum 1:9 (ed. Rusch, 3.413b)
D.3 c.43	R1	cf. *Gl. ord. in* Deut. 32:22 (*interlin. et marg.,* ed. Rusch, 1.421a)
D.3 c.44	R1	*Gl. ord. in* Naum 1:9 (ed. Rusch, 3.414a)
D.3 d.p.c.44 conscientia peccati	R1	cf. *Gl. ord. in* Ps. 118:137 (ed. Rusch, 2.618b)
D.3 c.45	R1	directly from material source (*De uera*)
D.3 c.46	R1	cf. *Vt autem* ll.165–67
D.3 c.47	R1	cf. *Vt autem* ll.160–64
D.3 c.48	R2a	cf. 3L A4.21

D.3 c.49	R1	cf. F20, *Sententie Sidonis* 12.119
D.3 d.p.c.49 Illud autem ... non reiteratur.	R1	cf. Bh 37
D.4 c.1	R1	cf. F113–114
D.4 c.2	R1	cf. F125
D.4 cc.3–4	R1	cf. F115
D.4 c.7	R1	*Gl. ord. in Deut.* **24:16** (ed. Rusch, 1.407b)
D.4 d.p.c.7	R1	*Gl. ord. in Rom.* **9:23** (ed. Rusch, 4.294b–295a), cf. Ans. Laud., *Sententia* 34 (ed. Lottin, 35)
D.4 c.8	R1	directly from material source (Aug. Hipp.)
D.4 c.10	R1	*Gl. ord. in 2 Tim.* **2:19** (ed. Rusch, 4.415a)
D.4 c.11	R1	*Gl. ord. in Ioh.* **14:2–3** (ed. Rusch, 4.257b)
D.4 d.p.c.11 Vt enim ... benedictione etc.	R1	*Gl. ord. in Eph.* **1:3–6** (interlin. et marg., ed. Rusch, 4.369), cf. Ans. Laud., *Sententia* 11 (ed. Lottin, 22)
D.4 (c.12) Modo tantum ... beatitudinis eterne (Aug. Hipp.)	R1	*Gl. ord. in Rom.* **8:21** (ed. Rusch, 4.291)
D.4 c.13	R1	*Gl. ord. in Ex.* **34:7** (ed. Rusch, 1.196b)
D.4 c.14	R1	cf. F106
D.4 c.15	R1	cf. F117, F138
D.4 c.16	R1	cf. F138, *Gl. ord. in Ez.* 3:20 (ed. Rusch, 3.231a)
D.4 c.17	R1	cf. F139
D.4 c.22	R1	*Gl. ord. in Hos.* **7:2** (interlin., ed. Rusch, 3.362b)
D.4 c.23	R1	*Gl. ord. in Hos.* **7:2** (marg., ed. Rusch, 3.362b)
D.4 c.24	{post-R2a}	cf. Trip. 1.46.55
D.5 c.1	R1	directly from material source (*De uera*)
D.5 c.2	R2a	cf. Trip. 1.43.14, Ans. 11.121, 3L 3.19.22, 9L 9.5.21
D.5 c.3	R2a	cf. Trip. 1.43.15, Ans. 11.129, 3L 3.19.23, 9L 9.5.22
D.5 c.4	R2a	cf. Trip. 2.1.11
D.5 c.5	R2a	cf. Trip. 2.32.7
D.5 c.6	R2a	cf. Polyc. 6.19.29, 3L 3.19.62, 9L 9.5.60
D.5 c.7	R2a	cf. Ans. 11.122
D.5 c.8	R2a	directly from material source? (copy of Lateran II canons?)
D.6 c.1	R1	directly from material source (*De uera*)
D.6 c.2	R2a	cf. Ans. 11.23, Polyc. 6.19.9, 3L 3.19.18, 9L 9.5.17
D.7 c.1	R2a	cf. Trip. 1.43.11, 3L 3.19.36, 9L 9.5.35
D.7 c.2	R1	cf. 3L 3.19.37, 9L 9.5.36
D.7 c.2 Si securus ... Si autem	[post-R2a] (R2b)	cf. Trip. 3.28.2
D.7 cc.3–4	R2a	**3L 3.19.37**; cf. 9L 9.5.36
D.7 c.6	R1	directly from material source (*De uera*)

Bibliography

Primary Sources

Algerus Leodiensis. *Liber de misericordia et iustitia. Alger von Lüttichs Traktat "De misericordia et iustitia": Ein kanonistischer Konkordanzversuch aus der Zeit des Investiturstreits. Untersuchungen und Edition,* edited by Robert Kretzschmar. Quellen und Forschungen zum Recht im Mittelalter 2. Sigmaringen: Jan Thorbecke, 1985.

Ambrosiaster. *Commentarius in Pauli epistulam ad Romanos (recensio gamma),* edited by H. J. Vogels. CSEL 81.1. Turnhout: Brepols, 1966.

———. *Commentarius in Pauli epistulas ad Galatas, ad Ephesios, ad Philippenses, ad Colossenses, ad Thessalonicenses, ad Timotheum, ad Titium, ad Philemonem (recensiones alpha et gamma),* edited by H. J. Vogels. Turnhout: Brepols, 1969.

Ambrosius Mediolanensis. *De Apologia David ad Theodoxium Augustum,* edited by P. Hadot, 299–355. SChr 239. (Paris: Éditions du Cerf, 1977). Also ed. C. Schenkl. CSEL 32.2. Turnhout: Brepols, 1897.

———. *De Cain et Abel,* edited by C. Schenkl, 339–409. CSEL 32.1. Turnhout: Brepols, 1897.

———. *De fuga saeculi,* edited by C. Schenkl, 163–207. CSEL 32.2. Turnhout: Brepols, 1897.

———. *De Helia et ieiunio,* edited by C. Schenkl, 411–65. CSEL 32.2. Turnhout: Brepols, 1897.

———. *De Isaac vel anima,* edited by C. Schenkl, 641–700. CSEL 32.1. Turnhout: Brepols, 1897.

———. *De Nabuthae,* edited by C. Schenkl, 413–97. CSEL 32.2. Turnhout: Brepols, 1897.

———. *De paenitentia.* Under title: *La pénitence.* Ed. and trans. Roger Gryson. Sources chrétiennes 179. Paris: Éditions du Cerf, 1971.

———. *De paradiso,* edited by C. Schenkl, 263–336. CSEL 32.1. Turnhout: Brepols, 1897.

———. *Expositio euangelii secundum Lucam,* edited by M. Adriaen, 1–400. CCSL 14. Turnhout: Brepols, 1957.

Augustinus Hipponensis. *Contra Cresconium,* edited by M. Petschenig, 325–582. CSEL 52. Turnhout: Brepols, 1909.

———. *Contra Faustum,* edited by J. Zycha, 251–797. CSEL 25. Turnhout: Brepols, 1891.

———. *De consensus evangelistarum*, edited by F. Weihrich. CSEL 43. Turnhout: Brepols, 1904.

———. *De correptione et gratia*. PL 44:915–46.

———. *De diuersis quaestionibus octaginta tribus*, edited by A. Mutzenbecher. CCSL 44A. Turnhout: Brepols, 1975.

———. *De Genesi ad litteram libri duodecim*, edited by J. Zycha. CSEL 28.1. Turnhout: Brepols, 1894.

———. *De gratia et libero arbitrio*. PL 44:881–912.

———. *De libero arbitrio*, edited by W. M. Green, 211–321. CCSL 29. Turnhout: Brepols, 1970.

———. *De peccatorum meritis et remissione et de baptismo paruulorum*, edited by C. R. Vrba and J. Zycha, 3–151. CSEL 60. Turnhout: Brepols, 1913.

———. *De sermone Domini in monte*, edited by A. Mutzenbecher. CCSL 35. Turnhout: Brepols, 1967.

———. *De trinitate*, edited by W. J. Mountain. CCSL 50, 50A. Turnhout: Brepols, 1968.

———. *Enarrationes in Psalmos*, edited by E. Dekkers and J. Fraipont. CCSL 38–40. Turnhout: Brepols, 1956.

———. *Enchiridion de fid , spe, et caritate*, edited by E. Evans, 49–114. CCSL 46. Turnhout: Brepols, 1969.

———. *Epistulae*, edited by A. Goldbacher. CSEL 34.1, 34.2, 44, 57, 58. Turnhout: Brepols, 1895–98.

———. *In Iohannis epistulam ad Parthos tractatus*. PL 35.

———. *In Iohannis evangelium tractatus CXXIV*, edited by R. Willems. CCSL 36. Turnhout: Brepols, 1954.

———. *Quaestionum in heptateuchum libri septem*, edited by J. Fraipont. CCSL 33. Turnhout: Brepols, 1958.

———. *Sermones*. PL 38–39.

———. *Sermones de Vetere Testamento*, edited by C. Lambot. CCSL 41. Turnhout: Brepols: 1961.

Baptizato homine. In John Wei. "Penitential Theology in Gratian's Decretum: Critique and Criticism of the Treatise Baptizato homine." ZRG Kan. Abt. 95 (2009): 78–100.

Basilius Caesarius (trans. Rufinus). *Regula*, edited by K. Zelzer, 5–221. CSEL 86. Turnhout: Brepols, 1986.

Beda Uenerabilis. *In Lucae evangelium exposition*, edited by D. Hurst, 5–425. CCSL 120. Turnhout: Brepols, 1960.

———. *Homiliarum evangelii libri ii*, edited by D. Hurst, 1–378. CCSL 122. Turnhout: Brepols, 1955.

Biblia latina cum Glossa ordinaria: Facsimile Reprint of the Editio princeps, Adolph Rusch of Strassburg, 1480/81. Introduction by Karlfried Froehlich and Margaret T. Gibson. Turnhout: Brepols, 1992.

Caesarius Arelatensis. *Sermones ex integro a Caesario composite vel ex aliis fontibus haust*, edited by G. Morin. CCSL 103. Turnhout: Brepols, 1953.

Cassiodorus. *Expositio psalmorum*, edited by M. Adriaen. CCSL 97. Turnhout: Brepols, 1958.

Chromatius Aquileiensis. *Tractatus in Matthaeum*, edited by R. Étaiz and J. Lemarié, 185–489. CCSL 9A. Turnhout: Brepols, 1974.

Codex iustinianus, edited by Paul Krueger. Berlin: Weidmann, 1877.

Collectio canonum trium librorum. Pars altera: Liber III et Appendix, edited by Joseph Motta. MIC Ser. B. Vol. 8.2. Vatican City: Biblioteca Apostolica Vaticana, 2008.

Collectio nouem librorum. Berlin, Staatsbibliothek Preußischer Kulturbesitz, lat. fol. 553 and Città del Vaticano, Archivio di San Pietro C.118.

Collectio tripartita. Working edition by Martin Brett and Przemysław Nowak. Available at http://project.knowledgeforge.net/ivo/tripartita.html.

Concilia aevi karolini. Vol. 1.1, edited by Albert Werminghoff. MGH Conc. 2.1. Hannover: Hahn, 1906.

Concilia Galliae 511–695, edited by C. de Clerq. CCSL 148A. Turnhout: Brepols, 1963.

"Concilium Lateranense II." Ed. Thomas Izbicki, 95–114. COGD 2.1. Turnhout: Brepols, 2013.

"Concilium Nicenum." Ed. Giuseppe Alberigo, 1–34. COGD 1. Turnhout: Brepols, 2007.

Cyprianus Carthaginensis. *Epistulae,* edited by G. F. Diercks. CCSL 3B. Turnhout: Brepols, 1994.

Decretales pseudo-isidorianae et Capitula Angilramni, edited by Paul Hinschius. Leipzig: Tauchnitz, 1863.

Digesta. The Digest of Justinian, edited by Theodor Mommsen with Paul Krueger. Trans. Alan Watson. 4 volumes. Philadelphia: University of Pennsylvania Press, 1985.

Dionysius Areopagita (trans. Iohannes Scotus Eriugena). *De diuinis nominibus.* In *Dionysiaca: Recueil donnant l'ensemble des traductions latines des ouvrages attribués au Denys de l'aréopage, et synopse marquant la valeur de citations presque innombrables allant seules depuis trop longtemps; remises enfi dans leur contexte au moyen d'une nomenclature rendue d'un usage très facile,* edited by Philippe Chevallier et al., 5–561, line E. Paris: Desclée, 1937.

Gelasius. *Epistola ad Gerontium, Johannem, Germanum, et Petrum episcopum.* In *Epistolae romanorum pontificu genuinae et quae ad eos scriptae sunt a S. Hilaro usque ad Pelagium II,* edited by Andreas Thiel, 1.706. Braunsberg: Eduard Peter, 1868.

Gennadius Massiliensis. *De viris inlustribus,* edited by E. C. Richardson. TU 14.1a. Leipzig: J. C. Hinrichs, 1896.

Gratian. *Decretum magistri Gratiani,* edited by Emil Friedberg. Volume 1 of *Corpus iuris canonici.* Leipzig: B. Tauchnitz, 1879. Repr. Graz: Akademische Druck und Verlagsanstalt, 1959.

———. *The Treatise on Laws (Decretum DD.1–20) with Ordinary Gloss.* Trans. Augustine Thompson, O.P. and James Gordley. Introduction by Katherine Christensen. Studies in Medieval and Early Modern Canon Law 2. Washington D.C.: The Catholic University of America Press, 1993.

Gregorius Magnus (Gregory I, Pope). *Dialogorum libri iv,* edited by A. de Vogüé. SChr 260. Paris: Éditions du Cerf, 1979.

———. *Homiliae in evangelia,* edited by R. Etaiz. CCSL 141. Turnhout: Brepols, 1999.

———. *Homiliae in Hiezechihelem prophetam,* edited by M. Adriaen. CCSL 142. Turnhout: Brepols, 1971.

———. *Moralia in Iob,* edited by M. Adriaen. CCSL 143, 143A, 143B. Turnhout: Brepols, 1979–85.

————. *Registrum epistularum*, edited by D. Norberg. CCSL 140, 140A. Turnhout: Brepols, 1982.

————. *Regula pastoralis. La règle pastorale*, edited by F. Rommel. Trans. C. Morel. SChr 381–82. Paris: Éditions du Cerf, 1992.

Gregory VII, Pope. *Das Register Gregors VII*, edited by Erich Caspar. MGH Epp. 2.2. Berlin: Weidmann, 1923.

Haymo Antisiodorensis (wrongly attributed to Haymo Halberstatensis). *Sermones*. PL 118.

Hieronimus. *Aduersus Jovinianum*. PL 23:221–532.

————. *Commentarii in Danielem*, edited by F. Glorie. CCSL 75A. Turnhout: Brepols, 1964.

————. *Commentarii in Ezechielem*, edited by F. Glorie, 3–743. CCSL 75. Turnhout: Brepols, 1964.

————. *Commentarii in prophetas minores, edited by* M. Adriaen. CCSL 76, 76A. Turnhout: Brepols, 1969–70.

————. *Epistulae*, edited by I. Hilberg. CSEL 54–56. Turnhout: Brepols, 1910–18.

Ioannes Chrysostomus. *In epistolam ad Hebraeos homiliae*. Ed. J.-P. Migne. PG 63. Paris, 1860.

Isidorus Hispalensis. *De ecclesiasticis officii* , edited by C. W. Lawson. CCSL 113. Turnhout: Brepols, 1989.

————. *Synonyma de lamentatione animae peccatricis*. PL 83:827–68.

————. *Sententiae*, edited by P. Cazier. CCSL 111. Turnhout: Brepols, 1998.

Julianus Pomerius (wrongly attributed to Prosper of Aquitaine). *De vita contemplativa*. PL 59:415–520.

Die Konzilien der karolingischen Teilreiche 843–859, edited by Wilfried Hartmann. MGH Conc. 3. Hannover: Hahn, 1984.

Leo I. *Epistolae*. PL 54.

Lottin, Odo, ed. *Psychologie et morale aux XIIe et XIIIe siècles.* Vol. 5. *Problèmes d'histoire littéraire: L'école d'Anselme de Laon et de Guillaume de Champeaux.* Gembloux: J. Duculot, 1959.

Mercier, Paul, ed. *XIV homélies du IXe siècle.* SChr 161. Paris: Éditions du Cerf, 1970.

Origenes (trans. Rufinus). *In Exodum homiliae.* In *Origenes Werke*, edited by W. A. Baehrens. Volume 6: *Homilien zum Hexateuch in Rufin Übersetzung.* Part 1: *Die Homilien zu Genesis, Exodus und Leviticus.* Die Griechischen Christlichen Schriftsteller der ersten drei Jahrhunderte 29. Leipzig: J. C. Hinrichs, 1920.

Paulinus Aquileiensis. *Contra Felicem libri tres*, edited by D. Norberg. CCCM 95. Turnhout: Brepols, 1990.

Prosper Aquitanus. *Pro Augustino responsiones*. PL 45.

Pseudo-Augustine. *De uera et falsa penitentia*. PL 40 and in Karen Wagner. "De vera et falsa penitentia: An Edition and Study." Ph.D. diss.: University of Toronto, 1995.

Schmitz, Hermann J., ed., *Die Bussbücher und die Bussdisciplin der Kirche.* 2 volumes. Mainz: Franz Kirchheim, 1883–98.

Sententie de caritate et penitentia. Firenze, Biblioteca Medicea Laurenziana, Plut. V sin 7, fols. 70ra–84rb.

Summa sententiarum. PL 176:41–172.

Urban II, Pope. *The Councils of Urban II.* Vol. 1, *Decreta Claromontensia,* edited by Robert Somerville. Annuarium historiae conciliorum, Supplement I. Amsterdam: Adolf M. Hakkert, 1972.

Vt autem hoc euidenter. In John Wei. "A Twelfth-Century Treatise on Charity: The Tract 'Vt autem hoc euidenter' of the Sentence Collection *Deus itaque summe atque ineffabiliter bonus.*" *Mediaeval Studies* 74 (2012): 1–50.

Secondary Sources

Austin, Greta. *Shaping Church Law Around the Year 1000: The Decretum of Burchard of Worms.* Church, Faith and Culture in the Medieval West. Burlington, Vt.: Ashgate, 2009.

Brett, Martin. "Creeping Up on the *Panormia.*" *Grundlagen des Rechts: Festschrift für Peter Landau zum 65. Geburtstag,* edited by Richard Helmholz, 205–70. Paderborn: F. Schöning, 2000.

———. "Margin and Afterthought: The *Clavis* in Action." In *Readers, Texts and Compilers in the Earlier Middle Ages: Studies in Medieval Canon Law in Honour of Linda Fowler-Magerl,* edited by Martin Brett and Kathleen G. Cushing, 137–64. Church, Faith and Culture in the Medieval West. Burlington Vt.: Ashgate, 2009.

Brundage, James A. *Medieval Canon Law.* The Medieval World. New York: Longman, 1995.

———. *The Medieval Origins of the Legal Profession: Canonists, Civilians, and Courts.* Chicago: University of Chicago Press, 2008.

Buchner, Jürgen. *Die Paleae im Dekret Gratians: Untersuchung ihrer Echtheit.* Pontificium Athenaeum Antonianum, Facultas Iuris Canonici 127. Rome: Pontificium Athenaeum Antonianum, 2000

Colish, Marcia L. *Peter Lombard.* Leiden: Brill, 1994.

Constable, Giles. *The Reformation of the Twelfth Century.* Cambridge: Cambridge University Press, 1996.

Cushing, Kathleen G. *Papacy and Law in the Gregorian Revolution: The Canonistic Work of Anselm of Lucca.* Oxford: Oxford University Press, 1998.

Dillon, John Nöel. "Case Statements (*themata*) and the Composition of Gratian's Cases." ZRG Kan. Abt. 92 (2006): 306–39.

Eichbauer, Melodie H. "St. Gall Stiftsbibliothek 673 and the Early Redactions of Gratian's *Decretum.*" BMCL 27 (2007): 105–40.

———. "From the First to the Second Recension: The Progressive Evolution of the *Decretum.*" BMCL 29 (2011–12): 119–67.

———. "Gratian's *Decretum* and the Changing Historiographical Landscape." *History Compass* 11, no. 12 (2013): 1111–25.

Giordanengo, Gérard. "*Auctoritates et auctores* dans les collections canoniques (1050–1140)." In *Auctor et Auctoritas: Invention et conformisme dans l'écriture medieval: Actes du colloque de Saint-Quentin-en-Yvelines (14–16 juin 1999),* edited by Michel Zimmermann, 99–129. Mémoires et documents de l'école des Chartres 59. Paris: École des Chartres, 2001.

Giraud, Cédric. *Per verba magistri: Anselme de Laon et son école au XIIe siècle.* Bibliothèque d'histoire culturelle du Moyen Âge 8. Turnhout: Brepols, 2010.

Gujer, Regula. *Concordia Discordantium Codicum Manuscriptorum? Die Textentwicklung von 18 Handschriften anhand der D.16 des Decretum Gratiani.* Forschungen zur kirchlichen Rechtsgeschichte und zum Kirchenrecht 23. Cologne: Böhlau, 2004.

Kéry, Lotte. *Canonical Collections of the Early Middle Ages (ca. 400–1140): A Bibliographical Guide to the Manuscripts and Literature.* History of Medieval Canon Law. Washington D.C.: Catholic University of America Press, 1999.

Kuttner, Stephan. *Harmony from Dissonance: An Interpretation of Medieval Canon Law.* Wimmer Lecture 10. Latrobe, Pa.: Archabbey Press, 1960. Reprinted in idem, *The History of Ideas and Doctrines in the Middle Ages.* 2nd ed. Aldershot: Ashgate, 1992. no. 1.

———. "The 'Extravagantes' of the Decretum in Biberach." BMCL 3 (1973): 61–71.

Landau, Peter. "Neue Forschungen zur vorgratianischen Kanonessammlungen und den Quellen des gratianischen Dekrets." *Ius Commune* 11 (1984): 1–29.

———. "Research on Gratian: Act and Agenda." In *Proceedings of the Seventh International Congress of Medieval Canon Law, Cambridge, 23–27 July 1984,* edited by Peter Linehan, 3–26. MIC Ser. C–8. Vatican City: Biblioteca Apostolica Vaticana, 1988.

———. "Gratian und die Sententiae Magistri A." In *Aus Archiven und Bibliotheken: Festschrift für Raymund Kottje zum 65. Geburtstag,* edited by Hubert Mordek, 311–26. Freiburger Beiträge zur mittelalterlichen Geschichte, Studien und Texte 3. Frankfurt am Main: Peter Lang, 1992. Repr. in idem, *Kanones und Dekretalen: Beiträge zur Geschichte der Quellen des kanonischen Rechts.* Bibliotheca eruditorum 2. Goldbach: Keip, 1997. Pp. 161*–176*.

———. "Das Register Papst Gregors I. im Decretum Gratiani." In *Mittelalterliche Texte: Überlieferung, Befunde, Deutung. Kolloquium der Zentraldirektion der Monumenta Germaniae Historica am 28.–29. Juni 1996.* Hannover, 1996. Pp. 125–40.

———. "Burchard de Worms et Gratien: Â propos des sources immédiates de Gratien." RDC 48 (1998): 233–45.

———. "Patristische Texte in den beiden Rezensionen des *Decretum Gratiani.*" BMCL 23 (1999): 77–82.

———. "Gratian and the *Decretum Gratiani.*" In *The History of Medieval Canon Law in the Classical Period, 1140–1234: From Gratian to the Decretals of Pope Gregory IX,* edited by Wilfried Hartmann and Kenneth Pennington, 35–38. History of Medieval Canon Law 6. Washington D.C.: The Catholic University of America Press, 2008.

———. "Master Peter of Louveciennes and the Origins of the Parisian School of Canon Law around 1170." In *Proceedings of the Fourteenth International Congress of Medieval Canon Law, Toronto, August 2012,* edited by Joseph Goering, Andreas Thier, and Stephan Dusil. MIC Ser. C–15. Vatican City: Biblioteca Apostolica Vaticana, forthcoming.

Larrainzar, Carlos. "El Decreto de Graciano del codice Fd (= Firenze, Biblioteca Nazionale Centrale, Conventi Soppresi A.I.402): In Memoriam Rudolf Weigand." *Ius ecclesiae* 10 (1998): 421–89.

———. "El borrador de la 'Concordia' de Graciano: Sankt Gallen, Stiftsbibliothek MS 673 (=Sg)." *Ius Ecclesiae* 11 (1999): 593–666.

———. "La formación del Decreto de Graciano pore tapas." ZRG Kan. Abt. 87 (2001): 5–83.

———. "Datos sobre la antigüedad del manuscrito Sg: su redacción de C.27

q.2." *Panta rei: Studi dedicati a Manlio Bellomo*, edited by Orazio Condorelli, 3.495–515. Roma: Il Cigno, 2004.

———. "La investigación actual sobre el Decreto de Graciano." ZRG Kan. Abt. 90 (2004): 27–59.

———. "La edición critica del Decreto de Graciano." BMCL 27 (2007): 71–105.

———. "Métodos para el anàlisis de la formación literaria del Decretum Gratiani: 'etapas' y 'esquemas' de redacción." In *Proceedings of the Thirteenth International Congress of Medieval Canon Law: Esztergom, 3–8 August 2008*, edited by Péter Erdö and Anzelm Szabolcs Szuromi, 85–116. MIC Ser. C–14. Vatican City: Biblioteca Apostolica Vaticana, 2010.

Larson, Atria A. "The Evolution of Gratian's *Tractatus de penitentia*." BMCL 26 (2004–6): 59–123.

———. "Early Stages of Gratian's *Decretum* and the Second Lateran Council: A Reconsideration." BMCL 27 (2007): 21–56.

———. "The Influence of the School of Laon on Gratian: The Usage of the *Glossa ordinaria* and Anselmian *Sententie* in *De penitentia* (*Decretum* C.33 q.3)." *Mediaeval Studies* 72 (2010): 197–244.

———. "An *Abbreviatio* of the First Recension of Gratian's *Decretum* in Munich?" BMCL 29 (2011–12): 51–118.

———. "The Reception of Gratian's *Tractatus de penitentia* and the Relationship between Law and Theology in the Second Half of the Twelfth Century." *Journal of Religious History* 37:4 (2013): 457–73.

———. *Master of Penance: Gratian and the Development of Penitential Thought and Law in the Twelfth Century*. Studies in Medieval and Early Modern Canon Law. Washington D.C.: Catholic University of America Press, 2014.

———. "Gratian's *De penitentia* in Twelfth-Century Manuscripts," BMCL 31 (2014): 57–110.

Lenherr, Titus. "Die Summarien zu den Texten des 2. Laterankonzils von 1139 in Gratians Dekret." AKKR 150 (1981): 528–51.

———. "Arbeiten mit Gratians Dekret," AKKR 151 (1982): 140–66.

———. "Fehlende 'Paleae' als Zeichen eines überlieferungsgeschichtlich jüngeren Datums von Dekrethandschriften." AKKR 151 (1982): 495–507.

———. *Die Exkommunikations- und Depositionsgewalt der Häretiker bei Gratian und den Dekretisten bis zur Glossa ordinaria des Johannes Teutonicus*. Münchener Theologische Studien III, Kan. Abt. 42. St Ottilien: EOS Verlag, 1987.

———. "Die *Glossa Ordinaria* zur Bibel als Quelle von Gratians *Dekret*: Ein (neuer) Anfang." BMCL 24 (2000): 97–129.

———. "Zur Redaktionsbeschichte von C.23 q.5 in der '1. Rezension' von Gratians Dekret: 'The Making of a Quaestio'." BMCL 26 (2004–6): 31–58.

———. "Langsame Annäherung an Gratians Exemplar der 'Moralia in Iob'." In *Proceedings of the Thirteenth International Congress of Medieval Canon Law, Esztergom, 3–8 August 2008*, edited by Peter Erdö and Sz. Anzelm Szuromi, 311–26. MIC Ser. C:14. Vatican City: Biblioteca Apostolica Vaticana, 2010.

———. "Gratian und die Glossa zu den Psalmen und den Paulusbriefen: Beobachtungen und Fragen." Paper presented at The Fourteenth International Congress of Medieval Canon Law. Toronto. 11 August, 2012.

Le Bras, Gabriel. "Alger of Liège et Gratien." *Revue de sciences philosophiques et théologiques* 20 (1931): 5–26.

Morris, Colin. *The Papal Monarchy: The Western Church from 1050 to 1250*. Oxford History of the Christian Church. Oxford: Clarendon Press, 1989.

Noonan, Jr., John T. "Gratian Slept Here: The Changing Identity of the Father of the Systematic Study of Canon Law." *Traditio* 35 (1979): 145–72.

Pennington, Kenneth. "Gratian, Causa 19, and the Birth of Canonical Jurisprudence." *La cultura giuridico-canonica medioevale: Premesse per un dialogo ecumenico*. Rome: 2003. Pp. 215–236. Expanded version in *"Panta rei": Studi dedicati a Manlio Bellomo*, edited by Orazio Condorelli, 4.339–55. Roma: Il Cigno, 2004. Available online with manuscript image details at http://faculty.cua .edu/pennington/Canon%20Law/Causa19Rome.htm.

———. "The Biography of Gratian, the Father of Canon Law." *Villanova Law Review* 59, no. 4 (2014): 679–706.

Rider, Catherine. *Magic and Impotence in the Middle Ages*. Oxford: Oxford University Press, 2006.

Rolker, Christof. *Canon Law and the Letters of Ivo of Chartres*. Cambridge Studies in Medieval Life and Thought. Cambridge: Cambridge University Press, 2010.

Somerville, Robert and Bruce Brasington, ed. and trans. *Prefaces to Canon Law Books in Latin Christianity: Selected Translations, 500–1245*. New Haven: Yale University Press, 1998.

Van Engen, John H. "Observations on 'De consecratione'." In *Proceedings of the Sixth International Congress of Medieval Canon Law, Berkeley, California, 28 July–2 August 1980*, edited by Stephan Kuttner and Kenneth Pennington, 309–20. MIC Ser. C–7. Vatican City: Biblioteca Apostolica Vaticana, 1985.

Vaugn, Sally and Jay Rubenstein, eds.. *Teaching and Learning in Northern Europe, 1000–1200*. Studies in the Early Middle Ages 8. Turnhout: Brepols, 2006.

Vetulani, Adam. "Autour du Décret de Gratien." *Apollinaris* 41 (1968): 54–57.

Viejo-Ximénez, José Miguel. "La investigación sobre las fuentes formales del Decreto de Graciano." *Initium* 7 (2002): 217–39.

———. "Variantes textuales y variants doctrinales en C.2 q.8." In *Proceedings of the Twelfth International Congress of Medieval Canon Law, Washington DC, 1 August – 7 August 2004*, edited by Uta-Renate Blumenthal, Kenneth Pennington, and Atria A. Larson, 161–90. MIC Ser. C–13. Vatican City: Biblioteca Apostolica Vaticana, 2008.

———. "La composición del Decreto de Graciano." *Ius Canonicum* 45:90 (2005): 431–85.

———. "La recepción del derecho romano en la derecho canónico." *Annaeus* 2 (2005): 139–69.

———. "'Costuras' y 'Descosidos' en la version divulgada del Decreto de Graciano." *Ius Ecclesiae* 21 (2009): 133–54.

Wei, John C. "A Reconsideration of St. Gall, Stiftsbibliothek 673 (Sg) in Light of the Sources of Distinctions 5–7 of the *De penitentia*." BMCL 27 (2007): 141–80.

———. "Law and Religion in Gratian's *Decretum*." Ph.D. diss., Yale University, 2008.

———. "Gratian and the School of Laon." *Traditio* 64 (2009): 279–322.

———. "Penitential Theology in Gratian's Decretum: Critique and Criticism of the Treatise Baptizato homine." ZRG Kan. Abt. 95 (2009): 78–100.

———. "The Sentence Collection *Deus non habet initium uel terminum* and Its Reworking, *Deus itaque summe atque ineffabiliter bonus.*" *Mediaeval Studies* 73 (2011): 1–118.

———. "A Discussion and List of Manuscripts Belonging to the Σ-group (S-group)." Available online at https://sites.google.com/site/repertoriumi uriscanonici/home/gratian/s-group. Accessed 29 September 2015.

———. "A Twelfth-Century Treatise on Charity: The Tract 'Vt autem hoc euidenter' of the Sentence Collection *Deus itaque summe atque ineffabiliter bonus.*" *Mediaeval Studies* 74 (2012): 1–50.

———. "The Importance and Influence of Gratian s Tract *De penitentia.*" ZRG Kan. Abt. 101 (2015): 373–88.

———. "*Gratian the Theologian.* Studies in Medieval and Early Modern Canon Law 13. Washington, D.C.: The Catholic University of America Press, 2016.

Weigand, Rudolf. "Die Dekrethandschrift B 3515 Spitalarchivs Biberach an der Riss." BMCL 2 (1972): 76–81.

———. *Die Glossen zum Dekret Gratians: Studien zu den frühen Glossen und Glossen-kompositionen.* 2 vols. SG 25–26. Rome, 1991.

———. "Zur künftigen Edition des Dekrets Gratian." ZRG Kan. Abt. 83 (1997): 32–51.

———. "Chancen und Probleme einer baldigen kritischen Edition der ersten Redaktion des Dekrets Gratians." BMCL 22 (1998): 49–73.

Werckmeister, Jean. "Introduction." *Décret de Gratien, Causes 27 à 36: Le Mariage.* Ed. and trans. Jean Werckmeister. Sources canoniques 3. Paris: Éditions du Cerf, 2011.

Winroth, Anders. *The Making of Gratian's Decretum.* Cambridge Studies in Medieval Though and Life. Cambridge: Cambridge University Press, 2000.

———. "Recent Work on the Making of Gratian's *Decretum.*" BMCL 26 (2004–6): 1–30.

———. "Neither Slave nor Free: Theology and Law in Gratian's Thoughts on the Definition of Marriage and Unfree Persons." In *Medieval Church Law and the Origins of the Western Legal Tradition: A Tribute to Kenneth Pennington,* edited by Wolfgang P. Müller and Mary E. Sommar, 97–109. Washington, D.C.: The Catholic University of America Press, 2006.

———. "Innocent II, Gratian, and Abbé Migne." BMCL 28 (2008): 145–51.

———. "Marital Consent in Gratian's *Decretum.*" In *Readers, Texts and Compilers in the Earlier Middle Ages: Studies in Medieval Canon Law in Honour of Linda Fowler-Magerl,* edited by Martin Brett and Kathleen G. Cushing, 111–21. Burlington, Vt.: Ashgate, 2009.

———. "Critical Notes on the Text of Gratian's *Decretum.*" Parts 1–3. Available at https://sites.google.com/a/yale.edu/decretumgratiani/. Accessed 29 September 2015.

———. "Where Gratian Slept: The Life and Death of the Father of Canon Law." ZRG Kan. Abt. 100 (2014): 106–28.

Zanichelli, Giuseppa. "Work in Progress: Bologna and the *Decretum Gratiani.*" Paper delivered at the 40th Annual Saint Louis Conference on Manuscript Studies. Saint Louis University. 12 October 2013.

Biblical References

References come from the Latin Vulgate and follow the traditional sequence of books within that version of the Bible.

Gn 1:1, D.2 d.p.c.44
Gn 1:6, D.2 d.p.c.44
Gn 3:7, D.2 c.39
Gn 3:9, D.3 c.36
Gn 3:10, D.1 c.45; D.3 c.36
Gn 3:13, D.1 c.47
Gn 3:9–14, D.1 d.p.c.60
Gn 4:4, D.5 c.1
Gn 4:9, D.1 c.47, d.p.c.60; D.3 c.36
Gn 4:13, D.1 d.p.c.60
Gn 4:16, D.1 c.45
Gn 20, D.1 d.p.c.60

Ex 3:5, D.1 c.56
Ex 18:12, D.1 c.45
Ex 32:32, D.2 d.p.c.39
Ex 32:33, D.4 d.p.c.7
Ex 34:7, D.4 c.13

Lv 4:3, D.1 d.p.c.58
Lv 10:16, D.3 c.34, c.35
Lv 10:18, D.3 c.35
Lv 14, D.1 d.p.c.60
Lv 27:18, D.1 d.p.c.87

Nm 20:10, D.2 d.p.c.39
Nm 20:12, D.2 d.p.c.39

Dt 32:22, D.3 c.43

1 Sm 2:25, D.1 d.p.c.58
1 Sm 13:14, D.2 d.p.c.39
1 Sm 16:1, D.1 c.75
1 Sm 16:14–23, D.1 d.p.c.60
1 Sm 24:15, D.2 d.p.c.39

2 Sm 6:22, D.2 d.p.c.39
2 Sm 12:12, D.1 d.p.c.87
2 Sm 12:13, D.1 d.p.c.60, c.82; D.2
    d.p.c.39; D.3 c.24, c.25, c.26
2 Sm 24:15–17, D.3 d.p.c.26

1 Kgs 21:19–29, D.3 c.27
1 Kgs 21:29, D.1 d.p.c.60; D.3 c.28, c.29
1 Chr 21:17, D.3 c.26

Tob 4:11, D.1 c.57, c.76

Jb 4:17–19, D.2 c.40
Jb 7:1, D.4 c.8
Jb 9:28–31, D.2 c.40
Jb 15:15, D.2 d.p.c.45
Jb 29:14, D.2 c.37
Jb 31:33–34, D.1 c.44
Jb 31:37, D.2 c.15
Jb 40:14, D.2 c.45

Ps 6:1, D.1 d.p.c.34
Ps 6:4–5, D.1 d.p.c.34
Ps 7:5, D.2 d.p.c.39
Ps 7:9, D.2 d.p.c.39
Ps 25:1, D.2 d.p.c.39
Ps 25:1–2, D.2 c.40
Ps 31:3, D.1 d.p.c.60
Ps 31:5, D.1 c.4, c.90; D.3 c.26
Ps 33:17, D.4 c.23
Ps 36:5, D.1 d.p.c.87
Ps 36:27, D.1 d.p.c.87
Ps 37:6, D.3 c.24, d.p.c.24
Ps 37:10, D.1 c.84
Ps 50:1, D.2 c.40; D.3 c.24

Index of Material Sources

The following index makes no distinction between direct quotations and paraphrases. If a text is identified as being located in a *dictum* (e.g., D.1 d.p.c.87), the quotation is found at some point within the *dictum* and may be found with reference to the *apparatus fontium* on the Latin side and the usage of small caps for introducing the text within the edition on both the Latin and English sides.

Also in the Studies in Medieval and Early Modern Canon Law Series

Kenneth Pennington, General Editor

Printed in the USA
CPSIA information can be obtained
at www.ICGtesting.com
LVHW041433051023
760085LV00048B/797

9 780813 237848